D0536913

NO LONGER PROPERTY OF
SEATTLE PUBLIC LIBRARY
Southwest Branch

JUL 1 2 2010

9010 35th Ave SW
Seattle, WA 98126-3821

THE EXPLORER'S GARDEN Shrubs and Vines
from the Four Corners of the World

THE EXPLORER'S GARDEN Shrubs and Vines from the Four Corners of the World

DANIEL J. HINKLEY

with photographs
by Lynne Harrison
and Daniel J. Hinkley

TIMBER PRESS
Portland ▪ London

Half title page: After days of rain, snow, and clouds during our time in northern Sikkim in 2005, the skies cleared to reveal a dramatic landscape filled with nearly unparalleled botanical riches. (Photo by Daniel J. Hinkley)

Title page: The fabled and botanically opulent Yulong Shan in northwestern Yunnan Province, with the Yangtze River at its base. (Photo by Daniel J. Hinkley)

Opposite: The Taktshang Monastery above Paro, Bhutan, amid an intriguing eastern Himalaya flora. (Photo by Daniel J. Hinkley)

Copyright © 2009 by Daniel J. Hinkley. All rights reserved.

Published in 2009 by Timber Press, Inc.

The Haseltine Building
133 S.W. Second Avenue, Suite 450
Portland, Oregon 97204-3527
www.timberpress.com

2 The Quadrant
135 Salusbury Road
London NW6 6RJ
www.timberpress.co.uk

Printed in China
Text designed by Susan Applegate

Library of Congress Cataloging-in-Publication Data
Hinkley, Daniel J.
    The explorer's garden: shrubs and vines from the four corners of the world / Daniel J. Hinkley; with photographs by Lynne Harrison.
        p. cm.
    Includes bibliographical references and index.
    ISBN 978-0-88192-918-8
    1. Ornamental shrubs. 2. Climbing plants. 3. Exotic plants.
I. Harrison, Lynne. II. Title.
    SB435.H56 2009
    635.9′76—dc22   2008032993

A catalog record for this book is also available from the British Library.

Observe how system into system runs,
What other planets circle other suns . . .

ALEXANDER POPE
An Essay on Man

To my parents,
Ralph Kirkland Hinkley and
Vivian Clara Yunk Hinkley;
my brothers,
Kirk Hinkley and Terry Hinkley;
and to the memory of our sister,
Amy Hinkley Gregory

CONTENTS

The richly forested slopes of Chile's Mount Orsorno reveal, even from a great distance, the floral effects of *Eucryphia cordifolia*. (Photo by Daniel J. Hinkley)

ACKNOWLEDGMENTS

I GRATEFULLY THANK the following individuals and institutions for their cooperation, friendship, and assistance in my travels and pursuit of clarity while researching and writing this book. My apologies in advance for all blatant omissions; assuredly there are many.

Lynne Harrison for her diligent, patient, and talented efforts in compiling and sharing her splendid photographs.

Richard Olsen of the U.S. National Arboretum for our hikes together along the Blue Ridge, for kindly assisting me in literature searches, and for providing photos of *Chionanthus pubescens*.

Andrew Bunting of Scott Arboretum for being my touchstone to hardiness in zone 6.

Dave Demers, for so graciously supplying many of his photos of plants in situ from our joint ventures in China, northern India, Bhutan, and Chile, and for his companionship on the trail.

Bleddyn and Sue Wynn-Jones for their company— traveling companions often, friends forever.

Ozzie Johnson and Scott McMahan, Georgia on My Mind, for their steadfast companionship, which has made numerous trips abroad together nothing short of undiluted pleasure.

Sandra Reed, USDA plant geneticist, for providing such ample and generous information, photos, and plants for evaluation of the *Hydrangea/Dichroa* hybrids to which she is steadfastly devoted.

The Pendleton and Elisabeth C. Miller Library Charitable Foundation, sponsor of my 2006 Vietnam expedition.

The owners and staff of Monrovia Nursery for generously sponsoring my trips abroad since 2007.

The staff of the Elisabeth C. Miller Library, Center for Urban Horticulture, University of Washington.

The staff and faculty of the University of Washington Botanic Gardens, Center for Urban Horticulture, and Washington Park Arboretum, in particular Sarah Reichard and John Wott.

Uoc Le Huu, my loyal guide, and friend, during my seven trips to northern Vietnam.

Sonam Sherpa and his family, our guides during two trips in Nepal.

Liu Li and Guan Kaihun, botanists and guides during numerous trips in Yunnan and Sichuan Provinces.

Aleck Yang and Chieng Fan of the National Museum of Natural Science, T'ai-chung, Taiwan, for their warm welcome to and immense knowledge of the flora of Taiwan.

John Grimshaw, taxonomist, England, for his ready and astute answers to numerous and sometimes vague questions.

Julian Harber for his astute observations, dedication to the genus *Berberis*, and willingness to share his knowledge.

Traveling mates, seed cleaners, and good friends over many years: Kevin Carrabine and Jennifer Macuiba, Peter and Sarah Wharton, Ketzel Levine, Richie Steffen, Shayne Chandler, Riz Reyes, Jamaica Kincaid, Finlay Colley, Paul Jones, Carl Schoenfeld, Alan Bush, Darrell Probst, Frank and Laura Lu Bell, Randall Hitchins, Hans Hansen, James Compton, John Coke, John D'Arcy, Maurice Foster, Georg Ubelhardt, Bob Beer, and finally, a *good thing* to mention, Martha Stewart.

Doug Hamilton, producer of *First Flower*, and his crew from NOVA, for the remarkable opportunity to see Sichuan at its floral zenith.

Fellow plant and nursery people: Rodney Eason, Tom Hobbs and Brent Beattie, Panyoti Keladis, Terri Stanley, Tony Avent, Wade Roitsh, Tim and Hamish Prebble, John Massey, Paul Bonine, Greg Shepherd, Dave and Gail Halsaver, Dennis Schrader and Bill Smith, Keith and Roz Wiley, Bill Thomas, Jonathan Wright, Brian Upchurch, Marina Christopher, John Elsley, Roger Raiche and David McCrory, Roy and Sue Lancaster, Tom and Jo Hudson, Stephen Ryan, Sean Hogan, Philippe de Spoelboech, and Nick Macer.

Tom Ranney and associates of North Carolina State University Woody Plant Breeding Station in Asheville, North Carolina.

Nancy Heckler of Indianola, Washington, friend and fellow gardener, for allowing me the use of her lovely studio while finishing this book.

The staff of *Horticulture Magazine*: Sara Begg, Meghan Lynch, and Nan Sinton, editors, handlers, and friends.

Devoted, loyal, and dear employees from another life: Duane West, Alan Hanson, Connie Lammers, Sally Stubberfield, Myrna Ougland, Josh McCullough, Eric Hammond, Celia Pedersen, Darah Cole, Maria Peterson, Pat Figley, and Dustin Gimbel.

Especially to Timber Press and its saintly and patient editor-in-chief, Tom Fischer, with special thanks to my editor, Mindy Fitch, and editorial director Eve Goodman.

And mostly to Robert L. Jones, architect, honest critic, editor, pet handler, waterer, weeder, cook, friend, partner in crime.

INTRODUCTION

I find it ever more regularly so that if I take note of even the smallest of natural wonders, my mind begins to wander the Milky Way. And in response, so say I, Rejoice Evermore, Rejoice Evermore.

—John Adams

Through the summers of youth in northern Michigan, my older brother, Kirk, and I often found ourselves cheek to jowl and giggling along the sandy banks of the Muskegon, a lengthy and celebrated sinuate of water dissecting my home town of Evart en route to Lake Michigan. It was while listening to the whip and whistle of our father's fly pole as he cast for German browns through air scented by sweet fern that my sense and awe of the natural world cemented. On those now-gilded evenings of glittering wings of mayflies above a glint of rock-tumbled river, we listened to the haunting warble of the whip-poor-will at dusk, and the signature song of a warm midwestern evening, the lancing drill of mosquitoes in attack formation.

Somehow in the process, and miraculously so, imbibed by my consciousness at that time was a fascination with the plant life that enveloped us. My dad, who had grown up in these woods of his father and grandfather, knew well the trees and taught us the names; the smaller unacknowledged associates and Latin nomen-

My garden, Windcliff, sits above Puget Sound on the Kitsap Peninsula near the small village of Indianola. On the 5½-acre site, I have accumulated a reference collection from more than twenty years of active plant collecting in similar climates worldwide. (Photo by Daniel J. Hinkley)

clature were those things I would need to add to my retinue on my own. One by one, I continue to do just that, and for this fact alone, I can always go home again. There is something new there, a plant that had been transparent until it was learned of, often by means of a closely allied species on some mountain on another continent. Plants generally have that way about them, of not speaking until spoken to.

I am very appreciative of those times along the Muskegon, even more so now as I witness an ever-decreasing interface with the adventures of a natural world by a youth who explore the universe instead through the strokes of a keyboard. It was during that time along the Muskegon that the trajectory of my life took form, taking me to places that continue to affirm that the compelling connectedness of life is alone sufficient for my personal enlightenment. It is precisely this emotion that often gets my pen in trouble, as such wonderment tends to color my writing a cloying hue of purple.

If I may say so without appearing high and almighty in my understanding of the process and individual gardener, the inclusion of woody shrubs and vines in our landscapes seems to be impeded by our need for immediate gratification by way of the more highly advocated herbaceous border. Better off, I think, is the gardener who learns right off that a garden with permanent framework, no matter the size, is one that brings satisfaction to the four seasons while developing, along with its gardener, a sublime patina with age.

Indeed, the inclusion of the woody shrub and vine into the garden, whether integrated into the mixed border with herbaceous components or utilized as the anchoring elements of a home, provides the year-round garden a persisting effect by a simple refusal to surrender at summer's end. In truth, virtually anything remaining above ground during the off season becomes a platform of ornament when carrying the vagaries of the seasons—hoarfrost, a tracery of snow, or an embellishment of raindrops—along its limbs. By default the garden planted for year-round structure becomes a winter garden without any consideration of actual effect offered during such an unlikely time of year.

Yet with just a little consideration, a gardener can employ a palette of woody plants that will provide the landscape with contrasting seasons of interest throughout the calendar year. Through the effects produced by the form and silhouette of deciduous or evergreen foliage, colorful bark, flowers, and fruit, there is established a broad-based and lengthy tenor that may come and go throughout the year without sacrificing the impact of the high summer, when we are most likely to be in the garden. Filling in the surrounding voids with ephemeral treasures comes with a significantly smaller risk of seasonal staleness once the lasting woody composition is in place.

But with such an enormous palette of possibilities, precisely what do we select? We cannot possibly have one of everything in our gardens, a fact that does not seem to keep many from trying. The current inventory of woody plants and vines by specific rank, not to mention the countless cultivars and hybrids now commercially available, is colossal. Ultimately we have to gather around ourselves those plants that bring us the greatest personal satisfaction.

Nor could I possibly include everything between the covers of this book. In the highly celebrated cult Hollywood production *Sideways*, there exists a memorable scene between characters Miles (Paul Giamatti) and Jack (Thomas Haden Church) at a wine bar in California. Miles waxes poetic over the pinot that has just been poured, demanding his friend first study his glass, the viscosity and bouquet. After a brief attempt at indulging his friend, a more knavish Jack replies, "When do we get to drink it?"

Attempting to write this book, much, much too long in process, is analogous to that near-intolerable pause before that first sip. The subject at hand, shrubs and vines, has been explored on my part to a near-lunatic degree over the past 15 years, yet I am no closer to writing the complete and honest tome I set out to write than I was when I first agreed to the project. In fact, this subject only continues to open, like a good bottle breathed, taking on levels of complexities moment by moment. There are some very blatant omissions—*Camellia, Deutzia, Philadelphus, Rhododendron,* and *Rosa* to name just a few. I have seen and collected seed of these genera on numerous forays. Ultimately, however, I made the decision to write about those plants I most appreciate, stop thinking, and simply drink.

Making such decisions is often quite freeing, but in my case I was only left with more consternation. My return home from abroad each winter during the past two decades has been bittersweet. Of course there comes the contentment of home fires and snoring dogs and reunions with friends and family. My box of numbered glassine envelopes of seeds, representing weeks of work and instilled with sufficient memories for a lifetime, seems a just reward. Yet I have come to realize that these homecomings lack the sense of fulfillment one might expect from a lengthy exposure to plants in their rightful places. My experience is often quite the opposite, my feelings burdened by the paucity of knowledge I have managed to accumulate or build upon. Beyond the obvious limits of my cerebral aptitude, there exist those line items for which I hold accountable these low spirits.

Firstly, the system of classification within which are held my core beliefs as a plantsman has suddenly been turned on its head. While there has always been some plasticity to this umbrella of understanding, the advance of a more sophisticated means to construct the ultimate tree of knowledge has resulted in entire plant families turned inside out, in fact often fully discarded. On some fronts, significant numbers of closely related plant genera have been crafted into one by the so-called lumpers (whom I refer to, over a beer with fellow plantsmen, as "genus enlargers"), while in others, one-time and easily digested taxa have been splintered into an eccentric assortment of unpronounceable names.

I will ultimately content myself in the end product of this fermenting process, as I am cognizant that one must on occasion move heavy furniture in order to renovate or remodel. However, it is indeed intimidating to cut the ignition of this empirical engine, running at full throttle, for even a few moments to capture a universe of shrubs and vines as we, at this moment, comprehend it.

Secondly, the world of plant exploration, contrary to some popular beliefs, is far from its twilight years. The *Flora of China* (Wu et al. 1994 to present), an immense undertaking by the Chinese in collaboration with the Missouri Botanical Garden and others, is still being written. I could not possibly have attempted writing this book without its guidance, yet there is still much work to do before the *Flora of China* is complete.

Botanical studies of vast areas of Vietnam, Myanmar, the Arunachal Pradesh, Bhutan, and countless other locales are incomplete, and in some cases the process has not even begun. Even in our own back acreage, never-before-documented woody plants—let alone the more obscure taxa of lower plants—are still being discovered. This fact was brought home by the discovery of *Neviusia cliftonii*, a large deciduous shrub in the Rosaceae found in northern California in the late 1990s.

Lastly, of course, are two obvious questions whose answers are clearly nebulous. What exactly is a shrub, and further, what defines a vine? This dilemma has certainly become more apparent as I have carried on with my travels. The genus *Illicium*, for instance, inhabited the garden of my imagination through the templates of *I. anisatum*, *I. henryi*, and *I. floridanum*, which I cultivated in my woodland garden as subservient lower-canopy elements that knew their place. Then came trouble. In northern Vietnam, our trail led us through towering trees of numerous species of *Illicium*. Whether in Tas-

mania, New Zealand, Chile, or China, this same trail of dubiety has guided me through forests predominated by imposing specimens of *Pittosporum*, *Daphniphyllum*, *Drimys*, and other "shrubs." Precisely at what point does a large shrub transition to a small (or enormous) tree?

Through these forests that I have trekked grow an assortment of vines, each with their own plan of action to reach the upper reaches of a darkened forest floor. Yet, as with the shrubs, their definitive habit of growth transmutes considerably if grown in full sun. For numerous years I grew *Solanum crispum* as a vine in my first garden, while in my second and sunnier landscape it

Artificially categorized as a "shrub" under cultivation, *Eucryphia cordifolia*, seen here along a country lane south of Concepción, southern Chile, expresses itself in treelike proportions. (Photo by Daniel J. Hinkley)

behaves as a respectable freestanding shrub. The same applies to the "climbing" hydrangeas, some of which I require to stand upon their own two feet, and they do just that.

For the purposes of this book, it must simply suffice to say that I have considered well my inconsistencies and made judgments based on how the species I discuss have been historically tagged or the percentage of species in each genera with shrublike or vinelike growth habits. Not everyone will agree with this treatment, and I look forward to the dialogue and criticism that ensues. I know I will learn a tremendous deal in the process.

The hope is that the information I provide, with no intention of suggesting taxonomic completeness or systematic correctness, and without always staying within traditional borders of what shrubs and vines are, will inspire the exploration of an exciting, often overlooked palette of woody plants for the garden.

I write this from our dining room on a blustery winter's day with an expanse of sky and Puget Sound laid out in the distance. The sun dances like diamonds on the water and takes me back momentarily to those late August evenings along the Muskegon, when the sublime light of a Michigan sunset reflected upon its moving water.

Having just days ago returned from a lengthy survey of Australia and Taiwan, I have again been made to note the lavish and inexhaustible archive of plants that adheres so tentatively to the thin shag of our planet's surface, a reminder of its profound perfection. What I first came to regard as an insurmountable and infinite adversary, I have now, in attempting to write this book, come to embrace for its exquisite munificence, made more beautiful by the fact that I will never know much of it at all. And in that I will rejoice forever.

DANIEL J. HINKLEY
Windcliff
Indianola, Washington

NOTES ON PROPAGATION

ACH PLANT ENTRY in this book is followed by a concise description of how to propagate the subject at hand. As a nurseryman and long-time devotee of the subject, I am fully cognizant that my suggestions seem overly simplified. As I too must deal occasionally with the cockiness of techno-junkies when confronted with a computer meltdown, I am aware of how frustrating it can be when assumptions of base knowledge are made.

The following extremely truncated overview of propagation by seeds and cuttings is meant to augment the methods included in the text. Be aware that every plant species holds tightly its own secrets; it should not be considered a challenge but a pleasure and honor to unlock these mysteries through trial and error. Through each success, more competence and confidence are accrued. Be adventurous.

More explicit reading on the subject can be found in *The Reference Manual of Woody Plant Propagation* by Michael Dirr and Charles Heuser Jr. A dog-eared copy of this reference should sit on every serious gardener's shelf above the potting table.

Sowing Seed

Fresh fertile seed is as committed to germinating as a coddled, undisturbed egg on a lovingly tended nest is to hatching. Following a very few basic rules, you can easily marvel in the emergence of the next generation of

Overleaf: My accommodations in Vietnam awash with seed collections drying in coffee filters. (Photo by Daniel J. Hinkley)

garden plants; it is primarily through this sexual process that significant variation, sometimes resulting in a positive physical difference, is most readily revealed to your quintessential seed-of-your-plants gardener.

1. Clean your seed upon gathering. If it is a fleshy berry or drupe, you need to clean the flesh from the seed to effectively prompt successful germination. Use a Ziploc baggie to remove the flesh from the seed by a vigorous massage, then decant the flesh from the bag before draining in a sieve and temporarily drying on a paper towel. It is important to realize that in the decanting process the fertile seed will sink to the bottom of the bag, making decanting of the pulp and infertile seed from the top gratifyingly easy.

2. Sow immediately. Seed sown fresh will often ignore all abuse and stupidities and still germinate.

3. Choose or make the correct medium in which to sow the seed. Though annuals and vegetables are programmed to germinate within moments of encountering a safe environment, perennials and particularly woody plants wish for more assurance before fully awakening and braving the new world. Thusly, a soil medium must be provided that will forgive their delayed emergence, from six months to three years in some cases. Commercial mixes are often comprised of those elements that readily compress over a short period, removing the pockets of air in the soil so very important to successful germination and growth.

Though one can find recipes for seed composts, for general ease I start with a commercial propagation blend that does not contain vermiculite, and cut this with one-third, by volume, of a coarse sand (not mortar sand, which is too fine). This should be "horticulturally" sterile—that is, if you use a coarse native soil from your garden you will have immediate germination of countless weed species.

The bottom line is that if you add a "mineral" component to your soil mix—meaning a coarser blend of soil particles based on tiny bits of rock—the medium will less readily compact and will retain its structural integrity until germination is complete.

4. Don't oversow. How many of us, as gardeners—or even as owners of small nurseries—need four thousand *Clethra barbinervis*? If the seed is viable and sown fresh, it *will* germinate. Sow your pots as you pepper eggs.

5. Top-dress your pots with a thin ¾ in. (1.9 cm) layer of chicken grit or forestry sand after sowing. This discourages the growth of moss and liverworts during the often long germination process. In the case of extremely fine seeds, such as those frequently found in the Hydrangeaceae, prepare your pot of soil, tamp the soil to firm it, top-dress, and then sprinkle the seeds atop the grit. The first watering will take the seeds down to an appropriate level for germination.

6. Maintain the pots in a site protected from full sun and wind yet exposed to ambient air temperatures. Remember that once you have watered the pot of seed, you have embarked on a journey of no return. The pots will from that point need to be kept evenly moist throughout the summer months. Protect pots from extreme cold in the winter.

7. Don't hurry transplantation. Though you need to keep in mind that once you water a pot of seeds, you have awakened a sleeping gaggle of geese that will from that point forward require the essentials of life—water and nutrition—you need not hurry the transplantation process. The resulting seedlings will patiently remain in the seed flat awaiting the next phase of life after transplanting. Treat the transplants with respect, providing good soil in pots, a bit of added fertilization, and protection from desiccating wind and sun until they are established in their pots.

8. Now that you have 4009 established pots of *Clethra barbinervis*, the rest is up to you. (See number 4.)

Cuttings

What a miracle it would be if I could take my little finger and make another me. Cloning of animals is no longer fiction but is a relatively recent development, whereas cloning has been a method of increasing important plants for thousands of years. Propagation by this manner allows us the opportunity to precisely replicate a plant we want more of without the inherent variation found within seeds.

I often mention the terms softwood, semisoftwood, semihardwood, and hardwood cuttings. What I am referring to is the degree of readiness of the cutting: think of green, ripe, and overripe bananas. Though there are more variations in the length and style of any cutting than there are recipes for fruitcake, the "typical" hardwood or softwood cutting has two to four nodes—that is, two to four leaves or pairs of leaves. The leaves on the bottom half are removed before sticking.

Rooting hormones have been shown to provide a positive influence, especially for belligerent taxa. Though there exists commercially a wide range of concentrations in powder formulations, a single container of concentrated liquid hormone can be easily diluted with water to create an infinite number of variations depending on the needs of the individual taxon.

Dirr and Heuser's *Reference Manual of Woody Plant Propagation*, essentially a finely crafted cookbook for making new plants, gives specific hormone concentrations for hundreds of different trees and shrubs. These recommendations, based on years of research, are given in ppm (parts per million). Don't get frustrated. A liquid hormone whose label states 1% active ingredient (generally IBA, or indolebutyric acid) translates to 10,000 ppm. Dilute 50:50 with water and you have a solution of 5000 ppm, so on and so forth.

Rooting hormones, though thought benign in regard to toxicity, should be used with caution and all label instructions followed precisely.

Every nurseryman and keen gardener who propagates plants has his or her own rooting medium of choice, whether sand, vermiculite, perlite, peat, or a combination thereof. I have always been partial to a 2:1 perlite/peat blend. The peat can be slightly increased in the summer to provide more water retention to the medium.

1. Softwood cuttings are those whose current year's growth "snaps" like a pea pod when bent, generally in early to midsummer. If cuttings are taken too soon, the succulent tissue will not maintain turgidity until its new root system is readied. Softwood cuttings need a great deal of coddling. Though you can maintain a high degree of humidity surrounding the foliage by covering with a translucent plastic covering, the most straightforward approach is construction of a mist bench. Sensors or timers periodically mist the top growth of the cuttings to reduce loss of water from their tissue. Softwood cuttings generally root very quickly, in one to three weeks.

2. As a general rule of thumb, consider those plants that retain foliage during the winter as good candidates for hardwood cutting on bottom heat. Though in the Pacific Northwest our inherent summer coolness requires the use of bottom heat year-round, in most climates this is only necessary in the winter. Keeping the root zone slightly warmer than the air temperature encourages faster rooting of hardwood cuttings. That said, there are numerous deciduous species that lend themselves to propagation in the winter without leaves, and for those species there is no easier method of propagation. The trick in these instances is to take very long cuttings (12–15 in. [30–38 cm] long) of the current year's growth after the leaves have fallen. These can then be treated with hormone and stuck vertically in any well-draining loam in the garden proper or in a deep container, with only the very top inch of the cutting left above ground. Leave them undisturbed until growth is well underway the following spring, at which time they can be lifted and transplanted.

3. In many instances, getting new rooted plants to awaken into growth the following spring can be a disappointing challenge. In a nutshell, especially for the deciduous species, the stored carbohydrate in the stem tissue has been fully depleted by the development of a new root system. Attempting to fool them in late summer, before they have dropped their leaves, into thinking that spring has arrived by artificially extending the day length with incandescent light will force them into a late flush of growth and significantly increase their survivability.

NOTES ON PLANT COLLECTING
AND BIOINVASION

WHEREVER I TRAVEL AND SPEAK, I am asked the same question: how do I get these things home? My response is such: all of my collection work strictly follows the guidelines and regulations of my host country as well as the Department of Homeland Security and Animal and Plant Health Inspection Service in this country. My seed collections are inspected for insects and disease prior to shipment home and subjected to an even more thorough exam by American agents upon arrival in the United States. All import, exemption, and post-entry quarantine permits are maintained, and the provided list of plants prohibited from entry is precisely adhered to.

With the introduction of numerous new pathogens and insects into the North American landscape, I am very grateful for these tedious exercises, wrought as they are with bureaucracy. None of us wish to be responsible for the introduction of another pest that may impact our native ecosystems in any manner.

This process, however, does not identify those plants possessing potential for escaping into the wild and causing loss of habitat for our native plant species. Along the roads and in the forests outside my gate in Indianola, Washington, are dense thickets of Himalayan blackberry (*Rubus procerus*) and Scotch broom (*Cytisus scoparius*), as well as English ivy (*Hedera helix*) smothering huge swaths of native forest. Unless highly specific

Overleaf: Our route below Kanchenjunga, the world's third-highest peak, in Sikkim, northern India, in 2005. (Photo by Daniel J. Hinkley)

herbicides are developed in the future, these landscapes will never be regained, despite some local Herculean reclamation efforts. The seed bank of our local invaders is simply too high, while their distribution, often by birds or wind, negates any well-meaning attempts to keep them at bay.

The work that I and others do in regard to looking at plants in the wild and selecting those we feel might provide ornamental value to the landscape is often viewed as flagrant disregard for this potential peril of the plants running afoul outside our garden walls.

Personally speaking, I never gather a single seed in the wild without first mentally weighing this potentiality. As a gardener, and as I hope an astute naturalist, I have had a lifetime of interfacing with plant genera with unseemly reputations. In the garden itself one can observe their seeding habits, while awareness of what plants are locally considered noxious provides other important data that is put to use in exotic locales around the world. I have encountered and bypassed splendid species of, to name a few, *Rubus*, *Elaeagnus*, numerous *Viola*, and members of the Fabaceae and Boraginaceae, because I knew based on past experiences that they might prove troublesome. The bottom line is that few of us are interested in having an invasive plant permanently adhered to our legacy.

I wish the issue was more cut and dry than it turns out to be. I feel as displeased as anyone when weeding Scotch broom from my garden, yet I know this species arrived in the Pacific Northwest not via a nursery but in the ballast of ships. The plague of kudzu (*Puer-*

aria lobata) in southeastern North America is a result of a governmental soil stabilization program, while in my original stomping grounds of northern Michigan, thousands of acres of woodland and meadow have been overtaken by *Elaeagnus angustifolia*, distributed to landowners by the millions by the Department of Natural Resources for deer browse in the 1970s. (Incidentally, deer do not eat it.)

Though the ornamental horticultural industry is not off the hook completely, nor should they be held fully accountable for the situation that exists in many parts of North America. They must, however, acknowledge the lasting impact of thoughtless introduction of invasive plants. Now that we are quite aware of the stakes, it is profoundly irresponsible to not consider invasiveness as readily as production, marketing, and distribution.

Except in a few instances, bioinvasiveness is a climate-specific issue. English holly is not going to prove invasive in Vermont, nor *Euonymus alatus* in Oregon. Nationwide blanket regulations make little sense; voluntary compliance in identifying local potential candidates and removing them from production seems the better approach.

Philosophically speaking, and in the context of a geological time frame, will what we have planted in our gardens and what has gone astray matter at all? At a 2005 symposium at the Smithsonian, a fellow lecturer suggested that we have now entered into the Homogecene, a geologic era exemplified by the great mixing of all of life's forms by way of humans' ability to travel, acquire, and alter so dramatically the crust of this splendid sphere on which we hurl through space. In this, do we as humans set ourselves outside the systems of life, or do we accept that our ephemeral rise to dominance and alteration of our environment is nothing more remarkable than the transfiguration of the atmosphere by bacteria living in the guts of termites?

What I will continue to do to the best of my abilities is to garden responsibly and passionately while all the time realizing the need to step gently. By so doing, I feel that the process of gardening continues to do something intrinsically good for our planet and those living things that share it with us.

Kiwis and Kin: The Actinidiaceae

By 4:00 p.m. the skies were beginning to darken, as a cold front is moving in tonight and rain and sleet are due tomorrow. We regrouped and began the journey back toward our lushly tacky resort hotel in the highly visited area of Jiuzhaigou. Hans Hansen and I were examining our collections of Paeonia mairei *during our slog back to our accommodations when my eyes settled on the pewtered foliage of an* Actinidia *growing*

through a small tree along the road. I startled the driver by shouting for an immediate stop and ran up a small embankment to confirm my suspicions that what I had seen was indeed A. pilosula. *Knowing now where it grows, how it grows, will perhaps be the most important collection of this entire trip; feeling quite satisfied tonight under my fake silken bedspread on which is embroidered "Love Tender Me."*

Sichuan Province
October 11, 2003

I WONDER IF I SIMPLY HAVE too many associations with our small-town Michigan IGA, from all the time I spent as a young lad reluctantly in tow as my mom did her grocery shopping. In this small shop, the smell of freshly ground coffee blended with the sanguinary odors of the meat counter, and I purveyed the fruit and vegetable section for another new exotic species brought to the heathens of northern Michigan.

It was there that I saw my first kiwifruit (a clever New Zealand name used to market a plant that is native to China), and after enduring a few weeks of my begging, my mom finally gave in and purchased one for an outrageously high price. It was impossibly tart and had probably been picked and shipped weeks before it ripened. It would be another four decades before my life intersected again with the genus *Actinidia*.

Actinidia kolomikta. (Photo by Lynne Harrison)

It was through this genus that I learned of dioecism, monoecism, perfect and imperfect, complete and incomplete, during an advanced systematics class taught by Art Kruckeberg at the University of Washington. As an illustrative example, Dr. Kruckeberg had brought from his garden—or more precisely from the garden of Mareen Kruckeberg, his wife, a renowned horticulturist—a flowering stem of *Actinidia arguta*. This particular selection was a notably polygamous, self-fertile individual.

This, however, is not the norm for the genus *Actinidia*, which is primarily dioecious, requiring both male and female plants for fruit and seed to be formed. Though it is this fruit that seems to garner a lion's share of generic contemplation, the floral display of many of the species is patently underappreciated. I recall how I first encountered *A. deliciosa* in prime blossom while walking the landscape garden of Bishop's Close in Portland, Oregon,

A rare variegated selecion of *Actinidia deliciosa* in my garden. (Photo by Daniel J. Hinkley)

Actinidia kolomikta. (Photo by Daniel J. Hinkley)

with the late J. C. Raulston. I was baffled as to what might possess such substantial, prepossessing flowers of white. J. C. was not. Later I would come to appreciate the floral pageants of, most notably, *A. hemsleyana*, *A. latifolia*, and *A. pilosula*.

Found in the Actinidiaceae along with the genera *Clematoclethra* and *Saurauia*, the 50-odd species of vines and, rarely, small trees in *Actinidia* are found only in the Old World, geographically centered in China, north to Siberia, and south to Indochina. And it was in Asia, 10 years post-education, that my relationship with the so-called kiwi vines deepened while I began to fully appreciate their potential in North American horticulture.

During my first trip to South Korea in 1993, while in the northeastern part of the country along the demilitarized zone, I first encountered *Actinidia kolomikta* and *A. polygama*, often growing in the same niche. Though actinidias are abundant throughout most of Asia, the specimens "crown out" atop the overstory and are seen relatively infrequently by casual visitors to natural areas. The exception is along river beds and road cuts where sufficient light invites them to present foliage at or near ground level.

It was indeed along a river in Mount Sorak National Park that I first attempted to distinguish between the two species. Photos of the two might suggest otherwise, but enough variation exists between them to allow for plenty of second-guessing.

Actinidia kolomikta, hardy to zone 3, is well known in cultivation, with bold, oval foliage naturally and strikingly variegated with irregular blotches of pink and white, presumably a nonfloral advertisement for pollinators. It is often touted that this variegation is found only on male specimens, but I have collected fruit of this species on numerous occasions from variegated female plants, although this natural variegation exists in approximately half as many females as males.

The cymes of white or pink flowers of *Actinidia kolomikta* result in, on female plants, large clusters of small, ovoid fruits that are sweet and orange-yellow when fully ripened. This contrasts with *A. polygama*, whose small clusters of large, actually rather showy, cylindrical fruits are acrid even when fully ripened. This was a profoundly useful though somewhat painful method of identifying these two species while in the field.

Actinidia polygama, known as silver vine, is equally hardy as *A. kolomikta*, and as its name implies, it has bisexual flowers occurring on the same plant along with either solely male or female flowers. The foliage is naturally and consistently variegated with large, white to yellow markings, and the small clusters of white flowers in late spring are ethereally fragrant.

Interestingly, for the genus at large but most notably *Actinidia polygama*, a compound within the leaves is highly attractive to cats, who react to it as if it was industrial-strength catnip, once prompting an intern in our nursery to refer to *A. polygama* as "cat crack." This identical reaction has long been recorded in literature in Japan and is still alluded to in the saying *Neko ni matatabi, jorō ni koban*, "Silver vine to a cat, a coin to a beggar." It is widespread across mainland China and reported to be often cultivated; my Sichuan collection from 2004, DJHS 4203, was assigned to this species.

We also employed a second, more palatable method of distinguishing between the two species by splitting the stem between nodes. *Actinidia kolomikta* has a solid white pith, while the inner stem of *A. polygama* is brown and comprised of numerous layers.

While in Korea in 1993, on numerous occasions in both the north and south, we also collected *Actinidia arguta*, the Chinese gooseberry. Though it is touted as the hardiest member of the genus for fruiting purposes, I find it rather bland in ornamental appeal. The glabrous, unvariegated foliage on vigorous, twining stems is rather pedestrian, although the clusters of large, white, five-petaled flowers are showy if not ephemeral. These result in stout, oblong, lime green fruit (or a handsome dark plum in *A. arguta* var. *purpurea*) the size of a large grape, culinarily possessing the same acquired taste

Actinidia polygama. (Photo by Daniel J. Hinkley)

A compound in the foliage of *Actinidia polygama* makes the plant irresistible to felines. (Photo by Daniel J. Hinkley)

of the kiwi of commerce. There are numerous named selections; as a Spartan, I feel compelled to mention 'Michigan State', selected at my eponymous alma mater, with particularly large fruit. I do cultivate a striking variegated selection of this species, found at a nursery in Gotemba, Japan.

A closely related species known as *Actinidia rufa* is found in both Japan and South Korea. The bright red petioles of this species can help distinguish it from *A. arguta*; however, a more reliable identifier is the brown indumentum on the undersurface of young leaves, which diminishes to axillary tufts of hair by midsummer.

In China proper, with 55 species of *Actinidia*, 44 of which are endemic, putting proper names to any species collected becomes more challenging. Not so, however, with the king kiwi itself, *A. chinensis*, whose broad, oval-ovate, brown, velvety leaves and conspicuously reddish, pubescent, twining stems shout its identity. Because it is found virtually throughout China and possesses such a long history of cultivation, as with the ginkgo and apple, pinpointing its true natural range is difficult if not impossible. My collection of this species from above Baoxing in Sichuan Province, DJHC 0612, might have easily arisen from plants escaped from cultivation.

On Mount Emei, also in Sichuan, my notes are vague, as they have been with so many of the actinidias I have collected. This for DJHC 0565:

Very common twining species throughout this area of the mountain, from 2400 m [7874 ft.] down to the village. Most we observed had pink-variegated foliage; however, this trait was not observed (or noted) on this specimen. More than likely it is the same species. I opened the internode and observed a solid pith, showing affinity to *A. kolomikta*; however, the fruit is oblong, brownish green, to 1 in. [2.5 cm], not squat or top-shaped.

While in northern Sichuan Province in 2003, near the popular tourist destination of Jiuzhaigou Valley, I excitedly observed a plant, unfortunately without fruit, of what I believe was *Actinidia pilosula*. I have long cultivated a plant under this name from a plant originally received from a nursery in England (without collection data). The tips of the elegant and narrow dark green leaves are variegated brilliant white, a sensational contrast with the cymes of rose-red flowers in early summer. The *Flora of China* (Wu et al. 1994 to present), however, notes that this species occurs only in the Gongga Shan in northwestern Yunnan near Lichiang. Future travels to this locale will include a concerted effort to secure wild collections of this much-too-little-known species.

The mountains of northern Vietnam offer a sizeable sampling of the genus, if not the same degree of vagueness and, on my part, apathy toward their ornamen-

Actinidia pilosula. (Photo by Daniel J. Hinkley)

tal and edible application to Western horticulture. The Wynn-Joneses and I collected four species in 1999, most notably *Actinidia indochinensis*, HWJ 99672—notably, I say, as it was not necessarily the slightly tomentose foliage and rounded green fruit with raised brown protrusions that I found memorable, but the number of leaches that I discovered that day attached to my bloodied legs and arms midtrek.

In eastern Nepal in 2002 these same traveling companions, along with novelist Jamaica Kincaid (who later documented the trip for *National Geographic Traveler*), collected seed of *Actinidia callosa*, HWJK 2367, at slightly above 6000 ft. (1800 m) along the Mewa Khola river drainage. It is a widespread species across much of Asia, forming small, rounded, brown, tomentose fruit similar in effect to a miniature commercial kiwi, *A. chinensis*. This same species has been noted during travels in Taiwan in 1999 and again in 2007, where the botanists recognize two varieties: *A. callosa* var. *callosa* and *A. callosa* var. *ephippioidea*.

Despite the paucity of species that have made landfall into mainstream Western horticultural, there do exist sincere and knowledgeable proponents of the genus. "Kiwibob" Glanzman of Hansville, Washington, remains its foremost cheerleader, while major collections exist at the National Clonal Germplasm Repository in Corvallis, Oregon, as well as with Roger Myers in Fountain Valley, California. Within these remain an

Actinidia pilosula in Sichuan Province. (Photo by Daniel J. Hinkley)

Actinidia rufa. (Photo by Daniel J. Hinkley)

inventory of superb deciduous and hardy vines that, in terms of foliage, flower, and fruit, demand greater recognition as superlative components of our landscape.

HARDINESS: Several actinidias are among the hardiest of all deciduous vining plant species, with *Actinidia kolomikta*, *A. arguta*, and *A. polygama* leading the pack of those evaluated, all taking subzero temperatures in stride. The key phrase here is "those evaluated." Though *A. deliciosa* is considered hardy only in zones 6–9, many other species have not yet been sufficiently tested; regardless of provenance, it may be much too early to assume that these do not possess the hardiness inherent to other members of the genus.

CULTIVATION: Both sexes are required for successful pollination, and though so-called self-fertile selections exist, a more copious fruit set is promoted by a matched set. In my estimation, finding the correct light levels for the variegated species is paramount for optimal enjoyment. Too much sun and the colors bleach, while too much shade encourages unvariegated foliage. A few hours of direct early-morning or late-afternoon sun with bright, shaded conditions in between seems to be ideal. Well-draining, humus-rich soil with adequate moisture is the best edaphic condition. Though growing these plants on a fence, wall, or arbor is acceptable, the variegated forms are ideally displayed climbing through a dark-foliaged evergreen tree; if and when too much vine is achieved, prune it hard to 2 ft. (0.6 m) in late winter before growth resumes.

PROPAGATION: The tiny seed of *Actinidia* will readily germinate if sown fresh after a single cold stratification. Sexing the plants is problematic, of course, until their inaugural flowering. Softwood cuttings under mist during the summer can be easily employed in the propagation of named or already-sexed selections. Encouraging a flush of growth in late summer after rooting will enhance survivability after the first winter.

Clematoclethra

While the late Gerald Straley was curator of collections at the University of British Columbia (UBC) Botanical Garden in Vancouver, he introduced me to a genus of deciduous vines known as *Clematoclethra*. It was frequently a curious name, whether scientific or common, that piqued Gerald's interest and paved the way for further inspection, and there could hardly have been a more unlikely amalgamation of two well-known plant names than *Clematoclethra*. In truth, as *Klethra* was the Greek name for *Alnus*, presumably the moniker is meant to evoke more an image of a climbing alder than actual *Clethra*. From cuttings that Gerald shared with me at that time, I grew this vine under the name *C. hemsleyi* (it is now considered to be a variety of *C. scandens*) for numerous years in my first garden on the vine arbor that encircled our front yard. The round-ovate foliage to 3½ in. (9 cm) long, alternately held along its extremely vigorous stems, indeed possessed the overall gestalt of an *Actinidia*, while the clusters of small male flowers possessed only 10 stamens, as opposed to numerous stamens in the flowers of *Actinidia*. The fruits, which I have since collected at 10,000 ft. (3000 m) in Sichuan, are glossy black berries.

Though I too was intrigued by the plant's name and certainly by its affinity to the genus *Actinidia*, in time its too vigorous growth in combination with a not-so-heady list of ornamental attributes forced me to make room for a more "profitable" species. I hope the UBC Botanical Garden was not as ruthless; in my discarding of this species from my collection, I felt as if I had betrayed a fond memory of the plantsman who did not require a splash and dance from any plant to fully appreciate it.

HARDINESS: Of the 20 described species of the genus, many of which are from subtropical regions in central and western China and most of which have not been trialed in cultivation, it must be presumed that their hardiness echoes that of the actinidias. My specimen of *Cle-*

matoclethra scandens var. *hemsleyi* thrived in a particularly cold spot in the garden and never demonstrated any degree of cold damage after arctic outbreaks and single-digit temperatures.

CULTIVATION: Though my experience with successfully cultivating this taxon is limited to one species, my success with it was based on siting it in full sun on the south side of an arbor in draining soils that received supplemental irrigation during the growing season. As with *Actinidia*, both sexes must be present for successful fruit production; however, as the fruit possesses questionable palatability and certainly scant ornamental interest, there is little reason to risk having *Clematoclethra* unleashed into our native ecosystems by seeking out and planting both sexes.

PROPAGATION: We once easily rooted the sole representative of the genus by means of softwood cuttings under mist with no significant degree of attrition after potting. Considering, however, that our yearly projected sales of this little-known vine were in the vicinity of zero to three, we would not have been noticeably flummoxed should one have actually died. Propagation

Clematoclethra scandens, in fruit, in western Sichuan Province. (Photo by Daniel J. Hinkley)

by seed presents the same insignificant challenges presented by *Actinidia*, if sown fresh and granted one cold stratification.

Bold Foliage, Beguiling Berries: *Alangium*

Ferris [Miller] hosted us for dinner in his elegant home last night in Seoul, where I met for the first time my traveling mates for the few weeks ahead: Jamie Compton, who is working on his doctorate from Reading (Cimicifuga and Actaea), nurseryman John Coke of Green Farm Plants in Hampshire, John D'Arcy, a somewhat proper English gardener, and lastly a keen and down-to-earth horticulturist by the name of Marina Christopher. I felt an immediate rapport with Christopher and sensed we would get ourselves into heaps of trouble while together on this trip. From the others, I sensed in our initial conversations that my own botanical mettle would soon enough be measured by those around me.

This morning Kihun Song, a plantsman from Chollipo and our guide and interpreter, suggested we stop en route to visit an ancient and revered specimen of Ginkgo biloba in a small protected reserve about half the distance to Mount Sorak, our destination for this evening. Within minutes on the trail I was seeing familiar plants for the first time in the wild, with all the excitement that entails. Clerodendrum, Lindera, Acer, Symplocos, Aristolochia, and Carpinus, among others. It was a lovely autumn day, and I madly attempted to take pictures while keeping up with the troops.

As I caught up with our party once again, I found the lot of them, sans Kihun, gathered around a shrub, fondling its bold, three-lobed, maplelike leaves, which were developing buttery yellow autumn tones, and glistening sapphire fruit. All possessed that unmistakable vaguish posture of unfamiliarity, and as I approached I knew instantly that I was up to bat.

I told them that if I was correct, this was Alangium platanifolium var. macrophyllum, but that we should verify with Kihun when he came along. I said, for Compton, that I believed it was in the Alangiaceae but close to the Cornaceae; for Coke, that it should be more frequently found in the nursery trade; and for D'Arcy, that it seemed it would make a really good garden plant. I told Christopher she should not touch the seed, as it was known to cause a severe allergic skin reaction; believing me to be earnest, she backed away, and I started gathering all of the seed for myself, resulting in a minor concussion of laughter between us (note: none from D'Arcy).

It is duly noted before lights-out, now at our very nice accommodation near Mount Sorak, that I knew definitely that it was Alangium the moment I saw it, as we had first met only last week while I was visiting Gerald Straley in Vancouver. Gerald and I admired it together in the far end of the David C. Lam Asian Garden. He told me that it was the only member of the Alangiaceae, close to the Cornaceae, that he thought it would make a splendid garden plant and certainly deserved to be in the trade. And he said I would assuredly see it while in Korea.

Near Mount Sorak, South Korea
September 18, 1993

Alangium platanifolium var. macrophyllum
(Photo by Daniel J. Hinkley)

THE SPECIMEN OF *Alangium platanifolium* var. *macrophyllum* at the UBC Botanical Garden had been planted at the very back of their collection in the David C. Lam Asian Garden, making it seem almost secretive and thus even more seductive. The large trilobed leaves of this shrub, to 6 in. by 5 in. (15 cm by 12.5 cm), were a pleasant matte green, and when Gerald lifted them for me to peak beneath, I realized they were hiding the floral attributes of this genus. Held in cymes, the pendulous inch-long flowers of white, strongly reflexed petals and yellow stamens appeared to me superficially similar to those of a shooting star (*Dodecatheon*).

Yet my association with this genus was enhanced soon after my introduction to it, when I spent the autumn of 1993 in South Korea. Throughout the entire southern half of the peninsula, this shrub made itself known at virtually every stop and in every conceivable floristic association. According to my collection notes from that autumn, I collected seeds of this taxon on Mount Sorak to the far northeast, on Ulleung Island in the Sea of Japan, on Mount Chiri to the south, and on Taehuksan Island in the South China Sea.

As I became reacquainted with this shrub in the wild that autumn, its most endearing traits came into their finest moments. Those rather secretive flowers I had admired in Vancouver in late summer had transitioned to shimmering turquoise drupes, just as the foliage had begun to develop handsome autumn tints of golden yellow. What struck me then was a question I have returned to many times with regard to other plants in other areas of the world: considering the downright vulgarity of this species in the wild, and its inherent beauty, why was it not better known in cultivation?

Alangium is a genus primarily of the tropics and subtropics. Besides Korea, 21 species occur in Africa, Australia, Fiji, and Indonesia, with 11 species in China proper. My grasp of the physical variation among species—beyond having read the vastly riveting, illuminative botanical descriptions found in various floras of the world—is decidedly impaired. It does appear, however, when untangling these Latinized descriptors, that when one learns to identify one *Alangium*, most if not all others will make their identities easily accessible.

The leaves are large, alternately arranged, can be completely glabrous, completely pubescent, or somewhere in between, and are uniformly described as orbicular to suborbicular, simple, and three- to five-lobed. The flowers are produced in axillary cymes and result in fleshy drupes.

Once fully enamored with the Korean taxon of *Alangium*, I was keen on collecting the seed of *A. chinense*, an endeavor with which I found success in Yunnan Province in 1996, just above Kunming in the Western Hills, where I excitedly collected the fruit from upright specimens to 25 ft. (7.6 m). I soon realized, however, that it is difficult to *not* encounter *A. chinense* throughout China and Taiwan, especially below 7000 ft. (2100 m), where it is either native or, more likely, has naturalized from cultivated plants. *Alangium chinense* is one of the 50 fundamental herbs in traditional Chinese medicine and is used for a compendium of ailments, from snakebites to arthritis, and has thusly quickly germinated in the footsteps of wandering men.

A resulting plant from my Yunnan collection was soon enough established in my woodland garden, but as it gained heart, my interest in it waned. I was accustomed to the dense, rounded framework of *Alangium platanifolium*, and my new accession grew rampantly upright and sparse. In addition, it soon enough expressed its ability to produce root suckers far from the parent plant, while I came to expect that I would have considerable damage to the previous year's wood if we suffered hard frosts. Records indicate that I had removed it from the collection by 2000.

In the summer of 2007, while on the campus of Scott Arboretum at Swarthmore College near Philadelphia, I became acutely cognizant of how cavalier I had been in my dismissal of *Alangium chinense* as a good garden shrub. There, planted in full sun, grows a superlative specimen to 15 ft. (4.6 m) tall, providing topnotch textural qualities from its foliage. Through communication with friend and Swarthmore horticulturist Andrew Bunting, I learned that though this specimen does flower dependably, it does not fruit.

Of the additional 19 species, I can offer no anecdotal information regarding their ornamental attributes or introduction to Western horticulture.

HARDINESS: Communications with staff members of the Missouri Botanical Garden strongly suggest that *Alangium platanifolium* is hardy in zones 6–9, while *A. chinense* also thrives in zones 6–10. It is likely that *A. chinense* benefits from the heat of the eastern seaboard, which ripens the wood before autumn temperatures plummet.

CULTIVATION: In my experience with *Alangium platanifolium* var. *macrophyllum* in cultivation, it has been planted in partial to full shade, where it produces a handsome flowering shrub and dependably colors each autumn. With that said, I believe both *A. chinense* and *A. platanifolium* will perform admirably under full-sun conditions, tolerating any well-drained, evenly moist soils. Cross-pollination between clones will enhance seed production.

PROPAGATION: Seeds sown fresh in autumn germinate readily the following spring after a single cold stratification. The large leaves and substantial internode length present challenges in propagation by softwood cuttings; leaves should be substantially reduced in size and placed under mist. Root cuttings of *Alangium chinense*, taken in early to midwinter, are successful, as is simply removing root suckers.

Smart Design: *Aristolochia*

It has been a rather remarkable day, and my neck has what I will henceforth call a Kalopanax *crook. So uncannily does the foliage of this tree appear from the corner of the eye to be that of* Acer macrophyllum, *I found myself the entire day jerking my head right and then left in double takes, wondering if we were indeed in Korea or the Olympics back home. It was a good day of collecting, with dry weather and all in high spirits, with 41 good accessions by day's end.*

We hiked today in a particularly rich area with an overstory of Kalopanax pictus, Acer triflorum *(disappointingly, no seed present on either),* Hovenia dulcis, Acer mono, *as well as* A. mandshuricum. *Of the latter, we disturbingly encountered a very ancient specimen that had been recently cut, apparently by commercial seed collectors. The branches were neatly stacked in a pile with all seed stripped away; sadly, it felt much like coming across a fallen elephant killed for its ivory.*

There was a rich inventory of herbaceous plants throughout the area, including Jeffersonia dubia, Arisaema angustatum var. peninsulae, Lilium tsingtauense, L. cernuum, Polygonatum involucratum, *and* Smilacina japonica. *Along a moderate-sized river there was sufficient light to bring the lianas closer to ground level. The variegated leaves of* Actinidia polygama *and* A. kolomikta *both shown from a distance; however, what caught my eye especially was the immense, broad, heart-shaped leaves of* Aristolochia manshuriensis. *We searched through a tangle of stems on numerous specimens and ultimately found a large cluster of sausage-shaped fruit. Such a handsome foliage plant it is, just beginning to turn to buttery yellow, and so similar in appearance to* Aristolochia macrophylla.

There was a significant open, moist meadow adjacent to this fruitful pipevine, with an enormous colony of an orchid we believed to be in the genus Listera. *We had our lunch there on a large rock in the sun, gorging on a sack of perfectly ripened persimmons that Kihun had bought this morning. I sensed we all felt quite drunken by the perfection of the moment.*

Mount Chuwang, South Korea
October 3, 1997

I T IS HARD TO ARGUE that any flower of any plant is designed more perfectly than all the rest. Whether a flower is elaborate in appearance or ostensibly simple, the mechanics of pollination, fertilization, and seed dispersal of each plant have been operating quite smoothly without our admiration for hundreds of millions of years.

With that said, the survival mechanisms of some plant species can seem a bit more clever and possess a bit more intrigue than others. Some plants are simply more entertaining to the human brain, to be more to the point. And what could possibly be more intriguing than sex and bondage?

The elaborately designed flower of *Aristolochia gigantea*. (Photo by Daniel J. Hinkley)

Pollinator "domination" in the plant kingdom is probably more common than is acknowledged. The most notorious of these is *Araujia sericifera*, a tender vine in the milkweed family that entices moths with its sweet nectar, only to grab on to their proboscises and hold hostage their tongues until the next morning, when, now thoroughly dusted with pollen, they are released. Interestingly, while on a rooftop garden in downtown Tokyo, I saw the same scenario played out in a flower of *Cynanchum ascyrifolium*, a hardy herbaceous perennial also in the Asclepidaceae. Realizing that one is never certain when the friendship of moths could come in handy (as when one is faced with imprisonment atop a high tower in Middle Earth), I carefully extracted the moth from its captor and let it free.

In a more passive and ever more furtive tactic, the curiously shaped flowers in the genus *Aristolochia* are also in the business of full-scale insect exploitation without regard to their pollinators' fundamental comforts. Without realizing the carnage taking place inside (or perhaps while knowing full well), the gardener can take both folial and floral pleasure from this assemblage of hardy and tropical vines and herbaceous perennials.

The Aristolochiaceae is a family of eight genera, three of which are commonly encountered in plant-driven gardens in North America. In addition to the type genus, *Aristolochia*, represented by more than 400 species worldwide in both the New and Old Worlds and in both hemispheres, the hardy gingers, *Asarum*, and yellow-flowered *Saruma* share the ranks. Of those 400 species, 45 occur in China, with 33 endemic to its political boundaries (studies suggest that numerous taxa should be translocated to the genus *Isotrema*).

Besides the vernacular name of birthwort, two other common names, Dutchman's pipe and pipevine, are more descriptive of the flower of many species. The U-shaped flower possesses a wide-open mouth that quickly narrows and, before expanding again to an inflated tube, bends significantly upward.

In the depths of this inflated floral tube, the flower's innermost chambers, complex pollination strategies are played out. In the botanical version of *Hotel California*, scores of midges and flies are invited in through a one-way corridor by a promise of nectar (or in some cases an odor replicating rotting flesh, where eggs would be laid). The flower continues to amass its prisoners in surprisingly large numbers until, at last, one arrives with the pollen from another plant of the same species. Once fertilization has been completed (a false window has led the pollen-carrying insect to the stigma), the flower powders its residents with pollen, opens its doors, and sends them on their way. This represents yet another good reason to never be the first to arrive for a party.

It is interesting and important to note that all members of the genus possess aristolochic acid, which comes into play in the life cycle of butterflies, in particular the swallowtails, whose larvae ingest and assimilate the chemical as a defense mechanism, making them poisonous or unpalatable to predators. Species of *Aristolochia* have a lengthy history in traditional Chinese medicine, and more recently in Western weight loss regimens. In 2000 the FDA issued a warning against humans ingesting *Aristolochia* products after the genus was linked to kidney failure and specific cancers. This would of course suggest the obvious: make sure to safeguard children from ingesting anything from the garden.

I first came to know the genus as a young gardener in zone 4 north-central Michigan. *Aristolochia macrophylla* (syn. *A. durior*) was the vine of choice to cover arbors and screens in summer on the shaded north sides of homes, where assuredly nothing remotely ribald was happening inside. The bold, heart-shaped, deciduous foliage provides a textural relief unlike any other hardy native vine, while the curious brown-purple flowers are hidden beneath. Much later I observed this species in the mountains of western North Carolina near Asheville, growing through maples, oaks, magnolias, and ashes, while presenting visually a near-perfect rendition of the forest environments of the mountains of South Korea.

It was during my first trip to Korea that I came to know *Aristolochia manshuriensis*, which is seen climb-

Aristolochia manshuriensis. (Photo by Daniel J. Hinkley)

ing and twining 50 ft. (15 m) or more into the upper atmosphere of the canopy, brandishing large heart-shaped foliage to 8 in. (20 cm) across. Its handsome yellow flowers are freely produced in my garden now; however, it was through my encounter with this species in the wild that I came to appreciate the effects of its fruit—honking huge, sausage-shaped, lavender pods to 6 in. (15 cm) long.

After moving to western Washington, I became enamored with the only West Coast representative of the genus, which I first saw during a visit to the Carl S. English Jr. Botanical Garden at the Chittenden Locks. *Aristolochia californica* is a diminutive plant, to 12 ft. (3.6 m), and perhaps the most charming in flower of the hardy species. The smaller gray-green foliage appears in midspring, only after the relatively large, translucent,

Aristolochia manshuriensis growing together with *Hydrangea seemannii*. (Photo by Lynne Harrison)

Aristolochia californica. (Photo by Daniel J. Hinkley)

tawny pink flowers appear in abundance along a barren framework of green stems. I have chosen to grow this species through a specimen of *Callicarpa* 'Profusion', sited where the flowers are backlit by early morning sunlight in early spring. Though all *Aristolochia* species will tolerate a great deal of shade, this species seems to appreciate a greater degree of direct sun.

The flowers of a Japanese species, *Aristolochia kaempferi*, though relatively small, pack a punch with their shades of vivid yellow contrasting with a deep burgundy throat. The felted gray-green leaves are linear and trilobed to 4 in. (10 cm) long along stems to 8 ft. (2.4 m). I have observed this species both on Honshū and Shikoku in Japan as well as in central Taiwan when with friends Bleddyn and Sue Wynn-Jones in 1999, collecting it under the number DJHT 99105. It is closely related to

Aristolochia kaempferi. (Photo by Lynne Harrison)

another species that we saw together on Honshū, having collected its seed near Wakayama in 1997. *Aristolochia onoei* is somewhat more glabrous in leaf than the more pubescent *A. kaempferi*, and in the garden setting, in my experience at least, is somewhat thuggish in behavior with an aggressive, annoying habit of spreading by underground rhizomes.

I observed *Aristolochia* aff. *delavayi* in the mountains of northeastern Sichuan Province near the small village of Tao Yuan in 2003, and collected its seed under the number DJHS 4226 when I returned in 2004 with friends Scott McMahan, Ozzie Johnson, Dave Demers, and Riz Reyes. During the 2004 trip, we surveyed the amazingly rich inventory of plants in the surrounding landscape, at times in disbelief as to the degree of diversity revealed foot by foot. This collection is now firmly established in my garden in Indianola, where I await the first blossoming to verify its identity.

A year later, Scott, Dave, and I reconnoitered in Sikkim and Bhutan, where we saw numerous specimens of *Aristolochia griffithii*, a large-leaved, vigorous species that occurs also in Myanmar and Nepal. As this species grows at elevations of 6000 ft. (1800 m), I can only expect it to be fully hardy if trialed in the Pacific Northwest; however, it will not come from our collections, as not a single fruit remained on the vines.

Aristolochia cucurbitifolia, an extremely rare and endangered species from Taiwan, has perhaps the most distinctive foliage of any *Aristolochia* species I have grown. As its specific name implies, the foliage of this species, collected by Bleddyn and Sue from the Southern Cross-Island Highway in Taiwan at 3300 ft. (1000 m), are deeply lobed and squashlike in appearance. The "pipes" are relatively large and yellow-brown; however, its relative lowness in elevation would suggest a tender and heat-loving disposition. My experiences thus far in my garden have lent credence to this suspicion.

Not all aristolochias are vines; some of the most endearing species are herbaceous or evergreen perennials. *Aristolochia debilis* is a suckering, scandent shrublet from Japan that has proportionally large yellowish green pipes clustered along short stems to less than 1 ft. (0.3 m). It is commonly encountered as an artfully containerized "bonsai" in Japanese horticulture. *Aristolochia serpentaria*, known as Virginia snakeroot, can be found in undisturbed woodlands from Connecticut to Florida. The small, tubular, pinkish white flowers are held just above the ground, while the stems holding linear, papery foliage rise to 15 in. (38 cm). It is not particularly showy, certainly, though illustrative of the effulgent flora of eastern North America.

It is in the tropics, where the lion's share of this genus dwells, that the shapes, sizes, and biologies of *Aristolochia* species take on otherworldly auras. Perhaps best known is *A. gigantea*, successfully cultivated as a summer "bedding-out" vine on the East Coast. I have seen this grown to perfection at Chanticleer Garden near Philadelphia. Where sultry summer temperatures exist, its cultivator will appreciate the enormous, flared, purple-spotted flowers, which might be described as beautiful or simply beautifully suggestive. Vancouverian plantsman Tom Hobbs characterized *A. gigantea* succinctly as "an obscene flying tropical pancake with a scrotal pouch." Sadly, due to the perpetual coolness of our region, we cannot grow this species in the Pacific Northwest. I wish we could, though, if only to repeat that apt description to friends as we walk the garden in the evening.

Fortunately, however, I can grow other aristolochias successfully. And when—especially when—I am ushering children (our next generation of gardeners) through the garden, I will take a flower of any aristolochia when it is in blossom, and open it and watch a hundred midges

Aristolochia griffithii. (Photo by Daniel J. Hinkley)

Aristolochia debilis. (Photo by Daniel J. Hinkley)

fly away. As I perform this task I watch also the astonished look of undiluted amazement on the faces of these children. It makes me feel good. For the children. And the midges.

HARDINESS: Whereas W. J. Bean reported that there were six species hardy enough to grow outside in England, there are without a doubt numerous newly introduced species that can be cultivated in temperate climates even without factoring in global warming. *Aristolochia macrophylla* and *A. manshuriensis* are probably the hardiest and can be grown in zones 4–9, whereas generally speaking the Asian species occurring naturally at 6000 ft. (1800 m) and above are going to survive in zones 7–10. The tropical species can be grown as summer annuals as well as superlative container specimens; however, they will not perform in summer-cool areas of the country.

CULTIVATION: Aristolochias are primarily climbers and lianas and are therefore prepared to address the shade of their supporting cast. The scrambling species are better sited in full sun. Generally speaking, the temperate species are best established in draining, humus-rich soils: feet in the shadows, heads in the sun. Butterflies favor aristolochias as habitat on which to lay eggs. The resulting larvae will eat the foliage before pupating. Let them be.

PROPAGATION: The long, narrow, sausagelike fruits of the pipevines remain extremely hard until late autumn when they soften and dehisce the seeds. These will germinate readily after a single cold stratification. Semi-hardwood cuttings under mist will root; however, the large leaves and lengthy internodes of some species are unwieldy. The suckering species can be easily divided in late winter as growth resumes.

Stipuled Splendors: *Azara*

This morning it was proven again that there is nothing that elongates a mile more efficiently, or that more lays to ruin the enjoyment of the moment, than an empty gas tank, a cognizance that has arisen in human consciousness swiftly and that will hopefully depart in same fashion. We left our lodging in Temuco in the dark this morning at 5:30, and I had not filled the tank as planned when we had arrived in town the night before. Heading toward Conguillio for a long day's outing, lost and fogged by caffeine withdrawal, and hobbled by our pathetic command of the language, I watched the gauge drop from really low to really screwed. It was my fault. Coasting a Chilean secondary road on a prayer of fume, we finally found gas and Nescafé in an unlikely village. I celebrated by procuring a day-old potato and beef empanada for breakfast.

Our approach to the trailhead in our vehicle was by way of a dusty single-track road woven through the devastatingly beautiful landscape of a relatively recent lava flow, just as the sun rose above the ridge to the east, which blinded further still my driving abilities. I was ebullient, three hours after our departure, to be on the trail with the ordeal behind us.

We all drove the trail independent of one another, at different speeds, which was perfectly fine with me; I did not see my mates for most of the following eight hours. I was entranced by the immensity of the Nothofagus *along the lower reaches of the trail: the largest I had ever seen, with impressive* Araucaria *as well. A particularly full and pyramidal specimen of* Austrocedrus chilensis *had me looking for seed on the ground for a considerable time.*

At higher elevations, the low understory became a uniform blend of two plants: one I had met before and one I had not. The former was Maytenus magellanicus, *looking so uncannily similar to our native* Paxistima myrsinites *that I caught myself transported mentally to a hike in Olympia. Kevin, Jennifer, and I collected this further northward in 1997. The other, however, was familiar but curious. In foliage and fruit, there was no question that this was in the genus* Azara; *as I was approaching the alpine zone, I could only believe this was actually* A. alpina *that I was seeing for the first time, an assertion I confirmed minutes ago with my reference books back at our hostel.*

Temuco, Chile
March 3, 2005

W HEN I WAS A RELATIVE newcomer to the horticultural scene in Seattle, there was no question that I had to prove my mettle to those stalwarts who either anoint or eject young upstarts. Thusly I was asked to speak at a small, rarified private gardening club attended by some of the finest plantspeople in the area. I presented a few of my favorite plants, yet learned that these were only props for the purposes at hand. *Abeliophyllum distichum*, for example. "Exactly what does *distichous* mean?" I was asked. *Azara ser-*

Overleaf: *Azara lanceolata* and *Chusquea culeou* growing together in the *Araucaria* complex of southern Chile. (Photo by Daniel J. Hinkley)

42

rata, as another. "And what family does that belong to?" I answered without flinching: "The Flacourtiaceae, the same as *Idesia polycarpa* and *Poliothyrsis sinensis*." There was a satisfied bobbing of heads about the hall.

As it turns out, I was quite wrong and so were those who sat in judgment of my horticultural abilities. The genus *Azara* has been reassigned to the family of willows and alders, the Salicaceae. It brings to mind a quote I once read, unattributed, made by a retired Ivy League professor of physics in the early 1990s: " I shudder to think how many students I have failed for not knowing something that is now no longer true." This is particularly apropos in the contemporary state of plant taxonomy.

Well, I know a few willows and alders, and though botanists might explain what traits these two odd genera share with *Azara*, they are, to the layman, as far apart in appearance as *Idesia* and *Poliothyris* are from their former housemate. The genus *Azara*, commemorating Félix de Azara, a Spanish naturalist who traveled to South America from 1781 to 1801, is a conglomeration of small evergreen shrubs and trees that bellow for greater application in gardens from British Columbia to Southern California. It is not only the appropriate proportions they provide for integration into the mixed border but also their highly textural evergreen qualities and often showy, sometimes fragrant floral display that demand the attention of the keen gardener with an eye for quality and the uncommon. The flowers of all species are apetalous; what beauty they provide comes by way of myriad numbers of yellow or creamy-colored anthers.

Of the 12 species found throughout the southern Andes in Chile, *Azara microphylla*, the box-leaf azara, would be the most likely to encounter by chance in the landscapes of the Pacific Northwest. This species must have had some following by midcentury horticulturists; it can be found occasionally in mature landscapes in the older neighborhoods of Seattle, where according to plantsman Arthur Lee Jacobsen it has been grown in gardens since 1893. When one becomes familiar with its distinctive gloss and texture, there is little chance of mistaking its glittery presence with anything else.

Azara microphylla adheres to the foliage characteristics of the genus as a whole: evergreen leaves alternately arranged along the stem, with each leaf attended by a large, leaflike stipule at its base. To the untrained eye it appears that there are two very differently shaped leaves attached at the same point—and it is because of this that such superlative textural qualities are offered, as well as a very quick and easy field identification.

The box-leaf azara quickly creates a narrow, upright tree to 15 ft. (4.6 m) or somewhat more and offers seasonal delights well beyond its persistent folial luster. In late winter, small axillary clusters of yellow flowers, barely noticeable, pack a commanding punch in terms of fragrance, a characteristic that prompted the Chileans to christen this small tree with the name aromo.

Azara microphylla. (Photo by Lynne Harrison)

Described by some as vanilla and by others as white chocolate, it is a delicious, unexpected off-season fragrance that sets into motion the appropriate Pavlovian response of salivation. I refer to it as aromo-therapy.

Despite the secure position of *Azara microphylla* in horticulture, and the fact that I have developed a keen interest in the genus with two surveys into its natural territories, this species is among the azaras I have never met in the wild. It is known to occur in association with *Nothofagus obliqua*, a colonizing, somewhat coarse-looking Antarctic beech found in drier sites of Chile and adjoining parts of Argentina.

There exists a lesser-known, yet endearing, variegated counterpart of this species, and though it has been in cultivation for over a hundred years, it was for many years virtually unknown in the North American trade. *Azara microphylla* 'Variegata' carries demure, rounded, evergreen leaves exquisitely edged in creamy white, and has a graceful, lax habit of growth, particularly if grown in a bit of shade.

Azara microphylla 'Variegata'. (Photo by Daniel J. Hinkley)

It was in the shade where I grew this specimen in my first garden, believing it too tender to tolerate low winter temperatures without overstory protection. Though I digress here, the story of how this tree came to be in my garden deserves telling. Through communication with J. C. Raulston in the early 1990s, I learned of the existence of this same variegated form in the collection of the San Francisco Botanical Garden at Strybing Arboretum. During a visit a year later, I found the rather decrepit specimen in an overgrown section along the fence line. There was little doubt that it would soon be dead, and with the permission of the staff, I took two small cuttings from the tree.

Of these, both successfully rooted in the greenhouses at Edmonds Community College, where I taught plant propagation. I took one home and left the other for the plant collection on our campus. Mine, planted in the open, expired after the first hard frost of the year. Upon my return to the school after the holidays, I found the staff had cleared the propagation benches over the break, and all existing plants had been discarded. For nearly two hours I rummaged through a reeking dumpster on campus and ultimately found my rooted *Azara*, albeit in shock, at the very bottom of the heap. From that one plant, hundreds, if not thousands, were ultimately propagated and distributed up and down the West Coast, with a replacement sent to Strybing as well.

Aspiration is often the first step to revelation, and in that vein, I sincerely hope that a more compact form of this species will be found and successfully introduced. The species itself is fast to grow and is often improperly sited in the landscape, too close to the foundation or to other plants. A good dwarf form with the same sensational fragrance in midwinter would be a welcome addition to our landscapes.

I first came to know *Azara lanceolata* from a plant growing in the lathhouse at Washington Park Arboretum when I was a student at the University of Washington in the 1980s. I was attracted then, as I am now, to its sensational foliage arrangement, with lance-shaped leaves to 3 in. (7.5 cm) long attended by rounded stipules. In early spring this small tree or large shrub, to 12 ft. (3.6 m) in height, cloaks its textural foliage with a flurry of showy butterscotch-golden flowers, sadly barely scented, produced in the axil of every leaf along the stem. Later in summer, resultant crops of powdery blue fruit are so prolific that the stems are drawn downward.

In 1998 in southern Chile, friends Kevin Carrabine, Jennifer Macuiba, and I were able to collect fruit of *Azara lanceolata* (HCM 98130) at 4120 ft. (1260 m) near Huerquehue National Park, where the plants grew in dense thickets along forest margins. Despite its lack of fragrance, I still find it an exceptional plant: fast growing, graceful in habit, and outstanding in floral and fruiting effects.

On the same trip, and again in 2005, I found and collected seed of an *Azara* that I misidentified in the field on both occasions. Collected under the number HCM 98034 as *A. petiolaris* near Laga de La Laja at 2080 ft. (630 m), this species is properly known as *A. serrata* and has proven to be a marvelous small evergreen tree for the western slope of the Pacific Northwest.

The glossy, throaty green leaves of this species are rounded, and yes, serrate, to 1 in. (2.5 cm) across, while the stipules too are orbicular though more demure in proportion. The floral effects of this species are similar to those of *Azara lanceolata*, a rich tawny yellow, although the flowers come much later in the season. Frequently, it is not until the early weeks of June that

Azara lanceolata. (Photo by Lynne Harrison)

Stipuled Splendors: *Azara*

Azara serrata. (Photo by Lynne Harrison)

this well-behaved small tree casts its stroke of color to the garden. It wastes no time in becoming established, producing a 15 ft. by 10 ft. (4.6 m by 3 m) rounded small tree in four years from a small rooted cutting, making it an ideal candidate for a moderate-sized privacy screen.

While on the subject of *Azara serrata*, one must briefly discuss *A. dentata*, a similar species that is probably irrevocably muddled in commerce under the name of the former. With a leaf similar in appearance to *A. serrata*, it differs only in the felted underside of its emerging leaf and in its slightly longer pedicel. Its flowers are reportedly fragrant; however, I will confess to only having grown numerous specimens of *A. serrata* with labels reading *A. dentata*.

Being the taxonomic wizard that I am, I also collected in 1998 a species under the name *Azara* aff. *petiolaris* HCM 98066, at the relatively low elevation of 1680 ft. (512 m) near the town of Queco on exposed

north-facing slopes. The resultant seedlings of this collection were obviously a different taxon altogether, and one was retained for my arboretum in Indianola. It blossomed for the first time in early March of 2008, revealing, miraculously, that it is indeed *A. petiolaris*. The clone that I retained possesses a very dark quality to its foliage, which is somewhat smaller than *A. serrata* and more leathery and hollylike. W. J. Bean praised this species as one of the most beautiful in the genus, but though the flowers are good—a rich tawny gold—and have a pleasant vanilla scent, in our climate the foliage leans toward a rather sickly pallor, with spots and blotches by winter's end. Though I have had this in my garden for several years, it has become best known for its perpetual sulk and has been placed mentally into the category of those that first look ugly but then die.

In 2005 it was the bright red fruit of *Azara alpina* that caught our eye as we hiked beneath an overstory

Azara petiolaris. (Photo by Daniel J. Hinkley)

of *Nothofagus dombeyi* and *Araucaria* en route to the subalpine scree on the volcano Conguillio to see populations of the bizarre *Viola cotyledon*. Growing to less than 3 ft. (0.9 m) in height and commingled with *Maytenus magellanicus* in equal number, it was a very handsome species, I felt, and deserving of introduction as a small evergreen fruiting shrub. Though I collected a good number of seeds, to my knowledge these never germinated, or the seed pot was lost during the shuttering of the nursery.

I must briefly mention *Azara integrifolia*, a tender species from central to south-central Chile to 900 ft. (275 m) in elevation. As the name implies, the leaves are entire and larger than other azaras, to 3 in. (7.5 cm) in length. There exists in the trade a variegated selection with golden yellow and rose suffusions on the leaf blade; however, I have been unsuccessful growing it or any *A. integrifolia*. It is more appropriate for coastal southern Oregon south through California.

HARDINESS: The azaras are appropriate shrubs only for zone 7 and above, with *Azara microphylla* representing the hardiest of the lot. Overstory protection will push hardiness considerably, although this comes at the expense of creating a more lax, less full habit of growth. Fruiting seemingly is not dependent on cross-pollination, as single clones will fruit quite heavily.

CULTIVATION: All azaras appreciate a well-drained, humus-rich soil with even moisture, but demonstrate some drought tolerance when fully established. Plant them with their ultimate height and width in mind, as they resent hard pruning and are difficult to successfully transplant at a large size.

PROPAGATION: Very easily propagated by seed if provided a single cold stratification. Hardwood cuttings taken in late summer to early winter, on bottom heat, root readily with very little attrition during transplanting.

Flowers, Fragrance, Winged Finery: *Buddleja*

We crossed a river with children sitting upon contented water buffalo as happy as large, lazy puppy dogs. Then we rose again amidst devastated forests, following the rotted remains of Holboellia *fruit along the trail, eaten by Hmong porters, until we found its ripened clusters ourselves and collected its fruit. After six hours of climbing, I could take no more of the heat and petulantly demanded that we stop to eat our lunch. My legs were lined with grass cuts from the* Miscanthus *through which we hiked, and my socks were blotched with blood from leach bites.*

As our guide cut our apples and served us pork sandwiches, which they called pig bread, I noticed in the distance a play of movement that I have reflected upon over and over again. Two butterflies were flying together in a finely articulated cartwheel, over and atop and around one another like enormous electrons kept in perfect orbit by an invisible nucleus. It was not a slow, methodical rhythm but one of frenzied sex. This alone was beautiful enough, but it got better. Every minute or so a third butterfly would cut into the frenzy, and when that happened, the other suitor would depart and sit it out on a nearby branch as if these were well-understood rules of engagement and social protocol. I am sure that I could identify this butterfly, or at least its genus, by the description of its behavior, so extraordinary was the crafted grace it displayed.

Above Sa Pa, Vietnam
October 4, 1999

I T WAS FOR THE RECTOR of Farnbridge in Essex that this genus was named, a one Reverend Adam Buddle, an amateur botanist who, when not preaching, amassed large collections of grasses, lichens, mosses, and seaweed in the late 17th century. I acquainted myself with this genus by way of its American misspelling—*Buddleia*—and will admit to often perpetuating the error in times of haste and general laziness.

The genus of the so-called butterfly bushes has done remarkably well for itself. Its 150-plus species are distributed over a wide range: throughout Asia, where it is geographically centered, in the higher elevations of South Africa, and from western North America southward to Tierra del Fuego.

With no authority to support this theory, I maintain that the genus *Buddleja* may be successful in nature for precisely the same reason it has become synonymous with bioinvasiveness. Ongoing studies have illuminated the fact that many *Buddleja* species show a highly efficient utilization of soil nitrogen coupled with an exuberant fashion of manufacturing carbohydrates through photosynthesis. These attributes paired with simple fecundity—a typical flower head of *B. davidii* 'Potter's Purple' will release 40,000 fertile seeds each year—have

Buddleja loricata above the Mlambonja River valley in the northern Drakensberg Mountains of South Africa. (Photo by Daniel J. Hinkley)

resulted in a blitzkrieg of naturalization in temperate climates outside its natural range. For this reason, in a span of merely 50 years, *Buddleja* has become one of England's most wide-ranging weed species.

With caution and care, as well as proper selection of species and cultivars, one can still bring buddlejas into the garden setting with a clean conscience. Even if you choose to disregard these plants entirely as landscape subjects out of deference to the potential risk, the most splendid species deserve acknowledgment, which I will provide here.

All but one species, *Buddleja alternifolia*, possess paired leaves that are retentive during the winter season. *Buddleja alternifolia* and a few other species stand apart in that they blossom on the previous year's growth, in axillary clusters, rather than the norm of terminal panicles on the current or first year's wood. Though this genus is often associated with fragrant flowers loved by lepidopterans, I have long maintained that it should be considered as much for its foliage as for its flowers.

Like many, I first became enamored of the genus through the now notorious *Buddleja davidii*. During the formative years of my first garden and nursery, I grew numerous cultivars of this species, captured by its sub-

stantial range of colors, from pure white to pink, powdery blue, and black-purple, and by its pleasing fragrance and the fact that the flowers come on relatively late in the season.

The numerous selections of this species now available in commerce are based genetically on the collections of Ernest Wilson in Sichuan and Hubei Provinces during the early years of the 20th century. It is, of course, named for Père Armand David, a devoted and kind Lazarist missionary whose intense interest in the natural sciences while in China resulted in the discovery and documentation of hundreds of species of mammals, birds, fish, reptiles, insects, and plants, including the giant panda and the fabled dove tree, *Davidia involucrata*.

Buddleja davidii, like many other species, exhibits a particularly diverse phenotype in the wild, with variously sized panicles of lavender, yellow-eyed flowers occurring up to 10,000 ft. (3000 m) in elevation. During my first trip to Sichuan in 1996, I collected what I believed to be this species at 5800 ft. (1770 m) in the Wolong area under the number DJHC 577, noting that it was growing in open, somewhat degraded, dry sites among rocky outcrops. During this trip I made numerous other collections of *Buddleja* without a species designation, my reticence due to the length of the terminal racemes. When these first blossomed several years later, it was shown that they were indeed *B. davidii*, simply showing typical variation. The downside to learning taxonomy by means of plants under cultivation is facing this kind of reticence when it comes to accepting the nonuniformity of wild plant populations.

During the same trip, I was attracted to the silvery, felted leaves of *Buddleja nivea*, a species I had already grown in my garden for several years. It is primarily a foliage plant, and a good one at that, its small, terminal, light lavender heads of flowers barely noticeable. A tetraploid form of this species, *B. nivea* var. *yunnanensis*, possesses extraordinarily large leaves to 8 in. (20 cm) long and 4 in. (10 cm) wide. With this size, the concentration of indumentum is lessened as is the visual

Buddleja davidii 'Potter's Purple'. (Photo by Lynne Harrison)

appeal; still, the large leaves provide a good textural component in the landscape.

While in Yunnan Province above Lichiang at the base of Yulong Shan, I collected the seed of another startling white-foliaged *Buddleja*, this one identified by our Chinese botanists as *B. forrestii*. These were, after all, the stomping grounds of George Forrest, a sturdy, resourceful, rakishly handsome Scot who had given up a decade of panning gold in Australia for the even less profitable prospects of panning for horticultural plants in Yunnan. Descriptions for this species in literature, however, do not precisely fit the resultant seedling in my Indianola garden, which possesses arresting, silvery, tomentose foliage and lax, pendulous, terminal racemes of small lavender flowers.

Before leaving China (with disappointment, as I have done little justice here to enhance the cachet of buddlejas still to be introduced into cultivation), I must again bring your attention to the odd duck of the genus, *Buddleja alternifolia*. I have not yet had the opportunity to visit the haunts of this species as did Reginald Farrer in the early war years of the 20th century. Years after his death, the clever, cynical, and obviously frustrated Farrer remains an enigma, but his observations of plants are often spot on. He speaks of *B. alternifolia* ebulliently, describing it in blossom as embodying an elegant waterfall of purple, in foliage a doppelganger of an old olive.

I have found this to be the case, as I have frequently with Farrer's often sensitive, tetchy observations, and would not be without *Buddleja alternifolia* in my garden. Unlike the lion's share of buddlejas, this species blossoms on second-year wood. There can be no assault on its annual growth in autumn if one wishes to savor its cascade of flowers. Though many suggest tutoring this species to a single-stemmed small tree, I have found this to be a fruitless endeavor. New basal growth springs eternal during the growing season, and to my mind its elegance is not amplified significantly by the outlay of effort. It should be noted that *B. alternifolia* does spread stoloniferously in the garden, although I have yet to observe a self-sown seedling in the Pacific Northwest.

It was beyond the southern border of Yunnan into the northern reaches of Vietnam that I spent considerable time during the early years of the 21st century. At the relatively low elevation of 4000 ft. (1200 m), along high, disturbed roadsides, I was enchanted by the fragrant, late-autumn blossoming and elegant habit of *Buddleja asiatica*. It is a delicate species in appearance and constitution; having killed it twice during rather tame winters, I at last believe it does require a temperate glasshouse for successful cultivation. It has been a featured winter-blossoming subject in Longwood Garden's fabled conservatory for many years.

I collected *Buddleja macrostachya* at a slightly higher elevation, ranging to the top of Tram Ton Pass at nearly 7000 ft. (2100 m). In appearance, at least, this species is a far cry from delicate, possessing the largest leaves of any *Buddleja* I have encountered, 1 ft. (0.3 m) long and 6 in. (15 cm) wide, and a glabrous green upper leaf surface. It has generated a great deal of questions about

Buddleja forrestii. (Photo by Daniel J. Hinkley)

Flowers, Fragrance, Winged Finery: *Buddleja*

its identity during visits from keen horticulturists; *Buddleja* is generally not among the postulates offered up, while the loquat, *Eriobotrya*, is frequently suggested.

It is a dramatic species in blossom as well, producing substantial and fully erect panicles of very fragrant, light lavender, yellow-eyed flowers in late winter. Unfortunately, by the time this flowering commences, the previous year's foliage is tattered from winter's assault, providing visual clutter to the scene.

It is appropriate to note that in the early 1990s I received a plant under the name *Buddleja macrostachya* from the late Brian Mulligan, then director emeritus of Washington Park Arboretum in Seattle. Though a stately *Buddleja* it was, with strong growth, substantial foliage, and cascading terminal panicles to 2 ft. (0.6 m) carrying fragrant lavender flowers, it was most certainly not

B. macrostachya. I propagated this for years and distributed it under this name, adding yet another layer of confusion to the taxonomy of the genus. With Mr. Mulligan's death in the mid-1990s, and the lost ability to track this plant's provenance, it is unlikely that a proper name will be attached in the foreseeable future.

In 2005, during my first trip to Sikkim in northern India, I was excited to at last encounter *Buddleja colvilei* in the wild, between the outposts of Lachung and Lachang at 9800 ft. (3000 m). It was in this general vicinity that the young J. D. Hooker spent three years botanizing in the mid-19th century, and where he was briefly imprisoned by the Dewan of Sikkim. It was also here that Hooker discovered *B. colvilei*, which he later introduced into cultivation and ordained as one of the most beautiful flowering shrubs of the Himalaya.

Buddleja macrostachya near Sa Pa, northern Vietnam. (Photo by Daniel J. Hinkley)

Buddleja colvilei. (Photo by Lynne Harrison)

Blossoming on the previous year's wood in late May and June, *Buddleja colvilei* is as perplexing in flower as *B. macrostachya* is in foliage. Whereas the quality of most butterfly bushes comes from a collective wallop of numerous, tightly packed, small flowers, this species has loose racemes of very large, bell-shaped, rich rose-red flowers, more akin to a hybrid penstemon than to *Buddleja*. I grew the historically significant Kew form of this species—with somewhat more saturated flower tones—for many years beneath the temperature-moderating shelter of the woodland in my first garden and nursery, where it blossomed dependably. Unfortunately, I have lost track of the re-collections I made of this species, under the designation of DJHSi 7098; I would have greatly appreciated seeing the variation that exists in the wild with regard to flower color and size.

While in South Korea in 1993, we collected seed of *Buddleja venenifera*—a name, at least in my experience, of which I am suspicious. The plants I collected of this species on the west coast of the peninsula appear identical to what I have grown under the name *B. lindleyana*. And I have found insignificant difference between *B. lindleyana* and what is known in the trade as *B. japonica*. This being not a taxonomic treatise, it is remarkably easy to cast such aspersions on perhaps legitimate taxa; however, it is appropriate to suggest that taxonomists look into plants in the trade making the circuit under numerous aliases.

In any event, I had long ago abandoned all three buddlejas due to their annoying habit of suckering, when I again encountered this "species" in cultivation while visiting East Hampton on eastern Long Island. Once again I admired its long and elegant chains of purple flowers and glossy green foliage—almost, but not quite enough, to make me wish to have it once again in my garden.

I have become increasingly aware of the role of *Buddleja* in traditional Chinese medicine. The foliage and flowers are prized for their healing and antibacterial properties, and indeed, isolates of verbascosides in *Buddleja* have been shown to be effective in combating *Staphylococcus aureus*. I had not yet made this con-

nection when I first visited Chile in 1998. Along the streets of Puerto Montt were street vendors selling an array of dried herbage, and among this assemblage were the very recognizable foliage and flower heads of *B. globosa*. After struggling through a conversation using my pathetic Spanish, I understood that *B. globosa* was commonly used to treat respiratory ailments.

Common throughout southern Chile, and noted as well from Peru, *Buddleja globosa* is a very distinctive species with regard to both flower color and inflorescence. From an upright framework carrying foliage that is deep green above and coated with a tawny brown indumentum below, panicles of orange flowers, presented in globose heads, are produced in spring on the previous year's wood. These offer a light fragrance but not to the degree that I have come to associate with

Buddleja globosa. (Photo by Daniel J. Hinkley)

other members of the genus. I continue to include *B. globosa* in my garden from my first collections; however, as with many other species that blossom on the second year's wood, winter-damaged foliage detracts from its otherwise splendid attributes.

Hybrids between *Buddleja globosa* and *B. davidii* were created in England in the early 20th century and introduced as *B. ×weyeriana*, offering soft yellow, fragrant, and politically correct sterile or pollen-sterile flowers.

The medicinal benefits of the genus were not overlooked by the indigenous peoples and latter-day transplants to South Africa, where several native species have been put to use for a virtual epidemic of afflictions. I feel fortunate to have first visited the Western Cape with friends during an insanely good year for wildflowers, with flashback drifts of color so intense we were emotionally drained by the end of each day. One's eyes, I have learned, become rather gluttonous under such circumstances, seldom resting on anything other than the visual confections of color.

Thus I was fortunate to have *Buddleja salviifolia* pointed out to me, right in front of my nose, by our guides, Rachel and Rod Saunders of Silverhill Seeds in Cape Town. They had, perhaps, after so many years of visual feasting, become inoculated against fixation on color alone. The buddleja grew in a not-so-hospitable environment of rocky outcrops, with gigantic clumps of *Thamnochortus* and the honeybush, *Melianthus major*, growing nearby. Its soft, felted foliage of a muted ochre is a handsome addition to the garden.

As this blossoms on the current year's wood, it will take a surprising beating from the cold damp of the Pacific Northwest and still return from the base to blossom; however, I believe it is better adapted to a warmer and more arid climate. *Buddleja salviifolia* did not make the transition from my old garden to the new one, which I hold to be the hallmark of a good (versus not-quite-good-enough) garden plant.

Buddleja loricata, however, did come to Windcliff. A year after my month in the Western Cape, I returned with friends Ketzel Levine and Keith and Roz Wiley to examine the Drakensberg Mountains south of Johannesburg. Unlike the winter-dry scrub of the eastern side of this remarkable country, the Berg, as it is called, is a drama in green, with drifts of *Agapanthus*, *Eucomis*, *Gunnera*, *Kniphofia*, *Watsonia*, and elephantine heads of vibrant red *Amaryllis* running through rivers of grass.

On a particularly fine evening, with a colored expanse of sky absorbed by rousing and terrifying thunderheads, I hiked from our lodging for another survey of our exciting surroundings. This was a landscape of mostly herbaceous plants, with the occasional native tree or shrub imposing itself upon the scene, begging for attention. It was on this memorable evening that I first made my acquaintance with *Buddleja loricata*.

Its narrow, mainly evergreen leaves, rather sagelike in appearance, have a deeply impressed upper surface of green and a brilliant white undersurface, on a tidy, compact, rounded framework to 4 ft. (1.2 m). In early summer, rather open terminal panicles of small white flowers appear, bringing with them a powerful and delightful fragrance of honey. These appear on the previous year's wood. *Buddleja loricata* is sun loving and quite drought tolerant when established, and I have planted it in full sun in my new garden, bluff-side, allowing the prevalent breeze from the water below to carry the plant's scent throughout the landscape.

In a relative sense at least, my knowledge of the genus as a whole is miniscule, though of the species I have come to know and grow, I have formed a bevy of memories that will not soon be forgotten. With my promotion of this genus comes the insistence that all who include it in their garden remain vigilant with regard to the threat of bioinvasion and choose species that are deemed "safe."

HARDINESS: As a general rule—only general—buddlejas that blossom on the current year's wood, if in fact grown for their flowers and not just their foliage, will be hardy in zones 6–10, although *Buddleja davidii* is safely hardy to 0°F (−18°C). Tenderer species and those blossoming on the previous year's growth can be pushed by planting in protected locations or adjacent to rock or masonry walls.

CULTIVATION: Virtually all species can be cut back hard to rejuvenate from the base, and this is the recommended pruning practice for *Buddleja davidii*, in late winter before growth resumes. Species blossoming on second-year wood should be pruned hard directly after flowering. I recommend removing the flowering heads of all paniculate species directly after flowering. This serves to tidy the appearance of the plant and alleviates the chances of self-sowing while encouraging lateral growth. Although this may result in a small second flush of flowers, the resultant growth of foliage will be carried through the winter, providing visual appeal in the off season. I am not aware of any insects or diseases associated with this genus.

PROPAGATION: Softwood cuttings under mist root easily, as do hardwood cuttings during the growing season. Buddlejas, like hydrangeas, are fast growers, and resulting cuttings should be potted directly into gallon containers for establishment. Seeds are, of course (and somewhat unfortunately), easy to germinate and will require only a single cold treatment. First flowering commences in two to three years.

Allspice and Fivespice: *Calycanthus*

Such peaks and valleys. As weekends go, this one will remain forever a hallmark of both the zeniths and nadirs of life and living. Robert and I flew to San Francisco on August 1 for a long-anticipated reunion with friends, heading north to The Cedars to reconnoiter with Roger Raiche, David McCrory, Marcia Donahue, Mark Bulwinkle, and Chris Woods. We were at last in the midst of this celebrated landscape, an isolated, untrammeled expanse of inner coastal wildness with outcroppings of serpentine soils supporting a rarified flora. Along cool-watered pools and falls that sliced through and tumbled over a dramatic and parched land, grew many species I had never before seen in their nativity but had long grown in my garden. Dendromecon rigidum *and* Diplacus aurantiacus *were still in blossom, as were* Epipactis gigantea *and* Calycanthus occidentalis *where a bit more moisture still existed. I will recall seeing this latter species above all, and its growth in my garden will be eternally fused with the sentiments of this time.*

It was a weekend of fellowship and frivolity, long hikes, litanies of Latin, diving in cool pools, sublime food, and assorted vintages. There was a gibbous moon on Saturday night, filling the canyon with silvered light and our howls as we watched it rise and then fall; all at once we were again 19, with overly profound thoughts and that sense of sovereignty that is somehow abdicated in maturity.

Contentedly solemn and with a collective vow to return together, we repacked our gear the following morning and left to become adults again. I can now choose to either believe that the intensity of the past week has been a consequence of that brief lessening of my grip, or that I was granted by the planets a pithy interlude before meeting up with such deep trouble. Though it will be remembered— the disturbing number of calls waiting on my phone, the rush and uncertainty to return home, the pit and panic of learning of my sister's death, and now this valley of frosted shade—I will choose to believe the latter.

Wenatchee, Washington
August 9, 2003

THE CALYCANTHACEAE IS AN ANCIENT and rather rarified plant family comprised of only three genera of shrubs: *Calycanthus* and *Chimonanthus* in the Northern Hemisphere, and *Idiospermum* in Australia. It may be of some interest to mention the close taxonomic affinity this family has with the buttercup family, Ranunculaceae. Indeed, if you examine a

flower from a member of the Calycanthaceae, you will find a spiraling whorl of tepals that will suggest a *Ranunculus*, *Hepatica*, or *Anemone*, albeit in a larger form.

Though I have cultivated several taxa of the so-called wintersweets or *Chimonanthus*, both deciduous and evergreen, I possess a paucity of knowledge about the genus in the wild and little positive light to share in the garden setting. As delightful a punch of fragrance *C. praecox* provides the garden in late winter, its perfor-

Calycanthus floridus. (Photo by Lynne Harrison)

mance in the cool maritime Northwest does not begin to compare with its potential for summer-warm areas. For only a scant flowering, the shrub is too large, coarse, and monoseasonal to inhabit limited garden territory.

Until the early 1980s, Western botanists and horticulturists understood the genus *Calycanthus* through three superficially similar species native to North America: *C. floridus*, *C. fertilis*, and *C. occidentalis*. It was *C. floridus*, the so-called Carolina allspice, that found itself being utilized in horticulture more than others, though its introduction to Europe in the 18th century was based on its economic potential as a cinnamon substitute. Perhaps attesting to the commercial failure of this enterprise, all *Calycanthus* species possess an alkaloid that is poisonous to both livestock and humans (not so to horses and mules).

In fact it was this poisonous substance, identified as calycanthine, that led to the rediscovery of one of the rarest members of the Calycanthaceae. First discovered by loggers in the rain forests of Cairns, Australia, during the late 19th century, the tall evergreen tree was described at that time as *Calycanthus australiense*. Soon after, it was believed to have been extirpated by logging in the area, and was not seen again until 1971. A spate of sick and dying cattle south of Cairns led to veterinarian detective work, which ultimately led to finding the huge and distinctive seeds of this *Calycanthus*, now placed in the genus *Idiospermum*, in their guts. Brought back from the brink of extinction, in its present form, this extraordinarily rare taxon has remained unchanged for 120 million years.

More recent taxonomic detective work on the genus established justification for lumping *Calycanthus fertilis* and *C. floridus* together, with the former now known as *C. floridus* var. *glaucus*. However, not unlike a presidential recount, the story did not end there. The number of American species was resurrected to three when it was proposed that a rare population of greenish-yellow-flowered shrubs in Georgia be given species status and named *C. brockianus*. Nevertheless, this species,

too, is disputed by botanists as being only a variant of *C. floridus*.

I have seen both of the American species in their nativity: *Calycanthus floridus* growing adjacent to the American "weigela," *Diervilla sessilifolia*, on open rocky slopes in western North Carolina, and *C. occidentalis* growing along seepages, often on blazingly hot serpentine soils, slightly inward from the coast north of San Francisco. Both are similar in appearance, with broad, ovate leaves held in pairs along stems to 6 ft. (1.8 m) tall or more under cultivation. Plantsman Roger Raiche praises the duration of the buttery yellow autumn coloration of *C. occidentalis* in its natural range, which often lasts six weeks or longer. The flowers, very magnolia-like from a distance, are comprised of numerous blood-burgundy tepals arranged in spiral fashion, resulting in curious, flat-topped, dry capsules carrying numerous large seeds. In the Pacific Northwest, due to our summer chill, flowers from both American species are staggered throughout the growing season.

Calycanthus occidentalis. (Photo by Roger Raiche)

I know that I will be berated by some for suggesting that such a thoroughly American genus of shrubs possesses a lackluster appeal, yet had the status quo of *Calycanthus* continued unchecked, it is unlikely I would be writing about them, their 15 minutes of horticultural notoriety having evaporated decades ago. The somber burgundy flowers of *C. floridus* and *C. occidentalis* do not read from any distance, and the fragrance is more cloying—that of a fruit cellar in a heat wave—than sweet. Botanically interesting? Yes. Part and parcel to our natural ecologies? Absolutely! But definitely not possessing enough substance to warrant greater promotion for landscape use.

In the early 1960s, however, things were about to get a bit more interesting. On a wooded mountain slope in Zhejiang Province in eastern China, botanists discovered a 10 ft. (3 m) deciduous shrub with all the makings of a *Calycanthus* yet possessing larger flowers of white blushed with pink and a thick, firm texture. It was described in 1963 as *C. chinensis* and reclassified a year later as *Sinocalycanthus chinensis*, and it was under the name *Sinocalycanthus* that it made its debut into American horticulture in the early 1980s.

By 1985 there were only a handful of specimens in North America, mostly in botanical gardens, and all had caused a considerable stir (the specimen at the Brooklyn Botanic Garden was stolen soon after its inaugural blossoming in 1985). About this time a specimen reached J. C. Raulston, then director of the North Carolina State University Arboretum in Raleigh, North Carolina. Under J. C.'s tutelage in the late 1980s, student intern Richard Hartlage transferred pollen from *Calycanthus floridus* to the blossoms of *Sinocalycanthus* and in the process forever lifted the genus *Calycanthus* from ornamental mediocrity.

Exhilaratingly, this hybrid commenced blossoming three years later with large, somewhat magnolia-like, rose-red flowers, produced prolifically and precociously, showing a textbook intermediacy between both parents. This was ultimately named, after considerable and worldwide deliberation, and sadly after J. C.'s untimely death, ×*Sinocalycalycanthus raulstonii*. The original hybrid clone was given the cultivar name 'Hartlage Wine'. Thankfully, further taxonomic work has since returned *Sinocalycanthus* to *Calycanthus*, transferring the hybrid to the more euphonious *Calycanthus* ×*raulstonii*.

Though the entire concept of a *Calycanthus* breeding program would have been unthinkable as recently as the 1980s, the blossoming and subsequent introduction of 'Hartlage Wine' is now considered an entrée into a much-expanded selection program rather than an endpoint. Tom Ranney of the North Carolina State University Woody Plant Breeding Station in Asheville, North Carolina—appropriately located on the doorstep of natural populations of *C. floridus*—has fully embraced the genus, making additional crosses of, and backcrosses to, the same parents, as well as incorporating the genes of *C. occidentalis*. In addition, the yellow-flowered forms of *C. floridus*, most notably a well-distributed cultivar known as 'Athens', have been used to create yellow and

Calycanthus chinensis. (Photo by Daniel J. Hinkley)

Allspice and Fivespice: *Calycanthus*

Calycanthus chinensis. (Photo by Lynne Harrison)

cream-colored selections. Ranney's first release, 'Venus', represents the most exciting hybrid woody plant to be introduced into cultivation in recent history. Fast growing, it forms a dense, rounded framework to 6 ft. by 5 ft. (1.8 m by 1.5 m), with bold, dark green foliage and a smothering of 3–4 in. (7.5–10 cm) white flowers, stained basally in purple, throughout late spring and summer.

There are already other selections on the horizon to be released: yellows, deep reds, bicolored selections, and those with good fragrance. It is a story that will continue to unfold in the years ahead. It is also a story that speaks volumes of the pace and verve of global horticulture during this time as well as the importance of plant exploration and conservation. In a blink of the eye the genus *Calycanthus* has been elevated into a viable horticultural commodity by the discovery of a rare Chinese shrub, one that could have easily enough been extirpated before it ever became known.

HARDINESS: Though I believe the genus is more appropriate in summer-warm areas, where horticultural associates suggest the fragrance of *Calycanthus floridus* truly is agreeable, it does perform admirably in zones 5–10. Data is still relatively scarce regarding the overall adaptability of *C. chinensis* and *C. ×raulstonii.*

CULTIVATION: Plant *Calycanthus* in full sun or, even better, partial shade in humus-rich yet draining soils, with supplemental water provided during the growing season as needed. Roger Raiche notes that although *C. occidentalis* is recognized as an associate of seepages, seedlings emerging in drier sites will demonstrate con-

Calycanthus ×raulstonii 'Hartlage Wine'. (Photo by Lynne Harrison)

Calycanthus 'Venus'. (Photo by Daniel J. Hinkley)

siderable drought resistance. There have been widespread reports of a discoloration and disfigurement of the blossoms of *C. chinensis*. This begins as the buds swell and progresses through the tepals as each flower opens. As this appears worse some years more than others, and since I have never witnessed any fruiting bodies, I might suggest that this disease is environmental rather than cultural or pathological.

PROPAGATION: Softwood cuttings under mist of all species work easily, though obviously the leaf blade of *Calycanthus floridus* and hybrids should be reduced in size. Seeds are readily produced on all plants in my garden, although no assumption can be made about the seedlings remaining true to type if more than one species is present at the time of blossoming.

Calycanthus chinensis × *C. occidentalis* at the North Carolina State University Woody Plant Breeding Station in Asheville, North Carolina. (Photo by Daniel J. Hinkley)

Allspice and Fivespice: *Calycanthus*

Glorybowers and Beautiful Berries:
Clerodendrum and Other Verbenaceae

It was a very playful day today, perpetually lost on dusty dirt roads attempting to follow the route of botanists Sabina Knees and Martin Gardner by means of an article they had written for The Plantsman—*akin I suppose to using a photo essay in* Life *to navigate through New York City. Kevin was his usual upbeat, chirpy self, and we had good fun of it, letting the car take us where it might and in the process finding some exceptionally good habitat (though I am certain Jennifer had grown somewhat weary of our frivolity by day's end).*

Along the road in lower damp areas were stunning specimens of Drimys winteri *whose brilliant white undersides were exposed with gusts of wind. On drier ground, we stopped to admire* Tristerix *in blossom, a parasite on* Peumus *and* Cryptocarya *with blistering red spidery flowers appearing quite like* Embothrium *from a distance. I made the mistake of collecting a bit of its seed, more from curiosity than any intention of attempting to grow it, and spent the remainder of the day with its sticky resin adher-*

ing my fingers to the steering wheel: obviously a critical prerequisite for the seed of a parasite.

Three times I stopped the car believing I had seen Azara microphylla *only to discover each time that it was yet another specimen of* Rhaphithamnus spinosus, *which to my delight is a name Kevin now pronounces in a manner to suggest some Hindu deity. I am uncertain how I have thus far gone through life without knowing of this genus, which I gather through Hoffmann, though in Spanish, is in the Verbenaceae. Some are still in late flower with very pretty tubular flowers of light lavender, while seemingly all the specimens thus far encountered are weighted with enormous crops of shiny lapis-colored fruit.*

We found tonight a very clean and friendly (and ja, orderly) bed-and-breakfast run by a German woman. Somewhat overpisco'd, we sat outdoors after dinner, chuckling over our adventures and marveling over the plants of the day, and I saw for the first time the Southern Cross in the heavens above.

From Curacautín to Conguillio, Chile
February 16, 1998

T HE VERBENACEAE IS PROBABLY MOST notably represented in contemporary culture not by the vulgar, tangly, endlessly flowering annual verbena that serves as the type genus, commonly associated with the floral clock or flag, but through the tropical, rot-resistant, politically brittle timber of *Tectona* or

Clerodendrum trichotomum. (Photo by Lynne Harrison)

teak. The core members of the family, some 90 genera, are undergoing a taxonomic jerk between the Verbenaceae and the closely allied Lamiaceae, or mint family; time will ultimately determine whether I have linked my selected representatives to their correct families.

The genus *Clerodendrum*, providing the most girth of any genera in the Verbenaceae, gathers about it 560 species of mostly Old World tropical trees, shrubs, and assorted scrambling things. I both love and loathe its generic epitaph. I find intriguing that at its Greek roots lurk *kleros* ("chance") and *dendrum* ("tree"), referring perhaps to the fact that various members of the genus have been employed as both medicines and poisons—place your bets. I dislike the name because I first heard it incorrectly as *Clerodendron* rather than *Clerodendrum*, a commonly propagated mistake rooted in a spelling error made in 1737. The pronunciation of the word *Clerodendron* now conjures forth the same uncomfortable sensation as *Rhododendrum* and *Cotton Easter*.

Clerodendrum has a special place in my collecting history, being one of the first plants from which I gathered seed in the wild, at least in a professional sense. In 1993 in South Korea my eyes were not yet trained to decipher the more subtly colored fruits and seeds of my surroundings, instead resting on those natural elements that so brashly demanded attention.

And *Clerodendrum trichotomum* is just that type of shrub or small tree. Ultimately rising to 15 ft. (4.6 m) and spreading in a comely, rounded manner to about the same, its heart-shaped leaves emerge in spring with a purplish cast (and if broken reveal a characteristic peanut butter aroma that some regard as disagreeable). In mid- to late summer, cymes of white, jasmine-scented flowers, contrasting with an inflated purple-red calyx, are produced at the ends of each branch. After fertilization, the effects become decidedly more bawdy, when the sepal lobes swell, flare backward, and intensify in color to take on the appearance of red wax lips. In the center of this flamboyant, puckering calyx rests a single pea-sized fruit possessing a glimmering shock-and-awe coat of turquoise. It was this sensational fruiting effect that smacked this neophyte against the head while on Mount Sorak in northern South Korea not far from the demilitarized zone.

My seed collections from that year did not exactly change the face of Western horticulture. *Clerodendrum trichotomum* var. *trichotomum* had been in cultivation for more than 150 years and was abundant but relatively uncommon in gardens on the western slope of the Pacific Northwest. One of the seedlings from that trip did offer a short stint of bright yellow foliage in spring, and though it was preserved in my garden, the effects were too abridged to make it worthy of a name. *Clerodendrum trichotomum* var. *fargesii*, filling a near-identical ornamental niche, was already on the market in our climate. This clerodendrum, which has since been granted species rank as *C. fargesii*, hails from less accommodating elevations of southwestern China, where I have collected it at 6000 ft. (1800 m) on Mount Emei in Sichuan Province. It is promoted as returning from the ground to blossom if cut back by frosts. Having grown both of these clerodendrums, at least under

Clerodendrum trichotomum. (Photo by Daniel J. Hinkley)

two names, I can state with certainty that there is little visual difference between the two.

Four years later, in 1997, my eyes were better trained and more sensitive to the subtleties and variations within a natural assemblage of plants. Bleddyn and Sue Wynn-Jones, Darrell Probst, and I had spent the first weeks of that autumn in South Korea, and later continued onward to Japan. Traveling from northern Honshū to Shikoku, Darrell was hot on the trail of *Epimedium* and *Tricyrtis*, while Bleddyn and I were more catholic in our collective desires.

While on Shikoku that year, along a mountain road at a relatively low elevation, I recall my own double take and petulant demand to stop the car when we passed a shrub that appeared strangely familiar yet bizarre. Indeed, it was a broad specimen of *Clerodendrum trichotomum* with the typical sapphire fruit yet surrounded by pure white, fleshy sepals. Of the seedlings that emerged from that collection (HC 970591), I selected those with paler leaves, and these selections began to flower and fruit in my new garden a decade later. Of the two seedlings I selected with the palest leaves, one possesses a very light pink calyx fading to near-white, while the other proffers pure white calyces. Beyond simple curiosity and that compelling need to possess uniqueness, there does not exist any reason to seek out or grow this deviant form.

Though my recollections of time spent in southwestern China offer few encounters with *Clerodendrum fargesii*, my interface with *C. fragrans* (syn. *C. bungei*) has been sizeable, as fortunate or unfortunate as that might be. Whereas *C. trichotomum* might be described as a colorfully clad geisha, *C. fragrans* is more a samurai in drag. Its upright canes to 6 ft. (1.8 m) are clad in large, intriguingly purple-felted, pungently (some say nauseatingly) scented foliage, and capped in fragrant cymes of pink flowers in very late summer. The resulting crops of fruit, ripening in midautumn, are similar to those of *C. trichotomum* in terms of hue and texture but altogether larger and coarser in format. An unfortunate variegated form of this species is currently being promoted in commerce.

Though I cultivated this or a closely allied species in the woodland of my first garden, from collections in China and northern Vietnam, I did not invite it along when I left to begin a new garden due to its thuggish, stoloniferous habit of growth. It is probably best to recommend it only for more natural landscapes or gardens that are soon to be put on the market.

HARDINESS: Zones 7–10.

CULTIVATION: Clerodendrums thrive in full sun or very bright shade in well-drained soils. Avoid perpetually moist soils. Both *Clerodendrum fargesii* and *C. fragrans* will sucker; however, *C. fragrans* excels in this regard and should be avoided in landscapes requiring polite dialogue between garden subjects. The fruits of both species in their native haunts are frequently parasitized by insects, thusly care should, as always, be exercised if importing seed into cultivation.

Clerodendrum fragrans. (Photo by Lynne Harrison)

PROPAGATION: Seed germinates readily with a single cold stratification. Summer softwood cuttings under mist root easily, as do root cuttings. Can also be propagated by removal of suckering stems.

Callicarpa

I do not believe I had encountered the genus *Callicarpa* before my first autumn in Seattle, when I lived at the Stone Cottage at Washington Park Arboretum. A rather decrepit and forgotten portion of the collection was devoted to the Verbenaceae, and in this location grew a collection of species that were adaptable to the climate of the Pacific Northwest. I can recall being quite bedazzled that autumn by the unique color of *Callicarpa* fruit, ranging in hue from lilac-purple to rich mauve, possessing the exact chroma of the large, lavender Easter basket candies of my youth that tasted like the bottom of my mother's handbag. Even without a primer in the genus, I could, during those first encounters, ascertain that some species were better than others.

The name *Callicarpa*, like *Callista* and *Calycanthus*, refers to beauty, and in the case of our subject, befittingly, its carpels or fruit. These follow axillary clusters of lavender flowers that are quietly attractive though not of sufficient ornament to demand inclusion in the garden in their own right. The genus is rather large and geographically centered in tropical and temperate Asia, with more than 140 described species. It has not bypassed the New World, however, where *Callicarpa americana* exists, frequently encountered while hiking the moist, shaded *Taxodium* (bald cypress) swamps of the southeastern United States. Though like many *Callicarpa* species, it demands more heat during the summer than the Pacific Northwest can provide, it is still considered one of the best native shrubs available for fruiting effects, if not a bit on the frisky side in terms of self-sowing.

Once you have met one *Callicarpa*, you will always know when you are meeting another, whether it is under cultivation or in the wild, at least if the plant is in flower and certainly when it is in fruit. Its multistemmed habit

of growth produces 5–15 ft. (1.5–4.6 m) specimens, with oppositely arranged foliage and varying degrees of pubescence on the surface of the leaf. The rather pretty yet mostly underappreciated cymes of lavender flowers are produced along the entirety of each stem in the axils of the leaves in early summer, resulting in a fantastical display of fruit if fertilization goes according to design. White-fruited forms of all commonly grown species are encountered in the trade; in fact I will be wild and crazy enough to suggest that virtually every species exists in a white-berried form.

I went through a prolonged *Callicarpa* evaluation phase in my youthful arrogance, eschewing the more widely known and grown *C.* 'Profusion' as vulgar and unworthy in a garden devoted to valiant, pure-blooded,

Callicarpa bodinieri in northern Vietnam.
(Photo by Daniel J. Hinkley)

wild-collected species. From Japan and South Korea I collected *C. japonica*, *C. mollis*, and *C. dichotoma*. From China came *C. bodinieri*, itself the forebear of 'Profusion', while Vietnam, Nepal, Sikkim, and Bhutan proffered their own counterparts whose correct names, if they even existed, were never applied. It was less challenging to put good names to those we collected in Taiwan, with its well-studied flora, in both 1999 and 2007. The best of the lot was *C. formosanum*, found at high elevations, often with branches so plastered with gleaming purple fruit that they were pulled to the ground. Somewhere along the way, though I always appreciated their bodacious cloak of ripe fruit, I began to bypass them while in the wild. I had been forced to finally admit that 'Profusion' performed better than any of the species in delivering a punch of color to the autumn garden. Sometimes things labeled "new and improved" actually are. It must be noted that new variegated forms of *C. japonica* and *C. dichotoma* from nurseries in Japan have restarted my engines of interest in the genus as shrubs possessing more than a single, somewhat ephemeral season of interest.

A sprightly, variegated form of *Callicarpa dichotoma*. (Photo by Daniel J. Hinkley)

HARDINESS: Several species, such as *Callicarpa americana*, *C. japonica*, *C. dichotoma*, and *C. bodinieri*, are hardy in zones 6–10. Most respond favorably to summer-warm and humid regions.

CULTIVATION: Callicarpas should be planted in full sun for the best fruiting effects and to enhance a buttery lavender-infused autumn color in the foliage. Though more of a punch is offered by planting a trio or quintet of the shrubs together, one must be cognizant of the overall quietness of callicarpas during the majority of the year. The shrubs can be hard pruned to the ground each year and will blossom and fruit on new wood, although this practice is more recommended in summer-warm areas than in the Pacific Northwest where their rejuvenation is retarded. This cutting back, if done religiously before the fruit begins to drop from the branches, will alleviate the threat posed by this bioinvasive genus.

Callicarpa 'Profusion'. (Photo by Lynne Harrison)

Callicarpa

Callicarpa formosanum. (Photo by Daniel J. Hinkley)

PROPAGATION: Seed germinates readily with a single cold stratification. Summer semisoftwood cuttings for cultivars and hybrids root and survive the first winter easily, under mist.

Rhaphithamnus spinosus

During my first trip to Chile in 1998, I headed south from the Pacific Northwest with my great friends and frequent traveling companions Kevin Carrabine and Jennifer Macuiba, armed with relatively little expectation of what I would see in the southern Andes. Considering the profound adaptability of the flora of southern Chile to the Pacific Northwest, the paucity of native

Chilean plants in our landscapes seems peculiar. Of course, *Araucaria araucana* abounds, and a few species of Antarctic beech, *Nothofagus*, as well as the splendid Chilean flame tree, *Embothrium coccineum*, are occasionally encountered in plant collections. The greater share of the Chilean flora, however, which is top-heavy with evergreen shrubs and trees, has yet to be embraced by our horticultural community.

It was for this reason (or perhaps only an acceptable excuse) that I had never before heard of *Rhaphithamnus spinosus*. Its narrow habit of growth and small, glistening, dark green leaves caught my eye as we negotiated a very dusty gravel road between the villages of Curacautín and Pucón, ranging between 2000 ft. (600 m) and 3800 ft. (1160 m) in altitude.

I recall stopping the car rather excitedly because I was dead certain I had seen my very first specimen of *Azara microphylla*, a shrub in the Salicaceae. No deal. The leaves of this superficial look-alike, in pairs or threes, were small, broad, ovate, and possessing a purple cast when young. The ends of the branches held light brown spines, a feature that I later learned had led to the vernacular name *espino blanco* or "white thorn." *Rhaphithamnus* is a neat and tidy genus with only two species: *R. spinosus* from Chile and Argentina, and *R. venustus*, endemic to the isolated Juan Fernández Islands in the South Pacific.

It was not foliage nor thorn, however, that made me pause and wonder precisely why I had never before encountered *Rhaphithamnus spinosus*, despite it having been introduced to England by William Lobb in 1843. It was the shrub's burden of indigo-colored fruit and spotting of pretty, lavender, tubular flowers—still present so late in the season—that astonished me to such a degree.

From seed collections from that trip, I have *Rhaphithamnus spinosus* firmly established in my garden in Indianola, where it has achieved 15 ft. (4.6 m) in height; I expect very little more based on the height of the specimens I observed in the wild. The flowering effects in spring, just as the new growth has transmuted to a rather swarthy plum-bruise, have made its presence in

Purple new growth and lavender flowers complement one another in late spring at Windcliff, on my collection of *Rhaphithamnus spinosus*. (Photo by Daniel J. Hinkley)

my garden—and my acquaintance with it, at long last—a most gratifying experience.

HARDINESS: Zones 7–10. Historically this shrub was considered a tender species appropriate only for wall plantings or sheltered positions, an evaluation that does not hold true in my experience.

CULTIVATION: This genus seems to respond best to full sun and well-drained soils, though my time with it indicates it is far from desiring xeric conditions. Supplemental water during dry spells in the growing season appears to be necessary. Better fruit set will occur if more than one clone is present.

PROPAGATION: Very easy from seed, requiring only a single cold stratification for successful germination. Semihardwood cuttings in the autumn on gentle bottom heat will readily root.

Vitex

Though this genus has been officially banned from the Verbenaceae and placed in the closely allied Lamiaceae, it was within its original haunts that I first learned to recognize it, and it is within this edifice that I will discuss it.

Like the Verbenaceae as a whole, the 250-odd species of *Vitex* are primarily tropical and subtropical, with just a handful being sufficiently hardy to come out and play in temperate-minded gardens.

I became acquainted with the genus through *Vitex agnus-castus*, the most highly regarded of the hardy species, while touring Volunteer Park in Seattle with my plant identification classes during autumn term. It is not until September in the relative chill of the Pacific Northwest that this splendid shrub comes into blossom, with erect racemes of powdery blue terminating on square branches cloaked with pairs of fragrant, palmately compound, pleasingly gray foliage. White and pink flowering forms of this species can be found in the trade.

Native from the Mediterranean to southwestern Asia, *Vitex agnus-castus*, the so-called chaste tree (*agnos* being Greek for "holy" or "chaste"), is linked to a surfeit of myths, legends, and actualities about human sexuality. This makes it an ideal teaching tool, since talk of such things continues to garner undivided attention, especially when outside on a splendid autumn day in the Pacific Northwest.

This species was traditionally used as an anaphrodisiac by women of the Mediterranean, who would sleep upon its foliage while their men were away at war to keep themselves pure. Interestingly enough, Plan B was prescribed in the event that this did not work, using the seeds and leaves in teas as both a cure for venereal disease and as an abortive agent.

As is often the case, long-held plant myths often have some merit when empirically studied. If studies and claims of numerous Web sites devoted to natural medicines are to be believed, *Vitex* balances progesterone and estrogen in women while increasing testosterone production in men. As if men, who already go off to war far more than is necessary, actually need more testosterone . . .

Vitex negundo, from sultry south-central Asia, is somewhat hardier in disposition and coarser in appearance. Its palmate foliage of incised green leaflets, carried on stems to 10 ft. (3 m), provides a foil to the erect, terminal racemes of blue, similar to those of *V. agnus-castus*, which are produced in late summer, or earlier in summer-warm areas.

Vitex rotundifolia is a species I encountered during my first trip to South Korea in 1993. There it grew as a suckering beach shrub on the sandy western coast near Chollipo Arboretum, an immense woody plant collection founded by and later given to the Korean people by Ferris Miller.

In September and October during that visit, I can recall the sandy, ocean-side hummocks teeming with bees and butterflies as they worked the erect, blue terminal racemes of this species, atop 2 ft. (0.6 m) stems sporting pairs of compound leaves with rounded, grayish green leaflets. There was no seed for collection, which in retrospect was quite fortuitous.

Collections of this species made in the mid-1980s by American horticulturists were distributed and promoted as a beach stabilizer. The species has since colonized substantial stretches of the South Carolina coastline, where it is usurping sea turtle nesting sites and displacing native sand-stabilizing species. It is now an important reminder of the importance of methodically examining and evaluating a plant before releasing it. Unfortunately, the notoriety of prior "soil stabilizers" in the South, most notably kudzu (*Pueraria lobata*), seems to have been, in this case, overlooked.

HARDINESS: The *Vitex* species discussed here are primarily heat-loving species that thrive in zones 6–10.

Cooler maritime climates can accommodate them, but flowering will be significantly delayed until autumn.

CULTIVATION: These sun-loving shrubs thrive in well-draining soils and prove to be exceptionally drought tolerant once established. As they blossom on the current year's wood, *Vitex* species can be pruned hard in late winter or early spring.

PROPAGATION: Softwood cuttings on bottom heat and under mist in the summer, as well as hardwood cuttings during the winter, root easily.

Rostrinucula dependens

Like the genus *Vitex*, *Rostrinucula* is considered part of the Lamiaceae, or mint family, but much less vaguely so. That, however, did not prevent me from presuming I had come across a species of *Buddleja*, in a completely different plant order let alone family, when I collected seed of *Rostrinucula* in 1996.

I was in Sichuan Province with my friends Darrell Probst and Frank Bell, near Wolong, northeast of Chengdu, at about 5000 ft. (1500 m) in elevation. I recall that day being warm and sunny, and the three of us went our own separate ways to reconvene at a predestined locale at the end of the day. There were indeed numerous species of *Buddleja* in the drier sites, while a fantastic assemblage of trees and shrubs grew in the soils with more water, including *Salix magnifica*, *Cercidiphyllum japonicum*, *Tetracentron sinensis*, and *Helwingia chinensis*.

When I came upon this shrub, I was impressed with its long, pendulous, terminal racemes of flowers, not at all unlike *Buddleja lindleyana*. The gray-green leaves were held in pairs along the stems, which rose to 10 ft. (3 m) tall. Had I been more attentive I would have noticed that the seed capsules and seeds were not those of *Buddleja* at all, and I should have noted the somewhat camphorlike odor arising as I separated and cleaned my collections.

Late-summer drooping flowers of *Rostrinucula dependens*, from my collection in northwestern Yunnan, blossoming in my Indianola, Washington, garden. (Photo by Daniel J. Hinkley)

Later, after introducing *Rostrinucula dependens* through my catalog as *Buddleja* species DJHC 664b, staff of the UBC Botanical Garden contacted me to enlighten me of my mistake. Despite the error, they were pleased to report how exceptional the shrub had thus far performed in their garden.

Very late in the season, the tightly packed racemes of *Rostrinucula dependens* begin to open, revealing wiry flowers of pink or purple, while continuing to expand and gracefully droop downward (as can be predicted by the specific epithet) by as much as 10 in. (25 cm). It has become a well-noted shrub in my garden while in blossom, and to my gratification, most who observe it inquire as to what species of *Buddleja* it might be.

The *Flora of China* (Wu et al. 1994 to present) lists only one other species occurring in south-central China at moderate elevations: *Rostrinucula chinensis*, which I have not yet encountered in the wild or under cultivation.

HARDINESS: Zones 7–10.

CULTIVATION: Full sun or light shade in well-draining soils; it will prove to be quite drought tolerant when fully established. Growing this species in a very lean manner may increase its overall hardiness. As it blossoms on new wood, the shrub can be severely disciplined on a yearly basis.

PROPAGATION: Growing a single clone in the garden will result in little if any viable seed, pointing toward asexual propagation as the best method. Firm softwood cuttings under mist and on gentle bottom heat readily root and provide little challenge. *Rostrinucula dependens* has reportedly demonstrated an aggressive degree of reseeding in the Southeast; its use in summer-warm areas should be carefully monitored.

Summersweets and Autumn Delicacies: *Clethra*

There have been few days in my life thus far that I needed so badly a beer by the end of the day. We were all very weary from yesterday's hike into the medicinal plant station at Huadiamba, far above Dali on the Cang Shan, reportedly 16 miles but seeming more like 25 miles by day's end. The lot of us shared floor space dormitory-style last night, and Georg and I headed off directly after a surprisingly hearty breakfast served outside on the porch: deliciously sunny though fresh to the point of discomfort with our gloves off. We chose to explore a north-facing ridge we had seen during our hike the day before as it had seemed particularly rich in vegetation. I found a rather sizeable regenerated specimen of Magnolia wilsonii *that had been cut a few years, probably for the bark, and a single fruiting head possessed a single remaining seed. About us was a blaze of red from* Enkianthus deflexus *and* Pieris formosa *var.* forrestii, *while more exciting was the presence of another ericaceous shrub known as* Craibiodendron yunnanense *that appeared at first superficially identical to the* Pieris. *Several* Lithocarpus *species,* Skimmia, Daphne, *and rhododendrons are here in abundance.*

We followed a draw up until it narrowed and morphed into a small but annoyingly steep creek bed that slowed our ascent significantly. After a brief lunch to refuel at 11,240 ft., we continued up the slope and found ourselves in a disappointing thick expanse of Phyllostachys *with little diversity of plant material. For two hours we attempted to weave our way uphill to leave it behind but in the process only succeeded in getting ourselves utterly turned around in the density of the bamboo. Though neither of us verbalized our concern, the sense that we had managed to lose ourselves was rather palpable in our questioning of one other—did this or that downward-leading draw look remotely familiar? At last, upon a small knoll, we found a small opening that allowed for orientation, with a last bit of sun hitting us directly from the south. At that moment I brushed against a small tree above us, and its long terminal trusses of dry capsules dehisced their seed in enormous quantity; the entire universe seemed to sparkle as these flints of embryo interacted with the low-angled rays of sun, momentarily extinguished by the ridge in the distance. I gathered its seed and foliage, which under the gas lantern we excitedly identified as* Clethra delavayi *upon our return to the station, well after dark. Our comrades were just finishing the last beers brought up from Dali that afternoon by pack animals, and a gibbous moon was rising above the eastern horizon.*

Near Huadiamba Research Station
above Dali, Yunnan Province
October 6, 1998

I AM CERTAIN THAT I DID NOT GROW *Clethra* as a young gardener in Michigan, though I might have been aware of the genus through my perusal of plant catalogs each spring: Henry Field, Michigan Bulb Company, perhaps even Burpee when Burpee was Burpee. It was through these annual missives that the names of plants were often implanted, though it would be years hence before those letters would be transformed into actual living entities.

So it seemed that I already knew *Clethra alnifolia*, the

Clethra acuminata. (Photo by Lynne Harrison)

most commonly cultivated of the lot, as an old friend when I began to grow it, rather unsatisfactorily, after beginning my first garden in the Pacific Northwest. A suckering shrub with an affinity to water-soaked soils, it is found in dense thickets along waterways from Nova Scotia (where it is extremely rare) southward to Florida and west to Texas. There, reveling in the heat and humidity of the eastern seaboard, it scents the air with erect racemes in mid- to late summer. The standard fare of white has more recently been upgraded to pink ('Ruby Spice', 'Fern Valley Pink', and others), with a dwarf form known as 'Hummingbird' becoming popular in the trade. All together an acceptable yet fairly lumpy, somewhat pungently fragrant shrub that is perfectly acceptable for stabilizing soils on wet slopes.

As a young gardener I certainly would not have interacted with *Clethra acuminata*, another American species, as it is virtually ignored by the nursery industry, like so many other good, garden-worthy plant species. It was only after I moved to western Washington and encountered this species in a dank, overgrown grove of accessioned plants that I was able to marvel over its beguiling, beautiful, exfoliating bark and handsome, pendulous, fragrant flowers of white in late summer. Later, while hiking the Blue Ridge above Asheville, North Carolina, with friend Richard Olsen, I found that such a shaded position seems to be exactly its desired coordinates, though certainly its beefier limbs and apparent vigor were in response to the less frigid ambient air temperatures it was granted in its home turf.

So, long before my pilgrimage in plants had progressed terribly far, I had already come to know the only two species of *Clethra* native to North America. Waiting in the shadows to ambush the overconfidence of my accumulated knowledge, however, were some 70 additional species (the exact amount depending on which taxonomist you ask) from China, Indochina, Mexico, Central America, and South America, as well as one species from Madeira.

The Clethraceae comprises only two genera, the other being *Purdiaea* (a New World genus centered primar-

ily in the Caribbean), consisting of shrubs and trees, both evergreen and deciduous, whose flowers are characteristically presented in terminal racemes and often fragrant.

Besides the two species found within the confines of the geographical borders of the United States and Canada, very few of the Mesoamerican species have been trialed for use in gardens. In the early 1990s, a near-continuous flow of plants from J. C. Raulston brought *Clethra pringlei* into my garden, a species he had collected in northeastern Mexico with compatriots from Texas. I found the foliage of this species to be particularly handsome, with an accentuated ribbing atop the leaf blade. According to the staff of what is now the J. C. Raulston Arboretum in Raleigh, this species still thrives; in fact it appears to be the only *Clethra* trialed from south of our borders to have found the climate of the Southeast to its liking. Contrarily, *C. pringlei* quickly declined in vigor in the Frigidaire environs of the Kitsap Peninsula in Washington State, ultimately begging for, and being granted, a quick and painless death. It is highly regarded for its foliage, which emerges with reddish tones in spring, a trait that has been incorporated into a hybrid with *C. alnifolia* made by research geneticists at the U.S. National Arboretum.

While in Korea with Tony Avent, Bleddyn and Sue Wynn-Jones, and Darrell Probst during my second visit in 1997, my comrades and I stopped to admire a gentle slope solid with the glossy rosettes of *Heloniopsis japonica*, a late-winter-blossoming perennial that I hold in high regard. My eyes ultimately settled upon the handsome, exfoliating trunks of the small, shapely trees above the bank, and further study of the spent terminal clusters of dried capsules left little doubt that we had encountered the so-called Japanese clethra, *Clethra barbinervis*, in the wild.

I had first learned of this species during my years at the University of Washington while visiting the garden of the late and highly regarded plantsperson Mareen Kruckeberg, wife of taxonomist Art Kruckeberg and proprietor of MsK Rare Plant Nursery north of Seattle.

Ms. Kruckeberg had sung the praises of *Clethra barbinervis* for its numerous attributes: handsome, deep green summer foliage; a compact growth habit that allows it to fit into the smallest of landscapes; near-unparalleled autumn color even when cultivated in shaded positions; and last but certainly not least, the beguiling fragrance of its white flowers proffered in late summer.

Years later I would hike through expanses of *Clethra barbinervis* in north-central Honshū at moderate elevations. Still early spring, there was no distraction here from its foliage, making fully apparent its supremely handsome tricolored bark, which to my mind rivals that of *Stewartia pseudocamellia* though in an altogether more comely format.

Available forms of *Clethra barbinervis* include a handsome, yellow-splashed, variegated form; a tricolored pink, white, and green form; and one that makes the circuit among the cognoscenti as 'Dwarf Form'. Though these may indeed prove to be garden-worthy plants in their own right, I am profoundly more interested in simply raising awareness of the species itself, which deserves much greater recognition for zones 5–9.

My relationship with Gerald Straley, curator of the UBC Botanical Garden, and later with Peter Wharton, curator of the David C. Lam Asian Garden at the same institution, afforded me remarkable exposure to plants that might have easily passed my radar undetected. Both Gerald and Peter had a profound impact on my life with plants, and both died at much too young an age. It was at the UBC Botanical Garden that I first met *Clethra monostachya*, which forms a handsome, rounded shrub with elegantly long, somewhat pendulous racemes of fragrant white flowers in mid- to late summer. Though I grew this species for numerous years in the woodland of my first garden, taxonomic treatment now amalgamates it with *C. delavayi*, the species I had excitedly collected on that near-fateful day in Yunnan Province in 1998.

Interestingly, I had believed for many years that I knew precisely what *Clethra delavayi* was, because I grew *C. delavayi*, or at least a plant labeled as such. After receiving it in yet another gift box from J. C. Raulston, I unfortunately and mindlessly propagated and distributed it for several years without examining it to the degree that I should have. What J. C. had sent me had most likely been raised from mislabeled seed; it was simply another plant of *C. barbinervis*. Not until my collections of *C. delavayi* germinated and were transplanted in 1999 did I become aware of its significant physical differences, the gray-green foliage more felted and more

The handsome exfoliating bark of *Clethra barbinervis* near Kusatsu, Honshū. (Photo by Daniel J. Hinkley)

Clethra monostachya at the UBC Botanical Garden. (Photo by Lynne Harrison)

Clethra delavayi. (Photo by Daniel J. Hinkley)

deeply impressed. *Clethra delavayi* slowly and gracefully matured in my garden in Indianola, and a decade later the inaugural flowering allowed me to fully examine the floral differences of the real McCoy, with racemes of large, white, bell-shaped flowers.

Observing the propensity of *Clethra alnifolia* to create suckering, impenetrable expanses along streams on the eastern seaboard of North America just might prepare one for a similar, though decidedly disjointed, scene amidst Black Hmong villages in the far reaches of moderately low elevations in Vietnam. Oddly ungrazed by the villagers' livestock, the colonizing stems of *C. petelotii* held characteristic deeply veined leaves and pendulous, terminal trusses of dried fruit, in particular along river drainages near the remote village of Seo Mi Ty. Though I excitedly collected this species in the autumn of 2006, its relatively low elevations of 4000 ft. (1200 m) and below at this latitude would suggest it to be better adapted to the moderate climates of the southern states.

Throughout China, Malaysia, and Vietnam, and south of our borders into Mexico and South and Central America, there certainly exist other applicable species of this aristocratic genus for trials in our gardens. Though I am a plantsman with a supposedly beefy comprehension of the woody plants of the world, my knowledge of the breadth of the genus and how it applies "as is" to American horticulture is embarrassingly slight. I am aware of *Clethra arborea*, the only species to occur in what is technically Europe, on the island of Madeira, but I will admit that I am unable to recall ever having had an introduction. This shortcoming aside, my justification for writing about what little I know of this genus comes from the passion and commitment to the few species with which I am familiar. There are few other shrubs that I could so heartily demand you try in your garden.

HARDINESS: As the range of this genus is so broad, it is impossible to provide generalities about hardiness. The deciduous species from temperate areas of the globe are generally adaptable to zones 5–9, though those species hailing from warmer climates may easily request a climate more sultry than cool. *Clethra alnifolia* and *C. barbinervis*, from my angle, appear to have the most universal application to both baked and chilled climates.

CULTIVATION: In cooler climates, plants grown in full sun will be more floriferous and develop better autumn tints. In warmer climates, particularly in the Southeast, protection from sun during the afternoon and placement in moist, humus-rich soils seem to prevent leaf scorch, which can be problematic. Mark Weathington of the J. C. Raulston Arboretum in Raleigh, North Carolina, recommends *Clethra alnifolia* 'Sherry Sue' for its sun and soil tolerance. *Clethra barbinervis* colors nicely in even a moderately shady position.

PROPAGATION: Softwood cuttings taken upon ripening in midsummer and rooted under mist with gentle bottom heat present few challenges. Transplant the cuttings the following spring as growth resumes. The seed is dehisced from the dried capsules in autumn though seemingly remains viable for months afterward; I have collected seed from the infructescences of the previous year in midsummer and had full germination. A single cold period is required.

Where Fragrance Reigns: *Daphne, Edgeworthia,* and *Ovidia*

Last night was our first at elevation on the Milke Danda, and it seems none of us did very well with it; I woke continually during the night gasping for breath. It was cold and rainy when we gathered for breakfast, and I discovered that the four others had experienced the same problems. Sonam suggested we stay put here for a day to acclimate while he would take some of the porters to a village in the valley below us for supplies.

Kevin, Jennifer, and I left Bleddyn and Sue in camp and ventured downslope into an adjacent bit of undisturbed forest dominated by fir, Abies densa, *though the rain and cold did not infuse our party with a great deal of enthusiasm. The large rhododendrons here, primarily* Rhododendron arboreum, *prove to be refugia of numerous epiphytic plants:* Polygonatum oppositifolium *and P. cathcartii among them probably once existed commonly at*

ground level before the increase of yak grazing. We made several seed collections this morning, most notably Enkianthus deflexus—*coloring quite nicely even in the shade—and* Hydrangea anomala *subsp.* anomala.

Here was my first encounter with Daphne bholua *in the wild, and we excitedly searched for seed without success. In the middle of a clearing, quite magically, shone a brightly variegated sapling of this species. It made little sense to attempt a cutting from this so early in the trip, so left it untroubled where it grew.*

We were back to camp by late afternoon. The clouds had lifted along with our spirits and afforded dramatic, somewhat intimidating views of the Jaljale Himal to the north, where our route will lead us in the weeks ahead.

On the Milke Danda, eastern Nepal
October 12, 1995

FUNNY THING ABOUT THE THYMELAEACEAE, or at least those members that I have come to know. Forget the flower and foliage, growth habit, or fruit: this is one of those plant families that can generally be distinguished by the overall gestalt of its stems, which possess a visually and tactilely rubbery, flexible attitude. Consider my introduction to *Ovidia* in southern Chile. During my first trip to that country in 1998, my traveling chums Kevin Carrabine and Jennifer Macuiba and I were hiking amidst dwarf hummocks of *Embothrium* and admiring the ripening orbs of *Araucaria araucana*, the monkey puzzle, when I noticed a moderate-sized shrub clad with papery leaves and pretty white fruit. Upon further examination I noticed that the stem looked identical to that of *Daphne*, in that I could possibly, if so inclined, tie it into a knot without it snapping. It was this characteristic alone that led me to the plant's identity and the fact that the family is indeed represented in the southern extremes of South America.

Though I am not prepared to discuss the genus *Ovidia* in any depth, the two species there, *O. andina* and *O. pillopillo*, especially the latter, indeed have sufficient ornamental appeal and fragrance to consider trial and introduction to the western coast of North America and the

Daphne retusa in flower. (Photo by Lynne Harrison)

modified coastal gardens of Italy, France, England, and Ireland.

Despite the rather tidy nature of its generic representatives in ornamental horticulture, the Thymelaeaceae is relative large, with 700–750 species in 50 genera. North America is weak in representatives but makes up for the shortcoming by offering the rare and rarely encountered genus *Dirca*. *Dirca palustris*, leatherwood, is uncommon in the woodlands of the northeastern states into eastern Canada, though I have been fortunate to see it in its nativity growing with *Lindera benzoin*, within which it craftily conceals itself, just north of Boston. A few small populations of *D. occidentalis* occur in northern California, while a third species, *D. mexicana*, was discovered in northeastern Mexico in the late 1990s. The

Ovidia andina showing ripened white fruit and "daphne-like" stems. (Photo by Daniel J. Hinkley)

genus *Dirca* possesses coarse foliage and insignificant blossoms; its obscurity in nature and cultivation may justify its inclusion in the landscape, but to my sense of aesthetic, just barely.

The ornamental meat of the family is inarguably brought to the garden by *Daphne*. This complex genus is continually revised; some 50–95 species have been named, renamed, or amalgamated into existing nomenclature. I can generally use my collection notes of the past two decades to help me recall where and when I collected a particular plant species, but my notes do very little good with regard to this genus, as I have seldom collected their fruit, only at times cryptically noting their presence. *Daphne* includes both evergreen and deciduous shrubs throughout Asia, Asia Minor, Europe, and northern Africa. Since these shrubs possess primarily the good sense of blossoming in late winter or early spring, when little competition occurs among pollinating insects for available nectar, the resulting irritating-yet-logical ripening and distribution of their fruit happens long before my annual autumn forays into their range.

For the uninitiated, daphnes in the garden are no longer about undiluted species. Though daphne hybridization has been underway for decades, prolific and highly talented plant breeders have fashioned creative combinations using many rare species as their point of departure. Rising above the lot is the United Kingdom's Robin White, founder of Blackthorn Nursery in Hampshire, whose keen eye and steady hand have already perceptibly altered numerous genera of ornamental garden plants, including *Helleborus*, *Clematis*, *Epimedium*, *Anemone*, and *Hepatica*. His recombinations of *Daphne* species have resulted in a brimming inventory of dwarf, hardy evergreen shrubs proffering a dizzyingly long season of fragrant and colorful flowers.

Yet this book is meant to focus on the forebears of these hybrids, particularly those I have observed personally in the wild. It is a welcome excuse to conceal the limits of my depth on any subject, and most especially on the genus *Daphne*.

In northeastern Turkey, the Himalaya, China, Taiwan, and Vietnam, I have been at least afforded the opportunity to observe in their right place many of the species I have appreciated in my garden, undiluted, even though it must be said that it is often not so very long that I get to appreciate each individual. "Here on Monday, dead on Tuesday" seems to apply to most members of the genus, yet for fragrance alone, at often such an unlikely time of year, I will continue the game that often ends in inexplicable disappointment.

In the Pontic Alps of northeastern Turkey, I observed *Daphne mezereum*, perhaps the most celebrated species of the genus (in fact, it provides the common name of the Thymelaeaceae: the mezereum family). The so-called February daphne grew in summer-parched sites accompanied by *Datisca cannabina* as well as *Helleborus orientalis*, with much of its oblanceolate foliage shed by mid-September during my visit. The erect stems of this species put on a splendid showing in midwinter when the barren framework is completely clad in exceedingly fragrant flowers ranging in color from rich burgundy to ivory. Being quite variable in this regard, with some of the intermediate tones decidedly murky in effect, this daphne is best purchased in blossom. In my experience, the white-flowered forms begin to flower a full month before those with pigment.

Daphne mezereum, native across much of Europe and found primarily in chalky soils, is one of a few *Daphne* species that will dependably fruit—and fruit heavily and rather handsomely it does. Though adding an early-summer season of interest, the oft-reported toxicity of *Daphne* fruit is no exaggeration, and care must be taken to keep inquisitive toddlers away from fruiting specimens.

It was in the Atlas Mountains of Morocco, at moderate elevations, that I came upon *Daphne laureola*. It was a location in which I am certain the species actually belongs, as opposed to its role as an interloper among the natural landscapes of the Pacific Northwest, or even perhaps throughout much of western Europe; *D. laureola* is one of two species, including *D. mezereum*, native

Daphne mezereum in fruit. (Photo by Daniel J. Hinkley)

Daphne mezereum. (Photo by Daniel J. Hinkley)

Where Fragrance Reigns: *Daphne, Edgeworthia,* and *Ovidia*

to the British Isles. To my knowledge the so-called spurge daphne is the only daphne that has been officially nominated as being bioinvasive in North America.

Daphne laureola appears quite like *Euphorbia amygdaloides* var. *robbiae* from a distance, its matte green, obovate foliage clad densely on a rounded framework to 4 ft. by 3 ft. (1.2 m by 0.9 m). It can often be found appearing spontaneously in gardens and natural areas from British Columbia south to northern California, and of course through many locales in Europe. For many years I cultivated a lilliputian form of this species known as *D. laureola* var. *philippi*, hailing from the Pyrenees of northeastern Spain (a hiking destination nearing the top of my list), which rises to less than 8 in. (20 cm) tall while spreading stoloniferously, or at least by rooted stems, to 1 ft. (0.3 m) across. The green axillary flowers of *D. laureola*, held close to the stem and primarily hidden by foliage, are known to pulse with an intoxicating fragrance at dusk.

Daphne laureola and *D. mezereum* pair up to form the beguiling and too often obscure hybrid known as *D. ×houtteana*. The evergreen foliage, nearly identical in appearance to that of its evergreen parent, *D. laureola*, is deeply colored in tones of midnight purple, while the axillary flowers along the stem take on the personality of *D. mezereum*, though they are handicapped by the presence of leaves during the blossoming season. In my first garden, I attempted to replicate this cross by instead using *D. laureola* var. *philippi* as the evergreen parent, believing a dwarf mound of black-purple evergreen foliage might be well received.

Growing also in Turkey on the northern slope of the Pontic Alps, though on dry, rocky hillsides, is the eponymous *Daphne pontica*, an evergreen species whose deep red, fleshy fruit I collected in 2000 under the number DJHTu 0048. Its light, evergreen foliage is presented in a much less false-whorled fashion than *D. laureola*, forming an open shrub to 5 ft. (1.5 m) over time. The yellow-green flowers presented in open, spidery, axillary clusters, resulting in burgundy-red berries, are also known as possessing a pulse of evening fragrance, although I cannot honestly recall ever being driven

Daphne laureola var. *philippii*. (Photo by Lynne Harrison)

Daphne pontica. (Photo by Daniel J. Hinkley)

back into the garden for this added charm, suggesting its more proper siting would be nearer the house or terrace. Though indeed it was fascinating to see *D. pontica* in the wild, I had long cultivated it from a plant given to me by the late Kevin Nicolay of Seattle in the late 1980s. To my knowledge, my original plant still exists some two decades later in my original garden on the Kitsap Peninsula.

My several visits to southwestern China have resulted in both the observation of numerous species of *Daphne* and, on occasion, the luck of finding a few intact fruits late in the season. Two of those happened to represent a duo of evergreen species that I find to be among the most pleasing of the genus: *D. retusa* and *D. tangutica*.

At high elevations of over 10,000 ft. (3000 m) near Zhongdian in northwestern Yunnan Province, I collected fruit from a dense, rounded species known as *Daphne retusa*. I noted that it is common in this area, growing amidst *Berberis angulosa*, *Potentilla suffruticosa*, and numerous dwarf rhododendrons. Its dark green, lanceolate, ovate leaves to 2½ in. (6 cm) provide

a good foil for the terminal clusters of fragrant, deep lavender flowers for a long period in summer, resulting in crops of red fruit. In cultivation it will often create a mounded specimen to 4 ft. by 4 ft. (1.2 m by 1.2 m).

As an aside, I must mention an association with this shrub from my younger days, what I would call a milestone in my understanding and appreciation of the significance of plant nomenclature. I had had the pleasure of working with Brian Mulligan, director emeritus of Washington Park Arboretum, and on occasion took my plant identification students to his and his wife Margaret's garden in Kirkland, Washington. As proper English gardeners who took their roles as keen plantspeople seriously, the Mulligans wasted little time in coaxing a name for a plant from me, hesitant horticultural neophyte that I was at the time. While bidding them farewell during a visit early on in our relationship, I admired a *Daphne* outside their front door and wondered aloud if it were *D. tangutica* or *D. retusa*. Without a moment's hesitation, Mrs. Mulligan pulled off a leaf, thrust it toward my face, and asked whether the leaves did not appear quite retuse.

The two species are quite similar, although as Margaret Mulligan pointed out, the leaf edges of *Daphne retusa* do indeed curl under themselves. Perhaps it was the siting of this species in my own garden, at the base of a Douglas fir on the southern side of our woodland, but it never performed as admirably as did our specimens of *D. tangutica*.

It was *Daphne tangutica*, which I consider more robust but equally hardy, and perhaps with a longer season of bicolored lavender and cream, exceedingly fragrant flowers, that I observed also at higher elevations above the Zhongdian plateau on the western flank of Beima Shan at 12,000 ft. (3660 m). In my first garden I had sited this species near the front door of our home, in a somewhat shaded position, to invite the fragrance inside during late winter and spring when it was in blossom. I also grew it in a gravelly mound on the southern side of our home in full sun. Both spaces seemed to suit it. As with *D. mezereum*, it was perhaps the most heavily

Daphne retusa. (Photo by Daniel J. Hinkley)

Daphne tangutica. (Photo by Lynne Harrison)

fruiting species in my garden, and colonies of self-sown seedlings would need editing on a yearly basis from the beds in which they grew.

Before I get too far ahead of myself, I must take a moment to describe a small *Daphne* relative with which *D. retusa* associated itself in the dry alpine of Yunnan. In my collection notes I recorded it growing side by side with an indeterminate species of *Wikstroemia*, whose claim to fame, in my garden experience, has been its propensity to blossom itself to death with a steady smothering of terminal clusters of small, somewhat fragrant, yellow flowers. From this genus of about 35–50 species, 12 of which are endemic to the Hawaiian Islands, I have only had experience cultivating *W. terniflora*, which I received originally from J. C. Raulston. It made a demure deciduous plant in our woodland, with bright foliage and, except in the coldest of tem-

peratures, 12 months of perpetual flowers. I suspect it would perform better in a summer-warm climate and under brighter conditions.

But back to *Daphne*. Also in 1998, while with friend Georg Ubelhardt of Germany, we collected a deciduous species near the Tibetan border outside the frontier village of Dêqên in Yunnan Province. I have yet to put a name to this, collected as DJHC 98164, but I assume it is closely allied to *D. acutiloba*. A deciduous shrub to 5 ft. (1.5 m) with narrow, lanceolate foliage, it blossoms virtually nonstop between March and December, setting enormous quantities of orange-red fruit. It is primarily due to this prolific setting of viable fruit that *D. acutiloba* is valued as an understock in grafting the *Daphne* species and hybrids that are more difficult to root. Though this species is lovely in terms of fruiting effects, and far from shabby when it comes to floral ornament, it is dev-

Daphne genkwa. (Photo by Lynne Harrison)

astatingly devoid of any fragrance, a handicap that significantly compromises its desirability.

From eastern China (Henan, Shanxi, and Shandong), and some say South Korea, hails certainly one of the most distinctive *Daphne* species that exists. I can still recall my first interface with *D. genkwa* under cultivation in Japan in 1988. In view of its fragrant lavender-blue flowers cloaking upright stems to 2 ft. (0.6 m), I scoffed at the notion that it was properly named, though soon enough I was reminded of my shallow depth of knowledge. Though I have planted this species on numerous occasions in my garden, it has failed to establish; indeed, it is often dearly departed by the third year. Ernest Wilson professed "a thousand pities" after facing the same challenges with cultivating this species in gardens of the United Kingdom. Known as *yuán huā* in China, *D. genkwa* is important in traditional Chinese medicine and is the source of yuanhuacine and yuanhuadine, two alkaloids that show promise in the treatment of lung cancer.

In the autumn of 2007 at high elevations on Mount Morrison, Taiwan, Bleddyn Wynn-Jones, Finlay Colley of Dublin, and I found growing amidst krummholz of junipers and rhododendrons, fine specimens of *Daphne arisanensis*, a dense evergreen species somewhat similar in appearance and effect to *D. laureola*, with green, slightly scented flowers produced in late winter and resulting in red fruit. It is always gratifying to encounter an endemic species and make its acquaintance; however, I felt little regret over not being afforded the opportunity to gather its seed and cultivate it in my garden.

Not so with two "species" of Japan that I have, over the years, become quite enamored with. This does not include *Daphne odora*, perhaps the best-known, best-

Where Fragrance Reigns: *Daphne, Edgeworthia,* and *Ovidia*

Daphne jezoensis. (Photo by Daniel J. Hinkley)

Daphne pseudomezereum. (Photo by Lynne Harrison)

grown species in the genus, widely cultivated throughout Japan in countless forms despite the fact that it is rarely encountered in the wild (indeed, due to its lengthy and widespread use in horticulture in eastern Asia, its actual nativity is obscure). My attention has focused on a rare summer-dormant species and an uncommon dioecious member of the genus that may in fact represent its subspecies: *D. jezoensis* and *D. pseudomezereum*.

Indeed, *Daphne jezoensis* presents its papery, lime green leaves in an unlikely manner, just as temperatures drop in late autumn; it produces clusters of relatively large yellow flowers in early spring in the leaf axils along the stems, resulting later in red fruit, and sheds its leaves by June. It is found on the margin of woodlands particularly to the north and extends into the Kamchatka Peninsula. Current taxonomy suggests it is but a subspecies of *D. pseudomezereum*, which to my eye seems dramatically different from *D. jezoensis*, a superficial dead ringer for *D. mezereum* in regard to foliage. The oblanceolate leaves of *D. pseudomezereum* appear in false whorls along upright stems to 4 ft. (1.2 m), while clusters of yellow flowers appear in terminal clusters in very early spring. This species, too, attempts to fully uncloak during the summer months, though will stay partially dressed if provided a cool, humus-rich soil.

The *Daphne* species with which I have interacted in the wild more than any other, and whose perplexing rarity in the landscapes of the Pacific Northwest still confounds me, is a fine and exceedingly fragrant shrub with an unfortunate and intimidating Latin name. The species name *bholua*, pronounced *bo-loo-a*, comes from the plant's vernacular Nepalese name, *bhulu swa*. Indeed, *D. bholua* is found commonly in the high Himalaya, where I have observed it growing as an evergreen shrub to 8 ft. (2.4 m) in height in eastern Nepal, northern Sikkim, and Bhutan at elevations of 8000–10,000 ft. (2400–3000 m). I have also encountered it growing at lower elevations in the mountains of northern Vietnam and at very high elevations in western China. Throughout its range, its bark is used to make a fine-quality paper.

Oddly, it is likely due to this widespread distribution

Specimens of *Daphne bholua* in northern Sikkim. (Photo by Daniel J. Hinkley)

Flowers of *Daphne bholua*. (Photo by Daniel J. Hinkley)

Daphne bholua 'Alba'. (Photo by Lynne Harrison)

Daphne bholua var. *glacialis*. (Photo by Daniel J. Hinkley)

is far from readily available. Two of our clones remain completely evergreen, with elegantly narrow leaves to 6 in. (15 cm), each with a handsome undulate edge. Of these two, one blossoms in late December with clusters of fragrant, soft pink flowers, and the other, brought from England in 1996 under the name *D. bholua* 'Alba', offers pure white, intensely fragrant flowers borne in mid-February. The former may represent a seedling selected for its exceptional hardiness in England in 1982 and named 'Jacqueline Postill', although I purchased it in Seattle in 1998 with no associated cultivar name.

Additionally, we are cultivating clones from elevations of more than 11,000 ft. (3350 m) in eastern Nepal and Sikkim that are partially and completely deciduous. Often seen in literature, the fully deciduous forms are sometimes referred to as *Daphne bholua* var. *glacialis*, and references to this name and associated pictures suggest the flowers to be a rich pink. My own deciduous collections from high elevations have remained partially evergreen as pure white flowers are produced. It is these that should be considered by gardeners living at higher elevations or colder microclimates, as they will prove to be much hardier than the evergreen forms.

The rubbery texture of the wood and large, plump, pointed buds of these shrubs betray their identity in the depths of winter when they are without foliage, while the clusters of ethereally fragrant, large, white to lavender or pink flowers open from pink-blushed buds from late January through February. The growth habit of all forms is rigidly upright and quite narrow, to 10 ft. (3 m) tall while less than 3 ft. (0.9 m) wide.

In July of 2006, I found myself in far western Sichuan at a rather high elevation. There, at such an unlikely time of year, months earlier than I would normally be in the field to collect seed, I was treated to not only high-elevation Technicolor meadows of *Cypripedium*, *Primula*, *Iris*, *Rheum*, and *Mandragora*, but also to my first-ever opportunity to collect seeds of *Daphne bholua*, whose fruits disappear by September. Gratifyingly, these seed collections successfully germinated and are maturing nicely at Windcliff.

that *Daphne bholua* is generally absent from cultivation. The first attempts at cultivating this species probably involved plants grown from low-elevation collections—that is, less hardy parents. Old habits die hard, and even more boorish is the attempt to salvage the reputation of a plant that has been christened nonhardy.

There are now several reliably hardy clones of *Daphne bholua* in cultivation in the Pacific Northwest, though it

HARDINESS: I have made specific mention of the inhospitable climates many *Daphne* species tolerate in their native haunts. Expectations that the deciduous species might be hardier than the evergreen species should be cast aside. Daphnes are surprisingly adaptive and can tolerate the extremes and aridity of the inner-mountain states, the humidity of the Southeast, and the perpetual coolness of the Pacific Northwest.

CULTIVATION: Daphnes can be miffy creatures and give up the ghost overnight for no apparent reason, while others persist for decades. And while many species appreciate a deep, evenly moist, acidic loam, others thrive under alkaline conditions. A well-draining soil, however, is a nonnegotiable requirement. Full exposure to sun or at least bright conditions will promote better flowering. More than one clone of a species will also promote fruiting, but due to the acute poisonous nature of this fruit to humans and mammalian pets (not birds), fruiting should not necessarily be encouraged. With that said, serious poisoning from garden or house plants is extremely rare, so there is no need for overreaction to this threat.

PROPAGATION: Though seed presents little challenge, a double dormancy will develop if it is allowed to fully ripen before harvesting. Extracting and sowing seed while the flesh is still green (though the endosperm of the seed has turned white) will result in immediate germination. Otherwise seed allowed to fully ripen will require a single cold treatment before germinating the following season.

Cuttings are reasonably successful; however, the percentage that strike can vary dramatically and inexplicably from year to year. The wood should be beginning to harden though still flexible; some suggest erring on the side of soft tissue. Leaf drop will occur in the cutting flat regardless of timing, in both evergreen and deciduous species, and these rotting leaves can lead to secondary fungal infections of the living tissue of the cutting. It proves beneficial to remove as many leaves as possible when taking the cutting. In successfully rooting *Daphne*

bholua, some propagators remove all foliage from the cutting before sticking it in the rooting media.

Side grafts are often used for hard-to-root species, with *Daphne acutiloba* being the universal rootstock of choice. Tissue culture has also been successfully employed, particularly in the variegated clones of *D. ×burkwoodii* (*D. cneorum* × *D. caucasica*).

Edgeworthia

There is one thing I know for certain about *Edgeworthia*: no one seems to know what species they have, and few seem to know if more than one species actually exists. I include myself among the taxonomically challenged, though getting my sea legs, and I am among those guilty of propelling improper nomenclature through my writing and speaking.

I can recall the first time I saw *Edgeworthia* in blossom and fell head over heels in limerence with this winter-blossoming, vastly underknown shrub. It was in the gardens adjacent to the Imperial Palace in Tokyo during my first visit there in 1988. Oddly enough, what then caught my eye was the red-flowered form of what is now known as *E. papyrifera* (or *E. chrysantha*) 'Rubra' or 'Red Dragon', originally brought into the country under the name 'Akebono'.

We grew what we called *Edgeworthia papyrifera* for many years in my first garden, having received our specimen from J. C. Raulston under this name. It thrived in our woodland, each year setting enormous quantities of silvery buttons in autumn that would open to yellow, fragrant clusters of flowers in late January. We twice dug a single specimen for use in garden show displays in Seattle, and it sailed through both insults without harm while titillating attendees. Life seemed good.

Our plant formed a small, rounded shrub to 5 ft. (1.5 m) with slender, rubbery stems and bright green, deciduous leaves to 3 in. (7.5 cm) long. There was a slight but not overwhelming fragrance. It grew well in two locations of the garden, both in shade and in bright filtered light, in well-drained soils.

Things became more interesting when a Canadian nursery began selling another clone (or species?) of *Edgeworthia* that appeared miles apart in appearance, under the name *E. chrysantha*. Good enough. Stout in growth, with leaves and inflorescences double the size of our plant, and much more fragrant flowers. Unfortunately, at about the same time the *RHS Plant Finder* listed *E. papyrifera* as a synonym of *E. chrysantha*, leaving one of my plants quite nameless.

Tony Avent of Plant Delights Nursery shed some light on this ongoing investigation by sending me his knowledge of the original clones distributed by J. C. According to Tony, the original plant that J. C. grew was a clone that Don Jacobs of Atlanta, Georgia, collected on Yaku Shima in southern Japan and called *Edgeworthia papyrifera* 'Eco Yaku'. During Tony's stint as grounds manager of the North Carolina State Fairgrounds, he planted out numerous clones of this original collection throughout its landscape. His observations were that the flowers were rather small and fragrant, while the leaves were of less substance, visually similar to my original plant.

Piroche Plants of Vancouver, British Columbia, was seemingly responsible for the introduction of the larger-leaved, stouter-growing clone, though I was unable to ascertain the provenance of that material. For one of those plants, which possessed the largest leaves of all,

Edgeworthia gardneri lends its pith to the production of paper in remote areas of the Himalaya. (Photo by Daniel J. Hinkley)

Edgeworthia chrysantha 'Rubra' in the gardens near the Imperial Palace in Tokyo. (Photo by Daniel J. Hinkley)

Avent provided the name 'Snow Cream', and he has distributed it under this name through his nursery. Another Carolina nurseryman, Ted Stevens, later acquired seed of *E. chrysantha* and grew out many hundreds to maturity, with virtually all possessing the same stout stems, large leaves, and endearing fragrance associated with the Piroche clone, but differing significantly in the size of the inflorescence.

Avent's observations regarding the hardiness of the two forms is also in sync with my original observations. The smaller form of *Edgeworthia papyrifera*, which thrives in the maritime modified climate of the Pacific Northwest, is frequently killed by frosts in the Southeast, while the more robust clone can take temperatures to 0°F (−18°C) without damage while seemingly resenting (somewhat) the coolness of our maritime climate.

Both Tony and I believe it is possible that the so-called Piroche clone might represent a tetraploid form of the smaller-leaved, smaller-stemmed, less hardy 'Eco Yaku' form. However, the more I have observed it in the wild and grown its progeny to flowering age, while observing little variation in leaf or flower size, the more unlikely this seems.

Ultimately the mystery will solve itself, genetically or with the re-collection of wild populations exhibiting the traits of Don Jacobs's original introduction. For now the most important thing is to recognize the need to select forms most adaptive to particular climates.

In my experience thus far, the original clone of *Edgeworthia chrysantha* we received from J. C. is the best clone for cultivation in the greater Puget Sound, while the more robust form seems to appreciate the heat (and humidity) of the Southeast as well as summer-warm areas of British Columbia, Washington, Oregon, northern California, and surrounding environs.

The only time I have seen a plant resembling our original *Edgeworthia "papyrifera"* has been under cultivation in Japan. In particular, red- or orange-flowered forms frequently encountered in gardens in the Tokyo area seem to be identical in appearance but for the flower color. In 2008 I encountered for the first time a variegated form in Japan, with a hefty price and weighty ornamental presence.

The *Flora of China* (Wu et al. 1994 to present) lists four species, three of which are endemic to China and three of which are mostly evergreen. *Edgeworthia eriosolenoides* (southeastern Yunnan), *E. gardneri* (northwestern Yunnan, Nepal, Bhutan, northern India), and *E. albiflora* (southwestern Sichuan) are all known to retain their foliage, at least through the flowering season. *Edgeworthia chrysantha*, widespread across much

My guide, Pemba, standing below an immense specimen of *Edgeworthia gardneri* in Nepal. (Photo by Daniel J. Hinkley)

Edgeworthia

of China and naturalized in Japan, fully jettisons its foliage in autumn.

In eastern Nepal in 1995 and again in 2002, it was *Edgeworthia gardneri* that we frequently encountered, with some specimens approaching treelike proportions to 30 ft. (9 m). On occasion we found local villag-

ers using this species to make paper, a practice that was contemplated for North America during the early years of the 20th century, when *Edgeworthia* was introduced from the U.S. Plant Introduction Station in Chico, California, to a nursery owner by the name of W. T. Ashford. In 1906, near Wolf Creek, Georgia, a family named

Edgeworthia chrysantha from collections made in northeastern Sichuan Province, showing an usual pink blush at the base of the corolla tubes. (Photo by Daniel J. Hinkley)

Edgeworthia chrysantha. (Photo by Lynne Harrison)

A variegated form of *Edgeworthia chrysantha* found in specialty nurseries in Japan. (Photo by Daniel J. Hinkley)

Haynes planted a small plantation of *Edgeworthia* with the intent of producing paper and starting a printing business. Interestingly, though the plantation is now overgrown, the plants themselves are very intact and have perpetuated themselves to some degree throughout the general vicinity.

Edgeworthia gardneri paper is manufactured not by its bark, as with *Daphne bholua*, but by the inner pith of its stem—information provided by an ebullient connoisseur of handmade papers, Elaine Koretsky, director of the Research Institute of Paper History and Technology in Brookline, Massachusetts. However, although I find this fascinating, it has not helped to determine the actual discrepancies in taxonomy that the horticultural industry faces regarding this extraordinary plant.

In northeastern Sichuan Province in 2003 and 2004, we hiked through thickets of what we now believe was *Edgeworthia chrysantha* and were afforded the opportunity to collect its fruit. Those collections were sold through my enterprise under a DJHS designation in 2006, under the name *E. gardneri*, but this was certainly an erroneous name. In any event, the seedlings that blossomed from this collection have proven to be remarkable, with intensely fragrant orbs of butterscotch-yellow flowers transitioning to bright pink at the base of each tube. It is a vast departure from the clones currently in the marketplace and will ultimately be reintroduced under a cultivar name.

I am uncertain as to the taxonomy of the evergreen species, with specimens to 8 ft. (2.4 m), that I encountered in northern Vietnam in the autumn of 2008.

Despite its taxonomic confusion, I would not be without this genus in my garden. It represents the bounty of plants that bring interest to the temperate winter garden, and accentuates exactly how much there remains to learn of the plant world. That in itself is exciting.

HARDINESS: Though this deciduous "daphne" would seem to possess a certain degree of hardiness, that does not seem to be the case. Though there are reports of some surviving in protected sites in the Philadelphia area, in zone 6b, I do not believe one could expect consistent flowering in zone 6 or lower. The evergreen species, including *Edgeworthia gardneri* and others, may prove appropriate for summer-warm climates of the West Coast.

CULTIVATION: Full sun or partial shade in humus-rich, well-draining, slightly acidic soils seems to be the key to successful cultivation. Stronger growth can be expected under brighter conditions; however, this must be balanced with the ambient winter temperature and possible need for overstory protection from severe frosts. Waterlogged soils are to be avoided at all costs.

PROPAGATION: Seed, when produced, offers little challenge, and the seedlings will blossom in as little as two growing seasons. Cuttings of selected clones are more challenging. Encouragement of basal suckers by hard pruning offers the best cutting material, taken as the wood begins to harden in midsummer and placed under mist on gentle bottom heat. Any flower buds produced in autumn on the rooted cuttings should be removed immediately. Less attrition will take place if cuttings are left undisturbed in the cutting flat and not transplanted until growth resumes in spring.

Definitely Not Daphnes: *Daphniphyllum*

With my newfound friends, all in a very small Honda, with my pack crammed between my legs in the front seat, we happily made our way south from Chollipo toward the port city of Wando. Seemingly every 10 minutes today we stopped when spotting something of interest along the road and began the process of extricating ourselves from the kimchi'd air of our confines. The flora here is opulent, with numerous acquaintances of the past from cultivation making themselves known in the wild for the first time. We ate our lunch on a sunny rock under a sensational specimen of Pteroceltis tatarinowii *with a fabric of* Staphylea, Alangium, Lindera, Ilex, Camellia, *and* Deutzia *beneath that we slowly deciphered with sardine sand-wiches in hand. Overfed and running late, we reinserted ourselves limb by limb into the car and had proceeded only a mile before Bleddyn slammed on the brakes and the fire drill commenced again. Directly along the road to our right was a splendid colony of* Daphniphyllum himalaense var. macropodum *with female specimens clad in long axillary chains of glaucous blue fruit. It was the first time any of us had confronted this in the wild, and we contentedly, excitedly, gathered its fruit while wondering how we might fit even another single seed into our tiny transport.*

Near Wando, South Korea
October 8, 1993

FOR THOSE WHO HAPPEN TO KNOW just a scrappy bit of botanical Latin, the genus name *Daphniphyllum* might seem to refer to plants with leaves (*phyllum*) like *Daphne*. And if those same people happen to know just a tiny bit about daphnes, they would, before encountering their first *Daphniphyllum*, assume that this plant would have small, rather finely textured, perhaps evergreen leaves. But these people, upon at last encountering a *Daphniphyllum*, would not experience that "Aha!" validation of their preconceived notions. They would instead be gazing upon a shrub that appears deceivingly like a rhododendron. Perhaps the author of this genus, Carl Ludwig von Blume, who

died in 1862, had never encountered a rhododendron, a concept nearly unfathomable to us in the Pacific Northwest, where landscapes are insidiously infected with the genus. Yet he had obviously seen a laurel (*Prunus laurocerasus*), a plant known as *Daphne* by the ancient Greeks, and the rest is nomenclatural history. As is often said, a little knowledge is a dangerous thing.

Although they superficially resemble the cherry laurel and rhododendrons, daphniphyllums are much more closely related to euphorbias; in fact, *Daphniphyllum* shared the auspices of the family Euphorbiaceae until it was placed into its own family, the Daphniphyllaceae. Without exception, all 30-odd species are evergreen shrubs and trees, and all are dioecious, with male and female flowers borne on separate plants.

Despite the breadth of this genus, found through-

Daphniphyllum himalaense var. *macropodum* near Mount Chiri in South Korea. (Photo by Daniel J. Hinkley)

out the warmer regions of Asia, it is known to horticulturists in the West primarily through one species from Japan and Korea. And this is when it gets dicey, for the taxonomy of *Daphniphyllum* is as greasy as a mountain road in Vietnam during the monsoon. The species have been named, renamed, and in the process misspelled, so much so that I must content myself with the fact that I know what a *Daphniphyllum* is but haven't a clue what to call it.

Daphniphyllum himalaense var. *macropodum* (syn. *D. macropodum*) is frequently encountered at lower elevations of the Korean Peninsula and throughout the Japanese Archipelago. Despite its rather luxurious, temperate native environs, it holds its own when confronted with hostile climatic conditions while traveling abroad. From a vast contingent of broad-leaved evergreen shrubs, *Daphniphyllum* was among a handful that exhibited nary a niggling degree of damage after enduring the frigid tempest of the 1990–1991 Christmas storms in western Washington.

The foliage of *Daphniphyllum himalaense* var. *macropodum* is leathery in texture and extends to 8 in. (20 cm) long and 3 in. (7.5 cm) wide. It provides a bold, textural quality to the garden, in sun or shade, with an unblemished, varnished green and slightly bluish cast on top, and a lime-frost glaucous undercoating. Particularly striking is the bright red leaf petiole, which remains vivid throughout the year on new growth. The foliage is carried on this species along a vigorous, upright framework that is quite variable in height depending on its provenance. A seedling I raised from wild collections in South Korea in 1993 has resulted in a swarthy specimen to nearly 20 ft. (6 m) in height with no apparent desire to slow its upward thrust. In 2007 at nearly 9000 ft. (2700 m) in elevation on the Southern Cross-Island Highway in Taiwan, this species also made itself known, with spectacularly fruited female specimens to 40 ft. (12 m) tall, growing beneath virgin stands of *Chamaecyparis obtusa* var. *formosana*, *Tsuga dumosa*, and *Trochodendron aralioides*.

This vigorous growth habit compares unfavorably, in

A male specimen of *Daphniphyllum himalaense* var. *macropodum* coming into flower. (Photo by Daniel J. Hinkley)

A variegated form of *Daphniphyllum himalaense* var. *macropodum*. (Photo by Daniel J. Hinkley)

regard to garden adaptability, to the format adhered to in populations occurring on the northernmost Japanese island of Hokkaidō, where dense, rounded shrubs to no more than 3 ft. by 3 ft. (0.9 m by 0.9 m) are frequently found. This compact form was once provided its own name, under the affiliate of *Daphniphyllum humile*, but a more recent treatment amalgamates it with *D. himalaense* var. *macropodum*.

Attempting to define exactly what constitutes beauty in nature is anathema to those who (ultimately) come to understand that anything of substance, especially a living thing, possesses a sufficient sprinkling of magic to make it inherently pretty. The flowers of *Daphniphyllum* have routinely been, in literature, cavalierly dismissed as if the design was flawed or the product blemished. Of great notice they are not, but still quite perfect to be sure. Both male and female flowers are borne on numerous racemes from the leaf axils of the previous year's growth. Of the two sexes, the male flowers perform with more flair, providing a dense purple frill described as mulberry-like. If pollination is effected, however, the female plants then shine and provide a fruiting display that cannot possibly be deposed, no matter how suffused the horticultural writer may be with ruthless umbrage. The female inflorescences, initially erect, become weighted and lax by crops of succulent, showy drupes of blue or black, often waxed by a whitish bloom.

Variegated forms of this *Daphniphyllum* do exist, though they are hardly considered mainstream. I have encountered at least four colorful-leaved forms at nurseries in Japan (there are certainly many more) and was in 2000 presented with a gift "seto" of three while in Tokyo. No small largess—the retail value of the triad was more than $1000. More importantly, all three survived the rigors of root washing and plant inspection to meet the standards of the USDA and had established quite nicely by the time I left my first garden.

Daphniphyllum himalaense var. *macropodum* is not the only species I have come upon in the wilds of Asia. *Daphniphyllum pentandrum*, collected under the number DJHT 99140 and distributed under the name *D.*

glaucescens, is frequently found at rather high elevations in Taiwan where it forms tall, evergreen trees with foliage of a particularly beautiful glaucous blue. I "harvested" the fruit of these mammoth specimens from the forest floor through which we were hiking. I have used this vigorous species as a screening hedge along the property line of Windcliff in Indianola.

At lower elevations, also on Taiwan, indeed in the hills directly above Taipei, we collected fruit of *Daphniphyllum teijsmannii*, a somewhat more compact species to 25 ft. (7.6 m), with long chains of shiny black drupes on the female specimens. This is common throughout the lower elevations of southern Japan and was among the species I collected on Ulleung Island in the Sea of Japan in 1993. Though handsome, variegated forms of *D. teijsmannii* circulate in commerce in Japan, in my estimation, this tenderer species does not proffer anything beyond another name to justify seeking it out for inclusion in the garden.

Interestingly, taxonomists tell us that the *Daphniphyllum himalaense* that I observed in the mountains of

A variegated form of *Daphniphyllum teijsmannii*. (Photo by Lynne Harrison)

Taiwan and Japan is the very same species I encountered on a snowy day in Sikkim, in the vicinity of Lachang and Lachung, the climatically brutal stomping ground of J. D. Hooker where he was imprisoned by the Dewan: magnificent specimens of *D. himalaense* var. *himalaense*, forming Hollywood-handsome pyramidal structures of swarthy, glossy green, boldly textured foliage to 15 ft. (4.6 m).

As these specimens demonstrate, observed within small villages and adjacent agricultural land at elevations well above 12,000 ft. (3660 m), collections from this area (alas, we were there in late October, well beyond the envelope of ripened seed) are much hardier than other taxa currently in cultivation. I am a lay botanist only; however, my horticultural intuition tells me that this might be an entirely different taxon, and

efforts should be put into placing it into cultivation for more climatically provoked areas of North America and Europe.

My earlier assertion that "I know what a *Daphniphyllum* is but don't know what to call it" comes into full play during my travels in Vietnam. Bleddyn Wynn-Jones and I, both keen on the genus, have collected numerous species along Vietnam's border with China since our first visit there in 1999. At our second camp on Fansi-pan, on that trip, we camped amidst a sensational grove of shrubby daphniphyllums carrying exemplary unblemished foliage to 10 in. (25 cm) carried by radiant red petioles. We collected fruit of these specimens under the name *D. chartaceum* HWJ 99153, while during the autumn of 2006, approaching the village of Seo Mi Ti with my constant and loyal guide Uoc Le Huu, we

Daphniphyllum himalaense var. *himalaense* in northern Sikkim. (Photo by Daniel J. Hinkley)

Daphniphyllum chartaceum in northern Vietnam. (Photo by Daniel J. Hinkley)

paused to collect the fruit from handsome, pendulous racemes of what I later determined to be *D. longeracemosum*. Later the authorities weighed in heavily on both collections, suggesting that these names are, once again, but synonyms of the same species I observed in northern India.

It is certainly forgivable that the scientific community has not yet settled on certain names of the taxa deserving species status in this genus. With so many millions of life forms on this planet begging closer inspection, it will take a few lifetimes and an individual intrigued by

Daphniphyllum chartaceum. (Photo by Daniel J. Hinkley)

the taxonomy of *Daphniphyllum* to ultimately settle the accounts. Until then, I remain captivated by the genus and am profoundly content to call each of its members simply *Daphniphyllum*.

HARDINESS: This genus may very well represent one of the hardiest bold-foliaged, broad-leaved evergreens available to gardeners in zone 5 and above, though work in thoughtful collection from known provenance and considerable vetting must first take place. *Daphniphyllum himalaense* var. *macropodum* will easily tolerate the upper ends of zone 6, while my somewhat dubious suspicions are that the Sikkimese populations of *D. himalaense* var. *himalaense* will prove to be hardy to 0°F (−18°C).

CULTIVATION: *Daphniphyllum* can be grown in full sun or fairly dense shade but will prove more extravagant in foliage under brighter conditions. All the species appear to appreciate additional summer moisture. A very large grove of *D. himalaense* var. *macropodum* was decimated at Washington Park Arboretum in Seattle by honey fungus, *Armillaria* species, while a neglected, assuredly lonely male stalwart sallies forth in Volunteer Park after tolerating decades of compacted soil and not a drop of added water during our summer droughts. Hard pruning in late winter before growth resumes will encourage the growth of dormant buds and result in a more pleasingly dense habit of growth.

PROPAGATION: Cuttings taken in midsummer and kept under mist will root quite readily, though I have not yet had success propagating the variegated forms in this manner. The Japanese currently graft these selections; I am uncertain what rootstock they use, but it might be suspected that the Japanese also do not know what rootstock they use. Freshly sown seeds present very few challenges and will germinate the following spring.

Definitely Not Daphnes: *Daphniphyllum*

The Alluring Ancients: *Drimys, Tasmannia,* and *Pseudowintera*

It is called Place of the Messengers, and of all the shards of this planet I have seen or will ever see in my life, this day will dwell in my memory as one of wizardry. For several hours, we hiked among a grove of ancient-growth Araucaria draped in lichens that caught the sun and radiated a green of Middle Earth. An entire family of Magellan woodpeckers pranced on these corky-skinned monoliths, seemingly pretending to look for food while keeping pace with our progress along the trail. It seemed a vast and voluminous sunlit hall, like some kind of temple for gods no longer known, with a delicious, seductive, sweet coolness to an air of rare vintage. Along mountain lakes, like bones of fallen giants, bleached skeletons of Araucaria lay scattered along the shores. The understory here is not particularly diverse but perfectly composed and in peak performance. Myrceugenia chrysantha, Desfontainia spinosa, Berberis trigona, and B. serratodentata are prominent, adhered to by drifts of Drimys andina. The latter is charming in habit and flower and would assuredly make the most sensational splash in cultivation if it would somehow provide a key to its successful cultivation. Perhaps here, in this mystical, mysterious place, the secret will be proffered by the elves.

Lago Huerquehue, Chile
February 28, 2005

DURING MY ADVANCED SYSTEMATICS course at the University of Washington, I made acquaintance with the floral characteristics of the "ancients," the families of flowering plants believed by most to have first arisen during the early Cretaceous period. Of these characteristics, I remember mostly the beauty under a dissecting microscope of the seamless spiral arrangement along the receptacle of the tepals, stamens, and then pistils. Though examples of the Magnoliaceae and Ranunculaceae were most thoroughly represented, a few auxiliary families were included to appease our abbreviated attention spans.

One of these was the Winteraceae, a family of nine genera and about 120 species primarily found in the Australasian flora, though occurring in the floristic zone of Malesia as well as Madagascar and the Neotropics. Though it was primarily through the dusty herbarium sheets of *Drimys*, *Tasmannia*, and *Pseudowintera* that I first came to know this family, I distinctly remember also examining a species of *Bubbia* (and joking, much later over a beer with fellow graduate students, that it certainly must have been named in honor of two recent American presidents).

It is rather coincidental that at the time of my studies, and when I lived at the enchanting Stone Cottage at Washington Park Arboretum, I encountered a recently acquired living specimen of *Drimys winteri* var. *chilensis* in the arboretum's nursery. It represented Clement Hamilton and Sarah Reichard's collections made in Chile in

Drimys granadensis slightly below the páramo in Costa Rica. (Photo by Daniel J. Hinkley)

1985 and was not considered a prospect for long-term survivorship in the Pacific Northwest. Perhaps seeing an actual living plant conjoin the lifeless forms of herbarium study piqued my interest, or perhaps the trajectory of my life's pursuit was preordained for a direct collision. In either case, I have come to admire and appreciate the numerous species of *Drimys* that I have grown or encountered in the wild.

During my first trip to Chile in 1998, Kevin Carrabine, Jennifer Macuiba, and I coursed our way south from Concepción to the southern tip of Chiloé Island over a three-week period. It was during that time that I came to fully appreciate the foliar beauty of *Drimys winteri*. Its long, oblanceolate, evergreen leaves, carried on a dense, pyramidal framework to 25 ft. (7.6 m), were upturned by predictable afternoon winds to reveal a startling white undersurface. It should be noted that 25 ft. (7.6 m) is a mean natural height; bucking the norm, plants take on treelike proportions to 50 ft. (15 m) in the species' southern range (*D. winteri* var. *winteri*) and shrink to tall, multistemmed shrubs from Chiloé Island north to the southern edge of Atacama (*D. winteri* var. *chilensis*). The plants I saw were still in blossom, with clusters of starry white flowers in terminal clusters, while glossy black, oblong fruit had already begun to ripen. I made several collections of this species during that trip; one particularly fine plant with ruby red stems, found near Conguillio, appeared under the number HCM 98087.

This upright, large shrub or small tree, *Drimys winteri*, is the most typical species of this widespread genus, though taxonomists distinguish between very close allies from Brazil (*Drimys brasiliensis*) and those from the isolated Juan Fernández Islands (*D. confertifolia*). While traveling in Costa Rica on numerous occasions, at the high elevations of the Cerro de la Muerte, I have been struck by the similarities between *D. granadensis* and its Chilean counterpart thousands of miles to the south. Interestingly, at this elevation in the páramo it grows with numerous other southern associates, including *Gunnera* species, *Weinmannia racemosa*, and *Desfontainia spinosa*. Yet I digress.

Drimys winteri var. *winteri*. (Photo by Daniel J. Hinkley)

Drimys winteri var. *chilensis*. (Photo by Lynne Harrison)

Drimys winteri has a long and dignified association with the West. Its bark was gathered in 1578 from the Straits of Magellan by Sir William Winter while sailing with Sir Francis Drake in his highly vaulted one-way, round-trip voyage. Taking a cue from the aboriginal tribes of Patagonia, Winter used it for spicing the ship's bland cuisine, in the process finding it curative for scurvy. Indeed, two centuries later, when formally described from James Cook's second juggernaut, *D. winteri* became one of the first economically important agricultural exports from South America for its ascorbic acid content.

It was in southern Chile in 1998, and again in 2003, that I encountered and collected the seed of one of the most charming yet inexplicably difficult species of *Dri-*

mys. Drimys andina, which loiters in literature as *D. winteri* var. *andina*, has all the best features of other species rolled into one. Forming a dense, rounded globe of evergreen foliage to 3 ft. by 3 ft. (0.9 m by 0.9 m) and smothered in white flowers for numerous weeks, it seems more like the prepossessing product of a plant breeder's imagination than anything created by nature. Yet it holds close the secret of how to transplant it to an exotic garden: failure has been reported from fellow plantsmen worldwide. Unlike *D. winteri*, *D. andina* grows in a decidedly sheltered, shaded locale.

In the late 1980s, after we began our first garden, I took a trip to the pacifying climate of the Long Beach Peninsula in southwestern Washington State, where in a local notable nursery I encountered a specimen of *Dri-*

Drimys winteri var. *chilensis* in southern Chile. (Photo by Daniel J. Hinkley)

Drimys winteri var. *andina* in fruit, growing as a common understory shrub in the *Araucaria* forests of southern Chile. (Photo by Daniel J. Hinkley)

mys lanceolata. It is now accepted that this and other Australian species of *Drimys* should be transferred to the genus *Tasmannia*, a move for which I have found the same degree of euphoria as with all other recent taxonomic tergiversations. Despite warnings about its climatic temperament, I found this plant's rather demure, leathery, glossy green leaves and deep wine red stems irresistible. Perhaps it is yet another example of the value of ignoring self-perpetuating garden myths, or as my friend J. C. Raulston would have put it, the value of an adventurous spirit, or maybe it does in fact illuminate a profound change in climate; in any case, *Tasmannia lanceolata* has never demonstrated an ounce of resentment to winters in zone 8.

Tasmannia lanceolata hails from southeastern Australia, most notably in Tasmania, where I have met it in the wild. It forms a small tree or large shrub over time, with dense, pleasingly textured, evergreen, lanceolate foliage and very pretty, though mostly unsung, axillary clusters of fragrant, yellow-green flowers in late winter.

Upon my departure from Tasmania in 1998, horticultural associates presented me with a package of the dried leaves and flowers of this species, colloquially anointed the name mountain pepper, and I will admit to having it still intact upon our spice rack. Mostly I am fascinated by this coevolved culinary application, with so many thousands of miles of open ocean between *Tasmannia lanceolata* and the other closely allied genera.

Having grown only a female specimen of *Tasmannia lanceolata*, and *Drimys winteri*, adjacent in my garden, and having raised seed progeny of the former, I was surprised, though not wonderstruck, that several seedlings appeared in a seed flat that seemed a combination of the two. With the brilliant red stems of *T. lanceolata*, substantive flowers that are intermediate between the two species, in shades of creamy green with rose calyces, and the oblanceolate, glossy green foliage of *D. winteri*, the seedlings exemplify the affinity of both taxa, and make a case for revisiting their taxonomic divorce. (I will admit to having never seen a male specimen of *T. lanceolata*

A female specimen of *Tasmannia lanceolata*.
(Photo by Daniel J. Hinkley)

A plant raised from seed of *Tasmannia lanceolata* with *Drimys winteri* as a possible pollen parent. (Photo by Daniel J. Hinkley)

in blossom.) I have also grown a variegated form of *T. lanceolata* found and introduced by Bluebell Nursery in England, with irregular blotchings of bright yellow on its foliage. It is not to everyone's liking, although I have found it a pleasing permutation.

Knowing that *Tasmannia lanceolata* occurs throughout Tasmania and southeastern Australia, I was prepared to encounter it at high elevations while botanizing in eastern Victoria in 2007. Along the high reaches of the Great Alpine Road, above 7000 ft. (2100 m) in elevation, I was surprised to find hummocks not of this species but of *Tasmannia xerophila*. Recognizable immediately as a member of *Tasmannia*, yet with a more uniformly squat habit of growth and foliage that is somewhat less glabrous, it grew beneath a consistent overstory of the snow gum, *Eucalyptus pauciflora*, and amidst an array of other hardy Victorian plants including *Podocarpus lawrencei* and *Grevillea victoriae*. To my knowledge, *T. xerophila* has not been brought into cultivation.

In New Zealand, taxonomists bloodied the genus *Drimys* early on, assigning the three native species to the genus *Pseudowintera*. Here, too, the pungent quality of these plants' bark and berries has translated into the common name of mountain pepper. It was the best-known species of this triad, *P. colorata*, that I most frequently met up with while on the forested trails of the South Island, immediately recognizing the muted, ovate, coppery green foliage with a variable blotching of purple, densely held on a 5–15 ft. (1.5–4.6 m) chassis (as a matter a note, however, species of *Coprosma* grow here that are dead look-alikes). These often grew in very shaded and moist glades under a complex overstory of conifers and *Nothofagus*. I had cultivated this species for numerous years in the Pacific Northwest (as well as 'Red Glow', purchased from Ken Gillanders in Tasmania), though not with what I could describe as outstanding success. In retrospect I may have attempted growing them in conditions that were too lean.

Pseudowintera axillaris is similar to *P. colorata* in appearance, with ovate to obovate, burnished green foliage on a taller framework and axillary clusters of yellow-green flowers. It occurs in the lowland flora of both islands and overlaps territories with *P. colorata* in montane as well as subalpine zones, where the two readily hybridize. The third New Zealand species, *P. traversii*, is known only from the northwest corner of the South Island near Nelson. It is poorly represented in cultivation outside of New Zealand. Considering the appar-

Pseudowintera colorata. (Photo by Lynne Harrison)

Pseudowintera colorata 'Red Glow'. (Photo by Lynne Harrison)

ent promiscuity of the Tasmanian and Chilean species, attempts to hybridize the New Zealand species with their far-flung cousins could easily be justified.

HARDINESS: Though these evergreen shrubs have long been promoted as half-tender shrubs meant only for warm climates or for siting along protective walls, this no longer seems to be the case, due to ever-increasing temperatures and ever-adventurous gardeners. With that said, it is doubtful that any will thrive below zone 7, and a summer-cool, moist climate will assuredly be most advantageous. An unscientific survey of horticulturists in the Southeast has suggested that these shrubs are not appropriate choices for gardens in hot, humid summer climates.

CULTIVATION: Though *Drimys winteri* var. *chilensis* is noted for growing in moist, near-swampy conditions in the wild, it does not appear to demand that situation in the garden. I have successfully grown this species in well-drained, slightly acidic soils with supplemental water provided in the summer months; however,

W. J. Bean notes that it will tolerate alkaline conditions. I have grown both *D. winteri* and *Tasmannia lanceolata* in shaded as well as sunny conditions and would suggest the latter as being the better of the two for promoting strong growth and a handsome, intensely colored shag of foliage. The difficulty with cultivating *D. andina* may be due to the absence of a necessary symbiotic fungus naturally present in the soils of its natural range; however, this is complete speculation on my part, and justification for my failure with this plant.

Drimys winteri is best sited in the garden to take advantage of the brilliant white undersurface of its foliage. It is particularly striking if bottom-lit during the evening.

PROPAGATION: Seed of all species must obviously be cleaned from the flesh of the berry and if sown fresh will germinate readily the following spring; it should not be presumed that seed collected under cultivation will result in undiluted species. These shrubs provide little challenge with regard to hardwood cuttings taken in midautumn and placed on gentle bottom heat.

Antipodean Elegance: *Eucryphia*

I am currently aboard the final leg from Dulles to Seattle, delayed at the gate, beginning to feel somewhat human again after 24 hours of flying with food poisoning, assuredly from the ceviche I so foolishly ordered for dinner the night before my departure. I still possessed the presence of mind, upon wheels up from Puerto Montt, to examine the landscape below us, intending to see if the flurry of white flowers of Eucryphia cordifolia *could be perceived from a distance. I was dumbstruck by not only the sheer quantity—on the southern slopes of some mountains a solid snow-sweep of clean white—but also by the length of time and distance from which I could still recognize their characteristic glint. At first I wondered if anyone else on the plane had made the connection between the palpable hue of the dwindling landscape below and a tree in ample, sublime blossom. Shortly thereafter, I wondered exactly why it might be that I was beginning to feel so very green.*

Leaving Chile
March 2, 1998

I TEND TO LIKE A SMALL GENUS OF PLANTS, and even more so one with enough diversity in form to make it an interesting journey through the rank and file. Add to that mix ethereally beautiful flowers at an unlikely time of year and handsome evergreen or deciduous foliage, and you have the genus *Eucryphia*, which seems to have all it takes to draw me in.

It took some time to make an acquaintance. The climate of Michigan excluded such lovelies from consideration, as did the high desert of eastern Washington, where I relocated in 1980. It was in the summer of 1983, while living at Washington Park Arboretum and surveying its 230 acres as part of my master's thesis, that I was first bit. On a limpid August morning, I kneeled to tie my shoe. When I stood up, staring me in the face was a flower of *Eucryphia ×intermedia*. I recall thinking it was the most beautiful flower I had ever seen.

The genus *Eucryphia*, once sole tenant of the Eucryphiaceae, now must share a rambling pile known as the Cunoniaceae. It is a family of 26 genera part and parcel to the Antarctic flora, with only the genus *Caldcluvia* reaching into the Northern Hemisphere in the Philippines. (As an aside, I cultivate *C. paniculata* from my collections made in Chile in 2003, an interesting, moderate-sized, evergreen tree with terminal trusses of yellow-green flowers in late summer.) The name *Eucryphia* is a Greek derivative for "well concealed," referring to the small hidden sepals adjoined to the apex of the buds.

Again I must face in this chapter my inconsistent stance of including trees in a book devoted to shrubs. My justification comes from those commonly cultivated in the Northern Hemisphere that behave as large shrubs.

Overleaf: *Eucryphia cordifolia* blossoming at Windcliff from seeds collected in southern Chile in 1998. (Photo by Daniel J. Hinkley)

In the real world this is primarily and truthfully a genus of towering evergreen trees. Of the seven species, two are found in South America, while the remaining are Australian, including Tasmania. The foliage of these species is evergreen (except for *Eucryphia glutinosa*) and pinnately compound (except for *E. milliganii*).

The primary charms of this assemblage of—ahem—shrubs, are its flowers and timing of blossom. Pristine, silken white (very rarely pink), four-petaled cups to 2 in. (5 cm) across open in August and September to reveal a startling cache of dark filaments and, in some species, a beguiling fragrance. Two especially nectar-rich species, *Eucryphia cordifolia* in Chile and *E. lucida* in Tasmania, produce a monofloral honey considered unsurpassed by connoisseurs. Seeds are dehisced from woody capsules 12–14 months after flowering.

The two South American species and the hybrid between them are certainly the best known of the lot. *Eucryphia cordifolia* creates an evergreen, rounded-crowned tree to 50 ft. (15 m) or more. It is found as individual, perfectly proportioned specimens amidst denuded agricultural land (probably left standing for honey production) but forms solid stands along rivers and somewhat shaded southern-exposed slopes, below the *Araucaria* zone, sharing habitat with *Nothofagus*, *Saxegothaea*, and *Podocarpus*. The coarse, pinnate foliage provides a handsome texture, while a prolific late-summer blossoming of white flowers transforms the forests where it is prevalent to a tranquil scene of clean, freshly fallen snow, with drones of pollinating insects flickering about as they discover the nectar stores. *Miel de ulmo*, the honey produced from this species, is found on roadside stands and shops throughout Chile and is highly regarded for its distinctive taste.

Occupying the same general range in the temperate Valdivian rain forests, yet on soils less moist, is a species regarded as not only the hardiest but also the only true deciduous taxon in the genus. *Eucryphia glutinosa*, its species name referring to the rather gummy texture inherent to its terminal buds and new growth, has somewhat more finely textured foliage than its Chilean com-

patriot, which develops spectacular tones of amber and rose in autumn before leaf drop. Rising to 15 ft. (4.6 m) over time, it is also the only species that can be honestly referred to as multistemmed and shrublike in habit.

Amidst the collections of Washington Park Arboretum in the early 1980s were two somewhat forgotten yet exceptional forms of *Eucryphia glutinosa*. One of them seems to have spontaneously appeared there and may possess the potential to rewrite our perceptions of the genus. The other specimen, no longer extant due to an unknown decline, presented fully double to semidouble flowers every August, a phenomenon that had already been documented much earlier in literature from Europe (where, it might be added, the year-to-year offering of such flowers on this form, dubbed 'Flore Pleno', was known to be inconsistent).

Autumn color of *Eucryphia glutinosa*. (Photo by Daniel J. Hinkley)

Yet on the fringes of a planting mostly usurped by natural vegetation, I discovered a small hummocked individual no taller than 3 ft. (0.9 m) and spreading to 5 ft. (1.5 m) or more, covered in late summer with an ample-enough production of beguiling white flowers, followed in autumn by handsome tones in its foliage. The cultivar name attached to this plant, the rather awkward 'Nirrhe', was in actuality attached to several full-sized specimens of *Eucryphia glutinosa* in the collection; after further research, I realized that it was just the vernacular name for the species, taken from the Mapuche language. I propagated this at the time, despite very little cutting wood proffered on a yearly basis, and found that its superlative growth habit translated consistently to other sites, in my own and other gardens. Later, frustrated by the lack of cutting material each year, we began growing it from seed, which gratifyingly produced a spectrum of plants ranging from vigorous full-sized individuals to those even more compact than the parent. I have used the original and its more demure offspring in crossings with *E. cordifolia* and the lovely yet underknown *E. moorei*; the resulting seedlings are still too young to determine whether we might have a new generation of compact hybrid eucryphias.

Eucryphia glutinosa crossed with *E. cordifolia* gave rise to *E. ×nymansensis*, not surprisingly at Nymans in Sussex, a garden devoted to rare plants, in 1915. Intermediate in height between the two species, this large evergreen shrub or small tree is clad with foliage most resembling that of its fully evergreen parent and demonstrating added hardiness from *E. glutinosa*. Two seedlings of *E. ×nymansensis*, A and B, were ultimately selected and distributed. The former was ultimately given the name 'Nymansay' and appears to be the clone most often found in commerce in Europe, though I fear, as is often the case in such situations, putting the proper name to previously distributed plants is next to impossible. Autumn tones can develop on this hybrid in late summer, but its primary objective seems to be to remain entirely evergreen. For cool sites in the Pacific Northwest, it remains one of the most dependable of the ever-green species in terms of blossoming, putting on a terrific show in mid-August, though its ultimate size, to 30 ft. (9 m) over time, might make it too much of a good thing for the small urban garden.

Eucryphia glutinosa crossed with the Tasmanian *E. lucida* resulted in a highly touted and often awarded hybrid known as *E. ×hybrida* or, more correctly, *E. ×intermedia*. Found at Rostrevor, County Down, in Northern Ireland, and brandishing an eponymous cultivar name, it was given an Award of Merit by the Royal Horticultural Society in 1936. Resembling a somewhat more vigorous and free-flowering rendition of its Tasmanian parent, it is perfectly hardy in the coolness of the greater Puget Sound though more reticent in blossom, and should be sited in the warmest position possible. For years in my first garden it hosted *Clematis* 'Niobe' throughout its framework; the vining chains of ruby red flowers were in seasonal sync with the delicate white

Eucryphia ×intermedia 'Rostrevor'. (Photo by Daniel J. Hinkley)

flowers of the eucryphia, creating an opulent, jewel-like composition.

Though I have long cultivated the undistilled species, *Eucryphia lucida*, it was not until encountering it in 1999 in resplendent blossom on its home front of Cradle Valley, western Tasmania, where it is known colloquially as leatherwood, that I was made aware of exactly why it is held in such high regard. The puny, sporadically produced flowers of my cultivated specimens, amidst relatively demure pinnate to trifoliolate evergreen foliage, paled in comparison to the splendid pendulous racemes smothering the upright trees I saw in late summer during my visit, rising to 40 ft. (12 m) or more. Throughout Tasmania, leatherwood honey is "all the buzz."

A few distinctive cultivars have been selected from *Eucryphia lucida*, and these deserve mention. I was able to obtain from Tasmanian nurseryman and enthusiast Ken Gillanders, during my first visit, plants of *E. lucida* 'Pink Cloud', which represented the only pink-flowered *Eucryphia* currently available at that time. It has since been superceded by 'Carousel', with more deeply hued, more profusely offered flowers. Though still shy to blossom in our climate, these have offered enough flowers from which to secure pollen to transfer to flowers of our specimens of *E. glutinosa*. Resultant seedlings have yet to blossom.

Another superb selection from *Eucryphia lucida* is 'Spring Glow'. It represents the only known variegated member of the genus, with a clean and regular creamy white band of variegation encircling each leaf blade. Despite its reserved floral nature in my climate, this plant's texture and folial value have secured it a permanent place in my garden.

Eucryphia lucida is not the only *Eucryphia* to occur in Tasmania. Once regarded as a variety of *E. lucida*, *E. milliganii* is the only species in the genus to possess simple leaves, and very small ones at that. At first glance it may be hardly recognized as a member of the genus, appearing more like *Myrsine* or *Buxus*. Though it performs admirably enough in my garden, as does the purported cross between it and *E. lucida* (which appears to

my eyes to be simply another *E. milliganii*), I have never encountered it in its wild state, and flowers have never been produced on my garden specimen, which is 4 ft. (1.2 m) tall after 10 years.

Nor have I encountered what I consider to be the most distinctive species of all, *Eucryphia moorei*, though I have certainly botanized in its natural range of Victoria and New South Wales in southeastern Australia. The pinnate foliage of light, silky gray-green is comprised of sharply textured leaflets imparting a visual effect unlike any other species. Although literature suggests cultivating this supposedly extremely tender species in shaded, moist conditions, in my Indianola garden it has matured to a superb flowering specimen in full sun and sharp, draining soil, while tolerating temperatures in the mid-teens. In 2006 I crossed this species with the dwarf form of *E. glutinosa* and await evaluation of the resulting seedlings. In 1953 a self-sown seedling between this species and *E. lucida* was identified at the celebrated Hillier Nurseries of Hampshire, United Kingdom, and given the eponymous name *E. ×hillieri*, though it has created minimal stir in the waters of the horticultural industry.

The remaining two species, both narrow endemics discovered in Queensland, have a well-deserved following among native plant enthusiasts from Down Under; since both are part and parcel to a tropical clime, however, it is unlikely they will find, at least prior to hybridization with their sturdier relations, any application to temperate gardens of the Northern Hemisphere. *Eucryphia wilkiei*, discovered in 1984, can best be described as a much larger version of *E. moorei* with satiny white pinnate foliage and delicate white flowers on a framework to 50 ft. (15 m). *Eucryphia jinksii*, discovered only in 1994 on the border with New South Wales, represents the most recently described flowering tree in Australia and is highly protected due to its rarity. The fact that its delicate white flowers are produced atop the crown of the tree, some 80 ft. (24 m) above ground level, is certainly one of the reasons this species remained anonymous for so long.

The question must certainly be posed as to whether there remain species to be discovered. Even if the entire contingent is now accounted for, unquestionably there will be additional pairings of the species in the future, with selections having larger flowers, a range of color, and a varied habit of growth. Whether or not this actually plays itself out, I will remain content in growing those I already know, whose flowers I still believe to be among the most beautiful I have ever seen.

HARDINESS: Unquestionably the hardiest of the lot is *Eucryphia glutinosa*, though this too will refuse to grace gardens below zone 7. Outside their native haunts, cultivated eucryphias seem most content in the moderated and moist climate of Ireland, where superlative garden specimens give their untamed counterparts a run for their money. This response to the Irish climate presents a double edge; those under a bit more climatic distress might fit the bill as a "shrub," rather than as a tree, for the smaller urban garden in zones 7–10.

CULTIVATION: Despite the fact that eucryphias can be found as an understory component where they are native, they will not begin to fully express their charms until allowed additional light by the attrition of nearby competing trees. It is therefore in a brighter situation in the garden that they will perform and blossom to their full potential. Well-drained yet humus-rich, slightly acidic soils appear to be to their ultimate liking. I have observed no problems with insects or disease.

PROPAGATION: Hardwood cuttings taken in late autumn and put on gentle bottom heat root readily and can be potted in spring. Some attrition can be expected from root disturbance during potting, so if room allows, it is advisable to stick cuttings directly into plugs. The dwarf form of *Eucryphia glutinosa* offers a paucity of cutting material due to its extremely short internodal length. A heavier-than-normal application of nitrogen fertilizer applied in late winter will promote internode elongation while providing more cutting wood. Air or trench layering may be applicable, but I have not attempted either. Seeds ripen a full year after fertilization, with the woody capsules generally opening while the plant is in flower. As the species tend to be self-fertile, emasculation and bagging of the flowers for breeding purposes is recommended.

Spinning Tales: *Euonymus* and Other Celastraceae

Last night seemed, despite the incongruity of our surroundings, a family reunion! Our old friend John Gallagher arrived on the island, and we arranged to have dinner together after meeting him at his hostel this afternoon. We had a lovely day on Mount Halla, and the weather has been sublime, with excellent autumn color from the maples, oaks, dogwoods, and Sorbus; *hoping it will stay that way. We reconnoitered two hours later at a highly recommended restaurant on the harbor that specializes in local seafood and had a splendid feast, with dozens upon dozens of small dishes brought to our table. Rather surrealistically, the music system played Elton John's tribute to Diana; that tragedy seems to have impacted even the most unlikely outposts of Korea this autumn. We ate and toasted well beyond the comfort level of some of the party (Tony finally got up and hovered next to the table until our resolve broke).*

Today five of us entered a highly weathered volcanic cauldron called the Alovorum amidst a near-mystical terrain that seemed the perfect, though unlikely, hybrid of Ireland crossed with Campania. At the base of the cauldron, a near-perfect circle of conifers grew, probably planted decades ago to create a paddock for animals. While I looked across this remarkable landscape in the distance, that circle within a circle seemed both ancient and edgy.

We spent the entire day surveying the inner slope of the cone and discovered it to be more opulent and productive than we had at first sight assumed it would be. Interestingly, in the grassy, steep area, we found the decidedly diminutive versions of many familiar genera: Hosta, Hemerocallis, Aruncus, *and a charming, tiny-foliaged, scrambling form of* Euonymus fortunei *that compressed itself to the irregular features of rock outcrops, looking somewhat like a free-form topiary park.*

Sue and I found ourselves quite separated from the other three by midday and had our lunch in the sun on a large benchlike rock encrusted with a heavily fruited specimen of the aforementioned Euonymus. *It was a blessed afternoon that will long live in the collections I made.*

Letter to Robert Jones
sent from Cheju, South Korea
October 15, 1997

F ORGETTING FOR THE MOMENT the brilliant and ubiquitous orbs of autumnal fire from *Euonymus alatus* var. *compactus* in the landscapes of my

Overleaf: Specimens of *Euonymus oxyphyllus* growing at Windcliff from seed collected in southern Korea in 1997, showing the burgundy autumn color of the species. (Photo by Daniel J. Hinkley)

hometown—already common fare in the zone 4 nurseries of northern Michigan in the 1960s—it was through the American bittersweet, *Celastrus scandens*, whose colorful fruit was cut and brought inside for the winter by my mom, that I came to vaguely and unknowingly amalgamate the characteristics of the Celastraceae in my youth. Though there are departures from the

114

unique visual prompting the family as a whole projects, it is often a podlike berry that opens to reveal a bright orange- or red-skinned seed that screams the Celastraceae. It is precisely this fruit type that asserts itself to the field botanist throughout Eurasia, the Americas, Africa, and Australia.

Though this is a family of nearly 100 genera and 1200 species, with regard to temperate horticultural relevance, this is a relatively truncated journey through its ranks—especially if one bypasses the allure of both khat and ayahuasca, two well-known recreational hallucinogens derived from *Catha* and *Maytenus* respectively.

Despite the breadth of ornament and utility from the few genera that I include here, it must be put forward that the family is red-tagged for bioinvasive potential. Both *Euonymus alatus* and *Celastrus orbiculatus* (more widespread) have annexed troubling amounts of territory from New England, the Midwest, and the Southeast. It must be noted that this vexation is climate specific—that is, there has been no evidence that these genera will present problems, for example, in the Pacific Northwest. So I will walk the tightrope in this instance, reporting on my observations of the remarkable members of the family while remaining ambivalent with regard to their promotion for ornamental use.

Because of its bioinvasiveness, I will not provide *Celastrus* its own section of text, so I will briefly mention it here. I have encountered, and initially collected, numerous species of this genus from China and Korea, seduced by its charms and fueled by the overall excitement of encountering and identifying numerous species I had hitherto been unaware of. After becoming cognizant of the generic jeopardy that I entertained, I abandoned the genus while at the same time developing an interest in, and concern for, our native American bittersweet, *C. scandens*—the same plant my mother had employed to extend autumn in our home. Above all I wish this chapter to be useful in helping to distinguish between our native and its more abundant, more vulgar usurper. The handsome clusters of fruit of our North American native are formed at the end of each branch rather than in the leaf axils. In addition, the capsules of *C. scandens* are red-orange rather than yellow-orange, as in its Asiatic counterpart. If this insight saves a single living specimen of *C. scandens* from murder by mistaken identity, it is worth this mention.

The overall breadth of this family is reduced by my personal encounters to four genera and their ultimate transition to my garden: *Euonymus*, *Maytenus*, *Tripterygium*, and *Paxistima*. My apologies to those assuredly exceptional species found outside of this limited envelope.

Euonymus

When I lived in Washington Park Arboretum in Seattle, I had immediate access to one of the most comprehensive collections of woody plants in North America. Not far from my tiny Stone Cottage on the southern edge of this 230-acre horticultural archive, in a rather forgotten and ill-kept location, grew a large grove of deciduous *Euonymus*, or spindle trees (an associate during that time blithely referred to this grove as the "euonymeetum"). In early October, when the fruits of these individuals were at their finest, I would chart my course to the arboretum offices by way of this small but seasonally magnificent medley, an effort that brought forth nothing short of undiluted admiration. Upon owning my first bit of land to make a garden, I replicated this grove in order to replay this moment each autumn.

Encompassing a vast degree of variation within its ranks, the 180 or so species from both the New and Old Worlds are represented by evergreen groundcovers with minute foliage, tall deciduous shrubs, and subtropical trees to 50 ft. (15 m). They are extraordinarily popular for landscape use; I would venture to guess that every garden center between Seattle and Edinburgh has at least one for sale.

The omnipresence of this variable genus in landscapes parallels its prevalence in the wild. Since 1987, whether I have been in Nepal, China, Korea, Japan, Taiwan, Turkey, or Vietnam, euonymus have made themselves known by way of their distinctive dangle of colorful fruit and leaves always held in pairs. A corky ridge is often found to some degree along the stems of numerous species, lending itself to the fashioning of spindles for spinning wool and thusly providing the common name of spindle tree.

Though I was fully primed on the essentials of the genus before my first trip to Korea in 1993, it was not until my confrontation with so many closely related deciduous species that I realized the challenges involved in sorting them out.

A few provided little work indeed. *Euonymus pauciflorus* (DJH 002) is a charming species that we collected on Mount Sorak to the far northeast. On this small deciduous shrub, one or two relatively large, coppery flowers are held on wiry pedicels that lie directly across the surface of the leaf, superficially resembling *Helwingia* from a distance. Later the bright red capsule, which exposes orange seed upon opening, spills gently to the side.

I found numerous botanical varieties of *Euonymus alatus* growing in Korea, each a far cry from the graceless, clunky expression of this species' compact form sold by the millions in North American garden centers. Among these, and one that grew for numerous years in my garden for its winter interest, was *E. alatus* var. *monstrosus*, with slender but substantial wings running the length of each of its stout stems. Its autumn coloration, reds and oranges that are shed to reveal the plant's beautiful framework, is nearly enough reason in itself to grow this. Though this variety has not shown potential for invasiveness in the Pacific Northwest, it should not be considered for gardens east of the Mississippi.

I can still recall 15 ft. (4.6 m) specimens of *Euonymus oxyphyllus* (DJH 027) growing riverside on the eastern coast of Korea, so shockingly loaded with bright carmine red fruit that, despite having mentally prepared myself for such a spectacle, I was certain that I was, this time, seeing a flowering apricot or cherry in full blossom at a very unlikely time of year. This collection has matured to fruiting size in my garden in Indianola and performs spectacularly in terms of fruiting and autumn foliage each autumn. It is appropriate to note that some self-sown seedlings appear beneath these shrubs even in the uninviting chill of our climate; this species could prove as bioinvasive as *E. alatus* in summer-warm regions of North America.

Euonymus bungeana (DJH 325) grew on the magnificent south-inland mountain called Mount Chiri. I have long admired this little-known species. It forms a shrub to 10 ft. (3 m) tall, with crops of fleshy pink capsules, and there is a decided gloss to its foliage that seems to suggest an evergreen disposition, until the leaves garner splendid yellow tones in autumn and drop.

Ubiquitous across the peninsula was *Euonymus japonicus*, growing as a freestanding shrub or scrambling groundcover with glossy evergreen foliage and not-so-stunning crops of light yellow-green capsules.

In late summer the rose-colored capsules of *Euonymus oxyphyllus* open to expose orange seeds. (Photo by Daniel J. Hinkley)

This euonymus is so firmly ensconced in cultivation through a long inventory of popular and garish variegated forms that the thought of collecting and promoting the raw form of the species seemed akin to reintroducing Neanderthal man. I fondly remember Christopher Lloyd discussing the merits of *E. japonicus* 'Ovatus Aureus', which still grows in the long border at Dixter. As he once told me, "It looks good 364 days a year; nothing should be expected to look good on Boxing Day." Indeed, there are few more handsome evergreen shrubs available to the gardener than this species when it is well grown and appropriately sited.

It was during my first trip to Cheju, an island formerly known as Quelpart, that I initially met up with *Euonymus fortunei* in the wild. It is the most widespread and polymorphic of all *Euonymus* species, found across the entirety of Asia, while representing one of the hardiest broad-leaved evergreen shrubs available in the nursery trade.

Euonymus fortunei, in its many phenotypes, can be found growing as a freestanding shrub, groundcover, or self-clinging vine. Its vining nature tends to manifest itself at middle age or when support is provided. While on Cheju, I collected what is close in appearance to *E. fortunei* 'Kewensis', a scrambling form with tiny matte green foliage. This form develops the curious habit of growing up itself if not provided vertical support, acquiring over time the appearance of an angry, deep green ocean surface.

In the autumn of 1996 I found a lovely form of this same species growing in a narrow river canyon below the mountain town of Wolong in Sichuan Province at

Euonymus fortunei 'Kewensis' showing the curious habit of building upon itself if left to its own devices in the landscape. (Photo by Daniel J. Hinkley)

5600 ft. (1700 m). Wolong is known for its most famous mammalian resident, the giant panda, and for the widely grown, frosty blue *Corydalis* 'Blue Panda'. Among this *Corydalis* on a moss-covered bank grew the striking evergreen *Euonymus fortunei*, its dark, lustrous leaves the shape and size of a little finger, each with a skeletal veining of striking pewter. Named *E. fortunei* 'Wolong Ghost', this selection has seemingly found favor among gardeners of both coasts for its durability and handsome foliage; it will adhere to vertical surfaces as it matures. I grew this as a groundcover in my first woodland, interplanting pewter-foliaged forms of *Cyclamen hederifolium* amidst its wiry stems and complementing variegated foliage.

I have since collected additional patterned-leaf forms of *Euonymus fortunei* from China, with a couple perhaps possessing potential for landscape use. It is timely to note that I have also collected pleasing-foliaged forms that did not turn out to be this species at all. In 1999 on the slopes of Fan-si-pan, in Vietnam, at about 7000 ft. (2100 m), I took cuttings of a very handsome evergreen

groundcover, collected as *E. fortunei* HWJ 99546, that I noted as growing in dense shade. When this blossomed in my garden in Indianola in 2002, it proved to be in the closely allied genus *Microtropis*, though I have thus far been unable to provide a species name. It is perfectly hardy in the Pacific Northwest.

Yet I have digressed again. During the same year and in the same province in which I collected 'Wolong Ghost', I collected seed of an upright evergreen species to 6 ft. (1.8 m) that carried distinctive, highly textural, bamboolike foliage to 6 in. (15 cm) long but exceedingly narrow, to ½ in. (1.25 cm), later identified as *Euonymus cornutus* var. *quinquecornutus* (DJH 98439). It carried good quantities of the signature fruit that absolutely shouts to which genus it belongs, with four-sided capsules of pink opening to expose seed coated in a bright

Euonymus cornutus var. *quinquecornutus*, one of the few members of this genus with showy flowers. (Photo by Daniel J. Hinkley)

Euonymus fortunei 'Wolong Ghost'. (Photo by Lynne Harrison)

orange skin. Those collections first blossomed in my garden in 2006, and to say I was surprised by their floral effects would be an understatement. Contrary to most *Euonymus* species, which produce clusters of small, sleepy, greenish white flowers, this taxon offered an airy mass of large purple flowers carried among its handsome foliage. I am extremely excited about its future potential as a multiseasonal semievergreen shrub for gardens in the Pacific Northwest and beyond.

In northeastern Sichuan in 2003, I was gobsmacked to encounter for the first time *Euonymus phellomanus*, a narrow, upright, deciduous species to 15 ft. (4.6 m). It possessed a woody framework clad by corky ridges of an insane width; on many branches the ridges were three times wider than the stem itself. Disappointingly, there was no seed to be found during that year, though my return to the region the following year resulted in a successful collection of the species (DJHS 4244).

In 1996 I collected a curious deciduous species under the number DJH 318 in northeastern Yunnan east of Zhongdian above Napa Hai at nearly 10,000 ft. (3000 m) in elevation. This *Euonymus* forms a shrub to 6 ft. (1.8 m). Its stems have slightly raised ridges and are clad with extremely narrow, needlelike leaves to 3 in. (7.5 cm) long. I have attempted on numerous occasions to key this to the correct species, but though I have been without success, I am gratified to have a triad of this species secured in my garden, where someday a correct name may be found. In foliage this species appears very similar to the evergreen, ground-covering *E. nanus* var. *turkestanicus*, of the Tian Shan, which I grew for many years in a dry, shaded site below a specimen of *Acer palmatum* on the south side of our home.

In 1998 in the same general vicinity, near Weixi, Yunnan, I collected *Euonymus vagans* (DJH 98251), feeling uncharacteristically confident about its identity since I had already grown a specimen from Roy Lancaster's

Euonymus phellomanus in northeastern Sichuan Province, showing autumn color and outrageously broad wings along the stems. (Photo by Daniel J. Hinkley)

Euonymus vagans. (Photo by Lynne Harrison)

garden, which had come from his own collections made on Mount Emei. It is a handsome species with a light green, moderate-sized leaf held on wayward stems that gladly direct themselves upward into trees if provided the opportunity. I have appreciated this species for its

Euonymus latifolius. (Photo by Daniel J. Hinkley)

durability as well as its drought tolerance in the garden and have been rather pleased by its reluctance to set viable seed.

In the autumn of 2000, with friends Bob Beer and Richie Steffen, I was pleased to encounter *Euonymus latifolius* in northeastern Turkey growing on the arid southern side of the Pontic Alps. It was a splendid three-night stay on the top floor of our host's home; we dined while sitting on (and later slept upon) finely woven rugs, with no walls or windows between us and the quiet peace of the surrounding valley. It was not far from our lodging on the first day that we found this species garbed in the dazzling ornament of its fruit, and I was grateful to have at last seen it in its own environs.

A trio of *Euonymus latifolius* had long grown in our woodland garden, and I had considered it to be the earliest of the fruiting *Euonymus* species, with its colorful displays of large and typical bright pink capsules, opening to display orange interiors, dependably ripening by Labor Day each year. The autumn foliage color is also notable, taking on tints of orange and red as the leaves senesce in mid- to late October. My own collections (DJHTu 0109), planted again as a triad for purposes of cross-pollination and hence better fruit set, grow in full sun along the drive in my new garden and have thus far dazzled us with this early autumn fruiting effect.

It was a gratifying opportunity in Taiwan in the autumn of 2007 to be reintroduced to a euonymus that I had once held in high regard but had lost contact with over time, as sometimes happens in our lives as gardeners. I had first encountered *Euonymus carnosus* in the collections of the Arnold Arboretum, with my good friend Gary Koller making the introductions. It was early autumn, and I recall how the glossy leaves, appearing quite evergreen—though decidedly deciduous—were taking on splendid autumn tones of deep burgundy as the capsules were just beginning to ripen to light pink. Later I would admire this same species at the entrance to the David C. Lam Asian Garden at the UBC Botanical Garden, where it was presented front and center due to the seductive qualities of its foliage and fruit, and highly touted by Peter Wharton, superb plantsman and curator of the garden.

In Taiwan we encountered this same *Euonymus* (DJHT 7013) at rather high elevations, over 6000 ft. (1800 m), on Babokulu Mountain near Siyan in the Central Mountain Range, where it grew as splendid specimens to 15 ft. (4.6 m) tall on forest margins along the trail. Interestingly, nearby grew yet another climbing evergreen species, *E. spraguei* (DJHT 7014), which had plastered itself to a vertical rocky ledge, possessing moderate-sized leaves of high-voltage green. I have had no experience with it under cultivation.

This is but a short sampling from *Euonymus*, an immense and highly diverse genus of plants, many of which deserve inclusion in our landscapes (though, again, gardeners should remain ever vigilant to make sure they stay within garden boundaries).

HARDINESS: The genus *Euonymus* is perhaps more applicable to gardens across North America than any other significant conglomeration of woody plants.

CULTIVATION: Best grown in well-drained soils in full sun or light shade. Once fully established, nearly all euonymus demonstrate a great deal of drought tolerance. Though there seems to be a substantial degree of cross-pollination between closely related species, the best fruiting effects are achieved by planting more than one clone of a species. For plants grown primarily for foliage or stem effects, planting only one clone will lessen the possibility of fruit production and bioinvasion. Euonymus scale, an Asian insect firmly established on the eastern coast of North America, can be problematic with *Euonymus* as well as other taxa. Biological control by use of a predatory lady beetle has been an effective deterrent.

Euonymus carnosus. (Photo by Lynne Harrison)

PROPAGATION: Clean euonymus seeds of their orange aril to the best of your ability before sowing, as it prohibits the imbibition of water by the embryo. Seed sown fresh in autumn will germinate readily the following spring and present no real challenge to the propagator. Cuttings of the evergreen species root extraordinarily easily if taken in early autumn and placed on gentle bottom heat. The deciduous species, if taken after ripening in early summer and placed under mist, will often strike readily, but there will be some attrition the following spring. Encourage growth in the rooting media before transplanting.

Paxistima

Though indeed the genus *Euonymus* does occur in North America, with the so-called heart's-a-burstin', *E. americanus*, native from New York to Texas, and the western burning bush, *E. occidentalis*, found from British Columbia to California, they possess a somewhat languid ornamental appeal. The Celastraceae, however, is represented in fine form on this continent by the genus *Paxistima* (from *pachy*, "thick," and *stima*, "stigma"), which includes a total of two species and gives equal billing to both coasts with one species each (although both species also share digs in Texas, a state big enough to deal with two species of *Paxistima* and numerous cowboys to boot). The flowers of paxistimas are tiny and often rudely referred to as insignificant. More than once I have plucked the stems from this genus to examine the minute purple flowers up close and personal, and I find their perfection in doing what is asked of them as significant as any other flower.

Paxistima canbyi is the East Coast representative from high elevations of the mid-Atlantic and Appalachian states, and is known as both Canby's mountain-lover and rat stripper (the reasoning for the latter common name seems to have been momentarily misplaced). I have always found it a charming plant, forming rather dense, suckering mounds of finely textured, linear, evergreen leaves held in pairs along stems to 10 in. (25 cm).

It makes a superlative groundcover for dry, shaded conditions but has never been as well known in cultivation as I believe it should be.

For numerous years Baldassare Mineo, former proprietor of Siskiyou Rare Plant Nursery near Medford, Oregon, propagated a dwarf form of *Paxistima canbyi* that I grew in my tiny scree garden. It was a clever selection, rising to only 4 in. (10 cm) high and spreading laterally to 2 ft. (0.6 m).

Paxistima is represented in the western half of the country by *Paxistima myrsinites*, referred to commonly as box huckleberry or Oregon boxleaf. This is a fine evergreen shrub to 4 ft. (1.2 m) in height with pairs of small, glossy leaves along its stems and tiny, brownish red, axillary flowers in late spring. Though it is seldom found in nurseries, it is far more common in the Cascades and Olympics than most think; hikers often misidentify it as our native evergreen huckleberry, *Vaccinium ovatum* (the leaf arrangement of *Euonymus* and *Paxistima* are always opposite, in pairs, while the foliage of *Vaccinium* is always alternate).

There will never be an enormous future for this species, I fear, unless something especially aberrant befalls its genetic makeup to create some ghastly contorted, variegated, or prostrate creature. In truth, we had for years growing in our garden a variegated sport with yellow foliage that plantsman Chuck Rogers had found on his property near Hood Canal. It was extremely slow in growth and generally looked rather sickly. Yet we kept and nurtured it just the same, for no other reason than to celebrate a too often overlooked minion of our native forested flora.

HARDINESS: Zones 4–9.

CULTIVATION: Dry, shaded, or partially shaded difficult locations in well-draining soils suit both species.

PROPAGATION: The tiny capsules of both species presumably release even tinier seeds, which I presume work perfectly fine, though I will confess to having never set my eyes, nor fingers, on one in my life. Cuttings taken in early fall and placed on gentle bottom heat without mist root readily.

Tripterygium

There was a time when I was terribly interested in *Tripterygium*. I had grown *T. wilfordii* (under the name *T. regelii*) and found its familial relationships fascinating. The terminal clusters of white flowers on its polite, rambling, climbing stems, carrying bold, oval or ovate foliage, were worthy of conversation when touring the garden with likeminded plant folk at the end of a long day; a glass of wine would perhaps add a bit of undeserved, though not unwelcome, flavor to the species that we hovered over in our walkabout.

Over time, however, I came to know the genus better, and found that a bit of unfamiliarity in many relationships goes countless miles. While in South Korea in 1993, I would, seemingly relentlessly, find myself

Tripterygium wilfordii. (Photo by Lynne Harrison)

hopelessly entangled in *Tripterygium* in places where it formed immense thickets, then skirmish to extricate myself, my backpack providing further grasping material for its arching canes. The result was a litany of expletives that would be inappropriate to document.

Tripterygium is now considered to be a monotypic genus, with *T. wilfordii* the sole occupant. It is widespread across Asia, from Japan and Korea to Myanmar. The terminal clusters of creamy white flowers result in what I think to be its most ornamental season of interest, when heads of papery, three-winged samaras take on a tawny-rose translucency.

Perhaps the most intriguing aspect of the genus is not its ornamental attributes at all but its pharmacogenetic applications. Though it has been employed in traditional Chinese medicine for a multitude of maladies, it has also recently been shown to produce temporary antifertility in male mammals, a finding that has raised interest in its possible use as a male oral contraceptive. Initial tests indicate that full fertility returns within a short period after treatment ends, though there is still work ahead to determine potential side effects.

HARDINESS: Though *Tripterygium wilfordii* remains untested in many climates, because of its wide distribution, the provenance of the collection will probably determine its overall hardiness. Collections from Korea and northeastern China will certainly prove adaptable to zones 5–9.

CULTIVATION: On a wall or fence or through a moderate-sized tree in full sun or partial shade in moderate, moist but draining soils. This species should be thoroughly tested for bioinvasiveness before introducing it to your climatic zone. Though our single clone did display heads of ornamental samaras, the seeds were not viable.

PROPAGATION: The species seemingly requires two clones for viable seed. Though my initial wild collections of this species from South Korea readily germinated in a single season, I would suggest propagating this by summer softwood cuttings under mist and maintaining only a single clone to reduce possible bioinvasion.

Maytenus

Despite the relative size and extraordinary natural distribution of the genus *Maytenus*, only a handful of the 200-some species are known in cultivation. These plants are primarily distributed in the tropics of the New and Old Worlds, though representatives that might show hardiness, occurring in the Canary Islands, Mexico, and China, have been proffered little attention by Western horticulture. The genus pokes its head into the flora of North America by way of *M. phyllanthoides*, a durable, heat-tolerant evergreen shrub found from Florida to Texas.

The leaves of *Maytenus* are held alternately along the stems, and the small flowers, sometimes fragrant, are unisexual and can be dioecious or monoecious. The resulting fruiting effect puts little doubt in the mind of the field botanist as to what family has been encountered, as the capsules, splitting to reveal orange seed, can be a dead ringer for a lilliputian version of *Celastrus*.

Interestingly, this genus too yields a complex inventory of natural compounds that have been historically used by cultures for medicinal or cultural purposes. *Maytenus ilicifolia* from Brazil, known as *espinheira santa*, has been employed by women in Brazil and Paraguay as both a fertility regulator and abortive agent. A hallucinogenic shamanic brew known as *ayahuasca*, used by peoples of the Amazon but primarily by pagan cults of Catholicism, is in part made with *M. ebenifolia*. As an interesting aside, a colleague of mine who has partaken in the ceremony said that the hours-long experience took him to life-altering plateaus in which choices of life and death were clearly presented. To my mind, his journey seemed eerily similar to my own experiences with air travel in modern-day America.

Birth control and religious ritual aside, certainly the best known in commerce is *Maytenus boaria*, an elegant, weeping, evergreen small tree or large shrub to 20 ft. (6 m) with narrow, glistening green leaves. It is precisely this high-gloss varnish that makes it so evident in the natural landscape in south-central Chile, where it is frequently encountered growing on woodland margins. It is perfectly hardy in the Pacific Northwest though is very infrequently encountered in landscapes or commerce, enjoying a more devoted following throughout California.

Three other intriguing species that I encountered in southern Chile, all decidedly shrublike in habit of growth, remain to this day emblematic of the impor-

Maytenus disticha. (Photo by Daniel J. Hinkley)

tance of recognizing familial traits for field identification. In a seemingly parched yet beautiful landscape at the base of the volcano Villarica, I found myself in a dense, low thicket of an evergreen shrub with minute, linear foliage to less than ½ in. (1.25 cm) in length. At the time I thought it was a superficial dead ringer for *Paxistima myrsinites*, yet the foliage was arranged alternately, not oppositely, along the stems, which rose to 3 ft. (0.9 m).

Upon further inspection I found female specimens clad with tiny yellow capsules that had split to reveal seeds covered by a bright scarlet-orange aril. Not realizing the breadth of the *Maytenus* at that point in my career as a world-class plantsman (that is, *no sabía nada*), I made my introduction by way of first inquiring into members of the Celastraceae in the Chilean flora. My collection on that day, HCM 98126, identified as *M. disticha*, has performed remarkably well and is sited directly adjacent to a specimen of our native *Paxistima* for comparative studies (to prove to visitors exactly how brilliant I truly am).

It was interesting, then, that the very next collection of that Valentine's Day, 1998, was an "unidentified evergreen shrub" adjacent to the former species, collected under the number HCM 98078 with the following description:

> To 10 ft. [3 m], leaves narrow lanceolate to 4 in. [10 cm], acuminate, margin sparsely dentate, petiole short, red, fruit axillary, flattened yellow drupes, two seeds per fruit. We found this to be a lovely, evergreen shrub growing in a wide range of habitats and altitudes.

It was not until much later on that trip that the switch flipped and my low-wattage light bulb illuminated the fact that the handsome yellow fruit crowding the stems of *Maytenus magellanicus* were not drupes at all but large, fleshy capsules possessing sufficient visual cues for any self-respecting horticulturist to have initially seen similarity in. In my defense, having spent my life nearer the pole than the tropic, where species diversity plummets like milky glacial water from a cliff, I am not accustomed to thinking two species of the same genus would grow adjacent to one another without, over time, simply melding into one and the same.

Despite the fact that I found this plant so very comely in it natural haunts, I somehow lost track of the collections—if they germinated at all, I do not recall. Though I have not seen this species in blossom, it is reported to possess small crimson flowers with an arresting scent of orange peel. I had every intention of re-collecting it during my time in the same general vicinity in 2005, but as luck would have it, I never once encountered it during our numerous forays into the bush.

I did, however, collect during the second trip another species known as *Maytenus chubutensis* (HS 069), which I duly noted as being extremely similar to *M. disticha* though somewhat taller, to 4½ ft. (1.4 m), crowded with tiny linear leaves, and having very colorful crops of yellow capsules splitting to reveal the innards of bright red seed.

HARDINESS: Even the hardiest of the species (or so my suspicions say) will not be appropriate for anything less than zone 7, while possibly tolerating zone 12 or higher.

CULTIVATION: As I observed these species of *Maytenus* growing in both fully open sites and shaded situations, I will take a gamble by suggesting the same rule will apply in cultivation. Obviously, in colder and untested climates, providing a bit of overstory protection will push their hardiness. They are best suited for well-drained soils and will exhibit drought tolerance when fully established.

PROPAGATION: My collections of *Maytenus chubutensis* and *M. disticha* were sown fresh in late February and germinated by August of that year. Hardwood cuttings taken in autumn and placed on bottom heat will root with little difficulty and demonstrate little attrition during transplanting the following spring.

Tassels of Silk: *Garrya*

Robert and I hiked 11 miles today, from our overnight stay at World's End to just north of Llangothen, which included a tortuous unnecessary mile at the end of the day when we lost our way just as a cold pint of lager had seemed well within reach. We stopped at an old ruined castle well above the surrounding valley for a rather meager lunch of bread and cheese at midday; I poked around the old walls afterward, admiring the dreamy haze of Calluna vulgaris that melded into the horizon and robust colonies of navelwort growing between the weathered mortar. We decided to splurge on a bed-and-breakfast for the evening after chatting briefly with a couple hiking northward with their dog, who highly recommended the hospitality and cooking of the Baker's Green Bed-and-Breakfast, another five hours ahead and directly along the trail. We arrived at 6:30 p.m., tired to the core and grateful for the vacancy. It is a charming cottage in a quiet setting surrounded by an expansive garden. Obviously very keen after learning where we lived and of my interests, our hostess offered us lemonades and asked rather furtively if we would like to see something she was sure we would—wink, wink—recognize. We were led to a far corner through a concoction of asters, anemones, and dahlias, grown to perfection in the way only an English garden is able. The endpoint revealed a sincerely despondent specimen of Garrya elliptica with a life status so questionable that I wondered if there was to be a wake conducted at that very moment. Our cushty hostess beamed with pride as we doused our smiles with lemonade.

Offa's Dyke Path, Wales
August 23, 1984

N OT UNTIL I MOVED TO WESTERN Washington did I confront the small, underutilized contingent of evergreen shrubs known as *Garrya*, which blossom so bravely and beguilingly in the depths of winter. It is a genus that demands attention, on the one hand for its graceful floral effects and weighty evergreen presence, and on the other hand because the potential for cultivating it badly is so great—there is no question that the genus *Garrya* is as specific in its cultural needs as it is stunningly beautiful when grown to perfection.

Garrya ×*issaquahensis*. (Photo by Lynne Harrison)

The Garryaceae houses the 18 species of *Garrya*, named in honor of Nicholas Garry of the Hudson's Bay Company, who assisted the young David Douglas in his North American travels during the early 19th century. (The genus *Aucuba*, formerly assigned to the Cornaceae, has been shuttled to this family by some taxonomists.) During that trip, Douglas introduced to cultivation *G. elliptica*, the so-called coast silk tassel, which remains— perhaps regrettably—the most commonly encountered species in cultivation.

The genus is linked primarily, with one exception, to the Pacific slope extending from Washington State southward to Panama, with numerous species occupying the hostile niches of the inner-mountain west up to 7000 ft. (2100 m) in elevation. One species breaks rank by occurring in the West Indies. *Garrya fadyenii* has been collected in Haiti, the Dominican Republic, and Cuba; for this reason alone it is a species I would like very much to study in the wild, especially for lengthy periods during the winter months.

Without exception the genus is dioecious and evergreen, with leaves either entirely glabrous or covered with white indumentum. Of the two sexes, the male plants are considered the showiest by most contemporary references, though I find this mildly misogynistic. If macho duration of blossom is preferred, then yes, the manly persuasion wins, but if duration of effect is considered—including waxy, pendulous racemes of purple fruit that ripen in August—females carry the day. The gracefully pendulous catkins, up to 10 in. (25 cm) long on selected male plants, appear from late January through February and are, not surprisingly, wind pollinated.

The species that Douglas introduced in 1828, *Garrya elliptica*, is a ubiquitous part of the upper-dune flora, extending into upper elevations of the coastal ranges, from Southern California north through Oregon and the very southwestern tip of Washington. Its decidedly undulate leaf margin has provided one of its common names, wavyleaf silk tassel. My swipe at its reputation and prevalence in commerce is based primarily on the well-known 'James Roof', named in honor of the botanist devoted to California's native flora; the extra long, pendulous male catkins of this cultivar smother its ever-gray-green framework from January to early April. Despite its popularity, 'James Roof' was selected from the southern part of the species' natural range far south of San Francisco; it does not exhibit sufficient hardiness in the greater Puget Sound area to warrant such a devoted following.

An inland species with a range sometimes overlapping that of *Garrya elliptica* is *G. fremontii*, which has a penchant for drier eastern-slope environments from Southern California through much of Oregon, crossing to the north side of the Columbia River into Washing-

ton. The foliage, carried along a rounded framework to 15 ft. (4.6 m) in height, can vary from entirely glabrous to very pubescent. This shrub is known as fever bush, and its intensely bitter leaves have been used by First Nation tribes throughout its range as a febrifuge. Modern-day investigation has revealed an alkaloid in its foliage called garryine, which may be the compound associated with its effectiveness.

It was in the garden of Pat Ballard, a well-respected horticulturist in the Seattle area, in 1957, that a sole female specimen of *Garrya fremontii* produced viable seed. With no other possible paternal suspect than a nearby, innocent-appearing *G. elliptica*, the resulting male seedling possessed both added hardiness and male inflorescences to 10 in. (25 cm) long. Named *G. ×issaquahensis* for Ms. Ballard's community of Issaquah, Washington, a clone is frequented upon in commerce under the cultivar name 'Pat Ballard'. What has never been clear is whether more than one original seedling was raised and distributed.

Whether knowingly or unknowingly, this cross between *Garrya elliptica* and *G. fremontii* was replicated at Malahide Castle in Ireland, resulting in 'Glasnevin Wine', a seedling that exhibits a suffusion of red pigment in its stems and flowers. I will admit to initial disappointment over its performance in my garden, where in its youth its leaves exhibited a propensity to burn during severe frosts. As it has settled into place, however, it has revealed itself as a splendid selection that I would not be without.

In the mid-1990s I was sent a plant of *Garrya laurifolia* from J. C. Raulston raised from seed he had collected in the mountains of northeastern Mexico with Texan plantsmen John Fairey and Carl Schoenfeld. It possessed a stunning mantle of glaucous blue, leathery leaves and demonstrated over the course of the following decade an admirable constitution. When it ultimately blossomed several years later, it revealed its masculinity with 6 in. (15 cm) chains of greenish white flowers in January and February.

Seven additional species, all of which I have had limited interaction with, exist in Baja, Utah, Arizona, California, and New Mexico. None garners the amount of press one might expect for a drought-tolerant, hardy, evergreen shrub. More germane, very little attempt has been made to pair these species through hybridization to create plants that are more adaptable to a broader climatic range or that possess more ornamental buoyancy. Other than *Garrya ×issaquahensis*, the only other published hybrid is *G. ×thuretii*, a cross between *G. fadyenii* from the West Indies and the familiar *G. elliptica*. It is seldom if ever encountered in commerce.

Garrya fremontii. (Photo by Daniel J. Hinkley)

Garrya ×issaquahensis. (Photo by Daniel J. Hinkley)

Until innovative plant breeding takes the genus *Garrya* to new levels of appreciation, those who possess the climatic coordinates necessary for successful cultivation should more fully examine and put to use this vastly overlooked contingent of resilient, winter-blossoming, evergreen shrubs.

HARDINESS: The broad geographical ranges of many of these species demand an examination of provenance of material before any can be declared inappropriate as garden subjects. Other than *Garrya fadyenii* and *G. laurifolia*, whose home in the tropics would suggest a tolerance for heat and humidity, the West Coast species could easily be written off as evergreen shrubs for arid or tempered cool environments only.

CULTIVATION: *Garrya elliptica*, and thus *G. ×issaquahensis*, is tolerant of both sun and shade, though its finest flowering will be achieved under brighter conditions. The inner-mountain species will appreciate full sun. Edaphic conditions in the wild include clay, serpentine, and rocky, well-draining soils. Above all it is drainage that must be addressed, as excessive water in the soil will lead to certain failure. The shrubs are not easily moved; though I have had success in this arena on one occasion, I have lost numerous mature specimens upon transplanting. These vigorous shrubs respond well to heavy pruning and can be rejuvenated on occasion by cutting directly to the ground in later winter.

PROPAGATION: The species can be easily raised by seed if given a single cold treatment; the seed will germinate readily in the first spring after sowing. Unfortunately, sexing of the resultant seedling cannot happen until the inaugural flowering after four to six years. Named forms or sexes can be propagated by hardwood cuttings taken in September and October and placed on gentle bottom heat. Although the cuttings strike with relative ease, transplant shock can lead to a high attrition rate; care should be exercised in lifting and potting to reduce root disturbance.

Winter Feasts and Autumn Finery:
Hamamelis and Other Hamamelidaceae

We returned to Guest House No. 5 in Dali yesterday afternoon from Huadiamba, a long hike of 17 miles. Ozzie was suffering from the flu and had a real slog of it; he rode a horse for a while, but I think that it was as much work as simply hoofing it on his own. I ventured off the road on the way down and was excited to find seed of Magnolia wilsonii *from a stooled but resprouted specimen, good collections of* Primula, Enkianthus, *and particularly good quantities of* Corylopsis aff. yunnanensis, *which was quite abundant on the west-facing hillsides, turned primarily amber by its autumn color. The fruits were still quite green; however, I believed them sufficiently mature to justify the collection.*

Jamaica was waiting for me in my room when we arrived at dusk, and we had a good reunion, catching up on her days while staying behind in Dali; she was excited to have someone to talk to again. Her photographer (inter-estingly it is Chris Baker, whom I worked with in Mississippi on an article on Sarracenia!*) and his assistant are to arrive in the morning and are bringing two bottles of Lagavulin from duty-free in Hong Kong per our request. We are feeling rich.*

After dinner last night (quite a jovial affair despite our collective exhaustion) we came back to find the beds and carpet of our room literally covered in what I first thought were mice droppings (the look of horror on Jamaica's face was particularly precious). It took only seconds to realize that my Corylopsis *capsules had all opened in a matter of hours, discharging the seed over every bit of our dark and very dank room. It took the two of us over an hour to gather them; however, we rewarded ourselves with a glass of (no longer so precious) scotch in the end.*

Dali, Yunnan Province
October 4, 1998

THE HAMAMELIDACEAE IS MY KIND of plant family—small enough to get one's hands around yet possessing sufficient diversity within its ranks to make it interesting. Though *Hamamelis* (witch hazels), *Corylopsis* (winter hazels), and *Fothergilla* are generally well known and often encountered in nurseries, numerous other genera in this family of deciduous and evergreen shrubs and small trees are worthy additions to mixed borders and adaptable to a wide range of climates.

Hamamelis virginiana. (Photo by Lynne Harrison)

Within the ranks of the Hamamelidaceae are some 33 recognized genera and about 140 species, all in the constant taxonomic motion of being lumped or split. Despite the popularity of its temperate, deciduous species in the landscapes of North America and western Europe, originating in the Arcto-Tertiary Geoflora of eastern North America and northeastern Asia, the family is geographically centered in the semitropical, broad-leaved, evergreen forests of Asia, where numerous, mostly underknown, yet highly ornamental genera and species exist, while making appearances as well in eastern and southern Africa, northeastern Australia, and

Central and South America. The flowers of many family members are borne either in autumn, winter, or very early spring and can be with or without petals. Those lacking petals bring forth ornament to the garden—and assuredly pollinators to the flowers—by means of numerous colorful stamens. The resulting woody capsules in numerous genera contain seeds that are explosively discharged.

I will forever associate the Hamamelidaceae, or witch hazel family, with the concept of hunting, whether or not I still support the tradition. *Hamamelis virginiana* grew in great abundance in the sandy hills of north-central Michigan, where its distinctive silhouette, a multistemmed, rounded shrub to 15 ft. by 15 ft. (4.6 m by 4.6 m), made itself readily apparent in winter and summer alike. It is regarded as the last of the deciduous trees or shrubs of the northern temperate region to blossom, presenting its rather small, pungent blossoms of spidery yellow petals in November and December. The flowers were presented along stems still clad in russetted leaves as enormous battalions of red-coated warriors descended on the woods for the taking of white-tailed deer.

In addition, the ruffed grouse, or "pats" as we called them, could always be counted on being somewhere close by, as they ate the flower and leaf buds of this species throughout the year. I would approach a grouping of witch hazels in spring in anticipation of the sudden thundering departure of this bird, a signature startle well known for its ability to induce massive coronaries among smoking, overweight hunters, and hikers alike.

The common name "witch hazel" is rooted in the fact that *Hamamelis virginiana* became the wood of choice for water witching by early colonists in New England. The European hazelnut, *Corylus avellana*, which was used for dowsing in England, was not available to the colonists. The newly encountered *Hamamelis* not only appeared quite similar in foliage but also worked its water-detecting magic with equal ability. Later, a distillate of the sap of this species, extract of witch hazel, became an economically important crop of early American commerce; when I was a lad, it was still a frequently sold commodity in my father's drug store.

The genus *Hamamelis* is home to only four or five species worldwide, with two (or three) of these occurring in North America (just for the record, the *Flora of China* [Wu et al. 1994 to present] suggests an even six). This amorphous body count is due to the current argument over whether populations of *Hamamelis* in the mountains of northeastern Mexico represent another species (*H. mexicana*) or, as current thinking has it, only a southerly distribution of *H. virginiana*. The Ozark witch hazel, *H. vernalis*, is similar in appearance to *H. virginiana* but with flowers that appear in spring rather than winter, as its specific epithet implies. As with its more easterly cousin, the flowers are not particularly showy; however, there are some exceptional forms of this species commercially available, such as 'Lombarts' Weeping' and 'Sandra'. I have not yet traveled to the botanically fantastic Ozarks, a destination high on my list.

Two Asian *Hamamelis* species complete the quartet or quintet, though hybrids between the two have certainly made the most noise in contemporary horticulture. In the oak and maple forests of the central mountains in Honshū, in a flora deceivingly similar to the overall gestalt of the uplands of northern Michigan—distant views of Mount Fuji discounted—I have encountered beautifully balanced specimens of *H. japonica*. With its late-winter display of crumpled yellow-petaled flowers plastered along the stems, generally after leaf drop (though this too is annoyingly variable on the Japanese and Chinese species), *H. japonica* is a notch up in ornament from *H. virginiana*. In the wild this species is in serious decline from a fungal disease of unknown origin.

There is no question that *Hamamelis mollis*, from north-central China, occurring at the relatively low elevations of 1000–2600 ft. (300–800 m), is the reigning queen of the genus. Despite an astounding inventory of time-tested as well as novel hybrids sharing common blood with *H. vernalis*, *H. mollis*, and *H. japonica*, could I only choose one to grow, it would still be

Hamamelis vernalis 'Lombarts' Weeping. (Photo by Lynne Harrison)

Hamamelis vernalis 'Sandra'. (Photo by Lynne Harrison)

H. mollis in its undiluted state. There is no greater pleasure than to confront the vivid yellows of a mature specimen in full blossom in early February, its intoxicating fragrance often alerting you to its presence long before you actually see it. The foliage—large and felted beneath when fresh in spring, coloring up to vivid yellows in autumn—is reason, too, to have this in the garden.

I am saddened by the fact that I have never seen *Hamamelis mollis* in the wild, since the experience would, as it has with so many other plants, apply yet another layer of high-gloss varnish to my appreciation for the species in my garden.

Yet enough. Tomes such as *Witch Hazels* (Lane 2005) say more about this genus, and with more authority, than I can possibly add. I will instead devote my time to discussing those taxa that cannot so readily belie my overall shallowness of knowledge.

The northern temperate forests of both the New and Old Worlds offer additional, and in my estimation aristocratic, garden plants from this family. In North America the only other representatives of the hamamelids are two endemic species of the genus *Fothergilla* (*Liquidambar*, or sweet gum, was once included but has been reassigned to the Altingiaceae).

Fothergilla major is a robust, somewhat suckering shrub to 12 ft. (3.6 m) or more, with broad, scalloped leaves ranging from a deep glossy green to a matte glaucous blue and transforming to fiery tones of red, orange, and yellow in autumn. In many a gardener's mind, this species' autumnal performance outshines its floral season, when, just as the leaves are emerging, erect, lightly scented, bottlebrush-like, apetalous spikes of white stamens are presented. I find it a refined yet admittedly reserved presentation.

Naturally occurring plants of *Hamamelis japonica*, growing with *Rhus sylvestris*, in the mountains north of Nagoya, Japan. (Photo by Daniel J. Hinkley)

Fothergilla major is native to elevated sites in the Carolinas, Georgia, Alabama, Tennessee, and Arkansas. Its lowland counterpart, *F. gardenii*, is from moist savannas of the coastal plains of both Carolinas, Georgia, Florida, and Alabama. To my mind *F. gardenii* is smaller in all aspects, with leaves possessing a similar shape held along a less upright, more spreading, more suckering framework, and smaller upright spikes of white flowers. I frame its description in this subjective manner for two reasons: first, I have not observed its natural variation throughout its range, which is substantial; and second, its performance in the coolness of the Pacific Northwest, where it often proves to be a weak performer, reveals its affinity for heat and humidity.

It is somewhat ironic that Dr. John Fothergill, the namesake for this genus, is credited as the first person to record coronary arteriosclerosis in humans, as the variation found within natural populations of *Fothergilla* and the ease with which the two species hybridize with one another have resulted in artery-hardening consternation regarding its nomenclature, both in literature and commerce. A third species, *F. monticola*, often encountered in literature, is now universally accepted as a synonym for *F. major*. For the plant enthusiast, it matters less what species or combination thereof you actually have than whether it performs to your expectations in the garden. Summer-cool climates will favor selections leaning toward *F. major*, while *F. gardenii* blood will respond to more sultry conditions.

One does encounter several named forms in the trade, all of which I have grown and only two of which demonstrate sufficient difference in character to suggest seeking them out (although this opinion possesses a cool maritime climatic bias). Both are the steely-blue-

Hamamelis mollis. (Photo by Lynne Harrison)

Hamamelis and Other Hamamelidaceae

foliaged forms of each respective species: *Fothergilla gardenii* 'Blue Mist' and a more recently introduced *F. major* 'Blue Shadow'.

Although the genus *Fothergilla* is indeed endemic to the New World, a trekker in the western Himalaya, including Pakistan and Afghanistan, might beg to differ if encountering *Parrotiopsis jacquemontiana* at just the right stage of flower. While the foliage has a superficial resemblance to that of a more rounded, somewhat more scalloped *Fothergilla* leaf, the inflorescence is best described as a cross between *Fothergilla* and dogwood, with creamy white spikes subtended at the base by four white bracts.

Maturing at 8 ft. by 5 ft. (2.4 m by 1.5 m), this taxon is appropriately described as a botanical curiosity by some, yet I for many years admired it in my garden, never passing up the opportunity to share it with my plant identification students when it was in flower. (This generally came toward the end of a full year of spending numerous hours together every week, garnering identification tools and botanical names, by which time my students were tempted to believe they had at last learned all there is to know.) In western Nepal and Kashmir, the tough, friable wood of *Parrotiopsis jacquemontiana* is often crafted into rope traditionally used for building suspension bridges over rivers and ravines.

Further west still, in the Elborz Mountains of northern Iran, north and west to the Caucasus, is found the Persian ironwood or *Parrotia persica*. In its native haunts this species reportedly produces dense thickets of mul-

Fothergilla major. (Photo by Daniel J. Hinkley)

Autumn color of *Fothergilla major.* (Photo by Daniel J. Hinkley)

tistemmed trees with branches that graft themselves to one another, creating miles of living fence, a scene that to me sounds both exciting and daunting.

Although *Parrotia persica*, which has been firmly established in Western horticulture since 1840, would hardly be considered rare in cultivation, nor could it be remotely considered commonplace. In midwinter—more precisely, during the second week of February in the Pacific Northwest—one finds the stems cloaked with small clusters of blood red stamens that collectively offer a pleasant haze of color at an unexpected time of year. It is in the autumn, however, when the foliage takes on breath-taking tints of orange and scarlet, that this species is at its finest. Though *P. persica* can easily reach 25 ft. by 25 ft. (7.6 m by 7.6 m) over time, it is a politely

slow-growing species, and as this tall shrub matures it makes known yet another ornamental virtue: its bark exfoliates with an effect similar to that of *Stewartia* or *Platanus*, revealing patchwork patterns of greens, grays, and tawny browns.

Although *Parrotia persica* is now occasionally encountered as a single-stemmed lawn or street tree specimen, inspecting the stems of these at ground surface will erase any doubt that this species has a steadfast desire to grow with multiple stems. Two other forms of this species, both more demure and pendulous, are seen in commerce under the name 'Pendula'. Only one of these, occasionally denoted as Kew Form, does indeed possess a graceful weeping habit. More narrow and upright is 'Vanessa', which delivers the same punch of autumn

Parrotiopsis jacquemontiana. (Photo by Lynne Harrison)

Exfoliating bark of *Parrotia persica*. (Photo by Daniel J. Hinkley)

Hamamelis and Other Hamamelidaceae

Autumn color of *Parrotia persica*. (Photo by Lynne Harrison)

Parrotia persica 'Pendula'. (Photo by Daniel J. Hinkley)

color as the species yet in a decidedly more columnar format than the species.

The genus *Parrotia* doubled in size, to two species, in 1998 when Chinese botanists reassigned to it the critically endangered taxon formerly known as *Hamamelis subaequalis*. Known from only a few locations in the montane forests of eastern China (Anhui, southern Jiangsu, and northern Zhejiang Provinces) at relatively low altitudes of 2000–3000 ft. (600–900 m), it has been successfully brought into cultivation through the efforts of Mikinori Ogisu of Japan. I have seen small specimens thriving in the private garden of friend Ozzie Johnson of Atlanta, Georgia, where its foliage indeed superficially resembles that of its Persian cousin. It has also appeared for sale at a nursery in the Netherlands. (Admittedly, this is a scanty bit of information for an extremely rare yet exciting new addition to Western horticulture.)

Although this is not the ideal time to leave the deciduous species in this family, I must digress momentarily to discuss the genus *Sycopsis*. Though there is substantial variation in the number of *Sycopsis* species believed to exist, recent work has pared the number down to one, perhaps two. *Sycopsis sinensis* is a finely textured, evergreen, small tree or large shrub that I have long had an affection for, years before encountering it in the mountains of Taiwan in 1999. In a short altitudinal band on both slopes of the Central Mountain Range, at about 10,000 ft. (3000 m), superb specimens of this species can be seen growing directly adjacent to the Central Cross-Island Highway. The glossy, ovate leaves, to 3 in. (7.5 cm), are borne along very dark stems rising to 25 ft. (7.6 m), offering good proportions for the smaller urban garden. In late winter, tawny clusters of orange stamens open from bronze-felted buds amidst the foliage. Though *S. sinensis* is not considered a highly ornamental flowering tree, I find its durable qualities and handsome evergreen foliage to be vastly underrated for climates that can accommodate it. A lovely grove of this species grows at the Washington Park Arboretum, in the witch hazel section directly along the southern end of Arboretum Drive.

Parrotia persica 'Vanessa'. (Photo by Daniel J. Hinkley)

Sycopsis sinensis. (Photo by Lynne Harrison)

Nearby this grove is a single specimen of a shrub that represents the only bigeneric hybrid to have thus far been created from within the witch hazel family. ×*Sycoparrotia semidecidua* was raised in Switzerland in the mid-20th century as a result of crossing *Sycopsis sinensis* with *Parrotia persica*. As its epithet implies, it is partially evergreen, with the foliage resembling a somewhat bolder version of its *Sycopsis* parent. Those that shed their leaves in autumn pick up decent tones of yellow, while the orange flower clusters are borne along the spreading *Parrotia*-like framework in February and March. As pointed out so aptly in *The Hillier Manual of Trees and Shrubs* (Hillier Nurseries 1992), it has not proven to be an improvement on either parent, though I still find it worth growing, if for nothing other than as

Autumn color of *Disanthus cercidifolius*.
(Photo by Daniel J. Hinkley)

a reminder to be more adventurous in pairing together unlikely candidates.

For the effects of autumn color, *Disanthus cercidifolius* is nearly unparalleled in other taxa of deciduous shrubs, particularly those wishing to grow in shaded locations. Forming a small, multistemmed shrub to 10 ft. by 10 ft. (3 m by 3 m), it brandishes heart-shaped leaves that, as the species name implies, are dastardly good impersonators of *Cercis*, the redbud.

Taxonomists have divided this disanthus into two subspecies: *cercidifolius* and *longipes*. *Disanthus cercidifolius* subsp. *cercidifolius* occurs in Japan, primarily in Nagano and Gifu Prefectures, the latter of which is where I at last came upon it in the rich mountain flora slightly east of Nagoya in the spring of 2008. In 1894, celebrated American botanist Charles S. Sargent wrote the following after seeing this plant in its natural haunts:

> *Disanthus cercidifolia* is not rare in the valley of the Kisogawa on the Nakasendō, in central Hondo, where it is occasionally found, covering steep hillsides with thickets sometimes a quarter of an acre in extent. In habit and in the autumn color of its leaves *Disanthus* is one of the most beautiful shrubs which I saw in Japan, and if it flourishes in our gardens it should prove one of the best plants of its class recently introduced into cultivation.

Disanthus cercidifolius subsp. *longipes* represents the mainland populations of the genus occurring at moderate elevations in mixed evergreen and deciduous broad-leaved forests in Hunan, Jiangxi, and Zhejiang Provinces, where it is listed as an endangered species. I have seen both growing side by side under cultivation and find them easy to distinguish by foliage alone, with the mainland plant lacking the deeply impressed veins of the Japanese subspecies.

Small, rather uninteresting clusters of ruby-red flowers—sessile to the branches on Japanese plants, while carried on ¼ in. (0.6 cm) pedicels on Chinese plants—possess a faint but somewhat disagreeable pungent quality and are borne in axils along the stems in autumn,

Disanthus cercidifolius subsp. *cercidifolius* is a commonly occurring element in the deciduous forests north of Nagoya, Japan. (Photo by Daniel J. Hinkley)

The leaves of the Chinese populations of *Disanthus cercidifolius* subsp. *longipes* do not show the deep veining present on the Japanese variety. (Photo by Daniel J. Hinkley)

just as the foliage explodes into a shining burgundy-red spectacle that lasts for several weeks. *Disanthus cercidifolius* is one of the few deciduous shrubs that will develop excellent autumn tones even in shaded conditions. Though now relatively commonly encountered in the nursery trade, it is far from mainstreamed and should be utilized to a greater degree. I recommend it with only one caveat: in some situations it dies suddenly and inexplicably, perhaps as a result of endemic soil pathogens it has not evolved any resistance to. Several sprightly variegated clones are frequented upon in specialty nurseries throughout Japan, while dwarf, dwarf variegated, and extremely narrow upright cultivars are also on the horizon. I have personally found the most commonly encountered white-variegated selection to be very weak in growth.

While above the village of Tao Yuan in northeastern Sichuan, I collected seed capsules from the long, drooping racemes of a large shrub with broad, bristly edged leaves. Though I was certain at the moment that I knew the shrub, I could not mentally place it. It was later that evening, when recording the collections for the day and perusing again a pressed specimen, that its identity came to me with a bolt of delight.

I had cultivated *Sinowilsonia henryi* in the woodland of my first garden, where for numerous years it drew scant attention from visitors despite a prominent position along the drive. I rather admired its leaves, which resembled to a degree those of *Styrax obassia*, though admittedly the small, green, monoecious flowers were hardly cause for much excitement. As I had only one clone, fertilization was never effected, so observing *Sinowilsonia henryi* with fruit on the expanded female inflorescence was a novel experience.

As my garden and nursery grew, space to grow and trial an ever-increasing number of plants became an issue, and I felt compelled to jettison many taxa that were occupying arable land without contributing to the bottom line. However, *Sinowilsonia henryi* kept its due place and to the best of my knowledge is still there. For it was its generic epitaph, commemorating the nick-

Hamamelis and Other Hamamelidaceae

name of Ernest Wilson, aka China Wilson, that I appreciated above all. I have long abandoned any aspirations of achieving Wilson's level of plantsmanship, but I continue to imagine what it might have been like to walk with him among the plants he collected and introduced, while listening to his attending narrative. The species name *henryi*, of course, commemorates Augustine Henry, the esteemed botanist of Scottish heritage and contemporary of Wilson, who is perhaps best remembered for coauthoring with Henry Elwes the seven-volume *Trees of Great Britain and Ireland*.

Sinowilsonia henryi is widespread throughout much of central and western China, and has now been delineated by Chinese taxonomists into two varieties based on the presence or absence of pubescence on the leaf surface.

Nearby the *Sinowilsonia* in my garden grew *Fortunearia sinensis*, which regrettably did not make ample argument for its retention as space dwindled and decisions were made. Projecting a visual balance, in foliage, between *Hamamelis* and *Corylopsis*, it demonstrated the same somewhat maddening trait as the witch hazels in winter: that of refusing to drop its foliage. Terminal racemes of very small green flowers were produced in late February and March, but despite the fact that I meant no disregard for the memory and contributions of Robert Fortune, they were simply not sufficiently entertaining. Thumbs down.

Related to these two taxa, however, are the so-called winter hazels, or *Corylopsis*, which in most cases need not beg for accommodation in any garden. It is a widespread genus throughout Asia, showing significant diversity in nature as well as monumental nomenclatural difficulties in literature and commerce.

The *Flora of China* (Wu et al. 1994 to present) now recognizes 30 species, with 19 of those endemic to China itself. Of those, many that were previously considered varieties under the umbrella of *Corylopsis sinensis* have been given species rank. Without knowing the provenance of many of the plants currently in cultivation, the task of putting good names to existing material in our gardens is daunting.

Still, many *Corylopsis* species are worth growing, with or without names, for their signature characteristics. *Corylopsis pauciflora*, from the forests of both Japan and Taiwan, is a lovely species with a low, mounded habit of growth, buttery yellow flowers of considerable size, and bright green, oval-ovate leaves that emerge in emerald tones edged with red. It shares Taiwan with another species endemic to the island, *C. stenopetala*. Truly more of a small tree than a shrub, *C. stenopetala* is common on forest margins near Wuling Farm at moderate elevations, with orbicular, spiny-margined leaves to 3 in. (7.5 cm) and pendulous clusters of woody capsules to 4 in. (10 cm). My collections have yet to blossom in my garden.

Corylopsis spicata, from Japan, is well known and easily identified by its ungainly habit of growth. To my mind, though handsome enough with relatively long, pendulous spikes of large, soft yellow flowers, it is too large for most smaller landscapes, and its habit of growth does not allow for graceful shaping.

While on the southern coast of South Korea near Wando in 1993, Eric Hammond, who would later return to Washington to become my head propagator, and I found a single specimen of *Corylopsis glabrescens*, with a single remaining capsule, containing a single seed. The resulting seedling now dependably blossoms in mid- to late February in my current garden, possessing a reddish stamen that contrasts nicely with the soft yellow flowers; unlike any other *Corylopsis* I have grown, it also develops splendid autumn tones of claret and orange. For its fragrance as well as its tidy mounded habit of growth, I find this species, which Korean botanists refer to as *C. koreana*, to be among the most worthy of cultivation.

The same Eric Hammond traveled to China as my propagator in 1997 and returned with a single seedling of *Corylopsis* sp. EDHCH 97342, collected near Baoxing in Sichuan Province. This ultimately blossomed in our woodland, and we keyed it to *C. omeiana*, with drooping spikes of ridiculously small flowers barely visible to the naked eye. We eventually abandoned it in favor of more acceptable species, a decision I now regret, hav-

Corylopsis pauciflora. (Photo by Lynne Harrison)

Corylopsis spicata. (Photo by Lynne Harrison)

Corylopsis glabrescens. (Photo by Lynne Harrison)

Corylopsis glabrescens I collected in South Korea. (Photo by Daniel J. Hinkley)

ing become more keen on sorting out the genus more carefully.

While in Yunnan Province during my second trip in 1998, we hiked a considerable distance up the western slope of Cang Shan above Dali, the historical stomping ground of George Forrest at the turn of the 20th century, and of Jean Marie Delavay before that. It was during that trip that I collected *Corylopsis yunnanensis*, DJHC 98320, a 6–8 ft. (1.8–2.4 m) shrub that we found common on the drier west-facing hills. Though we had sufficient germination from this collection, and distributed the seedlings through my enterprise, I sadly lost track of this plant before securing for it a place in my garden. Fortunately, patrons scattered about North America have it in cultivation, and I hope to one day meet up with it again, at precisely its peak of blossom.

My experiences with the evergreen genera within the ranks of the family have been mixed. These are generally of the mindset that summer is a time for exuberant heat and humidity, and so they rebel in the face of the ongoing hypothermic conditions of the Northwest.

That I continue to attempt to grow *Loropetalum chinense* in the garden after having failed so many times attests to the ornamental virtues of this species, which has long been cultivated in the southeastern United States and for that matter throughout much of Asia. For years I admired and coveted these splendid, dense, rounded shrubs cloaked with small, ovate, slightly pubescent leaves and smothered with ivory white, witch-hazel-like flowers in late winter. With the rather sudden arrival in the early 1990s of the purple-foliaged and vibrant pink-flowered forms, the species took on an even greater seductive allure. 'Sizzling Pink' is a particularly good selection, with inky foliage and a spidery sizzle of pink flowers appearing over a long time in late winter.

Worldwide there are three known species of *Loropetalum*, though despite the popularity of *L. chinense* in cultivation, the remaining duo are virtually unknown in cultivation. Though *L. chinense*, of the three, occurs naturally at the highest elevations (to 3500 ft. [1070 m]) throughout much of south-central and western China

A celebrated mature and weeping specimen of *Loropetalum chinense* at the Tokyo Botanical Garden, planted more than a century ago. (Photo by Daniel J. Hinkley)

Seedlings of *Loropetalum chinense* showing the variation in foliage color inherent to the species. (Photo by Daniel J. Hinkley)

Hamamelis and Other Hamamelidaceae

west to northeastern India, and is therefore predictably the hardiest, *L. lanceum*, at 3000 ft. (900 m), does not occur so low as to be completely written off as potentially hardy. This species has glabrous rather than bristly foliage, setting it apart from the other members of the genus, while achieving the greatest height, ultimately forming a moderate-sized tree to 40 ft. (12 m). It would be worth trialing in the summer-warm areas of North America.

Loropetalum subcordatum is encountered, though not frequently, at low, tropical elevations in northern Vietnam, 300–600 ft. (90–180 m), where it forms a large shrub or small tree with foliage similar in appearance to that of *L. chinense*. It also occurs in the adjoining provinces of southern China, where it is considered to be a highly threatened species. My collections from the autumn of 2006, which began to germinate in 2008, require a warmer locale for evaluation than I can provide.

Much bolder in foliage than *Loropetalum*, yet seemingly as tuned in to the need for summer baking, is *Exbucklandia*. This genus is comprised of three species, the best known of which is *E. populnea*, the species through which I came to know the genus while in Yunnan in 1996.

The leaves of *Exbucklandia populnea* superficially resemble those of the tulip poplar, *Liriodendron*, in terms of shape, but are evergreen, glossy, and leathery-textured, with a very prominent stipule at the base of each leaf. I encountered this species growing as a tall shrub at about 3500 ft. (1070 m) in western Yunnan near the village of Weixi. Though my own plants of this collection have long since failed, there are encouraging reports of the species thriving near Raleigh, North Carolina. In 2005, while in a pristine locale in central Bhutan, I again had the fortune of meeting up with this splendid species, which this time showed its full potential in regard to ultimate size. I was flabbergasted when I realized that the mammoth-girthed tree trunk in front of me, towering well over 100 ft. (30 m) above, was none other than the same taxon I had come to know as a "shrub."

In 1999 I recognized this genus again on the slopes of Fan-si-pan in northern Vietnam, but it was *Exbucklandia tonkinensis* that this time caught my eye. Along Tram Ton Pass at about 6500 ft. (2000 m), it grew as a small tree or large shrub to 15 ft. (4.6 m) tall. In 2006, however, I located stands of this species as fruiting specimens rising to 75 ft. (23 m). *Exbucklandia tonkinensis* has a rather broad distribution in south-central China and Indochina, though it is known to occur at much greater altitudes than *E. populnea*. Literature cites it as occurring between 2700 ft. and 5000 ft. (820 m and 1500 m), but my collection notes record an altitude of 6100 ft. (1900 m). I am hopeful that this high provenance will reveal a plant with a broader appeal to temperate areas of North America.

Though *Exbucklandia populnea* is evergreen, the previous year's leaves color nicely before being jettisoned. (Photo by Daniel J. Hinkley)

Another species, *Exbucklandia longipetala*, is considered vulnerable to extirpation, existing at relatively high elevations around 5000 ft. (1500 m) in China's northern Guangxi and southern Guizhou Provinces. Unlike the other known species, the flowers of this species possess petals. I have had no interaction with it, though its provenance would suggest justification for trialing it for possible use in our gardens.

It was while in Tokyo in the autumn of 2004, on a quaint and quiet city alley, that I had my first face-to-face encounter with *Rhodoleia championii*. A branch of a tall evergreen shrub, carrying decidedly rhododendron-like leaves with a brilliant silvery white cast beneath, was arching over a fence, while presenting at eye level a cluster of large and exceptional electric pink flowers.

It is an inexplicable phenomenon frequently shared by those who submerse themselves fully in any subject, and a phenomenon that when reported runs the risk of seeming boastful or self-congratulatory: the case of bringing forth a name from somewhere deep and long forgotten, as if the name had always been lodged in your memory bank. I believed that this tall evergreen shrub encountered in Tokyo must be *Rhodoleia*.

Of course I had read of the genus. I had also once seen a specimen, though in foliage only, growing at the UC Davis Arboretum, and recall having been intrigued by this first encounter. It may have been its high-voltage pink flowers, so similar to those of the pigmented forms of *Loropetalum*, that dislodged its name from some cavelike recess in my brain and brought it forth.

Since that time I have collected this same species of *Rhodoleia* in Vietnam, adjacent to specimens of *Exbucklandia tonkinensis*, at elevations far higher than its cited range in literature. It is a genus of about six species, known primarily from western and southwestern Yunnan as well as Vietnam, Malaysia, and Indonesia.

Surprisingly, several species, including *Rhodoleia forrestii* and *R. henryi*, are reported to occur at elevations nearing 8000 ft. (2400 m), putting them well within the margin of probability in terms of hardiness. *Rhodoleia*

championii is appropriate only for mild locales in zones 8–12 and responds favorably to heat and humidity.

Although the genus *Distylium*, including some 18 evergreen species from across South Asia, responds with more assuredness in the sultry states of the Southeast, the two species I have grown have made a valorous attempt at overcoming the coolness of my Pacific Northwest garden.

Distylium racemosum, which occurs naturally on the southern coast of Korea, southern Japan, and Taiwan, possesses a long tradition in cultivation, making an interesting modestly sized shrub for the mixed border or for foundation plantings in shade to partially shaded sites. In late March, bundles of intensely red flowers open in the axils of glossy, ovate, 3 in. (7.5 cm) leaves along stems rising to 8 ft. (2.4 m). I cultivate two named forms of this species, both of which were kindly shared with me years ago by Phil Normandy of Brookside Gardens in Maryland. 'Akebono' enlivens the spring garden with new growth that is pure white, fading to green as the summer progresses. 'Guppy' is smaller in aspect, with miniature leaves carried along congested stems to 3 ft. (0.9 m) when mature.

The rarely encountered *Rhodoleia forrestii* is from high elevations in western China and should possess more hardiness than would be expected from the genus as a whole. (Photo by Daniel J. Hinkley)

Hamamelis and Other Hamamelidaceae

Distylium myricoides, with a broad distribution in western and southern China, is a very comely tall shrub or small tree with a blue-green cast to the foliage that, at 3 in. (7.5 cm) long and ¾ in. (1.9 cm) wide, provides a pleasing textural quality to the lightly shaded garden. It is poorly represented in Western horticulture, though it has been propagated and distributed by Gossler Farms Nursery in Springfield, Oregon, for numerous years.

During a trip to Taiwan in the late autumn of 2007, I encountered a genus name that had been utterly unfa-miliar to me until that point: *Distyliopsis*, a compact assemblage of six species, mostly classified as small trees. After a bit of detective work, I discovered that I had in fact once grown a member of the genus, a one *D. tutcheri*, when it made its horticultural rounds under the alias of *Sycopsis tutcheri*. In Taiwan, however, it was *D. dunnii* to which I was introduced. Though this species also occurs on mainland China, where it may express itself in a more treelike fashion, here it grew as a dense, upright, pyramidal, evergreen shrub to 8 ft. (2.4 m). Its demure, ovate foliage, to less than 2½ in. (6 cm) long, possessed a light mustard-green color that made the scattered specimens of this rarity readily apparent. The yellow or orange apetalous flowers of *D. dunnii* are borne in axillary clusters along the stem in late winter. My assumptions are that this species, which grows in central Taiwan above Sun Moon Lake at 8550 ft. (2600 m), will prove hardy and forgiving of summer-cool regions, as has *D. tutcheri*.

There are other genera of plants in this remarkable family that are of immense interest, including those from South Asia, South America, and Africa, but sadly, none are appropriate for our climate. With regard to the Hamamelidaceae, it seems we cannot have them all, yet we can at least revel in the fact that for those we can grow, we can grow well. Our gardens would be vastly less opulent if not for the ornamental strengths provided by this aggregate of profoundly garden-worthy plants.

HARDINESS: A quick-reference guide to the hardiness of the taxa included in this family follows. Please note that I have indicated those genera that are appropriate only in summer-warm areas. I must also add that in my experience, though *Corylopsis* species tend to demonstrate hardiness as a whole, with *C. glabrescens* being the hardiest of the lot, they do not tolerate late frosts. Whereas numerous shrubs may lose flower buds or flowers or experience minor leaf damage from such events, *Corylopsis* can be severely damaged or killed outright. If late frosts are part and parcel to your gar-

Distylium racemosum. (Photo by Lynne Harrison)

Distyliopsis dunnii. (Photo by Daniel J. Hinkley)

dening experience, consider providing overstory protection for these species.

Corylopsis: zones (5)6–9
Disanthus: zones 6–9
Distyliopsis: zones 7b–11(12)
Distylium: zones 7b–12
Exbucklandia: zones 8–12 (summer-warm)
Fortunearia: zones 6–9
Fothergilla: zones 4–8
Hamamelis: zones 5–9
Loropetalum: zones 7–12 (summer-warm)
Parrotia: zones 4–9
Parrotiopsis: zones 6–9
Rhodoleia: zones 9–11(12) (summer-warm)
Sinowilsonia: zones 6–9
Sycopsis: zones 7b–12

CULTIVATION: As a general rule of thumb, the deciduous species of this family appreciate bright, sunny, or lightly shaded conditions; autumn display of these species will be more intense under more direct exposure. Exceptions include *Disanthus cercidifolius*, which will color nicely in a fully shaded site, and *Corylopsis pauciflora*, which will bleach if grown in excessive sunlight; both appreciate some overhead protection. The evergreen members of this family, by and large, are understory shrubs or small trees that are more content in slightly sheltered positions, despite the fact that they will tolerate full sun if given adequate summer water.

Members of the Hamamelidaceae prefer acidic to slightly acidic soils, though *Parrotia persica* shows a great deal of tolerance to alkaline conditions. As a whole, these plants perform best in humus-rich, well-drained soil and benefit from regular applications of supplemental water during the growing season, especially prior to full establishment.

PROPAGATION: Since many of the taxa in this family release their seed with considerable explosive force, collecting the capsules before they dehisce is obviously rather important. Keep them in a closed paper bag until the action is complete. The capsules can be collected as soon as the endosperm of the seed is white. Germination will occur after two cold moist treatments, interrupted by a single warm moist treatment.

The evergreen genera present little challenge with regard to rooting or overwintering the first year, when ripened wood is taken in late summer or early fall and placed on gentle bottom heat. I have not had experience in attempting to root *Exbucklandia* but would recommend that leaf reduction be considered to reduce moisture loss.

The deciduous genera of this family are decidedly more unforthcoming in aiding and abetting the propagator. High concentrations of rooting hormone (IBA [indolebutyric acid], NAA [naphthalene acetic acid]) have a positive influence on root formation on the deciduous hamamelids. We often used undiluted liquid hormone (10,000 ppm of IBA) to induce rooting of *Hamamelis*. Though this concentration burned the lower tip of the cutting, root initials appeared above the damaged tissue. Attempting to get these species rooted under mist by midsummer, and promoting a late-season flush of growth by artificially extending the day length and applying a nitrogen-based fertilizer, helps reduce attrition the following spring. Withhold transplanting from the rooting media until growth resumes in the spring.

Though *Hamamelis* species would ideally be produced on their own roots, due to the nuisance of rootstock suckering, this is not yet a commercially viable approach. Witch hazels are nearly all (supposedly) grafted on *H. virginiana* rootstock, the universal choice of nurserymen. With that said, anecdotal evidence suggests that many rootstocks sold as *H. virginiana* are indeed *H. vernalis*, an inferior choice due to its propensity to sucker from both the stem and roots. *Parrotia persica* has been used as a rootstock for *Hamamelis*, and though it suckers less than *H. vernalis*, it does reduce the vigor of the scion. Seedling or cutting grown *Disanthus cercidifolius* is used as an understock to its variegated and dwarf clones.

Befuddled Fusion: *Helwingia*

Today the bus dropped us like unwanted cargo at the base of a mountain they called Ninety-Nine Dragons—as far as I can tell, about three hours north of Dali. The ceiling of cloud was low and heavy as we disembarked with our packs, pilfered through sacks of provisions to assemble the makings of lunch, and scattered in ones, twos, and threes with a set time to reconnoiter before dark. I chose to enter a small wooded area and hike up a steep north-facing draw that was strewn with large boulders and canopied by rather sizeable trees. I immediately noticed seed on a limb of Acer franchetii *(syn.* A. sterculiaceum *var.* franchetii*), with enormous leaves, and went about collecting the seed, which entailed climbing the tree with a rock so as to weigh down the limb sufficiently to collect from the ground. It took much longer than I had imagined, and I was irritated to have wasted so much time; the others were assuredly now much higher in richer hunting grounds. As I began to slog up the slope, I studied a curiously smoky-purple-stemmed shrub that appeared to be*

something of merit. A quick inspection of the remaining foliage revealed a raised midrib from the leaf base to the middle of the blade, with some vestiges of connective tissue, betraying its identity as Helwingia, *but disappointingly without fruit.*

Yet it has been during this trip that I have, quite at last, and successfully at that, drawn the conclusion that one specimen does not often speak openly of the state of affairs (especially considering dioecism in this case). I traversed the draw laterally to a dense thicket comprised chiefly of more of the same species, where I was rewarded with finding a female specimen still clad in yellow foliage, each leaf with one or two fully ripened black fruits adhered to the dead center of the blade. It seemed a treasure to me to at last see this in the wild, and I paused for a considerable time to take pictures and savor the moment before again resuming upslope.

Ninety-Nine Dragons, Yunnan Province
October 21, 1996

I T WAS FOR A GERMAN, Georg Andreas Helwing, a pastor and professor of both the genus *Pulsatilla* and the plants of Prussia, that *Helwingia* was named; however, Helwing almost certainly never laid eyes on any member of his namesake genus. It was not until 1830, nearly 82 years after Helwing's death, that Philipp Franz von Siebold introduced *H. japonica* to Europe from Japan. Since that time, this genus of shrubs has had

Helwingia japonica. (Photo by Lynne Harrison)

an obscure presence in horticulture. It has been grown as a novelty for its unusual morphology rather than for its ornamental appeal, and in fact has been denigrated as an undesirable for a garden setting and accused of possessing a significant vacuum of merit.

Yet this dismissal was set in motion when relatively little was known of the genus. As late as 1980, in the eighth edition of the mighty W. J. Bean's *Trees and Shrubs Hardy in the British Isles*, *Helwingia* is referred to as a group of wholly deciduous shrubs, but the more horticulturally plucky evergreen species have since been introduced. I make a case for the utilization of *Helwingia*, no matter the species, evergreen or deciduous. They offer an unobtrusive charm with a kind of botanical sortilege that demands a second look, resulting in the dazzled realization that beauty is fabricated across an absurdly wide spectrum of styles. In addition, I would never bypass the opportunity to share this novelty with children visiting my garden. Such kickshaw is precisely the thing that invites a youthful mind to explore more fully the mysteries embodied by the plant kingdom.

Taxonomically, the genus *Helwingia* snuggles somewhere between the dogwood family, Cornaceae, and the araliads, Araliaceae, and has been provided digs of its own in the Helwingiaceae. The leaves on all species are alternately arranged along a multistemmed, often suckering framework to 6–8 ft. (1.8–2.4 m) in height. It is in the flowering and fruiting effects, however, that things get, well . . . interesting. Happening upon any species of *Helwingia* in full blossom for the first time is somewhat startling, as it appears that the inflorescences, rather small umbels, are arising directly from the leaf blade. I say startling because one's immediate take is that the foliage is under full assault by some insidious infestation.

This morphology, rare in the plant kingdom, results from the leaf stem (the so-called petiole) and the flower stem (pedicel) being fused up to the midpoint of the leaf blade. This somewhat bizarre natural design should not be confused with the similar appearance of some species in the genus *Ruscus*. In that genus, the flowers arise on flattened, leaflike stems referred to as cladodes, with the flowers produced, quite naturally, at the nodes. As all species of *Helwingia* are dioecious, if male and female plants are planted in proximity, pea-sized drupes ripen atop the leaf blade in early autumn.

Helwingia japonica, the species that Siebold brought into cultivation, occurs in a broad range across eastern Asia. I have found this species a commonly encountered understory component in the moist, damp woods of northern Japan as well as in Yunnan and Sichuan Prov-inces of China some 3000 miles (4800 km) to the west. The Japanese, being fond of such oddities, have selected several variegated forms of *H. japonica*, with the all-golden-foliaged selection, 'Ogon', being the most readily found in commerce, though rarely at that. The fruit, produced when both sexes are present, is a black drupe that is quite handsomely displayed while the leaves transition to bright yellow in autumn. It is somewhat satisfying to note that I have observed, since my first visit to Japan in 1988, a growing appreciation for this species in its own right.

In the 1990s I received two evergreen helwingias from J. C. Raulston at North Carolina State University, though the provenance of those cuttings remains somewhat sketchy. Poorly armed with literature dwelling on the genus, we settled on calling both plants *Helwingia chinensis*, distinguishing between the two by calling one "broad-leaved form" and the other, ingeniously, "narrow-leaved form." The broad-leaved form possessed broad, glossy leaves to 3½ in. (9 cm) long and 2 in. (5 cm) wide, emerging in spring with a handsome purple blush, along suckering stems to 6 ft. (1.8 m). It was a male clone. The narrow-leaved form, which we subsequently removed from the garden, carried lancelike leaves to 5 in. (12.5 cm)—superficially rather bamboo-like—with a dull purplish green cast. This female clone would occasionally set seed for us, though in general paucity and not of particular note.

In 1996 in the Wolong area of Sichuan, northwest of Chengdu, I encountered our narrow-leaved form in its native haunts and was able to collect a small number of seeds, from deep purple, fleshy fruit, under the collection number DJHC 695. The resulting plant offered a much more glossy leaf surface while retaining the narrow, finely textured foliage. It is an often-asked-about shrub that we now grow in a north-facing courtyard at Windcliff, planted among culms of Mark Bulwinkle's welded bamboo to provide the visual cue of bamboo foliage without its exuberant sprint through the garden. The flowers of *Helwingia chinensis*, rather small, spidery umbels of dark purple, are borne both on the foliage and

My collection of *Helwingia chinensis*, a peculiar evergreen shrub from Sichuan, growing on the protected northern side of my home at Windcliff. (Photo by Daniel J. Hinkley)

in the leaf axils in early summer, and though they do not shout in ornament, they certainly would have impressed even W. J. Bean.

It is rather interesting to note that in 2008, while visiting the San Francisco Botanical Garden at Strybing Arboretum, I met up again with our narrow-leaved form, which the garden had purchased from my nursery years before. There, in the Bay climate, it had matured into an immensely handsome specimen with highly textural lanceolate foliage, while possessing none of the dullness I had associated with it in our garden on the Kitsap Peninsula. Nonetheless, without a proper suitor, it was not performing the song and dance that possesses the potential to bring it the notice it deserves.

In the autumn of 2002, in eastern Nepal at the relatively low elevation of 6000 ft. (1800 m), my trekking companion, Bleddyn Wynn-Jones, and I faced the frustration of dropping much too fast in elevation to perform a proper job of botanizing the slopes. A combination of things—mixed signals, our inability to communicate, and perhaps even a horse with his nose pointed toward home—had propelled our porters ahead of us at breakneck speed. In driving rain and with darkness

Helwingia chinensis. (Photo by Daniel J. Hinkley)

Helwingia chinensis "broad-leaved form."
(Photo by Lynne Harrison)

Befuddled Fusion: *Helwingia*

The startling fruit of *Helwingia himalaica* in northeast Sichuan Province. (Photo by Dave Demers)

fruited shrub alongside the trail where I walked. Expecting that it would prove to be a holly or photinia, I was dumbfounded to discover upon approaching it that it was indeed a *Helwingia*. An evergreen to 4 ft. (1.2 m) tall, it had elegant, glossy green, narrow leaves to 5 in. (12.5 cm), each leaf holding upward of three succulent ruby red berries. My collections of this species, which Chinese botanists somewhat controversially refer to as *H. himalaica*, grow in my new garden and blossomed for the first time in 2008. Excitingly, this species seems to cross that boundary between simply botanically intriguing and horticulturally ornamental.

It is odd that after so little natural interface with this genus, I seem capable of recognizing *Helwingia* species with relative ease in the field, probably due to their distinctive horizontally planed stems and often distinctive purple branches. Such was the case during the autumn of 2007 when my suspicions about the identity of a shrub along a mountain stream on Babokulu Mountain, Taiwan, at 4000 ft. (1200 m) proved to be accurate. Taiwanese botanists treat their sole deciduous inhabitant of the genus as *H. japonica* var. *formosana*, which appears superficially identical to the specimens of *H. japonica* I have observed in both China and Japan. In early December it was much too late to consider finding fruit, yet I was satisfied to have seen this in the wild.

There is still much to learn about this genus of shrubs. Where does the broad-leaved form of *Helwingia chinensis* exist in the wild? Are there other species that have yet to be brought into cultivation? How adaptable are those that we have in cultivation to conditions across North America? These questions will ultimately be answered, though I need no additional time to gather up my appreciation for this small family of plants. Its rather zany approach to perpetuation has in it enough beauty for me.

HARDINESS: The deciduous *Helwingia japonica* will assuredly be the hardiest species of the genus, thriving in at least zone 6b and above; however, the issue of provenance must again be addressed here. Collections of this

fast approaching, we fell past a tantalizingly good flora that we were unable to study. With that said, however, we were not entirely out of luck. Literally seconds after Bleddyn wondered aloud whether we were in the altitudinal range of *Helwingia himalaica*, a species we had failed to find during our 1995 expedition to eastern Nepal, we came upon just that. With deep purple, fleshy seed carried atop its jagged-edged, deciduous foliage, this species is somewhat akin to *H. japonica*, though its fruit might be likened to that of its evergreen cousins. I now have this collection secured in my garden, growing adjacent to both *H. japonica* as well as *H. chinensis*, though it has yet to set fruit.

A year later, in Sichuan Province near the border with Gansu, my eyes caught sight of a sensational bright-red-

species from Hokkaidō, for instance, to my knowledge have never been brought into cultivation, and these might broaden this taxon's adaptability to colder climates. The evergreen species have tolerated temperatures in my gardens as low as 15°F (−9°C) without leaf damage.

CULTIVATION: These plants do have a tendency to sucker and should be controlled on a yearly basis, either to reduce the size of the colony or to produce new plants. There is some indication that the lifespan of an individual stem might be quite ephemeral, so coppicing on occasion, as one would a shrubby dogwood, might be in order. An evenly moist but well-draining, humus-rich soil, slightly acidic, is recommended in a bright aspect. Of course, if the curious fruiting effects are to occur, both sexes must be present. To date, I have not seen evidence in my garden that interspecific pollen transfer results in fruit set. As the natural pollinators may be entirely absent, it may be necessary to transfer pollen by hand. That would be a drag.

PROPAGATION: Each fruit possesses numerous small seeds that require two periods of cold, moist stratification before germination; seed sown fresh will germinate in 18–20 months if exposed to ambient winter temperatures after sowing. Cuttings, particularly of the evergreen species, are easy to strike in late summer or early winter on gentle bottom heat. The deciduous species should be struck after hardening of the wood in midsummer under mist and not transplanted until growth resumes the following spring. Of course, division of the entire shrub or removal of the suckers in early spring is a viable alternative.

Beyond Mopheads: *Hydrangea*

We drove again today from our small, elegant ryokan, owned by a stern mistress (who is very cross each evening upon our arrival home, we assume because of the general filth of our clothing after yet another full day of hiking in the rain), into the mountains to the south, reaching sufficient elevation by midmorning. It was a quintessential late-autumn day: drier, and though not particularly cold, made to seem more so by that pervasive fragrance of this time of year. We were adjacent to a boisterous river virtually all day, and its vocalizations are still audibly present this evening.

What will remain most intact in my memory of today will be the luminous yellow leaves of Hydrangea anomala *subsp.* petiolaris *through a dense, blue morning fog, their self-clinging stems scaling scores of tall trees surrounding us. An herbaceous* Hydrangea *relative,* Deinanthe bifida, *was prominent on the forest floor with stems to 4 ft. and capsules offering a surfeit of ripened seed. This was only a wake-up to the richness of the Hydrangeaceae that we*

would ultimately encounter today; at one point, in midafternoon, I mentally noted those species readily apparent without moving: H. hirta, H. paniculata, H. serrata, H. involucrata, *and* H. anomala, *as well as* Schizophragma hydrangeoides.

If there was any vexation to such a red-letter day (other than again being scolded by our hostess), it came near dusk when I came upon our first specimen of Hydrangea sikokiana, *growing adjacent to the river's edge where an ebbing light still provided sufficient illumination to make a positive identification. It is a rare species that my traveling companions and I had sought passionately and unsuccessfully, primarily on Shikoku, during the previous three weeks of this trip. It had become somewhat of a competition to see who might ultimately find it. On a very quiet ride home this evening, I became acutely aware of the downside of slicing the goal posts in the last seconds to win the game.*

Southeast of Gojo, Kii Peninsula, Honshū
November 5, 1997

A S A GENERAL RULE, gardeners tend to repeat the things they have heard their mentors say about virtually all things in the garden, whether or not they themselves have enough personal experience to support the assertion. With that in mind, I will repeat what I heard an accomplished gardener exclaim when I first moved to western Washington in the 1980s:

Hydrangea paniculata 'Grandiflora'. (Photo by Daniel J. Hinkley)

hydrangeas do something for the garden in late summer that no other shrubs can. Yet in truth I am not just parroting this proposition. Over many years I have become a devotee of this remarkably diverse genus of shrubs and vines, while garnering sufficient data in regard to their taxonomy, nativity, and garden performance to feel—at least somewhat—qualified to sing loudly their praises.

My experiences with hydrangeas actually began much earlier in my career while I was a sapling gardener in the icy zone 4 of northern Michigan. On the northern side of my parents' home, I planted a pair of *Hydrangea paniculata* 'Grandiflora' and three *H. arborescens* 'Grandiflora', virtually the only available representatives of the genus that were suitable for our climate. Some 40 years later those same undemanding hydrangeas remain intact, offering my parents a generous display of flowers in July and August, and the white-tailed deer a bit of welcome nibble in the winter months.

Four decades later, while working a summer position at Washington Park Arboretum in Seattle, I significantly increased my appreciation for the genus after performing a feat any horticulturist worth his or her oats would have done: dumpster-diving to retrieve a discarded bouquet of hydrangea blossoms. The stems easily rooted and became the foundation for the sizeable collection of species and named forms I ultimately assimilated.

The hydrangea family, Hydrangeaceae, is a respectable conglomeration of shrubs, vines, and herbaceous perennials that once belonged to a behemoth institution known as the Saxifragaceae. The herbaceous components, in the genera *Cardiandra*, *Deinanthe*, and *Kirengeshoma*, proffer ornamental species for cultivation, although it is the woody taxa of shrubs and lianas of this family, in the genera *Hydrangea*, *Schizophragma*, and *Decumaria*, that are far and away the most familiar. Less well known are *Platycrater*, *Dichroa*, *Pileostegia*, and *Broussaisia*. Recent molecular work casts doubt on these ancillary species, which may be ultimately usurped by the large umbrella genus and subject at hand.

With the exceptions of *Hydrangea paniculata* and *H. quercifolia*, the prototypical *Hydrangea* inflorescence is a corymb, a rounded disk of numerous small, fertile flowers that possess insignificant sepals and four to five small yet often colorful petals of white, pink, or blue. Getting down to the business of procreation, this cluster of utility is surrounded by an advertising agency of sterile florets, or ray flowers, that provide the stuff of ornament. The ovaries are, as a rule, inferior—that is, enclosed in the receptacle—while the dehiscent capsules, sometimes in the shape of a Grecian water jar,

give rise to the genus name (*hydro*, "water"; *angeion*, "vessel"). The foliage is, without exception, held along the stems in pairs.

This floral composition, involving sacrificing the fertility of a few flowers to provoke the curiosity of commuting pollinators, has coevolved in other unrelated plant genera, most notably the genus *Viburnum*. Thusly it would not come as a complete surprise to those who have grown a doublefile viburnum, *V. plicatum* var. *tomentosum*, that the second Asiatic hydrangea to be noted by Western botanists, in Japan in 1777, was named *V. serratum*. That nomenclatural error marks the beginning of what would become a long and preposterous excursion into a field full of taxonomic landmines.

The first hydrangea described from Asia that same year, by Carl Peter Thunberg while in Japan, was in actuality a mophead or hortensia cultivar, but Thunberg, having never before encountered such a lovely creature, christened the plant *Viburnum macrophyllum*. For those who have become familiar with hydrangeas through the paradigmatic mophead form, it is important to underscore the fact that although mophead hydrangeas are highly ornamental, they are also supremely unnatural. What I mean to say is that the naturally occurring hydrangea flower is indeed a lacecap; mopheads essentially represent mutant, mostly sterile forms. This type of mutation in the hydrangea flower must be differentiated from a doubling or tripling of the number of sepals in each ray flower. In the latter case, the resulting, and often beguiling, roselike florets surround a central core of customary fertile florets.

The inebriated taxonomy of the hydrangeas that exists to this day can be ascribed to several unfortunate circumstances. To begin, much of the material first named, including Thunberg's *Viburnum macrophyllum*, was based on clonal selections with no botanical standing. Add to this the fact that many *Hydrangea* species occur across an immense geographical range, and that the natural, often significant variation found within each taxon is problematic even when the study of live material is readily accessible—which, to Thunberg and others, it was not. Remote and politically insular, the hot-beds of *Hydrangea* speciation in Japan and China have offered modern Western botany petite and ineffectual data. Though Elizabeth McClintock's highly regarded 1957 "Monograph of the Genus *Hydrangea*" remains the most comprehensive monograph to date, it would be evenhanded to say that a lion's share of her astute observations came from a small selection of overfried herbarium specimens. The topping to this tangle involves the nurserymen and lay authors (in the midst of which lies yours truly) who have simply taken matters into their own hands, laying low in great sweeps the attempts of systematics to provide a sturdy grip to the genus.

In this book I attempt to formulate my personal observations of many of the species in the wild, as well as those of known provenance that I have personally grown, within the broader academic context of the treatise by McClintock. Though I purposely divert my course from the minefield of cultivars that have arisen from the complex of *Hydrangea macrophylla* and *H. serrata*—as these have been thoroughly covered in published monographs—I note selected forms where I feel it is important to do so. In no way do I feel sufficiently licensed to suggest that my meager commentary be considered anything more than an informal discussion of a genus of plants that I greatly admire and whose breadth is not known to horticulturists to the extent that it should be.

Taxonomists have tackled the genus through the creation of two sections: *Hydrangea* and *Cornidia*. The former, all shrubs or small trees, has been further broken down into six subsections. *Cornidia* represents the climbing species and has been dissected into two subsections. Although contemporary genetic analysis somewhat undermines the foundation of these taxa, I prefer to traverse the vastness of this remarkable genus by the user-friendly globetrotting approach rather than adhering to any taxonomic treatise. This is accomplished by discussing the shrubs, vines, and closely related genera in three separate sections, beginning in this chapter with the shrubs.

The Shrubby Hydrangeas

In 2007 *Hydrangea macrophylla* was listed by the USDA as the fourth-highest-selling flowering shrub in the United States, generating some $32 million in sales. With such a rebirth of interest in the genus *Hydrangea*, once hugely popular during the Victorian era, it might as well be here that my story begins. Yet instead it begins, as with many other plants, with an argument over a proper name. Through the untangling of a legion of sticky webs, a rather interesting story unfolds that possesses all the parameters necessary for a perfect storm.

As already noted, the hydrangeas first described from Japan, through Thunberg in 1777, were christened *Viburnum macrophyllum* and *V. serratum*. The former, a selection later named 'Otaksa', possessed an inflorescence comprised of virtually all sterile florets; it is thought that this form was imported into Japan from China, where it was already a popular garden plant in the courts of Imperial China. The latter probably came to Thunberg's attention by way of fodder brought for animals on the island of Deshima, an artificial archipelago in Nagasaki harbor where all visitors to Japan during the 18th century were forced to live. (As an interesting aside, it was on Deshima that Philipp Franz von Siebold fell in love with Otaki-san, his Japanese lover whom the Japanese government forbade him from marrying. When Siebold left Japan in 1828, he took with him Otaki-san and the daughter they had produced. However, a ship wreck led to the finding of a forbidden map of Japan that Siebold had acquired. He was arrested and later banished; Otaksa and their daughter were not allowed to leave with him.)

About the same time, the French botanist Lammark published the name *Hortensia opuloides*, the moniker given to a plant that the naturalist Philibert Commerçon had sent to Paris from the island of Mauritius, where it grew in the garden of explorer Pierre Poivre. This invalid genus name is still used to some degree in French commerce to represent those cultivars possessing mostly infertile florets. There remains a great deal of speculation as to exactly whom the name *Hortensia* was meant to commemorate. Commerçon's mistress, Jeanne Baré, who accompanied him dressed as a man on Louis Antoine de Bougainville's round-world voyage, is ruled out. Queen Hortense was born several years after Commerçon's death. Madame Lepaute, the wife of a clockmaker and herself a respected mathematician, is often cited; however, her Christian name was Nicole-Reine. Most likely, *Hortensia* was named for the daughter of the Prince of Nassau-Siegen, whose father had accompanied Commerçon on Bougainville's juggernaut.

Later, in 1788, Sir Joseph Banks presented to Kew a sterile-floreted form he had procured from China. This was properly placed in the genus *Hydrangea*, described in 1792 as *H. hortensis*. This clone is still common along the mild southern coast of England, where it is now grown as *H. macrophylla* 'Sir Joseph Banks'.

It now very apparent that trying to sort out and rename *Hydrangea macrophylla* and *H. serrata* while adhering to the rules of priority only causes more damage than good, but it is understandable and meritorious that many have attempted to do just that. Ernest Wilson, Michael Haworth-Booth, and Elizabeth McClintock have all weighed in heavily to make things right. Though there is still plenty to be learned, we have gained a better understanding of the two species.

Hydrangea macrophylla 'Sea Foam'. (Photo by Lynne Harrison)

Hydrangea macrophylla, with its typically large, glossy, somewhat fleshy leaves, is common throughout coastal Japan at relatively low elevations, frequently found hugging windswept beaches. In 1995 and 1997 I observed large populations of this species growing in the Chiba Prefecture south of Tokyo. Of course, the normal form in the wild possesses both fertile and ray florets. *Hydrangea macrophylla* 'Sea Foam', a sport from 'Sir Joseph Banks', with rather large cymes of blue fertile flowers and white-fading-to-blue sterile florets, is probably the closest thing to true *H. macrophylla* in cultivation. There have been subsequent introductions from the wild, including Wilson's 1917 collection from Ōshima, but they have made little if any impact on Western horticulture. Pure *H. macrophylla* blossoms on second-year wood, making it inappropriate for use in any climate where winter damage will occur. But more on that in a moment.

For those blessed with warmer gardening climates, there exists a voluminous list of *Hydrangea macrophylla* cultivars from which to choose. Many in the trade adhere to the refreshing approach of simply designating each cultivar (L), lacecap, if the cultivar possesses the traditional fertile inflorescence, or tagging it (H), hortensia, if it offers globose heads of mostly sterile florets.

Despite the devotion to the mophead or hortensia types of *Hydrangea macrophylla* in the gardens of North America, it is my personal belief that what these lack in simple grace is made up for by an obesity of gaudiness, and therefore I must confess my partiality to the lacecaps. Although there exist too numerous cultivars to delve into, were I to name a favorite it would be *H. macrophylla* 'Veitchii', with large, clean white florets surrounding a central disk of fertile, powdery blue flowers. It blossoms well along our bright, sunny drive in Indianola and always elicits a response from visitors to the garden. Even though I have grown this cultivar for nearly two decades, I often find myself stopping my car along the driveway adjacent to where it grows, to appreciate its finest moments in early to late July.

A surge of interest in *Hydrangea macrophylla* for a

broader market has come forth through the introduction of 'Endless Summer'. It is one of several new cultivars, including 'Forever and Ever', now promoted for the ability to blossom on new growth, with names as cloying as their overweight blossoms. Still, I am certain that gardeners in zones 4–6, heretofore unable to appreciate hydrangeas in their climates, would rightly categorize my observations as zonally arrogant.

Though it is still quite in dispute whether *Hydrangea serrata* is simply a variety of *H. macrophylla*, or conversely whether *H. macrophylla* is a variety of *H. serrata*, Thunberg's *Viburnum serratum* did indeed represent a different taxon hailing from the higher elevations of Japan and Korea. *Hydrangea serrata*, as I will refer to it in this book, is thusly a much hardier species and possesses the ability to blossom on new wood, making it more adaptable to more challenging climates.

I have encountered and collected seed of this species on numerous occasions on Hokkaidō, central and northern Honshū, Cheju, and most notably while on Mount Chiri on the southern tip of the Korean Peninsula, in 1993 and 1997, at 4900 ft. (1500 m). Here, this species smothers the hillsides to a much greater degree than I have ever witnessed in Japan and must be a dazzling sight when in blossom. I have come to expect the typical wild form of this, from both Japan and Korea, to offer blue fertile flowers in a slightly dome-shaped corymb, encircled with ray florets of blue when provided acidic soils, or suffused with pink when grown under more alkaline conditions.

A collection from our time on Mount Chiri in 1997, under the number HC 970416, was a self-layered lower branch from a specimen possessing sterile florets with double sepals. I entered it into the trade under the cul-

Hydrangea macrophylla 'Veitchii'. (Photo by Lynne Harrison)

The Shrubby Hydrangeas

tivar name 'Chiri-san Sue' in honor of Sue Wynn-Jones, who had accompanied us on the trip and waited an inappropriate length of time for us to return to our preordained meeting spot, in the dark, on that chilly, rainy day.

It was, however, in Japan that I first observed a vast array of *Hydrangea* cultivars based upon this taxon. Unlike the European hybridization of hydrangeas, which focused primarily on increasing the flower size of *H. macrophylla*, the Japanese breeding programs selected for delicate subtlety, which translates to pure charm in the garden. Unfortunately, hydrangeas from Japan are forbidden from entry in the United States. However, Europe does not ban their importation, and since hydrangeas can come into the United States through Europe under post-entry quarantine, these exciting new plants will ultimately be made available

Hydrangea serrata 'Chiri-san Sue'. (Photo by Daniel J. Hinkley)

Hydrangea serrata 'Chiri-san Sue'. (Photo by Lynne Harrison)

through the trade, though not necessarily at the pace I would prefer.

Consider *Hydrangea serrata* 'Izu No Hana', one of dozens of classical cultivars from the Japanese tradition, each with a name nearly as enticing as the floral effects it produces. With this cultivar, the flattened disk of indigo-blue flowers are surrounded by sterile florets of a similar hue, much in the same fashion as other lacecap hydrangeas. In this cultivar, however, each sterile floret possesses a double dose of sepals, creating miniature blue "roses" that arc from the flower heads on wiry stems, suggesting intricate fireworks at precisely the moment of ignition.

This charming flower type is seen in numerous named Japanese cultivars, including the beguiling, large-headed, pure white *Hydrangea serrata* 'Miyake-Tokiwa'. A single stem of this cultivar, with miniature white tassels opening from chartreuse buds, could by itself be carried as a tastefully exquisite bridal bouquet.

Flower heads possessing sepals richly edged in contrasting hues comprise another substantial subset of the Japanese mountain hydrangea. The blossoms of *Hydrangea serrata* 'Beni Gaku' open with sepals colored brilliant white bordered in rich cerise. As the floral effect matures, the definition between these two colors dims, while melding to enchanting shades of rose-pink.

In foliage as well as flower, *Hydrangea serrata* offers numerous irresistible selections. The leaves of 'Kiyosumi' emerge in tones of rich burgundy, retaining these colors throughout spring and early summer. In near-perfect combination, its flowers open from deep crimson buds, later broadening to heads of startling white picoteed with rose. 'Beni Nishiki' brandishes intensely colored blossoms of cherry red held amidst a flurry of sprightly cream-splashed leaves.

It has been primarily in Japan that I have encountered in the wild one of the hardiest and most handsome of *Hydrangea* species grown in North America and Europe. *Hydrangea paniculata* has a large geographical range from Sakhalin and northeastern China to Taiwan through the entire Japanese Archipelago. The flow-

Hydrangea serrata 'Izu No Hana'. (Photo by Lynne Harrison)

Hydrangea serrata 'Beni Gaku'. (Photo by Lynne Harrison)

The Shrubby Hydrangeas

Hydrangea serrata 'Kiyosumi'. (Photo by Lynne Harrison)

Hydrangea serrata 'Beni Nishiki'. (Photo by Lynne Harrison)

ers, as one would expect, are carried in panicles with a infusion of sterile florets throughout the inflorescence. These are borne at the ends of each branch and are produced on the current year's wood.

In the autumn of 2001, while on the chilly mountain slopes of Mount Daisetsu, I collected seed from specimens of *Hydrangea paniculata* rising to nearly 25 ft. (7.6 m) in height. Charles S. Sargent's collection from Hokkaidō in 1893 resulted in 'Praecox', which blossoms nearly six weeks earlier than the much-celebrated *H. paniculata* 'Grandiflora', while emitting a fragrance that

has been aptly described as a heady infusion of horse and Chanel No. 5. My collections have not proven to be as precocious.

Hydrangea paniculata 'Grandiflora', the so-called pee-gee hydrangea, was imported from Japan in the later years of the 19th century and, with its startling heads of nearly all sterile florets and its tough demeanor, was practically the sole representative of the species in cultivation for about a century. Selected forms such as 'Floribunda', 'Pink Diamond', 'Greenspire', 'Brussel's Lace', and 'Unique' have since grabbed market share. I have not grown the highly touted 'Tardiva', which is reported to blossom much later than the lot, often not commencing until mid-September.

In 1997, on central Honshū southwest of Hasimoto at above 8000 ft. (2400 m), I collected seed from immensely broad thickets of this species, with stems to 15 ft. (4.6 m) in height. These have since flowered, and one clone is particularly magnificent, presenting 18 in. (45 cm) lacy heads of pure white flowers, with a sizeable proportion of sterile florets. Still under evaluation, it probably deserves a name and introduction into the marketplace.

In 1999 and again in the autumn of 2007, our collections of *Hydrangea paniculata* from Taiwan were from plants more demure, 8–10 ft. (2.4–3 m), with foliage of an intriguing bluish green. This comely effect has carried through to the next generation, but the panicles of flowers are disappointingly small, and selection work appears necessary to achieve more in the way of charge from the flowers.

In the southern part of its range, *Hydrangea paniculata* shares digs with a most unusual species. *Hydrangea sikokiana* is scarce in cultivation—virtually unknown in the gardens of Japan—which is surprising when considering its decisively handsome foliage and large white lacecaps to 1 ft. (0.3 m) across. I first observed it in the autumn of 1997 while in the moist, cool highlands of central Honshū on the Kii Peninsula with comrades Bleddyn and Sue Wynn-Jones and *Epimedium* specialist Darrell Probst. Growing on the shore of a rapidly moving mountain stream was a tall shrub with large, felted, light-textured, jagged-edged leaves that appeared superficially similar to those of *H. quercifolia*. As we had, without success, spent more than a week on Shikoku specifically searching for this species and were nearing the end of a second rainy, cool autumn day searching for the same species in this location, I was certain I had found what we sought.

From seed collected at that time, we were able to reintroduce *Hydrangea sikokiana* into cultivation in North America and Europe, although we have received few reports thus far as to how it has fared. It has proven to be a distinctive late-summer-blossoming species in the Pacific Northwest, though somewhat sluggish in growth. I have successfully crossed it with *H. aspera* subsp. *villosa*, to which it is closely related, using *H. aspera* as the female parent. The resultant seedlings do demonstrate

Hydrangea paniculata 'Floribunda'. (Photo by Lynne Harrison)

Hydrangea paniculata 'Unique'. (Photo by Lynne Harrison)

The Shrubby Hydrangeas

some lobing; however, they are still too young to evaluate for garden performance.

Also closely related to *Hydrangea sikokiana*, in the subsection *Asperae*, is one of my favorite Japanese species, *H. involucrata*, which I have encountered on numerous occasions during my travels, most notably in 1995 along the coastal forests of the Chiba Prefecture south of Tokyo. As its specific epithet implies, it sets itself apart from all other species in section *Hydrangea* by possessing involucral bracts that enclose its plump, rounded flower buds before opening. The bracts dehisce as the flattened corymbs of lavender-blue fertile flowers, surrounded by creamy white ray flowers, open. The ovate foliage to 5 in. (12.5 cm) long is held along stems to 12 ft. (3.6 m) tall. There are several forms in cultivation that possess an aberrant doubling of the sepals in the ray flowers, in particular the lovely 'Hortensis',

which also surrenders a greater number of its fertile florets to the cause of ornament. My collections of this species from numerous locales throughout Japan demonstrate a great diversity with regard to height, with one collection barely achieving 3 ft. (0.9 m) after 10 years. It should also be noted that *H. involucrata* resents full-sun situations and should be sited with some overhead protection.

Like *Hydrangea sikokiana*, *H. involucrata* hybridizes readily with *H. aspera*, a complex taxon found in the eastern Himalaya and the mountains of western China south to Taiwan, Java, and Sumatra. I still consider a hybrid between these two raised by friend Mark Fillan of the United Kingdom to be among the most exceptional hydrangeas I have ever grown, and I believe it deserves a cultivar name and wider distribution in commerce.

The handsome, jagged-edged, felted foliage of the rarely cultivated *Hydrangea sikokiana*. (Photo by Daniel J. Hinkley)

Hydrangea sikokiana. (Photo by Daniel J. Hinkley)

A curiously beautiful seedling of *Hydrangea involucrata*, uncharacteristically producing both terminal and axillary cymes, grows in the Belgium garden of Philippe de Spoelberch. (Photo by Daniel J. Hinkley)

Hydrangea involucrata in the Kii Peninsula on Honshū, Japan. (Photo by Daniel J. Hinkley)

Hydrangea involucrata 'Hortensis'. (Photo by Lynne Harrison)

In the same general vicinity where I collected *Hydrangea sikokiana* in 1997, I collected another species that is rarely encountered in the gardens of North America: *H. hirta*. It grew in great abundance here in moderate shade beneath a canopy of deciduous and evergreen trees at approximately 3000 ft. (900 m) elevation. The ovate leaves of this species, to 3 in. (7.5 cm), are very distinct in possessing an extremely dentate leaf margin. In May, profuse terminal flowers of light blue are formed in compact corymbs to 3 in. (7.5 cm) across atop 4 ft. (1.2 m) stems, lacking the expanded sepals on sterile florets that we have come to associate with hydrangeas as a whole. Since my first encounter with the species, I have stumbled upon it in full flower during lovely spring hikes in the marvelous woodlands of Hakone in the vicinity of Mount Fuji. It is not held in very high esteem in most garden literature.

Hydrangea hirta shares some of its Japanese territory with *H. angustipetala*, an upright, shrubby species quite distinctive in foliage. This hydrangea possesses an enormous range of leaf sizes and shapes in any given population, from narrow, lance-shaped leaves with a very jagged leaf margin to ovate, entire leaves. It is this plant, though treated by some as *H. yayeyamensis* and others as *H. scandens* subsp. *chinensis* f. *angustipetala*, that I have observed in blossom in very early spring both on extreme southern Kyūshū and on Yaku Shima further to the south. Specimens from this area are very distinctive, with lancelike, extremely dentate leaves to 4 in. (10 cm) long that appear more like the foliage of a forsythia than a hydrangea. The airy inflorescence is of a

Hydrangea hirta in the wild at moderate elevations north of Nagoya, Japan, blossoming in mid-May. (Photo by Daniel J. Hinkley)

On this collection of *Hydrangea angustipetala* from Taiwan, the characteristic jagged-edged sepals of the sterile florets surround striking chartreuse fertile florets. (Photo by Daniel J. Hinkley)

respectable size, with loose corymbs, to 5 in. (12.5 cm) across, of chartreuse flowers surrounded by scalloped white sepals.

I also cultivate collections of this variable species made in Taiwan in 1999 and again in 2007. These collections represent a wide range of altitudes, from 3000 ft. (900 m) to over 8000 ft. (2400 m), though consistently prove to be an early-blossoming species, with striking white lacecaps showing enormous variability in size and shape produced in April and May. *Hydrangea angustipetala* has become a highly valued component of my garden in Indianola, forming a deciduous shrub to 4 ft. (1.2 m) tall. It is dependably hardy only in zones 6–10.

Having briefly mentioned the taxonomic ambiguity surrounding *Hydrangea angustipetala*, I must enter into the nuclear minefield known as *H. scandens*, another rare species that deserves more recognition than it currently enjoys in the West. This species is represented in herbaria and literature by no fewer than 15 recognized varieties, most of which originated on the mainland of China, though they are certainly represented in the floras of Japan, Taiwan, and the Philippines—a wide range of distribution that translates by default into a nomenclature in a constant state of fusion and fission.

As an umbrella description, *Hydrangea scandens* is indeed a scandent shrub (not to be taken to imply that it is always a prostrate shrub) carrying pairs of linear or lanceolate leaves that may be fully deciduous or semi-evergreen. Like *H. angustipetala*, it blossoms in early spring, from late April to mid-June, and in fact is one of the earliest-blooming hydrangeas, presenting relatively large, white to creamy yellow corymbs of fertile flowers surrounded by highly variable though showy sterile florets.

Our collections of this species from Honshū in 1997 (HC 970561) were from specimens up to 6 ft. (1.8 m) tall. In full-sun situations, the foliage had transformed to lovely tints of burgundy in good complement to the characteristic brownish purple stems. Numerous specimens observed that autumn on both Shikoku and the Kii Peninsula were still in flower and quite handsome,

with quantities of 4 in. (10 cm) corymbs surrounded by the creamy white sepals (later fading to yellow) of the sterile florets.

It is the variably pigmented stem of *Hydrangea scandens* that seems to throw a stick in the spokes when attempting to understand the names of this taxon. Whereas some taxonomists refer the purple-stemmed forms to *H. scandens* subsp. *liukiuensis*, Japanese botanists have erected another species entirely: *H. luteovenosa*.

I cultivate in my garden both a variegated and a double-sepaled form of *Hydrangea scandens*, originating from nurseries in Japan, both of which emit a beguiling fragrance from their precocious blossoms.

The flowers of *Hydrangea luteovenosa* (or *H. scandens* subsp. *liukiuensis*) are beguilingly fragrant for weeks after first opening. (Photo by Daniel J. Hinkley)

The Shrubby Hydrangeas

While on the border of Sichuan and Yunnan in mid-October of 2000, I observed a hydrangea in full blossom at lower elevations, possessing narrow, coriaceous foliage and large, flattened cymes of white flowers surrounded by white florets. This was collected under the numbers 00-0492 and 00-0499 and assigned temporarily to *Hydrangea scandens* subsp. *chinensis*. Thus far this hydrangea has enchanted everyone who has seen it in our garden at Windcliff, where it blossoms very early in spring; however, its name is dubious as best. As a brief aside, confusing even more the taxonomy of the genus, Taiwanese taxonomists refer their endemic form of *H. scandens* to *H. chinensis*. My collection from Sichuan does not in any manner resemble those plants growing on Taiwan.

Considering all of this taxonomic uncertainty, who really knows what *Hydrangea* Bleddyn Wynn-Jones and I collected in the autumn of 1999 on Fan-si-pan, in Vietnam, at elevations over 7000 ft. (2100 m)? It was an evergreen species common on the lower slopes. The lance-shaped leaves to 5 in. (12.5 cm) were glabrous above and a striking purple beneath, while the cymes of white fertile flowers and lavender sepals were quite handsome. It was collected under the number HWJ 99736 and assigned the name *Hydrangea scandens* subsp. *indochinensis*; however, Bleddyn's nursery, Crûg Farm Plants, gives it species rank as *H. indochinensis*. Superficially it resembles *H. scandens* subsp. *lobbii* (sometimes seen as *H. lobbii*), which we observed at lower elevations in Taiwan a month later. I have attempted to grow the latter in our zone 8 woodland, and it has proven too tender; however, it has made a splendid late-winter-flowering addition to the spectacular, kindly climated woodland of Tom and Jo Hudson's garden, Trehegan, near Par, Cornwall, United Kingdom.

It was in Vietnam, also, that we collected *Hydrangea aspera* subsp. *strigosa*. Anyone traveling to the areas of Asia inhabited by this hydrangea, in lower elevations in mountain valleys, will encounter it before any other species, and more frequently. I have seen it in eastern

Hydrangea scandens subsp. *chinensis*. (Photo by Daniel J. Hinkley)

Hydrangea chinensis shows great variation in its natural range throughout northern Vietnam; individuals can be either fully evergreen or deciduous. (Photo by Daniel J. Hinkley)

Nepal at 5900 ft. (1800 m), in Vietnam at 5000 ft. (1550 m), and in Sichuan Province at 3100 ft. (950 m). In addition to its low-elevation digs, it is easily recognized by its very narrow leaves, which are strigose beneath, and by its very late blossoming habit—in fact, when I have observed it in the field it has often still been in blossom in October.

In 1998 I successfully sent cuttings home (DJHC 98464) from a specimen on the lower slopes of Mount Emei that was clinging precariously to a small plot of ground between an asphalt highway and a steep cliff to a river below. I had observed this very same plant in the autumn of 1996, but because of its perilous position was unable to secure material. The plant possessed globose heads nearly entirely comprised of sterile florets. Interestingly, Michael Haworth-Booth reports that Ernest Wilson collected a similar type from Emei in the early years of the 20th century under the number 4902; however, it has apparently been lost to cultivation. I later introduced this plant under the clonal name 'Elegant Sound Pavilion' to commemorate the Buddhist temple near where it grows, and it has proven to be fantastic in effect for zones 7–9, with almost fully sterile floreted cymes opening in chartreuse tones in late summer, ripening to creamy white and later transitioning to lime green. The original plant had been lost to a landslide when I visited Emei in 2008.

It is important to briefly mention two other double forms of this species in cultivation. Darrell Probst sent me cuttings of a double-flowered form he collected in eastern Sichuan, which appears to also be *Hydrangea aspera* subsp. *strigosa*. Interestingly, his form has only partially expanded sepals surrounding the fertile florets, while maintaining the lavender pigment. Though it produces a lovely effect, this flower type is inconsistently presented throughout the shrub.

While traveling in northeastern Sichuan in 2004, Ozzie Johnson encountered another mophead form during our foray into the mountains surrounding Tao Yuan. Though I am not certain, I believe this fits into *Hydrangea aspera* subsp. *villosa*, which, if true, will prove—irri-

tatingly so—to be hardier than 'Elegant Sound Pavilion' despite all of its other substantial ornamental shortcomings and cultural pitfalls (he says with a wicked grin).

It is indeed *Hydrangea aspera* subsp. *villosa*, which represents this species at higher elevations, that can be appreciated in a broader range under cultivation. There are few shrubs as beautiful as this taxon when it flowers in July and August. The leaves indeed possess a velvety villosity, carried along stems to 10 ft. (3 m) and smothered with 10 in. (25 cm) lacecaps of lavender-purple fertile florets surrounded by creamy white ray flowers. The woodland floor where this plant grows is blanketed with

Hydrangea aspera subsp. *strigosa* 'Elegant Sound Pavilion', from my collection from Mount Emei in 1998, puts on a remarkable late-summer showing in my garden at Windcliff. (Photo by Daniel J. Hinkley)

The Shrubby Hydrangeas

a striking purple snow as the petals dehisce during late summer.

My collections of this subspecies (DJHC 636), found in the Wolong area of Sichuan at 9800 ft. (3000 m), have proven to be sensational plants in our garden, with cymes to 1 ft. (0.3 m) across. In 1998 I collected DJHC 98443 from a similar elevation on Mount Emei, describing it as possessing ovate, villous foliage to 8 in. (20 cm) long and 7 in. (18 cm) wide. This collection displays a superb, deeply colored petiole of crimson and is worth cultivating for its foliage alone.

Taking red-infused body parts to a new level, while in Japan in the spring of 2008, I at last encountered a plant I had heard rumors of for numerous years. While visiting Yamaguchi Plantsman's Nursery near Nagoya, I was dumbstruck when faced with a swarthy purple-foliaged form of *Hydrangea aspera* aff. subsp. *villosa*. It was a celebrated plant collected by Mikinori Ogisu, an authority on Chinese plants and a welcoming presence in contemporary horticulture, in Hunan Province, China. Unlike a somewhat similar clone of this species collected and shared with me by plantsman Darrell Probst, of *Epimedium* fame, which possesses an undercarriage of near-iridescent red, this fantastic find exhibits a top blade sensationally infused with pigment. I am certain that nothing in the near future will more enthuse interest in the genetics of the genus *Hydrangea* than this single plant.

Though Elizabeth McClintock chose to reduce *Hydrangea sargentiana* to the subspecies rank of *H. aspera* subsp. *sargentiana* (a name I also use), W. J. Bean provided it species rank, and Hillier Nurseries referred it to a clonal selection, 'Sargentiana'. It was introduced by Ernest Wilson in 1908 from western Hubei Province, an area of China that I have not yet botanized; if any additional collections have been made of this *Hydrangea*, I am unable to verify it.

Hydrangea aspera subsp. *villosa*. (Photo by Lynne Harrison)

But again, with a plant so seductively beautiful, who cares? *Hydrangea aspera* subsp. *sargentiana* chiefly differs from *H. aspera* subsp. *villosa* by possessing what has been well described as a mosslike coating of hairs on its young stems, as well as large, ovate, substantive leaves of deep green surfaced with a seductive, black, velvety indumentum. The cymes, produced in mid- to late summer, are large and flattened, with purple fertile flowers surrounded by sterile flowers having somewhat concave, cream sepals.

I have raised this taxon from seed collected under cultivation and have seen little variation among the progeny, other than a nicely golden-variegated seedling that we have named 'Binti Jua' ("daughter of sunshine"). The species itself is a beautiful addition to the garden, though proper pruning is required in its youth to bring forth its fullest potential; I prefer to plant several of these together on 3 ft. (0.9 m) centers to provide

The sensational purple-foliaged *Hydrangea aspera* aff. subsp. *villosa* was found in central China by Mikinori Ogisu. (Photo by Daniel J. Hinkley)

A particularly fine seedling of *Hydrangea aspera* collected near the summit of Mount Emei in Sichuan Province in 1998. The red-suffused stems and petioles are nearly more striking than the flowers. (Photo by Daniel J. Hinkley)

Hydrangea aspera subsp. *sargentiana*. (Photo by Daniel J. Hinkley)

The Shrubby Hydrangeas

greater visual presence in a much shorter time frame.

On moderate to high elevations in Taiwan, with my friends the Wynn-Joneses, I have collected seed of *Hydrangea aspera* subsp. *kawakamii* that impressed us in both foliage and flower. One particular specimen at 7858 ft. (2395 m) carried felted foliage to 10 in. (25 cm) long and 8 in. (20 cm) wide, while the cymes to 15 in. (38 cm) across were held atop sturdy stems to 20 ft. (6 m) tall. It does not come as a surprise to find that Haworth-Booth described this subspecies as the most spectacularly fine of its subsection.

A specimen of *Hydrangea aspera* subsp. *kawakamii* of unknown provenance growing in my first garden was consistently damaged during severe arctic episodes, despite being grown in our woodland with overhead protection. It may be the circulation of less hardy clones in commerce that has given this form a reputation for tenderness. My own collections, growing in the open at Windcliff, have never been harmed and are, in full blossom late in the season, nothing short of magnificent.

It was not until the autumn of 2000, while north of Baoxing in Sichuan Province at elevations of 6600 ft. (2010 m), that I finally came to grips with a mostly misunderstood taxon known as *Hydrangea longipes*. While hiking through a damp wood in a mostly degraded agricultural area, I came across three specimens of this startling hydrangea, with colossal foliage carried on 1 ft. (0.3 m) petioles. The cordate leaves were 1 ft. (0.3 m) long and 13 in. (33 cm) wide. In the autumn of 2002 in eastern Nepal, the Wynn-Joneses, Jamaica Kincaid, and I found this same species, though at elevations of 8700 ft. (2655 m). In 2006 I observed and collected it at similar elevations in Sikkim, where the Wynn-Joneses have also made separate collections. It has proven to be a marvelous garden addition in regard to both flower and foliage.

Hydrangea aspera subsp. *sargentiana* 'Binti Jua'. (Photo by Daniel J. Hinkley)

Hydrangea aspera subsp. *kawakamii*. (Photo by Daniel J. Hinkley)

In literature *Hydrangea longipes* is frequently confused with a superficial look-alike, *H. robusta*. To my mind, the appearance of this low-elevation (5000 ft. [1500 m]), very late blossoming species could be described as intermediate between *H. aspera* subsp. *sargentiana* and *H. longipes*. It would only be appropriate for cultivation in zone 10 and above.

At moderate to higher elevations in Vietnam, Yunnan, Sichuan, northern India, and eastern Nepal, I have encountered a tough and durable species that remains light years away from being appreciated to the degree it deserves. It is called *Hydrangea heteromalla*, the blanket name for a rather large assemblage of variable ecotypes occurring from the eastern Himalaya through the interior to eastern China. It grows to immense proportions in central and eastern Nepal, where I collected it in 1995 and 2002 under numerous numbers at elevations of 6500–11,500 ft. (2000–3500 m). The leaves of the Himalayan forms are nearly 1 ft. (0.3 m) long, ovate-linear, glabrous above and with adpressed hairs beneath, and perhaps a bit coarse. The inflorescence is a terminal cyme of white fertile flowers and white or pink (or white turning to pink) ray florets.

From my observations, the leaf shape and petiole color change dramatically as one crosses Kanchenjunga from Nepal to Sikkim, with reddish-suffused leaf stems intensifying as one travels further east into China. In western China I have collected numerous forms possessing dark green, nearly orbicular foliage and striking lipstick-red petioles—a far cry from forms in the Himalaya. *Hydrangea heteromalla* 'Bretschneiderii' represents a form collected in the mountains near Peking and possesses a framework with handsome, exfoliating, cinnamon-colored bark, while *H. heteromalla* 'Snowcap' (grown under the name *H. robusta* for many years in England) is touted for its large, cordate foliage and sub-

From seed collected above Baoxing in Sichuan Province, the large-leaved *Hydrangea longipes* now puts on a splendid show in mid-June in my garden. (Photo by Daniel J. Hinkley)

Hydrangea robusta in full blossom in late October at low elevations in northern India. (Photo by Daniel J. Hinkley)

The Shrubby Hydrangeas

stantive, flattened, white cymes. As a whole, the species has yet to find favor in American commerce, where I believe its potential hardiness could expand the utility of the genus across much of the interior Midwest.

I must not forsake those things made in America; after all, though severely limited, our portion of this genus is not without garden worthiness. The North American species, though there are only two, have experienced more than a modicum of acceptance in Western horticulture. *Hydrangea arborescens* is distributed up the East Coast from Florida to New York and west and southwest to Iowa and Louisiana, often found growing under exceptionally shaded conditions. It is a deciduous shrub rising to 10 ft. (3 m) in height, carrying ovate, smart green leaves of a papery texture. The northern populations, though far from awe-inspiring in their pure state, with mostly fertile, dingy white flowers, have infused at least two selections with consider-

able hardiness. *Hydrangea arborescens* 'Grandiflora' and the more compact *H. arborescens* 'Annabelle', both with frilly heads of sterile flowers, begin their blossoming sequence in June with tasteful tones of lime green, later turning pure white, and transitioning again to verdant tones. 'Grandiflora' was the first hydrangea I grew as a young gardener in Michigan's frigid zone 4 interior, where its somewhat sloppy habit of growth was overlooked by the innocent eyes of ignorance. The somewhat stronger-stemmed, later-blossoming 'Annabelle', with flower heads to 1 ft. (0.3 m) across, was selected at the University of Illinois by J. C. McDaniel. It has justifiably superceded 'Grandiflora' in commerce and is one of the top-selling North American shrubs of all time.

Breeding work instigated by Richard Olsen in 2005 after he found a pink-flowered form of *Hydrangea arborescens* in the wild, and later carried to completion by Tom Ranney and others of North Carolina State Uni-

With a wide natural range of distribution comes a great deal of variability. This photo of *Hydrangea heteromalla* was taken at moderate elevations in Vietnam near the border with China. (Photo by Daniel J. Hinkley)

A particularly good form of *Hydrangea heteromalla* raised from seed I collected on Cang Shan in Yunnan Province in 1998. (Photo by Daniel J. Hinkley)

versity by using Olsen's 'Wesser Falls' and Don Jacob's 'Eco Pink Puff', resulted at long last in a pink-flowered 'Annabelle'. More than one talented breeding program has had their eye on this prize, however, as nearly concurrent with this long-awaited breakthrough was Michael Dirr's announcement of his own fully double pink form. Though neither has been released to the public, and comparisons have not been made, these will certainly provide another chapter in the appreciation of this sincerely American species.

In the southern Appalachians, *Hydrangea arborescens* subsp. *radiata* makes up for an all-around lackluster floral display with foliage undersurfaced with a brilliant white indumentum—best displayed by placement atop embankments or retaining walls. It is one of my favorite hydrangeas and deserves much greater recognition. I have observed it along the Blue Ridge in western North Carolina, with my friend Richard Olsen in tow. We puzzled over the delineation of this variety from *H. arborescens* subsp. *discolor*, also known to possess foliage with a white undersurface. The latter is poorly represented in cultivation, known by the better-known cultivar 'Sterilis', with frosty heads of mostly sterile florets.

The Cherokee, and later the early European settlers, were known to have used *Hydrangea arborescens* medicinally for the treatment of kidney stones. Modern-day analysis of this species has shown the presence of a cyanogenic glycoside called hydrangin. Poisonings from hydrangeas are rare, although there are reports of serious effects from ingestion by horses.

The oakleaf hydrangea, *Hydrangea quercifolia*, has experienced a prolonged rise to favor among this continent's horticulturists in the landscapes of zones 5–9 where it can be grown. Plantsman and superstar Michael Dirr is probably responsible for much of this reborn interest due to his selection work at the University of Georgia. Though *H. quercifolia* is one of only two *Hydrangea* species possessing flowers borne in panicles rather than corymbs, it is its foliage that sets it apart. Very leathery in texture, the boldly lobed, jagged-edged leaves to 8 in. (20 cm) long do indeed resemble those

A pink-flowering mophead seedling of *Hydrangea arborescens*, from Dr. Michael Dirr's breeding program. (Photo by Ozzie Johnson)

Hydrangea arborescens subsp. *radiata*. (Photo by Daniel J. Hinkley)

Foliage of *Hydrangea arborescens* subsp. *radiata*. (Photo by Daniel J. Hinkley)

Hydrangea quercifolia. (Photo by Lynne Harrison)

of a red oak and develop intense, prolonged tones of glossy burgundy in autumn. This species is native to the Gulf States, and I have seen it growing in Mississippi in semishaded sites with more than adequate water, though in cultivation it appears to tolerate a great deal of drought when established. Dirr recommends always providing *H. quercifolia* a modicum of protection from full sun, but this does not seem to be the case in the Pacific Northwest, where it becomes annoyingly rangy, with leaves that are adamant in their refusal to develop autumn tones or tidily undress in late autumn.

Hydrangea Cultural Information

SOIL: Hydrangeas thrive in a wide range of soil types but in the wild are generally found in woodland situations with humus-rich, well-drained soil. Flower color and intensity often depend on soil pH, which can be adjusted if you have either moderately acidic or moderately alkaline soil. If you want darker, blue-purple flowers, make the soil more acidic by incorporating a generous amount of peat moss before planting. Lighter colors of pink can be achieved by adding lime, approximately two cups per planting hole, to make the soil more alkaline. It does take time for either application to change the soil pH, and colors may also change on hydrangeas that have been recently transplanted; manure with patience in these instances. Please note that many *Hydrangea* cultivars are stable in color and will not change, or will change only slightly, if the pH is adjusted. It is also important to understand that soils that are very acidic (below 5.5) or very alkaline (above 7.0) are virtually impossible to modify enough to change the color of any hydrangea. If you are not content with the colors that result in such instances, you can grow the hydrangea in a container, allowing for total control of the soil pH.

FERTILIZER: A correct fertilizer program for your hydrangeas will not only assure more robust and healthier plants but will also aid in color intensity. For the best blues, apply a nitrate-based, rather than an ammonium-based, fertilizer, with an NPK ratio of 25-5-30.

Even better blues can be achieved with a yearly application of aluminum sulfate, available through garden centers (follow application rates carefully!). Avoid using bone meal or superphosphate when planting. For the best pinks and reds, use a nitrate-based fertilizer with an NPK ratio of 25-10-10. Or if all of this is too complicated, just plant 'em and enjoy 'em. You generally will not be disappointed.

WATER: Provide regular supplemental water during their first two years in the garden, and during dry spells thereafter. Literature often claims that hydrangeas are drought tolerant, but my experience with these remarkable plants does not lend much credence to the claim.

LIGHT: In cooler climates such as the Pacific Northwest, hydrangeas can be grown in full sun and will be none the worse for wear. In warmer climates, however, they must be protected from hot sun and drying winds or they will become leaf-scorched and unsightly. The best of all worlds is a bright situation under trees or on the north side of a house. Too dark a situation will not promote strong flowering, and brighter conditions will cause plants to become dense and stiff, while slightly shaded sites allow hydrangeas to become more lax and, in my opinion, assume more grace. In my experience in the Pacific Northwest, *Hydrangea quercifolia* should be planted in full sun or very lightly shaded positions rather than in the shade, as recommended by Dirr and others for gardens in summer-warm climates. *Hydrangea macrophylla* is more sun tolerant than *H. serrata*. *Hydrangea aspera* and its relatives will burn if provided too much direct sun.

PRUNING: This is difficult to get a handle on at first, as every *Hydrangea* species responds a little differently to pruning. Pruning can be performed right after flowering and certainly no later than early spring.

Hydrangea macrophylla, H. quercifolia, some *H. serrata*: The flowers appear *mostly* on stems produced during the previous growing season. Thusly, if you shear your plants in early spring to make a balanced plant or

to keep it in bounds, you will be removing virtually all flower buds for that year. It is better to entirely remove older branches that have already blossomed and leave younger, strong stems that have yet to produce blossoms. If these younger stems are multibranched, remove some of the branches to create fewer flowers and consequently less weight, which tends to pull the plant apart. Cultivars differ in this regard; each will tell you what it needs as it matures and blossoms in your garden. *Hydrangea serrata* is intermediate; some forms blossom on the current year's wood, others on the second year's growth.

Hydrangea angustipetala, H. arborescens, H. heteromalla, H. hirta, H. luteovenosa, H. paniculata, H. scandens, some *H. serrata*: These species blossom on the current season's growth, making it possible to prune severely and still have flowers produced that year. During the first few years, simply remove the flowering heads directly above a strong bud. As the plant grows taller, reduce its size as needed.

Hydrangea aspera and relatives: These respond to heavy pruning for the first three years after planting. Though they do not blossom during this time, many more branches are produced at ground level, ultimately forming a much fuller and more pleasing specimen.

Hydrangea anomala, H. integrifolia, H. seemannii, H. serratifolia: The vining hydrangeas and their close relative are self-clinging and will not generally need pruning beyond an occasional deadheading.

Growing Hydrangeas in Containers

Those gardening in less benign climates will be pleased to know that hydrangeas respond very well to pot culture. A gallon-sized plant should be moved directly into a 15- to 25-gallon (57- to 95-liter) container using a bark-based soilless compost, which can be purchased through gardening centers. Move the containers onto an unheated porch, garage, or greenhouse during the winter season, protecting them only during the coldest temperatures. Fertilize and water as for plants grown in the ground, and replace the compost every three years or as needed.

Looking Up: The Climbing Hydrangeas

Though for the past week I've been without virtually a soul to communicate with, I have been so overwhelmed by the incomparable richness of this island, both culturally and botanically, that not for an instant have I felt alone. I am absolutely knackered tonight, having set out before dark on the first boat of the morning, which dropped me on the far side of the island, about one and a half hours of sailing time. The journey was not particularly comfortable: a gale blew in overnight, and the sea was very choppy, and the passenger cabin was suffused with the cloying presence of squid and diesel oil.

By 7:30 a.m. the sun was up, with blue skies and a refreshing breeze, and I was already in rich oak woodland with incredible views to the surrounding waters and the smaller island of Jukdo. I collected seed of large specimens of Camellia japonica *with enormous red fruit that I was certain, from a distance, were in fact flowers.* Acer pictum subsp. okamotoanum *was also in seed, and its large leaves held by enormously long petioles, in this wind, could be easily identified from a considerable distance.* Sorbus commixta *and* Fagus multinervis *were also present and in ripened fruit.*

I reached the summit of Seonginbong (about 3300 ft.) at 1:00 p.m. and had lunch, already with 30 collections for the day. Herbaceous plants included Campanula takesimana *(fairly common in bright open areas),* Lilium hansonii, *and* Hepatica maxima. *Of the latter, I was very glad to have found it in perfect ripeness of fruit and spent considerable time harvesting the seed.*

By 2:00 p.m. I was getting distant views of Dodong and kicking myself for not having brought enough water; it was much warmer once on the leeward side of the mountain. I came upon a clearing of naturally felled trees with a tangle of vine covering their fallen trunks and found growing in one incongruous tangle Actinidia polygama, Hydrangea anomala, *and* Schizophragma hydrangeoides. *Of the latter two, I was surprised—and I cannot say exactly why—that two such closely related allies would be competing for the same habitat, with such similarity in form and flower.*

The distance was deceiving, and I was slower getting down than I had expected, finally cresting the hill above town and breaking into the open just as the ambient light was becoming too low for comfortable hiking. I was very glad for my tardiness, despite my thirst, as the fleet of squid boats were heading to sea for the night, like a thousand flashing stars against a blue-black sky.

Dodong harbor
Ulleung Island, South Korea
September 23, 1993

South Korea's Ulleung Island is isolated enough from the mainland to have developed a distinctive flora of its own. (Photo by Daniel J. Hinkley)

I CANNOT THINK OF ANY FINER and more widely applicable deciduous vine than *Hydrangea anomala*. A well-grown specimen of this species in blossom in June, with a shag of lacey white heads held amidst glossy, deep green foliage in hard shade, is difficult to improve upon. Further, this is a scene I have admired in gardens across North America, from hypothermic zone 4 in Vermont to zone *whatever* in Southern California (I would prefer not to know).

In the same manner as the shrubby hydrangeas, taxonomists have delineated the climbing species into two sections that divide the deciduous species from the evergreens, with the evergreens further split into two subsections. Though the one deciduous species, *Hydrangea anomala*, is well known, if perhaps not well named, by the horticultural community at large, the evergreen species chiefly fly below the radar but for three species with which some gardeners in zones 8–12 have become better acquainted. As with the shrubby hydrangeas, not all climbing species possess sterile florets surrounding the central disk of fertile flowers. When present, the four expanded sepals readily distinguish the hydrangea from the closely related genus *Schizophragma* with its single, large, tear-shaped bract.

From a distance at least, the taxonomy of *Hydrangea anomala* appears fairly straightforward, though I have found a surfeit of pitfalls here if one loiters too long. The subsection is segregated from other hydrangeas by its unique jettisoning of the corona (flower petals) in one bonnetlike structure.

I have observed *Hydrangea anomala* subsp. *anomala* and *H. anomala* subsp. *petiolaris* in the wild in numerous localities, collected seed, and grown the resulting seedlings. Though there is no question that there are enormous differences between the two—and provenance should indeed govern exactly what taxon is grown where under cultivation—these differences do not seem extraordinary when considering their expansive natural range.

The most northerly of the two, and thus presumably the hardiest, is *Hydrangea anomala* subsp. *petio-laris*. It is under this name that the preponderance of all climbing hydrangeas are grown in North America and Europe, whether or not the name has been legitimately applied. This hydrangea hails from Sakhalin in northeastern Russia through the Japanese Archipelago extending southward to Taiwan. It was common to encounter it during my time botanizing Korea, the central highlands of Hokkaidō, Honshū, Kyūshū, Shikoku, Yaku Shima, and the north-central part of the Central Mountain Range of Taiwan. Interestingly, in Taiwan it sprawled over stumps and up trees amidst the stems of *Schizophragma integrifolium*, rather than alongside *S. hydrangeoides* as on Ulleung Island. On more than one occasion I have admired the shine of this vine's golden autumn foliage as it climbed high into the overstory on virtually every available tree trunk, often appearing through the fog as gilded columns.

It is important to note that the southerly populations of the species tend toward a smaller, more glabrous leaf often suffused with a great deal of red pigmentation. This color can translate into the ray flowers as well, providing an overall light pink cast to the inflorescence, especially so when first expanding. My seed collections from Taiwan express this trait—along with a noted degree of tenderness—as have the wild collections of Bleddyn and Sue Wynn-Jones, who have put the name 'Crûg Coral' to an exceptional form of *Hydrangea anomala* subsp. *glabra* collected from the Central Mountain Range of Taiwan.

After nearly two centuries under cultivation, and no departure from the norm with regard to foliage, it is rather bizarre that two nearly identical golden-variegated sports occurred spontaneously at virtually the same time on both coasts of North America. *Hydrangea anomala* subsp. *petiolaris* 'Mirranda' and 'Firefly' each possess orbicular foliage that is nearly identically yellow-margined. Though their entrance into commerce produced all the noise that might have been expected, I have thus far been discontented with the lack of vigor they demonstrate in the garden, at least in the cool climate of the Pacific Northwest.

Cheju is a large volcanic outcrop approximately 50 nautical miles from the southern tip of the Korean Peninsula. It boasts a large inventory of endemic species in addition to sharing a number of species exclusively with the Japanese Archipelago directly to the south. Geologically it seems a somewhat bizarre mongrel, a cross between tropical Fiji and the Salisbury Plain of England, with tidy rock walls surrounding mossy green pastures and numerous volcanic cones that rise from the flattened landscape like druid mounds. Among the endemic species that grow here, so-called *Hydrangea quelpartensis*, a deciduous climbing species, is frequently found clambering up the oaks and pines in the

Hydrangea anomala subsp. *petiolaris*. (Photo by Daniel J. Hinkley)

In the mountains above Nagano, Japan, at moderate elevations, both *Hydrangea anomala* subsp. *petiolaris* and *Schizophragma hydrangeoides*—with leaves just emerging—grow side by side. (Photo by Daniel J. Hinkley)

Hydrangea anomala subsp. *petiolaris*

Looking Up: The Climbing Hydrangeas

dry woodlands of the volcanic slopes. I do not believe it to have any botanical standing, despite the fact that I have collected seed under this name while on Cheju and purchased plants under this name while in Europe. The claim that it possesses foliage one-quarter the size of *H. anomala* subsp. *petiolaris* can be attributed entirely, it seems, to juvenility.

I find it important to bring this rather esoteric fact to the fore due to my culpability in distributing a deciduous self-clinging vine for several years under the name *Schizophragma hydrangeoides* 'Brookside Littleleaf', having received it under this name from J. C. Raulston in North Carolina, who in turn had received it from Brookside Gardens in Maryland near Baltimore. After numerous years of climbing a tree in the garden, by which time it proved itself quite capable of producing entirely normal-sized leaves, it blossomed, authenticating itself as *Hydrangea anomala*.

It is of some interest to note that in Paris in 1922, Henri Cayeux exhibited a cross he had created between *Hydrangea anomala* subsp. *petiolaris* and *H. macrophylla* var. *rosea*, showing intermediate traits between the two. All plants of *H.* ×*hortentiolaris* were reportedly destroyed by the bombardment of Le Havre at the end of World War II.

Hydrangea anomala subsp. *anomala*, too, is quite commonly encountered in the mountains of western China and the eastern Himalaya, and as with its more coastal counterpart, demonstrates a great deal of variability. I have collected seed of this species above 7500 ft. (2300 m) in central and eastern Nepal and from similar elevations in Sikkim, where the foliage is glossy and appears to be winter retentive. At slightly higher elevations in Sichuan and on Cang Shan in Yunnan, the large lacey heads of flowers are carried among foliage that is more matte green and that is completely shed in autumn.

Hydrangea anomala subsp. *anomala* came from an individual that I noted as having very lustrous foliage and cymes to 10 in. (25 cm) across. It has maintained this beautiful foliage in the garden setting, but unfortunately has attempted to keep its leaves during winter and

Hydrangea anomala subsp. *anomala* growing on old-growth *Tsuga dumosa* in far western Sichuan Province. (Photo by Daniel J. Hinkley)

The lustrous foliage of *Hydrangea anomala* subsp. *anomala*. (Photo by Daniel J. Hinkley)

demonstrates some dieback after sharp freezes. Crûg Farm Plants in Wales has introduced a fully evergreen form collected in Sikkim as *H. anomala* subsp. *anomala* 'Winter Glow'; though indeed a handsome foliage plant, it is probably not applicable to more inhospitable climates.

Finally now, with numerous collections having been made of this continental counterpart, with known provenance, a comparative evaluation of the differences exhibited in cultivation is underway, though it will be many years before details about blossoming habit and hardiness are forthcoming.

Before moving on to the evergreen species, a brief note on another taxon that is quite perplexing. In one of the countless boxes of plants I received from J. C. Raulston over the years was a deciduous vine labeled *Schizophragma corylieum*. It had very distinctive, large, ovate, felted foliage, somewhat reminiscent of *S. integrifolium*, and we distributed it under the name *S. corylieum* for over a decade, though it had not blossomed by the time the garden closed in 2006 (the *Flora of China* [Wu et al. 1994 to present] does indeed include *S. corylifolium*, from Anhui and Zhejiang Provinces).

In late 2006 I came upon large, blossoming specimens of this very same plant for sale at a well-respected garden center in Seattle, appearing in foliage identical to my garden clone. Though it was exciting to see this in blossom for the first time, it was indisputably a hydrangea, with each ray flower possessing four small, white, expanded sepals. Now widely propagated and distributed under the erroneous name under which I distributed it, it will assuredly take decades to clarify the matter. It may ultimately be proven that this taxon is simply exhibiting further variation held within the ranks of *Hydrangea anomala*.

The evergreen climbing hydrangeas, which self-adhere to trees or rocky surfaces through the same adventitious roots found in the deciduous species, occur naturally, but for one exception, entirely in the New World, ranging from Mexico to southern Chile.

I will begin with the exception to the rule. *Hydrangea integrifolia*, one of the finest vines I grow, is the only evergreen climbing species of *Hydrangea* to occur in the Eastern Hemisphere. I first happened upon it as a scrambling terrestrial specimen in the garden of Marlee Hedges in Edmonds, Washington, in the late 1980s, and the oldest specimen in my garden originates from the cuttings she offered me at that time; its provenance is certainly lost.

Much later, in 1999 and again in 2007, I collected seed of this species on Tayuanshan as well as Yü Shan in Taiwan at elevations over 8000 ft. (2400 m), where it is frequently seen climbing 50 ft. (15 m) or more into trees as well as adhering to shaded, rocky outcroppings. Occurring in the Philippines in addition to Taiwan, it is a remarkably hardy and durable species that has only recently found itself in wider cultivation in milder climates of North America and Europe.

Hydrangea integrifolia. (Photo by Daniel J. Hinkley)

Looking Up: The Climbing Hydrangeas

The leaves of *Hydrangea integrifolia*, to 6 in. (15 cm) long, are deep green, linear-ovate, very leathery in texture, and held in pairs along the stems by way of a richly hued red petiole. In late June, terminal cymes of white flowers open from buds that are curious in appearance but that also conjure a bit more expectation than is warranted. As the attending bracts fall and the flowers expand, for a short period it appears as if large popcorn balls have been stashed among the greenery. When the flowers are fully expanded, however, the effect is much like the better-known deciduous species while generally, not always, lacking the outer row of sterile florets. Specimens grown under too much shade produce a paucity of flowers.

Hydrangea seemannii, even in shade, has been anything but reticent to blossom in our woodland, now smothered on a yearly basis with flattened cymes of creamy white flowers without ray florets. It is very closely allied to *H. integrifolia* despite the enormous range differential. *Hydrangea seemannii* occurs naturally in the mountains of southwestern Mexico in the Sierra Madre Occidental at approximate elevations of 7000–8000 ft. (2100–2400 m); in fact, it is the only member of the genus to occur within the political boundaries of this country. The leaves on the clone that we grow are broadly ovate, to 6 in. (15 cm) long and 2 in. (5 cm) wide, and extremely glossy on the upper surface. The plant is vigorous in growth and climbed more than 35 ft. (11 m) in our woodland in fewer than 10 years.

Hydrangea asterolasia is the only other American species in this subsection to possess flowers of white rather than pink. It occurs naturally from Costa Rica south to the Andes of Ecuador and Columbia. The ovate foliage of the clone that we once cultivated, from wild-collected Ecuadorian stock, was broadly ovate and coriaceous to 4 in. (10 cm) long, while both the new stems and leaf petioles were coated in a characteristic brownish tomentum. Though I have traveled through the mountains of Costa Rica where this species is reported to occur, my only horticultural experience with it has been through the young specimen we integrated into our woodland garden, which did not survive the winter of 2003–2004.

While in Costa Rica, however, I delighted in encountering my first pink-flowered, evergreen, climbing

Hydrangea integrifolia flower bud. (Photo by Daniel J. Hinkley)

Hydrangea seemannii. (Photo by Daniel J. Hinkley)

Hydrangea species, both along the canopy walks of Monteverde and at high elevations of the Cordillera de Talamanca south of San José. Though I presumed these plants to be *H. peruviana*, subsequent reading suggested that they were one of two very closely related species that occur in the same geographical range.

Hydrangea oerstedii and *H. peruviana* both possess very showy cymes of pink, fertile flowers surrounded by large, sterile florets. The difference between the two is based entirely upon the length of the stamen, and this difference may not stand the test of time as more material becomes available for study. Since the plants I observed were in full flower, in February, I was unable to gather seed, but during subsequent trips to the Cerro de la Muerte, including a trip in the winter of 2008, I successfully imported cuttings for trial. *Hydrangea* aff. *peruviana* will assuredly not be hardy for us in the Pacific Northwest, though it might be an exciting landscape addition for northern California. Through genetics it might also offer an opportunity to create a truly hardy pink-flowering hybrid.

Elizabeth McClintock's monograph retains three additional species in this subsection: *Hydrangea preslii*, *H. diplostemona*, and *H. steyermarkii*. All three reportedly possess pink flowers and naturally occur from Guatemala south to the Andes of Ecuador, Columbia, and Peru, though I have no personal experience with these species to offer.

Hydrangea serratifolia has purchased a rather schizophrenic episode in taxonomy, though as is always the case, this malady originates not from the plant itself but from the progenitor of its name. The young J. D. Hooker, having come upon this liana in Chile in 1833, placed it in a new genus, *Cornidia*, while tagging on an apt specific epithet, *integerrima*, which translates to "smooth" or "entire." Indeed, the leathery, ovate, matte green leaves of this species, to 4 in. (10 cm) long, do not possess the degree of jag found on the other evergreen species I have observed. Never mind the fact that the name *H. integerrima* might be confused with *H. integrifolia*; this is a conflict that mature gardeners could have coped with.

Hydrangea peruviana blossoming along a stream at high elevations south of San José, Costa Rica. (Photo by Daniel J. Hinkley)

My seed collection of *Hydrangea serratifolia* from southern Chile growing on a stump at Windcliff. (Photo by Daniel J. Hinkley)

Looking Up: The Climbing Hydrangeas

Exactly why, however, this species consummated its classification with exactly the opposite and erroneous reference will never be fully understood. Nonetheless, the accepted name of this hydrangea with smooth-margined leaves, *Hydrangea serratifolia*, conjures forth an image of dentation that does not actually exist!

In the southern Andes in 1998, Kevin Carrabine, Jennifer Macuiba, and I encountered this species growing upward of 60 ft. (18 m) along the main trunk of a *Nothofagus*, while later observing it upward of 100 ft. (30 m) in mammoth specimens of *Eucryphia cordifolia*. We were able to collect its seed from the large heads of flowers only in instances when its host tree had retired to a decidedly less intimidating horizontal stance on the floor of the Alercean rain forest.

The species has flourished in my garden, ascending to 40 ft. (12 m) in less than a decade along the main trunk of a second-growth Douglas fir. Admittedly it has not yet put on a stupendous performance with regard to floral effects, but I have no doubt that it will do this in time.

Literature cites three species closely related to *Hydrangea serratifolia*, all from the mountains of northwestern South America. *Hydrangea tarapotensis* is noted from the Andes of Colombia, Bolivia, and Peru at 3000–5000 ft. (900–1500 m). *Hydrangea felskii* is found in the Andes of southern Ecuador and northern Peru at 6500 ft. (2000 m). *Hydrangea mathewsii* was first collected in the Andes of northern Peru at an unknown altitude.

HARDINESS: *Hydrangea anomala* subsp. *petiolaris*, from northerly latitudes, is appropriate for zones 4–10, and certainly some forms of *H. anomala* subsp. *anomala* possess similar hardiness. The evergreen species are not nearly as forgiving, with none appropriate below zone 7.

CULTIVATION: Assuredly there will be appropriate questions raised in the Pacific Northwest about introducing another tree-climbing evergreen into a region where *Hedera helix* has done such considerable damage. Though I have seen a few self-sown seedlings of *Hydrangea seemannii*, these have been very few and far between. Additionally, with regard to the health of the host tree, hydrangeas do not "crown out" as do hederas—that is, the upwardly mobile stems stay adhered primarily to the main trunk, eliminating the potential for a sail effect and avoiding compromising the health of the tree through reduction of photosynthesis.

These will all require patience. As the adage goes, the first year it sleeps, the second it creeps, and the third it leaps. In the case of climbing hydrangeas, they sleep for a year or two longer. This is often due to gardeners assuming they must site their plant immediately adjacent to the trunk of the selected host tree. (Obviously, climbing hydrangeas are also appropriate for use on trellises and walls.) It is perfectly acceptable to plant further away, where more friable soil can be found, and let the vine grow to its support.

It is also acceptable to use a climbing species to conceal a stump (or sundry debris) or to grow as a freestanding shrub; though these will want to escape laterally, regular pruning will encourage them to build upon themselves.

Moderately moist but well-draining soils are best. The heaviest blossoming will occur under the brightest conditions, though an acceptable performance can be had without any direct sunlight.

PROPAGATION: Hydrangea seeds are minute and will easily cross-contaminate nearby pots, so consider sowing them far from the propagation area. Seeds sown in autumn will germinate readily in spring.

Though the presence of adventitious roots on the stems of the climbing species might seem to present the opportunity to simply remove a piece at any time with success, this is not the case. Softwood cuttings of the deciduous species are most successful taken early in the season and rooted under mist. The evergreen species should be taken as semihardwood cuttings in late autumn and placed on bottom heat. Older established plants will proffer self-layered stems that can easily be removed and transplanted in late winter.

Family Gathering: *Hydrangea* Relatives

Today it rained all day and was miserably cold. It started poorly when Bleddyn, irritated that I was taking precious moments attending to a three-legged dog, backed the car over Sue's foot. She was in pain and did not get out of the car all day. In a dense fog that morning our eyes had been drawn to a macaque stealing a large head of cabbage from a farmer's field above Tyuling. In the cloud that hung above this mountain, the monkey first appeared to be a grown man working frantically to harvest his cabbages before some dread would befall his land. We all got a good laugh when it dawned on us all at once what it was we were seeing. At 11:30, Mrs. Yu happened upon us on the road near the pass, and we headed down to the village to have lunch together. I had warm soup in a Styrofoam bowl with tasteless buds of daylily floating atop. Sadly, the village is filled with mangy, starving dogs, none of which still have four limbs.

After lunch we climbed back to the summit, where we collected sodden heads of Schizophragma integrifolium var. fauriei (DJHT 99160) and Pileostegia viburnoides (DJHT 99159), both covering the same rocky hillside as Hydrangea integrifolia (DJHT 99134), while often climbing trees with their stems comingled. I am very pleased with both collections from this altitude. Bleddyn and I were soaked to the skin, but neither of us wished to be the first to suggest bagging it for the day. I turned us back at 4:30 p.m., much to Sue's pleasure and to Bleddyn's mock disdain.

We are currently holed up in a hostel with no heat and lukewarm water. Everything in my world is wet, and my wads of saturated seed heads are scattered about the room, looking like some horrid experiment in germ warfare. We are an oddity here. The entire cafeteria went quiet and stared when we entered, and all studied us as our meal was served to see if we would pass muster with chopsticks; they all seemed rather disappointed that we did not drop the first piece of bony chicken into our laps.

Taipingshan, Taiwan
November 4, 1999

D URING THE SUMMER OF 2007, while attending the first-ever International Hydrangea Conference in Ghent, Belgium, I was made aware of how precisely dynamic the world of plant taxonomy has become, when papers read on the DNA analysis of members of the Hydrangeaceae suggested a major lumping of woody as well as herbaceous genera into the genus *Hydrangea*. Vanquished would be many genera names I had reserved space for in my ever-diminishing gray matter, while other familiar shrubby taxa, such as *Jamesia*, *Carpenteria*, *Philadelphus*, and *Deutzia*, would come under the greatly expanded umbrella of this family. Most interesting to me was that it was now believed that the entire family probably evolved under xeric con-

Overleaf: My 1993 collection of *Schizophragma hydrangeoides* from South Korea, blossoming for the first time in 2005. (Photo by Daniel J. Hinkley)

190

ditions and that the hydrangea family was very closely allied to the Loasaceae. (This latter tidbit will only prove interesting to those who have had the misfortune of brushing against the foliage of *Loasa triphylla* var. *volcanica* in the southern Andes, causing outrageously painful eruptions on the skin.)

I appreciate what taxonomists bring to our understanding of the world about us, but in numerous ways such drastic amalgamations hinder the ability of seat-of-the-pants gardeners to communicate with one another. For the purposes of this book, I will discuss the following genera using the currently, perhaps diminishing, accepted nomenclature.

Schizophragma

Being superficially very close to the climbing hydrangeas, *Schizophragma* differs primarily by the presence of one large, tear-shaped, petaloid sepal associated with the sterile florets around the perimeter of the corymb. In ornamental value, the flowers of *Schizophragma* offer a greater presence to the shaded garden, while selection work within the genus has offered at least two highly recommended and distinctive cultivars from one of the two species, *S. hydrangeoides*.

It was this species that I first observed in the wild on Ulleung Island in the Sea of Japan in 1993. There it grew together with its superficial look-alike, *Hydrangea anomala* subsp. *petiolaris*. That such two seemingly identically equipped species would coevolve for adaptation to precisely the same habitat seems quite odd to me, although I will admit to not having studied their pollination ecology, which may indeed explain the reason for the redundancy.

The foliage of *Schizophragma* does indeed differ considerably from that of *Hydrangea*, and after a few encounters one can distinguish between the two quite easily without having to search for their flowers, fresh or dry, which quickly surrender their identities. The orbicular leaves to 3 in. by 3 in. (7.5 cm by 7.5 cm) possess a dentate edge, while there is a varying degree of silver

veining on the upper surface. This trait, in its extreme, was the basis for selecting *S. hydrangeoides* 'Moonlight', which offers a very pleasing folial effect of bright mercurial variegation. When this plant is grown in a darkened situation on the north side of a building or up the trunk of a moderate- to large-sized tree, the showing of luminescent foliage is quite significant.

A well-grown specimen in full blossom is sensational and is taken a step further in *Schizophragma hydrangeoides* 'Roseum', with flowers that emerge with moderate pigmentation of red, fading rather quickly to a light pink. My experience with this pink-flowered form thus far in my garden suggests that it possesses significantly less vigor in growth than the standard species I grow; however, this may be due to the gardener and not the plant.

As a quick aside, in 2008 I acquired a very handsome variegated form of this species at a specialist nurs-

Schizophragma hydrangeoides. (Photo by Daniel J. Hinkley)

Schizophragma hydrangeoides 'Moonlight'.
(Photo by Lynne Harrison)

Schizophragma integrifolium var. *fauriei*.
(Photo by Daniel J. Hinkley)

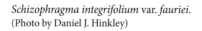

Schizophragma hydrangeoides 'Moonlight'.
(Photo by Daniel J. Hinkley)

A single sterile floret from the immense heads of *Schizophragma megalocarpum* in Sichuan Province. (Photo by Daniel J. Hinkley)

ery south of Tokyo. Each leaf is bright, splashed with both pink and creamy white, and possesses, thus far, an encouraging degree of vigor. Several other variegated forms of this species exist in specialty collections in Japan.

While in Taiwan in 1999, I encountered for the first time *Schizophragma integrifolium*, which, interestingly, grew side by side with *Hydrangea integrifolia* at elevations just above 6500 ft. (2000 m). Taiwanese botanists suggest this should be given the varietal rank of *S. integrifolium* var. *fauriei* to distinguish it from continental populations. I have also collected a superficially similar species, *S. megalocarpum*, above Baoxing in Sichuan Province with Bleddyn Wynn-Jones, where it also grew with what we believed to be *H. integrifolia*, both covering a substantial rocky cliff.

The foliage and flower of *Schizophragma integrifolium* is as distinctive as it is highly ornamental, considered by many to be the loveliest of the temperate lianas. Each cordate leaf, 4 in. by 4 in. (10 cm by 10 cm), possesses an overlay of grayish green tomentum with a rosy cast, a feature most apparent upon emergence in spring. It has been my experience that this new growth is highly seductive to slugs arising from winter's torpor, which will devastate young plants. In midsummer, corymbs of creamy white flowers are surrounded by sterile florets possessing a single large, ivory, tear-shaped sepal. I have this collection in fine form in my garden in Indianola, where after seven years it has reached nearly 30 ft. (9 m) on a trunk of *Abies grandis*.

With seven other species, all in China, the genus possesses greater breadth than most realize, a fact brought home in 2008 when I collected two additional and variable species from the mountains of northwestern Sichuan. Over time, hopefully, an opportunity will present itself to observe these in the wild or trial them under cultivation for garden worthiness.

HARDINESS: *Schizophragma hydrangeoides* is hardy in zones 4–12, using success with *Hydrangea anomala* as a general guide to suitability. Being of a more south-erly distribution and of relatively low elevation, *S. integrifolium* possesses distinctly less hardiness and is appropriate only in mild, temperate areas.

CULTIVATION: Grow as per the climbing hydrangeas, in bright shade and draining yet moderately moist soils or provided occasional supplemental water during dry periods in summer. I have not witnessed any attempt to grow *Schizophragma* as a freestanding shrub, though certainly by choice or circumstance it has been done; I cannot envision any reason it would not be successful. Care should be taken to protect members of this genus from slug damage in early spring.

PROPAGATION: Though seed is certainly a viable method, and one that should be handled as per *Hydrangea*, the most practical method of propagation, and of course the mandatory method for the selected forms, is by softwood cuttings after hardening under mist. The window of opportunity for success is quite limited as soon as the new growth begins to harden off in early summer.

Pileostegia viburnoides

In 1999 and again in 2007, Bleddyn Wynn-Jones and I found specimens of the monotypic, evergreen climber known as *Pileostegia viburnoides* growing at the same elevation as the Taiwanese species of *Schizophragma* and climbing *Hydrangea*, though it also extended to somewhat lower elevations.

I had first come to admire the genus during my frequent visits with the late Gerald Straley during his time as curator of the UBC Botanical Garden. Gerald was fascinated by botanical relationships, and it was through his infectious curiosity that I too wished to more fully examine the breadth of many plant families I knew only in a peripheral sense. On one particular visit, Gerald led me to one of the enormous specimens of Douglas fir in the David C. Lam Asian Garden, on which grew a handsome, dark, glossy-foliaged vine.

Pileostegia viburnoides, at first glance in the wild or in cultivation, could very well be mistaken for one of the evergreen climbing hydrangeas (a mistake I have often made myself when observing a specimen without fruit or flower!), with glossy, linear-ovate leaves of dark green held in pairs along stems outfitted with adventitious roots for vertical leverage. When in blossom, however, the conical, open cymes of off-white flowers are devoid of the showy sepals that often surround the inflorescences of *Hydrangea*, indicating that this vine is clearly a horse of a different color. Though not overly flashy in floral effects, this species offers good value in year-round lustrous foliage for ornamenting a tree trunk or protected wall.

Though *Pileostegia viburnoides* is the only species commonly encountered in cultivation, two other species are known to exist, including *P. tomentella*. This low-elevation species from southern China, where I have seen it in the hills on the outskirts of Kowloon, has both new foliage and stem covered in dense, brown indumentum. My attempts to bring this species back by means of cuttings have failed.

HARDINESS: Zones 8–12 or in protected sites in zone 7.

CULTIVATION: *Pileostegia*, like *Hydrangea* and *Schizophragma*, exhibits some obstinate tendencies in getting established and down to the business of growing. Simply provide an ample amount of patience in this regard. It is best grown in moist, humus-rich soil and provided some overstory protection, although I have observed

Pileostegia viburnoides in Taiwan. (Photo by Daniel J. Hinkley)

Pileostegia viburnoides. (Photo by Lynne Harrison)

very floriferous specimens growing as wall plants in full sun in England.

PROPAGATION: By seed, as per *Hydrangea*, or by semi-softwood cuttings in mid- to late summer, under mist and on gentle bottom heat.

Decumaria

Another genus of self-clinging lianas, *Decumaria* includes two species, one each from the New and Old Worlds. Both species are very close in appearance to *Pileostegia* though more closely related to *Hydrangea* and *Schizophragma*. From these, *Decumaria* differs in producing panicles of small flowers, all of which are perfect, as well as up to 10 sepals, petals, and carpels. This quantity—10, or *decimus*—put forth the genus name.

Certainly the best known and best understood of this duo is *Decumaria barbara* from the mid-Atlantic coastal states south to Florida and west to Louisiana. Known as both the wood vamp and climbing hydrangea, it is a deciduous species in its native haunts; however, in the maritime climate of the Pacific Northwest it remains entirely evergreen. The rather large, oval leaves add a highly textural polish, while the small heads of white flowers are more readily produced in the sultry native climate. A larger-leaved form known as *D. barbara* 'Vicki' has been selected. Though I have included this form in my new garden, I have not deciphered any significant degree of difference from the species, at least in our climate, where they both remain decidedly unflowered after a full decade.

As has often been the case with the pursuit of plants, the quest to find the Old World representative of the genus, *Decumaria sinensis*, brought considerably more pleasure to my life than the living entity itself once finally captured. At the time I made chase for this species, it was a highly sought commodity by J. C. Raulston of the North Carolina State University Arboretum, now the J. C. Raulston Arboretum. He had seen it in cultivation only once, years before, growing quite neglected on a fence at the San Francisco Botanical Garden at Strybing Arboretum. His desire for this species was quite contagious, and I joined him in attempting to find it. After numerous false starts, I was finally able to locate a small specimen in a nursery in England.

Decumaria sinensis seems a completely different beast from *D. barbara* and has thus far performed poorly in my climate. Known to hail from low to moderate elevations in west and central China, where according to Ernest Wilson it often associates with rocky outcroppings, it seemingly desires and deserves more summer heat than we are able to provide it. The narrow, persistent leaves are of a dark, glossy green, while the flowers are white and fragrant. Though it has yet to blossom in our garden, I have met up with it in peak blossom on several occasions, most notably at Crûg Farm in Wales where it is cultivated in a tunnel. Indeed, perhaps because it is in a confined space, the flowers pack a powerful punch.

Though sadly I did not locate this species until after J. C.'s untimely death in 1996, I suspect it would have served him much better in the Southeast than it ever

Decumaria sinensis. (Photo by Daniel J. Hinkley)

will in my own climate. With that said, I will always keep this species in any garden I tend, as it brings to mind the all-consuming passion with which J. C. pursued his plants.

HARDINESS: Summer-warm regions in zones 7–12 are seemingly best for both species.

CULTIVATION: As for *Schizophragma* and *Pileostegia*. In the wild *Decumaria* is frequently found hanging from rock ledges. It might thusly find such an application in the garden setting.

PROPAGATION: As for *Schizophragma* and *Pileostegia*, though I have only had personal experience in rooting species of these genera from cuttings.

Dichroa

Though other shrubby genera of the Hydrangeaceae exist, if not ultimately usurped by *Hydrangea* itself—most notably *Broussaisia arguta* from Hawaii—my experience with them is too little (or nonexistent) to shed any light on their ornamental attributes. However, though I have had a personal relationship with only one of the approximately 12 species of *Dichroa*, I feel there has been sufficient depth to our interaction to warrant discussion here.

Dichroa febrifuga, one of the earliest known plants used for medicinal purposes, was provided its specific epithet because of its positive effect as a febrifuge. Chinese scholar Shen Nung wrote in 2735 BC of this plant's effects in reducing fevers in patients suffering from malaria, and a tea made from its roots is still commonly used in traditional medicine to control malaria-related fevers throughout the plant's large geographical area from southeastern Asia through the Indian subcontinent, including the Himalaya.

The leaves are deep glossy green, carried in pairs along stems to 6 ft. (1.8 m). Terminal heads of blue flowers with four reflexed petals appear in mid- to late summer, without the outer row of sterile florets we have come to associate with hydrangea flowers. The plant's most comely attributes follow, however, when a spectacular display of vibrant violet-blue berries ripen in early autumn. The fruit is held intact and remains colorful throughout much of the winter.

The Greek name *Dichroa*, literally "two colors," refers to the variability of hue in the flowers and fruit of members of the genus. I have encountered populations of this species throughout moderate elevations in Vietnam, Nepal, Bhutan, and western China, where fruit color changes from plant to plant from near-black to electric turquoise. Likewise, the flower color can vary dramatically from clone to clone, from white to deep blue.

Though I do not remotely suggest that I am an authority on the genus, my presumption is that due to the significant variation found within populations of *Dichroa*, there exists a quagmire in regard to its proper taxonomy. *Dichroa versicolor* is encountered in commerce on occasion. Whether this name is validly applied, I cannot say with certainty; however, the plant, which performs as a subshrub or herbaceous perennial in colder

Dichroa febrifuga in flower. (Photo by Lynne Harrison)

climates, with large heads of pink flowers, is indeed distinct from *D. febrifuga*.

My seed collections of *Dichroa febrifuga* from numerous locations throughout Asia have resulted in plants with rather disappointing grayish pink flowers and lackluster fruiting effects. Fortunately, I had already come to admire this plant in my garden through the clone originally collected in Guizhou Province by Peter Wharton, then curator of the David C. Lam Asian Garden at the UBC Botanical Garden.

Wharton's collection remains the best in commerce and is now frequently seen in garden centers and wholesale nurseries along the West Coast. It grows in a rather lax manner if planted in deep shade, more upright under brighter conditions, with the panicles of glistening sapphire berries remaining as effective in April as they had been upon ripening the previous October.

Illuminating the close affinity of *Dichroa* to *Hydrangea*, hybrids between the two genera have been produced by scientists at the U.S. National Arboretum, most notably Sandra Reed, using *D. febrifuga* and *H. macrophylla*. It is the intent of this program to produce

Dichroa febrifuga, in fruit, in Bhutan. (Photo by Daniel J. Hinkley)

shrubs with both showy summer flowers and colorful crops of winter fruit. I am currently evaluating these hybrids in my garden in Indianola for suitability to the climate of the Pacific Northwest.

It is interesting to note that spontaneous hybrids between *Dichroa* and *Hydrangea* have been reported from New Zealand; photos of the resulting plants in flower suggest we have not heard the end of this story. With such a diverse assemblage of hydrangeas from which to select parents, saying nothing of the possibility of bringing into cultivation other taxa of *Dichroa* for the purposes of breeding, the potential combinations seem nearly infinite.

Ending on that note, I have only knowingly observed one other species of *Dichroa*, in 2005 while botanizing in northern India. My colleague Dave Demers and I walked a considerable distance that day on the only road leading south from Lachung, where J. D. Hooker was arrested in 1849 by the Dewan of Sikkim. At 3500 ft. (1070 m), we were well below the altitude of possible hardiness when we found in blossom a roadside specimen of *D. aff. mollissima* with large, ovate foliage and, in October, beautiful heads of bicolored yellow and blue flowers. I took with me only the memory of having seen it.

HARDINESS: Though this would be considered a nonhardy shrub in climates below zone 7, I believe it would make a sensational containerized shrub if maintained in a cool, bright situation during the winter months.

CULTIVATION: Slightly acidic, humus-rich soils in either shade or partial shade are best, with supplemental water as needed throughout the growing season.

PROPAGATION: Semihardwood cuttings in late summer are as unchallenging as with *Hydrangea*. Due to dichroas' propensity to change dramatically in appearance, propagation by seed is not advised, though with that said, I have never had viable seed produced in my garden.

Platycrater arguta

There are often those "Aha!" moments in the fantastical world of plants, and I experienced just such a moment during a trip to Japan in the spring of 2008.

Let it be known that I had collected seed of *Platycrater arguta* during our time on the Kii Peninsula in the autumn of 1997, and before that I had imported plants of this species for the nursery I founded with my partner, which at the time was devoted to rare and unusual plants. Yet the seed never germinated, and the plants I imported failed to survive the rigors of USDA inspection. So for many years I remained acutely aware of this species only in terms of its name; its physical presence had not yet entered my consciousness.

During my first visit to Yamaguchi Plantsman's Nursery (a name given to the establishment by Roy Lancaster during his first visit in the early 1970s) in Gifu Prefecture, as we sat for the traditional welcoming cup of tea prior to commencing a tour about the premises, I noticed a single stem in blossom in a vase on the table. It was familiar—with opposite foliage and terminal cymes of few but relatively large flowers—yet it was certainly not a *Deutzia*, *Hydrangea*, or *Philadelphus*.

Seiju Yamaguchi assuredly knew the Japanese nomen-

clature of this species, but the gulf that exists between our languages diluted the opportunity to meet this at last at its finest, in person, with others who obviously appreciated its charms.

It was not until the following week, when encountering this plant at another nursery (where two forms are now offered, one with larger-than-normal, showy flowers and another with pink flowers), that the flip switched. Of course, this was what had graced our table.

Platycrater arguta is known to exist naturally on southern Honshū, Kyūshū, and Shikoku at moderate elevations. On the Kii Peninsula, slightly northeast of Ōsaka, where I found it growing with numerous species of *Hydrangea* at approximately 5000 ft. (1500 m) in elevation, I collected the seed from 4–5 ft. (1.2–1.5 m) specimens carrying terminal infructescences of numerous small capsules. In the world of plants, however, it is seldom the moment of gathering seed from uninspiring fruit that provides the "Aha." Those moments are provided more auspiciously and unexpectedly, over cups of tea or while purveying plants on display at a nursery.

HARDINESS: *Platycrater arguta* has been seldom trialed in North America, and its suitability in differing climates is little understood. Extrapolating from those plants with which it associates in the wild, I suspect it would perform with some resentment in the Pacific Northwest, but gladly so southward to northern California and certainly in the Southeast.

CULTIVATION: Again extrapolating, I would say that this is a shrub for humus-rich, cool, and evenly moist soils in shade or partial shade.

PROPAGATION: Reproduction by softwood cuttings under mist would present few challenges. Though I have not personally succeeded with wild-collected seed, one cannot account for lack of talent in this regard; it is certainly straightforward, although as per usual, tiny seeds must be treated more intelligently and sensitively than those with a greater expanse of endosperm.

Hydrangea macrophylla × *Dichroa febrifuga*. Recent hybrids made between these two taxa prove their close taxonomic relationship. (Photo by Keri D. Jones)

Seeing Stars: *Illicium*

We left our Alaskan comrades in Kunming for their imminent departure for home yesterday morning, and shortly thereafter, Bleddyn, our guides from the Kunming Institute of Botany, and I began our drive north toward the Sichuan border. It was a very long drive, but we did manage to get out a few times en route. It was interestingly very arid territory as we approached the border yesterday, with Wikstroemia *and* Ternstroemia *predominant. We arrived at Huali very late in the evening, road weary, yet a meal was somehow arranged for us at a local restaurant, and we ate a splendid dinner of "mock fish," crafted from eggplant, while surrounded by staring locals who had heard of our arrival in town.*

This morning, after an early breakfast of rice porridge and peanuts, we left for the summit of Longshou Shan, a rich botanical reserve with easy access by vehicle to 11,000 ft. It was a very satisfying day of collecting after nearly five days away from the process. The vehicle and our guides managed to get us to high elevation over bits and pieces of disintegrating road that had me at times white with terror. I was relieved when it was impossible to proceed fur-

ther and Bleddyn and I were jettisoned with our packs and a plan to reconnoiter with the vehicle at the base of the mountain at dusk.

We continued to hike up the road, now in places only a narrow path hugging the side of the mountain, through a truly fascinating flora quite unlike anything I had experienced before. Arisaema wilsonii, *with enormous trifoliate leaves, was common and found growing beneath fantastic specimens of* Rhododendron aff. rex. *Beneath were thickets of* Sarcococca aff. hookeriana var. digyna, Camellia pitardii var. yunnanica, *colonies of* Pachysandra axillaris, *and beautiful dark-stemmed forms of* Hydrangea scandens. *Seemingly carrying this "dark-stemmed" theme further was a magnificent species of* Illicium, *forming dense conical shrubs to 15 ft. with glossy green leaves carried along striking deep purple stems. Gratifyingly, after raking through the stems of numerous specimens of the latter species, we found an individual with sufficient quantities of seed, although as luck might have it, its stems were only slightly suffused with pigment.*

Huali, Sichuan Province
October 10, 2000

I WAS AWARE OF STAR ANISE long before I had learned of the ancient genus of evergreen shrubs known as *Illicium*. It was the long, frigid winters of Michigan, the same that kept me from appreciating these shrubs for garden use, that encouraged me to

take cooking classes at a local community college, in an effort to do battle against the endless nights of sub-zero temperatures. During that culinary enlightenment, I learned to use five-spice powder and garam masala, and ultimately became adventurous enough to use one of the primary ingredients of these concoctions—star anise, obtained from the starlike woody seed capsule of

Overleaf: *Illicium anisatum.* (Photo by Lynne Harrison)

I. verum—on its own to flavor Vietnamese pho and Italian Bolognese sauce.

It is precisely the same ester, anethole, that gives both *Illicium* and *Pimpinella anisum*, or aniseed, their characteristic licorice-like flavor, but the former has been historically the least expensive flavoring of the two. This temporarily changed in the early 1990s when shikimic acid, a compound found in quantity in star anise, became a key player in the production of Tamiflu, a drug that showed great promise in treating the particularly deadly strain of avian flu dubbed H5N1. Shikimic acid is now manufactured in the lab, and prices of *I. verum*, an agricultural commodity of four southern Chinese provinces, have again dropped.

For those involved in the investigation of naturally occurring compounds in the floral kingdom for potential medicinal value, it would have come as no surprise that this small monotypic genus of the Illiciaceae, with about 40 species, would yield positive results. Medicines and poisons often go hand in hand, and numerous species (with fruit appearing identical to that of star anise) are perilously toxic to humans.

While studying advanced systematics as I received my master's degree at the University of Washington, I was introduced, by way of herbaria—that is to say, sincerely dead, squashed plants smelling of mothballs—to the genus *Illicium*, while being tutored in regard to ancient versus more highly evolved floral structures. In that the spiral arrangement of the flower and undifferentiated perianth (tepals only) of *Illicium* is suggestive of *Magnolia*, we were meant to believe that this ancient assemblage of plants lay somewhere between the Magnoliaceae and the Winteraceae. The genus name is Latin for "allurement," an obvious reference to the aromatic oils in all body parts.

That same spring, taking my life in my own hands while trekking through the overgrown collection of woody plants at Washington Park Arboretum in Seattle, I came upon a somewhat sorry but nonetheless flowering specimen of *Illicium anisatum*, to wit a living and breathing classroom concept. I experienced its quint-essential primitiveness in flesh and blood. It was love at first sight.

In 1995, during my first organized collection trip to Japan, I collected seed of this same species from the Chiba Prefecture, just south of Tokyo. Had the characteristic starlike capsules not been present, its glossy, ovate foliage alternately arranged on the stems and the telltale licorice-scented oils released from a crushed leaf would have provided the verification I needed.

Those collections (DJH 441) now grow along the fenceline in my new garden, producing in early spring a spirited display of creamy yellow flowers; yet certainly it is the memory of my edification through this one species that I most value. Since that time I have acquired cultivars of this species from nurseries in Japan. A form with enduringly deep purple foliage—nonpareil in desirability quotient—has sadly turned out to be completely lacking in vigor. However, another form, whose new growth is as seductive as the former in new growth, though fading to burnished green for the winter, has tremendous ornamental potential to lift this species to a new level of appreciation. As a matter of note, I offered a pink-flowering form of this species in my former nursery, though I did not secure a specimen to follow it through under cultivation.

In 1988, already certifiably mad over the idea of amassing a respectable collection of *Illicium* in my new garden, I traveled to the Southeast with good friend Eric Nelson. With introductions arranged by J. C. Raulston, our time together took us to Woodlanders Nursery in Aiken, South Carolina, the mecca for rare native plants of the Southeast. Coproprietor Bob McCartney, perhaps one of the most unsung and directed plantsmen of our time, introduced me to not only our two native North American species but also superb selections he and others in the area had made.

Illicium floridanum, a rare species that occurs from Florida to Louisiana (federally endangered in Georgia, threatened in Florida) is part and parcel to the flora of shaded, moist ravines and steepheads, which, as anyone can tell you, are an endemic geological formation, essentially a migrating sand-based amphitheater. It is a tall evergreen shrub to 10 ft. (3 m) with relatively large, starry, red flowers. Both the foliage and flower deliver a commanding aroma of three-day-old fish, and for this reason the species is known in the vernacular as stink bush.

Though I personally do not mind the smell of rotting fish in my garden, this nuisance proved benign in my garden in the Pacific Northwest, as our temperatures are not warm enough to volatize the esters guilty of such an olfactory offense. Unfortunately, our lack of heat slowly but surely defeated this species and the several selections I had returned with from Aiken, including a white-flowered form and the highly regarded 'Halley's Comet', with flowers twice the normal size. All parts of *Illicium floridanum* are considered highly toxic.

At the end of our excursion to the Southeast in 1988, Eric and I were treated to the all-too-common madness of J. C.'s generosity, and took back with us an embarrassment of plants and cuttings. Among these was the newly acquired *Illicium mexicanum*, from populations from the mountains of northeastern Mexico. It is still disputed whether this is a species in its own right or simply a variety of *I. floridanum*, but the argument means little to a gardener whose climate, with its continual splash of cool air, causes the plant in question to suffer terminal shrinkage.

The same disappointing results came from my attempt to grow the only other American species, *Illicium parviflorum*, native to shaded streamside locales of central Florida. Though it might seem rather obvious that this would be an inappropriate choice for a Northwest mar-

Purple-leaved form of *Illicium anisatum*. (Photo by Daniel J. Hinkley)

Variegated form of *Illicium anisatum*. (Photo by Daniel J. Hinkley)

itime garden, indeed my first exposure to *I. parviflorum* came from a specimen growing at the University of Washington medicinal herb garden. Despite the fact that this yellow-flowering species is considered to be in imminent danger of extinction in the wild due to habitat loss, its carefree ability to tolerate general landscape abuse and the humiliation of imprudent shearing has propelled it into a starring role in clipped hedges and shopping mall horrorscapes of the greater Southeast.

It was in South Carolina at Middleton Place, one of America's oldest extant plantations, that I first witnessed the utility of *Illicium parviflorum* firsthand. There it is employed as a clipped hedge—certainly a contemporary choice rather than a historically accurate one—partitioning the formal areas of the garden. While perusing the interior of these spaces, I encountered a most handsome, dense, and conical evergreen shrub, which I might have initially believed had been formally clipped. This was my first encounter with the lovely, red-flowered, highly adaptable *I. henryi*, a wide-ranging species across much of China.

While on the eastern slope of Cang Shan in Yunnan Province in 2000, just above Dali, I collected the fruit of *Illicium henryi* at elevations of nearly 9000 ft. (2700 m) under the number DJHC 0454. The specimens there grew not as handsomely narrow, upright cones, as they do in the heat and humidity of the Southeast, but were slightly more open, as they are in the Pacific Northwest. To my mind, this allows for greater appreciation of the striking, carmine red, many-tepaled flowers produced in late spring to midsummer.

Illicium henryi, though the best known of the Chinese

The signature fruit of *Illicium* in the mountains of northern Vietnam. (Photo by Daniel J. Hinkley)

Illicium mexicanum growing in John Fairey's garden in Hempstead, Texas. Fairey was primarily responsible for the introduction of this species into American horticulture. (Photo by Daniel J. Hinkley)

Seeing Stars: *Illicium*

Illicium henryi. (Photo by Daniel J. Hinkley)

My collection of *Illicium simonsii* from Sichuan Province blossoming at Windcliff. (Photo by Daniel J. Hinkley)

Illicium lanceolatum. (Photo by Lynne Harrison)

Illicium simonsii in Sichuan. Note the deep purple of the stems and petioles. (Photo by Daniel J. Hinkley)

species, is certainly not the only red- or pink-flowered taxon of the 27 found within its geographical boundaries, 18 of which are endemic. One of these is *I. lanceolatum*, a species I have not encountered in the wild but grew for many years in the woodland of my first garden. Collected by Peter Wharton, curator of the David C. Lam Asian Garden at the UBC Botanical Garden, it is a splendid species with deep glossy green, elegantly narrow foliage to 6 in. (15 cm) on a framework to 8 ft. (2.4 m), though of course it is much taller in the wild. Quantities of wine red flowers are produced in late winter to early summer.

The seeds mentioned in my journal entry at the beginning of this chapter, under the number DJHC 0500, germinated readily the following spring, and I was duly gratified to find a few seedlings exhibiting the rich purple coloration seen in the population at large. These blossomed in my garden in Indianola for the first time in 2005 and were identified at that time as *Illicium simonsii*, a sensational and adaptable species worthy of greater appreciation. Though my collections proved to be primarily ivory white, previous collections made in Sichuan by Bill MacNamara and others of Quarryhill Botanical Garden in northern California have shown variability in flower color from pure white to creamy yellow.

Again later, while hiking through the midlevel forests of Fan-si-pan in northern Vietnam, I was dumbstruck when I realized that the plethora of *Illicium* fruit littering the forest floor had dropped from the evergreen canopy 50–75 ft. (15–23 m) above us. The severely outdated annotated checklist of Fan-si-pan records more than eight species of *Illicium* from this mountain alone; without the opportunity to compare foliage with the shape and size of the fruit we picked from the ground, it will be many years before proper names are applied, if proper names even yet exist. I have seen just one of these in blossom, in the sublime garden and arboretum of Tom and Jo Hudson in Cornwall, with lovely white flowers elegantly tumbling downward by means of pedicels a staggering 6–8 in. (15–20 cm) long.

I must end on yet another stern warning to consider all fruit from this genus, besides that which is verified to be *Illicium verum*, to be toxic. Poisons and cures aside, there are assuredly great things in store for this genus as more species are brought into cultivation, evaluated for heat and cold tolerance, and ultimately promoted through the nursery trade.

HARDINESS: Cold hardiness does not necessarily translate into garden worthiness. Many of the species are more horticulturally primed for summer heat and lots of it. As a general rule the genus will survive in zones 7–10.

CULTIVATION: Illiciums will tolerate a great deal of shade and blossom dependably, but I find that overall appearance and floriferousness improve under brighter conditions. A modicum of shelter from midday sun, especially in more arid climates, would be advised. Humus-rich, well-draining soils are ideal; however, my collections of *Illicium anisatum* thrive in difficult soils with root competition from adjacent trees.

PROPAGATION: The plump seeds expelled from the star-shaped capsules upon ripening germinate readily in a single season if sown fresh in autumn. Hardwood cuttings taken from September through November and placed on gentle bottom heat root readily and transplant easily. The Japanese continue to graft the purple-foliaged form of *Illicium anisatum*, presumably on the rootstock of the same species. Perhaps experimentation with using other rootstocks will translate into a more vigorous expression of top growth.

Sweetspires in the Old and New Worlds: *Itea*

Ozzie and I separated ourselves today from the rest of the pack and hiked up from Wuxian-gang, from midelevation on the mountain to about 8000 ft. I left the trail at 7500 ft. and headed up a river drainage at about midday, presuming Ozzie was directly behind, soon realizing we were irreparably separated for the day. The water was low in the river, and I was able to negotiate the rocky streamside by fording many times on slippery rocks with saturated boots. After an hour of hard work, I entered into a most amazing amphitheater surrounded by steep walls on both sides and an insurmountable tumble of water upstream.

This seemed to be a transition zone from mostly subtropical to temperate within only a few hundred yards; even the downward current of air seemed to change in temperature. Growing on the vertical wall on the opposite side of the river were spectacular clinging colonies of Mahonia gracilipes *whose undersurfaces of leaf shown brilliant white. With feet already wet, I collected what fruit I could by standing in water to upper thigh.*

Further upstream, on the same side of the river, was a rather small bowl with a stream entering the main flow. The diversity here was boggling; very few moments before have I felt such excitement in seeing so many species, recognizable and not, in one place. There were several specimens of Aucuba omeiensis *with its recognizably bold, jagged leaves, with female specimens presenting crops of not-yet-ripened green fruit. Atop a moss-covered rock*

grew Mahonia eurybracteata, *with a stunning, near-iridescent, pewter-colored leaf.* Asarum (caudigerum*?*), Impatiens (omeiana*?*) *and* Disporum *aff.* bodinieri *were loaded with crops of shiny black fruit.*

Up the very steep slope there were numerous trees, both evergreen and deciduous, that I was unable to identify from a distance. Jettisoned leaves of Tetracentron sinense *were scattered about on the rocks, but I could not discern what trees these were from.*

I made my way up the draw to a large evergreen shrub with leathery ovate leaves to 6 in. and narrow axillary racemes carrying small woody capsules. It was with a rush of remembrance that I realized this was the same plant J. C. had brought me under the name Itea yunnanensis. *We had discussed together, at length, this very species, and how I wish he could have been there today, on such a day, to share it with me.*

I sorted and bagged my numerous collections while having my lunch on a large rock along the river in the sun. One by one, a troupe of macaque monkeys appeared from the surrounding bush to sit and watch me eat. I was utterly enthralled by the whole of this scene, until what I presumed to be the alpha male bore his long incisors as I took a bite from my sandwich. I quickly gathered my seed into my pack, threw my food as far as I could in the opposite direction, and ran for it.

Mount Emei, Sichuan Province
October 13, 1998

Mount Emei in Sichuan Province, one of four sacred mountains in China, is home to more than 3000 species of higher plants. (Photo by Daniel J. Hinkley)

When I planted my first garden in Kingston, Washington, I sited *Itea virginica* 'Henry's Garnet' on the south side of the house, grown from a cutting given to me by J. C. Raulston. The common name, Virginia sweetspire, provided the inspiration to plant it so closely to the patio of the house. I knew virtually nothing of the genus at that time, and much like reading a novel by a previously unknown author and then seeking out other works by the same author, I was invited to its charms by this one plant.

Though the genus *Itea* is no longer found very far west of the Mississippi, had I lived in Washington State during the Eocene, some 50 million years ago (as many of my young friends presume I actually did), I would have seen at least one species growing in the mixed coniferous forests of the mountains in the area. This fact attests to how long the genus has been around, now comprised of about 27 species in warm temperate and tropical regions of both the New and Old Worlds.

First situated in the saxifrage family, the genus *Itea* has now been provided its own placeholder in the plant world, the Iteaceae. Both deciduous and evergreen species exist, all with leaves alternately arranged along their stems and flowers in slender racemes arising from the leaf axils, often fragrant.

The deciduous species that I first planted, *Itea virginica* 'Henry's Garnet', responded nicely to the full-sun, rather dry position where I planted it, though I soon found that it was equally at home in damp and shaded conditions. The floral display, in midsummer, was indeed showy, though I did not find myself overly aroused by its supposed perfumery. Not until early October of that year did I come to recognize its most sincere ornamental trait: the leaves transitioned to brilliant shades of red and orange, which remained intact and effective well beyond Christmas.

This autumn bravado was the reason behind this plant's selection by Mary Gibson Henry, field botanist and proponent of American native plants. A sport from this selection showing a more compact habit of growth has been dubbed 'Little Henry'. Woodlanders Nursery in South Carolina, long devoted to promoting the rich tertiary flora of the Southeast, and other nurseries within this species' natural range from New Jersey to Cuba west to Louisiana, have introduced several other selections, including 'Long Spire', 'Saturnalia', and the slightly pink 'Sarah Eve', though perhaps owing to their more southerly provenance, these have failed to perform to the degree of 'Henry's Garnet' in the Pacific Northwest.

I have come upon this in the wild only once, in the swampy terrain of southern Mississippi, where it grew adjacent to *Hydrangea quercifolia* and a very fat water moccasin that I nearly stepped on.

Not long after my introduction to *Itea virginica*, I acquired my first evergreen species, *I. ilicifolia*, as seed from my first trip to China in 1996, from the dry pine-covered hills near Lichiang in Yunnan Province. This species has had a long history of cultivation in the West, primarily as a wall shrub in plant collections of the United Kingdom. Literature implies that it is a decidedly tender species, a reference that does not seem to hold up after over a decade of cultivating it, during which time it has taken numerous episodes of single-digit temperatures. I consider it one of the finest evergreen shrubs that I grow, with glossy green, hollylike leaves and elegant, 10 in. (25 cm), pendulous racemes of powerfully fragrant green flowers produced in late summer.

Itea yunnanensis and *I. chinensis* soon joined the ranks from my second trip to China in 1998, though I was already acquainted with the former through material of unknown provenance. Both of these evergreen species are distinctly different in appearance, and the validity of their names remains questionable. *Itea yunnanensis* is a bold-foliaged plant with large, leathery-textured, oval leaves to 8 in. (20 cm) and rather short axillary racemes of white produced in midsummer. *Itea chinensis*, collected also on the slopes of Mount Emei at moderate elevations, is more finely textured, with leaves that emerge in early summer with a pleasing pale appearance, taking on a deeper green constitution before producing fingery white racemes in late July. I find both species worth growing, though I could not stand behind their names if challenged by someone more knowledgeable than I.

I struggled with *Itea oldhamii*, a species native to Taiwan and the southern islands of Japan, and finally sent it packing to a warmer climate. The foliage is dark green and leathery, while the flowers on the clone I grew were rather stubby and without particular merit. While in Taiwan during the autumn of 2007, I at last met up with this species in the wild, growing at the relatively low elevation of 4000 ft. (1200 m) on Babokulu Mountain in association with *Chlorandra*, *Ardisia*, and *Pileostegia*. It is probably more appropriately cultivated in the humid mid-Atlantic states southward.

A deciduous species, *Itea japonica*, offers yet another

Itea yunnanensis. (Photo by Lynne Harrison)

Itea virginica 'Henry's Garnet'. (Photo by Daniel J. Hinkley)

Itea ilicifolia. (Photo by Daniel J. Hinkley)

Itea chinensis. (Photo by Daniel J. Hinkley)

An evergreen species from Japan, *Itea oldhamii* is best adapted to summer-humid regions. (Photo by Daniel J. Hinkley)

A widely misunderstood taxa due to its confusion in commerce with *Itea virginica*, the real *Itea japonica* is distinctive, elegant, and readily identified. (Photo by Daniel J. Hinkley)

taxonomic minefield. For years *I. japonica* 'Beppu', a supposed dwarf form, was passed around the horticultural circles of North America. This "dwarf" probably originated as an imported bonsai from Japan, where *Itea* is a popular subject in that craft. However, it is *I. virginica*, in fact 'Henry's Garnet', that is the *Itea* of choice in Japanese horticulture. Thusly, though *I. japonica* does exist throughout the woodlands of Japan, much if not all of the material grown in the West under that name is actually the native American species.

It was not until the spring of 2008, while in Gifu Prefecture on Honshū, that I at last encountered the real McCoy. With a decidedly different appearance from *Itea virginica*, *I. japonica* has slender, horizontally held racemes to 8 in. (20 cm) or more on a spreading framework to 5 ft. (1.5 m). I was shown this by the celebrated plantsman Seiju Yamaguchi, who noted that his own native species did not receive due attention from his fellow countrymen.

The genus *Itea* has joined the ranks of numerous plant species that illuminate the flora shared by North America and eastern Asia, while providing a keyhole through which to peer into our geological past. Alternatively, without thinking at all, one can simply enjoy their sublime qualities in the garden.

HARDINESS: The deciduous species, *Itea virginica* and *I. japonica*, are considered hardy in zones 6–10; however, plants representing a more southerly provenance will prove to be less hardy in the north. *Itea virginica*

cultivars 'Henry's Garnet' and 'Little Henry' continue to represent the sturdiest selections under cultivation. The evergreen species are hardy only in zones 7–10 and might, as has been done historically in European gardens, be pushed in colder climates through cultivation as wall shrubs.

CULTIVATION: Cultivation of any *Itea* is not particularly difficult. *Itea virginica* is amenable to a wide range of habitats, from sunny and moderately dry to shaded and relatively moist. The best autumn color develops under brighter conditions and will be effective for numerous weeks from autumn through early winter. As all species are notably suckering in growth, the older branches should be pruned directly to the ground to encourage new stems to emerge.

PROPAGATION: Not particularly challenging. The seed is tiny and should be sown directly upon harvesting. It will germinate in a single season the following spring. The deciduous species are readily rooted as softwood cuttings under mist, while the evergreen species can be taken as hardwood cuttings in mid- to late autumn. As these cuttings will produce flowers the following spring, removal of the flower buds will enhance the vigor of the cuttings during the first season of growth. These are naturally suckering by nature; for small quantities of additional plants, simple division is foolproof and should be carried out in early spring before growth resumes.

Basket Weaving and Monkey Business:
Lardizabala and Other Lardizabalaceae

We were today just inside the ceiling of clouds, drizzling and quite cold, and I spent virtually all of it in dense shade, so I will have no photos of merit to help me recall, in the future, the memories of what I have seen other than those images conjured by these words. I left the bus with two of the now-notorious red-cellophaned hot dogs of ambiguous origin and two highly sugared rice crackers, not returning to meet the others at the vehicle, as planned, until dark. I chose a north-facing slope and entered into the woods on my own. It was a very rich and exciting flora with associations quite unlike any I had seen during the trip thus far. Numerous rhododendrons, with what I believe to be Rhododendron roxieanum *being dominant at this elevation, handsome and distinctive with its narrow, leathery foliage and an impressive bronze indumentum beneath. Immediately inside I found a tangle of* Holboellia *foliage, appearing identical to the UBC clone that I have grown under the name* H. fargesii. *There was not a fruit to be found, so I took a stem with foliage to press.*

The draw that I walked up was quite steep and rocky yet moist, deep soil. Other than some spectacular ferns, one of which appeared close to Polystichum braunii, *with glossy, plastic-like foliage, the ground was a solid expanse of* Chrysosplenium davidianum, *at least very similar to the plant Roy Lancaster had provided me under that name several years ago. It must be a glorious sight in spring when in flower, nearly radioactive in effect.*

It was so quiet at times, other than water dripping from the canopy to the vegetation and rocks below, that I would sometimes pause to simply listen. During one of those times, I heard a branch break to my right and turned slightly to find myself staring directly into the face of a Chinese man who was clutching in his arms an enormous bounty of ripened Holboellia *fruit still attached to their stems. I nearly jumped out of my skin.*

The gentleman recognized my startle and smiled broadly, toothlessly, while deftly tossing me a single fruit. He then demonstrated how to open it and eat the pulp inside, dropping the lavender rind on the ground. I nodded thankfully but did not want to eat it as I so wanted the seed inside.

I acknowledged his kindness and pointed in the direction I was heading. He continued downhill, certainly puzzled as to who I was and precisely where it might be that I was going. I took only 10 steps before I found another of his discarded rinds, and then realized I had been provided a Chinese version of breadcrumbs to find the mother lode. In just over an hour, I was standing below a gigantic specimen of this vine rising into the canopy surrounding an opening of a recently fallen tree. I had my lunch nearby and ate the fruit of Holboellia, *primarily to rid the taste of the hot-dog-like cylinders I had eaten earlier.*

Ninety-Nine Dragons, Yunnan Province
October 2, 2000

Decaisnea insignis. (Photo by Lynne Harrison)

As a lazy lay botanist, I have always appreciated those plant families that I can get my arms around without extraordinary effort. If, in addition, those succinct familial qualities are combined with ornamental value, I find myself obsessed with gathering about me for comparison and evaluation as many of the genera and species found within the family's ranks as possible. Thus it has been with my association with the Lardizabalaceae, a family of mostly evergreen vines and one shrub. The rather awkward phonetics of the family name can be blamed on its 18th-century namesake, Miguel Lardizábal, a patron of Spanish botany.

Though the Lardizabalaceae is geographically centered in Asia, there are two endemic, monotypic genera in southern South America, including the type genus, *Lardizabala biternata*. The remaining 7 genera and 48 recognized species occur in the Himalaya, Myanmar, Japan, Korea, and China, where 25 of those species are endemic to the political boundaries of China.

With a few exceptions, once you recognize the floral characteristics of even one species, the rest of the family offers few surprises, even to the untrained eye. This floral format is primarily monoecious, that is, male and female flowers are presented separately on the same plant. The calyx of the flowers (sepals) are generally expanded and provide the stuff of ornament, while the petals are greatly reduced. These flowers are offered in bundled (fascicled) racemes, with the bulk of each raceme comprised of smaller male flowers and (generally) two female flowers counterpoised on either side. Upon fertilization, the ovaries of the female flowers expand to leathery follicles that split open upon ripening to reveal a sweet, somewhat slimy pulp in which are imbedded numerous large seeds. The fruits of many of these species have made their way into indigenous diets and are also readily eaten by monkeys.

I have long harped on about the scarcity of good evergreen vines for our gardens, though I am fully cognizant that evergreenness is not appropriate for the inland climates of North America. For years, if one asked for an evergreen vine in nurseries of the Pacific Northwest, one was led to a back corner showcasing a single species: *Clematis armandii*. It is high time to renovate the nursery, expand the offerings, and make room for the lardizabalids.

The type genus, *Lardizabala*, is commonly found throughout southern Chile and is represented by a single species, *L. biternata*. The very leathery, compound leaves of this species are sufficiently distinctive to identify it by foliage alone, each leaflet a dark lustrous green and possessing a somewhat undulate edge. As the specific epithet implies (somewhat confusingly, I admit), rather than possessing a trifoliate leaf, with three leaflets, this plant has leaves often divided into three sets of three leaflets.

I first encountered *Lardizabala biternata* in the early 1990s growing in the garden of Elisabeth C. Miller in The Highlands, a gated community in northern Seattle. Her plant, still alive as I write this account, was certainly one of the only in the Pacific Northwest at that time, when its unjustifiable reputation for tenderness pervaded the horticultural consciousness of Pacific Northwest connoisseurs.

In 1998 and again in 2005, I collected seed from the green, leathery, elongated fruit of *Lardizabala* in the southern Andes of Chile at relatively low elevations of less than 860 ft. (260 m). I frequently saw its fruit for

Flower and foliage of *Lardizabala biternata*.
(Photo by Kevin Carrabine)

Lardizabala biternata is common in the forests of southern Chile. (Photo by Daniel J. Hinkley)

Boquila trifoliolata. (Photo by Daniel J. Hinkley)

sale by street vendors in villages throughout the country, where its sweet pulp is eaten fresh. In the same area, its vines were historically used for ropes.

My original collections of this species (HCM 98072) have matured to blossoming age in my garden in Indianola, growing on a shaded fence while presenting showy female flowers of deep purple-black attended by smaller male flowers of the same color. Though I have only a single clone of this, it is obviously self-fertile, as it regularly sets fruit (which is readily consumed by deer on the outside of the fence).

During my first visit to Chile, I sought the only other member of the family to occur outside of Asia. *Boquila trifoliolata*, once included in the genus *Lardizabala*, shares habitat with *L. biternata* on the western slope of the Andes and is endemic to Chile. Accustomed as I was to the large, leathery fruit of other members of the family, it comes as no surprise that my notes from that trip describe an unidentified evergreen vine collected under the number HCM 98069 as "a common species throughout area, leaves trifoliate, leaflets small, evergreen, fruit in long drooping racemes, fruit a fleshy berry."

In 2005 I again searched for this species that I had already collected seven years prior. My traveling companion Dave Demers, who has a very good eye, spotted the fruit of this species, which led to a positive identification. Upon second examination, the compound leaves held by deep red petioles along 20 ft. (6 m) twining stems possessed such an obvious similarity to that of *Akebia* that I wondered whether one should not truly hold as suspect my abilities in field identification. As a matter of note, the vines of *Boquila trifoliolata* are traditionally used throughout southern Chile for weaving into baskets (perhaps a profession for which I am better suited?). This species, in both basket and living plant, now ornaments my home and garden in Indianola.

Interestingly enough, I was with Dave Demers and others in northeastern Sichuan Province in 2004 when I first recognized the glaucous stems and compound, deciduous foliage of *Sinofranchetia chinensis* weaving through shrubs and small trees at higher elevations. Aggravatingly enough, it was also Dave Demers who found for us a specimen in fruit on that day.

Sinofranchetia is a monotypic genus that deviates from the majority of this family by possessing trifoliate and deciduous foliage, with each leaflet broad, ovate, and thin-textured. The genus name honors the highly regarded Adrien René Franchet, a French botanist attached to the herbarium of the Muséum National d'Histoire Naturelle in Paris in the mid- to late 19th century.

The shedding leaves of *Sinofranchetia* in autumn reveal what I for many years considered the bulk of its ornamental virtue: slender, twining new growth covered with a brilliant, glaucous white farina. The tangle of new stems at this time of year, ultimately growing to 50 ft. (15 m) or more in length, is reminiscent of the papier-mâché baskets we made as children by wrapping cornstarched string around inflated balloons.

The very small, greenish white flowers are borne on pendulous racemes, which result in fantastically long chains of light lavender, grape-sized berries. With only one clone in my garden for many years, this character flew under the radar; now with the addition of another seedling from our collection, DJHS 4326, my garden plants offer this handsome season of ornament on a yearly basis.

Throughout the limbs of trees in this same area of Sichuan that year, along rambunctious climbing stems clad with compound evergreen foliage, were the ripening crops of the large lavender-blue fruit of *Holboellia*, a representative of the same family. *Nightmare on Elm Street* pales in comparison to the horror I feel upon entering into a discussion of this genus, a conglomerate

The long white stems of trifoliate, deciduous *Sinofranchetia chinensis* clamber through the vegetation in far western Sichuan Province. (Photo by Daniel J. Hinkley)

Sinofranchetia chinensis in fruit. (Photo by Dave Demers)

of vines that is solely responsible for my initial attraction to the Lardizabalaceae, with such profound but underappreciated application to ornamental horticulture. So, first a primer on the subject.

Holboellia is a genus of about 20 species of evergreen (and rarely deciduous) climbers, all native to southeastern Asia. The genus name commemorates F. L. Holboell, one-time superintendent of the Copenhagen Botanic Garden. Found at low to moderate elevations, 2600–6500 ft. (800–2000 m), throughout the eastern Himalaya, indeed throughout western China and southward to Vietnam, this genus, along with *Stauntonia* and *Clematis*, represents one of the most frequently encountered vining plants in the natural landscapes of these areas. Under cultivation it represents a tangle of misidentified plants.

This is partially due to its close relationship with *Stauntonia*, a genus with which it is frequently muddled taxonomically and with which it differs only by having connate, or fused, filaments—that is, the stamens are bundled together at their base. From my experience with both genera, I rely more on their overall gestalt rather than this characteristic to set them apart: *Stauntonia* has five to seven large, broad leaflets and is generally more leathery in texture, while *Holboellia* has three to seven smaller, narrower leaflets. Of course, such lightheaded taxonomic diagnoses often have a way of going astray.

I first came to know the genus through exposure to *Holboellia coriacea*, with broad, trifoliate foliage and clusters of creamy white flowers in early spring, growing in the Carl S. English Jr. Botanical Garden at the Chittenden Locks, and later in the garden of Mareen Kruckeberg, of the MsK Rare Plant Nursery, who helped popularize it in cultivation. It has a wide distribution across much of China and because of its primarily trifoliate nature is easy to distinguish from the normally five- to seven-foliate *Stauntonia*.

The monoecious flowers of *Holboellia coriacea*, creamy white with some purple striations, are variable among individual clones in regard to the degree of fragrance, with some being powerfully strong. I have in my collection a forcefully yet pleasantly scented selection known as 'Cathedral' that was propagated from the walls of Winchester Cathedral in the United Kingdom.

In 1995 my collecting partners and I found the reddish purple fruit of *Holboellia latifolia* in eastern Nepal, where the species grew at the relatively low elevation of 8000 ft. (2400 m) on the botanically rich hogback known as the Milke Danda. Additional collections from 2002 (HWJK 2014) found along the Arun River grow in my new garden on the south-facing columns of our home; the handsome new foliage, with five to seven broad, ovate leaflets per leaf, appears in spring suffused with purple-bronze, while clusters of variably colored flowers with a slight bit of fragrance appear in late April. This too has had some commercial exposure in nurseries of the West, though recent collections of other more highly ornamental species have somewhat usurped this interest.

A particularly good flowering form of *Holboellia latifolia* from eastern Nepal. (Photo by Lynne Harrison)

Lardizabala and Other Lardizabalaceae

As an aside, in 1998 on Mount Emei in Sichuan, my friend Ozzie Johnson found alongside the trail a single fruit of either a *Holboellia* or *Stauntonia* that had somehow escaped the notice of the marauding, tormenting gangs of macaque monkeys in the area. I took this seed under the number DJHC 98442, and the resulting plant is nicely established on our eastern fence, though it has yet to blossom. I had presumed this to be a *Stauntonia* by the size of its leaf, but the inaugural blossoming of a plant I provided Crûg Farm in Wales has suggested that it is *H. latifolia* subsp. *chartacea*. It differs in possessing more ovate foliage with a greater leathery texture.

In 2002, while in Nepal with Bleddyn Wynn-Jones, Sue Wynn-Jones, and Jamaica Kincaid, I was able to collect a root piece of *Holboellia angustifolia* subsp. *linearifolia* (HWJK 2419) from a trailside specimen at a rather low elevation of the Mewa Khola drainage; the fruit had long before been consumed by the wayfaring citizens of the countryside or by wild bands of monkeys. It is a handsome plant with long, narrow, spidery leaflets to 6 in. (15 cm). I assumed it was this plant that I had also observed in Yunnan Province on Cang Shan above Dali, growing at higher elevations than the Nepalese plants, though again without fruit. My one-time lead propagator, Eric Hammond, was successful in finding fruit of this elegant taxon in 1997 in Sichuan Province, and it was from that collection that we were able to introduce it into general cultivation, albeit under the incorrect name *H. fargesii* Narrow Leaf Form EDHCH 97242. Eric's collection fits more neatly into the published botanical description than my own. My collection presents monoecious, light lavender, nearly white flowers in April, with strongly reflexed petals that are somewhat unimpressive in an ornamental sense; it is supremely worth growing, however, for the sake of its handsome, highly textural foliage alone.

I had first come to know *Holboellia angustifolia* subsp. *angustifolia* under the name *H. fargesii*, from an individual plant growing at the UBC Botanical Garden in Vancouver. It was this species whose clusters of lavender fruit we had admired in Sichuan (DJHS 4246), and that

The spidery foliage of *Holboellia angustifolia* subsp. *linearifolia*. (Photo by Lynne Harrison)

Holboellia angustifolia subsp. *angustifolia*. (Photo by Daniel J. Hinkley)

I had so curiously encountered on Ninety-Nine Dragons (DJHC 98217). My experience with it in the garden, in full sun as well as deep shade, suggests it to be one of the evergreen vines most worthy of cultivation in our mild maritime climate, while it continues to prove its durability on an arbor on the campus of Swarthmore College in Pennsylvania, zone 6.

The elegant, finely textured, compound foliage is comprised of five to eight elegantly narrow, bambool-ike leaflets to 6 in. (15 cm) long yet only ½ in. (1.25 cm) wide. Drooping clusters of tubular, lavender, fragrant flowers are offered in March and April and might result in plump lavender fruit if multiple clones are grown together.

As a matter of note, the *Flora of China* (Wu et al. 1994 to present) has chopped *Holboellia angustifolia* into two additional subspecies, *trifoliata* and *obtusa*. It seems quite unlikely that I will ever possess any confidence in distinguishing these from one another and will have to be content referring to them simply as *H. angustifolia* sensu latu. Good enough for me.

The slopes of Fan-si-pan in northern Vietnam have offered Bleddyn Wynn-Jones and me a highly ornamental but confusing array of *Holboellia* or *Stauntonia* species, of which many have yet to flower from seed to allow for a positive identification. One that has blossomed is my collection of *H. brachyandra*, HWJ 1023, which has been stunning in flower, with the male inflorescence, the largest of the genus, comprised of large white sepals with a purple stain on the base, and female flowers of dark purple. These result in crops of enormous purple fruit to 7 in. (18 cm) long. The foliage is primarily trifoliate with broad, papery, conspicuously veined leaflets. Despite its relatively low elevation provenance of 6500 ft. (2000 m), it has proven completely hardy in zone 8.

The bounty of this far-flung mountainous region has also provided us with seed of *Holboellia grandiflora*, HWJ 1024, found by Bleddyn near Y Ty on the border with Yunnan at 6300 ft. (1920 m), as Sue, his devoted, underappreciated wife, and I, equally underappreciated, labored intensely cleaning seeds in a bleak, cold hotel room. This species has since blossomed in the tunnels at Crûg Farm and proffers large, sweetly fragrant, pendulous bells of white blushed pink in late winter. Its range of adaptability in cultivation is mostly untested.

Most remarkable to date, however, at least in my garden, has been a taxon that I have not yet had the opportunity to place in either *Holboellia* or *Stauntonia*. I collected this as a root piece during our first trip to Fan-

Holboellia angustifolia. (Photo by Lynne Harrison)

Holboellia brachyandra, perhaps the most exciting *Holboellia* species to be introduced to cultivation in recent years, has tepals to 3 in. (7.5 cm) long. (Photo by Bleddyn Wynn-Jones)

si-pan in the autumn of 1999 as no seed was present. Now it is a rather sizeable vine with five-foliolate leaves, the new growth emerging each spring from enormous flowerlike bracts of soft yellow tinged with pink. Most people seeing the vine at this stage of growth believe they are indeed witnessing it in blossom and are quite in awe of its ornamental virtues. Currently growing under HWJ 99614, this may prove to represent *H. chapaensis* when it ultimately blossoms, though I would be quite content with this beautiful species should it decide to abandon the concept of flowering altogether.

Though I had certainly come to know *Akebia* from cultivation in the Pacific Northwest, it was not until my first trip to South Korea that I came to appreciate the degree to which the genus is knitted into Korean culture. In autumn, wild-gathered fruit of the five-fingered akebia, *A. quinata*, can be found in small fruit stalls throughout the country. Though it is eaten fresh as with other members of the family, in Korea it is primarily used to flavor the rice liquor *soju*, which Sue Wynn-Jones and I became rather fond of by the end of our trip.

The genus *Akebia* is represented by five species, all of which are native to eastern Asia. The best known is *A. quinata*, with small, palmately compound leaves comprised of five to seven obovate, evergreen to semievergreen, 2 in. (5 cm) leaflets. In late winter a pendulous inflorescence of handsome, black-purple, male and female flowers is produced just as growth resumes, reportedly possessing a lovely scent of chocolate. I personally have only detected this fragrance from the albino flowering form, *A. quinata* 'Shirobana', now popular in the trade, while a pink-flowered form, 'Rosea',

The curiously beautiful bracts of this species of *Holboellia* or *Stauntonia* from Vietnam, HWJ 99614, appear quite flowerlike. It has not yet blossomed in my garden. (Photo by Daniel J. Hinkley)

Akebia quinata is among the fruit for sale at a small stall in South Korea. (Photo by Daniel J. Hinkley)

possesses little in floral effects to recommend seeking it out. Various variegated forms circulate among collectors, primarily in Japan, but those that we have tried have proven very unstable in this regard.

The fruits of *Akebia quinata* fit the norm of the family at large, with large, pale purple, leathery follicles splitting open to reveal a white, succulent, seed-studded interior. I have collected seed of this species in South Korea on Mount Chiri on the southern part of the peninsula at moderate elevations, where I noted stems climbing to 50 ft. (15 m) in height, as well as in Chiba Prefecture, Japan (DJH 442).

Because of its vigorous growth, particularly in warm-summer climates, *Akebia quinata* has a checkered reputation in cultivation. It has been dubbed "the kudzu of the north" by many who consider it too aggressive

Akebia quinata 'Shirobana'. (Photo by Lynne Harrison)

for inclusion in gardens of the East Coast; it is relatively tame in this regard in the Pacific Northwest. Though fruiting is effected by the planting of more than one clone, it is with the white-flowered form that we have most come to anticipate fruit set, at least in the Northwest.

Akebia trifoliata, as its name implies, differs from *A. quinata* by having three-parted leaves, with the degree of substance depending on its provenance. Taxonomists have described three subspecies, all of which occur throughout eastern Asia. It was *A. trifoliata* subsp. *trifoliata* that I collected in Japan at 1400 ft. (430 m) near Egiri on the main island of Honshū, and it is this subspecies that is most encountered in cultivation in North America; it possesses a tendency toward deciduousness in autumn, and the margin of each leaflet is decidedly sinuate.

The purple, monoecious flowers on a drooping inflorescence are produced in late winter and early spring, resulting in sausagelike fruit very similar in appearance to *Akebia quinata*. The fruit, roots, and leaves of *A. trifoliata* have long been used in Chinese medicine for their analgesic, antibacterial, and antifungal effects, and contemporary analysis has revealed a remarkable array of complex and unique terpenoids.

On the west side of our home on a small trellis grows my collection of *Akebia trifoliata* var. *australis* from northeastern Sichuan Province. It was collected under the name *Archakebia apetala* DJHS 028, a taxon that indeed occurs in the same vicinity, and that differs from *A. trifoliata* primarily by lacking petals on both the male and female flowers, which result in yellow fruit. As I collected this by means of a self-layered stem with the foliage mostly gone, I was unable to put a name to it until the following spring. I was admittedly disappointed initially to discover its real identity, but the bronze new growth of this vine and its graceful, colorful racemes presented in late winter have grown well on me, as the plant has on the trellis.

I was given *Akebia* ×*pentaphylla* by J. C. Raulston in the late 1980s and grew it for many years on a trellis in the garden. It represents both of its parents (*A. quinata* and *A. trifoliata*) in an unbiased fashion, with each of the five leaflets per leaf appearing nearly identical to that of *A. trifoliata*.

Akebia longeracemosa is a vigorous species that superficially resembles a very small foliaged *A. quinata*, with deep green, leathery, five-parted leaves along vigorous twining stems to 50 ft. (15 m). It is commonly seen in the Wuling Farm area of north-central Taiwan at relatively low elevations, while also occurring in the southern coastal provinces of the mainland. As intriguing as its name and description, with purple flowers in bundled racemes up to 10 in. (25 cm) long, it has proven, after a decade of coaxing, to be utterly uninterested in revealing its floral charms under cultivation in the Pacific Northwest, and its somewhat suckering habit of

growth forbade its introduction in my new garden. It might prove a better performer in summer-warm climates. Bleddyn Wynn-Jones reports that his 1992 collections of this species have begun to blossom in the United Kingdom.

Akebia chingshuiensis, which is both extremely rare and little understood, is endemic to Taiwan, occurring at much higher elevations than the former species, to 7500 ft. (2300 m). The flowers of expanded black-purple sepals are borne in short axillary racemes, while the fruit has yet to be observed.

In 1792 the first embassy to China was taken by Lord George Macartney to the court of Emperor Qianlong in an effort to increase Chinese trading ties with Britain. He was accompanied by minister plenipotentiary Sir George Leonard Staunton, whose diaries would later

Akebia trifoliata var. *australis*. (Photo by Daniel J. Hinkley)

Flowers of *Akebia longeracemosa*. (Photo by Nick Macer)

become popular and well read throughout Europe and Asia, and for whom the genus *Stauntonia* is named.

It was, however, in the garden of Elisabeth C. Miller in The Highlands in northern Seattle that I first became familiar with this genus, through *Stauntonia hexaphylla*, the only one of the 25 species not endemic within the political borders of China and Taiwan. I have seen this growing in both Korea and Japan, most notably tangled among *Rhododendron schlippenbachii* and *Acer tschonoskii* on the rich and diverse slopes of Korea's Taehuksan Island in the autumn of 1993. In 1995, in Japan while en route to Nepal, Bleddyn Wynn-Jones and I collected seed of this species, as is often the case with members of this family, by finding its large, succulent fruit washed into drainage ditches along road cuts.

As with *Akebia*, the foliage is palmately compound but

Our collection of *Stauntonia hexaphylla* from Japan in 1997. (Photo by Daniel J. Hinkley)

Akebia longeracemosa in Taiwan. (Photo by Daniel J. Hinkley)

Stauntonia hexaphylla. (Photo by Daniel J. Hinkley)

Lardizabala and Other Lardizabalaceae

to a much larger scale, with five to seven leathery leaflets per leaf, each to 6 in. (15 cm) long and 2 in. (5 cm) wide. In early spring, clusters of showy, creamy white, pink-blushed flowers appear that add a substantive fragrance to the cool air of the season. It is a vigorous grower and will indeed compete with sizable trees over time if provided a fertile environment. We grew this for many years above a hot tub, where we could enjoy the fragrance in late winter as well as the year-round privacy provided by the romping ropes of tidy leaves. Where I have observed this species in its native haunts, the flowers have resulted in plum-sized fruits, lavender in color, which split open upon ripening to reveal a translucent, fleshy mass of seed inside. The single clone at the Elisabeth C. Miller Botanical Garden performs this feat as well, a characteristic that illustrates the propensity of *Stauntonia* toward being polygamomonoecious, meaning that it has male, female, and perfect flowers on the same plant. In a pinch, when without an appropriate suitor, it is able to produce viable seed.

As with the genus *Holboellia*, my relationships resulting from encounters with *Stauntonia* are mostly unresolved until an inaugural flowering provides a valid name. This is not the case with two species from Taiwan that appear significantly different in foliage and are thus, with no recorded species of *Holboellia*, difficult to confuse. *Stauntonia purpurea* possesses compound foliage of five to eight dark green leaflets with a decidedly undulate leaf edge. It is seen frequently throughout central Taiwan at moderate elevations, though infrequently in fruit due to the healthy population of monkeys on the island. I was able to secure a root sucker in 1999 to introduce to my garden. Handsome purple flowers with strongly reflexed sepals are produced in early spring on axillary racemes; however, this color may extend to yellow with purple staining at the base of the flower.

Stauntonia obovatifoliola is also common throughout the island and superficially resembles *S. hexaphylla*. The large, leathery, compound foliage of this species is readily distinguished from that of the only other species on Taiwan, *S. obovata*, by the presence of obvious spotting

Stauntonia purpurea from Taiwan is easily identified by its purple flowers and undulate leaf margins. (Photo by Daniel J. Hinkley)

Stauntonia purpurea. (Photo by Lynne Harrison)

on the undersurface. We were pleased to beat the monkeys to a bit of this fruit directly above Taipei, DJHT 7011, in the autumn of 2007. When flowering commences, I will expect relatively small racemes of yellow flowers stained purple within.

By means of the strikingly distinct and elegant foliage of *Stauntonia* DJHS 026, collected in northeastern Sichuan on the border with Gansu, I should be able to identify the taxon, but no *Stauntonia* reported to occur in this region fits the description. It is a beautiful species with trifoliate, compound foliage, each leaflet narrow, bamboolike, to 6 in. (15 cm) long, and less than 1 in. (2.5 cm) wide. I have this established through a small tree in my garden; however, it will be several growing seasons before its first flowering.

Stauntonia obovatifoliola growing at moderate elevations in Taiwan. (Photo by Daniel J. Hinkley)

In foliage, *Sargentodoxa cuneata* appears superficially to be an evergreen counterpart to *Sinofranchetia*, with three broad, deltoid leaflets along vigorous vining stems that ooze a characteristic and diagnostic red sap. It was one of the most frequently observed vining plant species during our time in western Sichuan in 2008. I have not successfully brought it home in the form of fruit or plant, though it is high on my shopping list during forthcoming visits to Vietnam and China. To my knowledge it is not in cultivation in the West.

Though not all lardizabalids scramble and climb, if a family reunion were to occur, only one member would be standing tall at the end. *Decaisnea insignis* seems an incongruous member at first look, with multiple stout, upright branches, generally 15–18 ft. (4.6–5.5 m) in height, carrying deciduous, odd-pinnate foliage to 18 in. (45 cm) that emerges in shades of an arresting blue. In spring, long, axillary, spidery racemes of separate male and female flowers appear, comprised of reflexed, yellow, blue-stained sepals. By autumn, however, the fruit—leathery, azure "fingers" to 6 in. (15 cm) long filled with a sweet, seed-studded, somewhat slimy pulp—gives little doubt to its affinity with the vines.

I first came to know this taxon by way of its former name, *Decaisnea fargesii*. The genus commemorates Joseph Decaisne, a 19th-century French botanist who described numerous plants, including *Vancouveria*, an herbaceous member of the barberry family native to my home state of Washington. After reexamination, the two species of the genus were amalgamated into one with the rules of priority favoring the retention of *D. insignis*.

Decaisnea insignis is commonly encountered throughout Asia, across much of China and particularly in the eastern Himalaya. I have made numerous collections from Nepal and Yunnan and Sichuan Provinces, where this plant's watermelon-like seeds and empty rinds are nearly omnipresent on any trail, snacked upon by humans and other beasts and birds. Specimens I observed in Sikkim in the rich woodland between Lachang and Lachung, while with Dave Demers in the autumn of 2005, stand out above all others not only in

Lardizabala and Other Lardizabalaceae

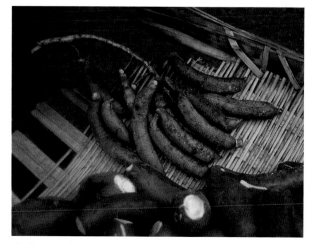

The leathery blue fruit of *Decaisnea insignis*. (Photo by Daniel J. Hinkley)

Decaisnea insignis. (Photo by Daniel J. Hinkley)

terms of size—to 40 ft. (12 m)—but also because the fruit ripened to yellow rather than the typical blue. This fruit color once played an important role in retaining the two original taxa.

HARDINESS: Though certainly a great deal of testing must be done before precise recommendations can be given for many members of the family not commonly encountered in commerce, I can state conservatively that the lion's share of these plants are appropriate for zones 8–12, while the deciduous members of the family, such as *Akebia* and *Sinofranchetia*, are appropriate for zones 6–12.

CULTIVATION: Though these taxa are primarily minions of the shaded forest, with their roots in cool, shaded, humus-rich soils and their stems climbing into the sunlight above the crowns of their host trees, I have found them willing to consider brighter conditions in the garden, even full sun, if provided supplemental water in the summer. As with all vines, if possibly they should be sited in shade—that is, on the north side of the tree, shrub, or arbor through which they will grow—to allow their stems to grow into the sun. These and other evergreen vines should be utilized more fre-

quently near pools and water features; though some foliage is discarded through the year, the maintenance in autumn is dramatically lessened.

Most members of the family will fruit more generously if more than one clone of the species is present in the garden. *Akebia quinata* has escaped into natural areas of the Northeast and should be monitored carefully for potential bioinvasion.

PROPAGATION: Seeds of members of the Lardizabalaceae require only a single cold period for successful germination and will appear the following spring after sowing. Propagation by cuttings of the vining members of this family, with softwood undermist for the deciduous species, and hardwood on bottom heat without mist for the evergreen species, is not difficult but somewhat challenging. This is due to the long internodal sections of the stem between leaves, requiring 12–18 in. (30–45 cm) cuttings: awkward at best when attempting to keep them upright in the rooting medium. A single node cutting—that is, one leaf, one bud, 1 in. (2.5 cm) segment of stem—has been successful. Interestingly, I have never failed in the establishment of root suckers, even if they are poorly rooted, if seed has not been available.

Identities Lost, Ornaments Found:
Mahonia and *Berberis*

Tonight we are in an extremely remote, though not even remotely extremely small, outpost in north-central Sichuan, at the only hotel in the area. It is painted a sickly color of pink that melds efficiently with the surrounding industries of this valley. Our room comes with hot water between 6:00 a.m. and 8:00 a.m., a vinyl shower curtain with a faded image of the Eiffel Tower, and a paper banner across the toilet bowl that says "alrecy disinfect." Seemingly we are in complete luxury: the bathroom towels are refreshingly absent of fungal fruiting bodies. It has

been a splendid day in the mountains, the air bracing and autumn colors lurid. We are all in good spirits.

There are pots evenly spaced along the balconies, each containing what I believe to be Mahonia eurybracteata, *so uniform as to suggest that they are being produced by tissue culture. It seems an unlikely place to encounter such a rarity, somewhat like finding truffles on a menu at Denny's. In any case, it is gratifying to see the commitment to cultivating plants at all. There are many motels and hotels at home that could not be bothered.*

Song Pan, Sichuan Province
October 11, 2003

MY SURPRISE IN THE ABOVE ENCOUNTER underscores the state of *Mahonia* appreciation in the West. Of all the shrubs I admire, mahonias are perhaps the least acknowledged of the lot. While a bevy of superlative species from Asia, Mexico, and Central America have flown under the radar of the collective horticultural cognoscenti for the last century, the taxonomy of widely grown species currently in cultivation is often vastly confused.

As garden writer Allen Lacy once quickly pointed out after I had written that the genus *Mahonia* was named in honor of a little-known botanist, the name of this genus in fact commemorates Bernard McMahon, a giant in early-19th-century gardening, horticultural mentor of

Overleaf: *Mahonia oiwakensis*. (Photo by Lynne Harrison)

Thomas Jefferson, and author of the classic *McMahon's American Gardener*. Much like the dismissal of Pluto as a planet, this generic epitaph is in threat of abandonment by contemporary botanists, who favor lumping it into the closely related barberries, genus *Berberis*.

Despite the fact that I can accept the argument for abandoning *Mahonia* in favor of *Berberis* on an intellectual level, physically they appear very distinctive, and in this book I will treat them as separate entities. Under any name, they offer a surfeit of species and hybrids that lend the American garden handsome textural foliage, off-season flowers, and colorful crops of fruit for year-round effects.

Whereas the genus *Berberis* possesses both evergreen and deciduous species, mahonias are unconditionally evergreen, with foliage that is pinnately compound (close observation of the anatomy of the barberries will reveal that their leaves also are compound, though the leaf rachis is so compressed that they appear to possess multiple simple leaves at each node). Mahonias lack the nodal thorns found in the genus *Berberis*; however, their stiff barbed leaves will bite if provoked.

The flowers of both *Berberis* and *Mahonia* are anatomically identical and, depending upon the species, offered in tones of yellow, white, orange, and rarely red. Flowers of both genera possess what are known as irritable anthers, which abruptly and quite visibly contract toward the stigma when stimulated at the base, in the process dabbing any nectar-seeking insect with pollen and delighting the astute observer. The flowers of the majority of mahonias are presented in terminal fascicles of erect, simple racemes, whereas the prototypical inflorescence of the traditional barberry is produced in leaf axils by way of solitary racemes. However, the fact that "bigeneric" crosses have been made, with *Mahoberberis miethkeana*, originating in 1957 at Miethke Nursery in Tacoma, Washington, being the most common in cultivation, makes certain their taxonomic relationship is very close.

Mahonia is a diverse but easily recognizable genus of approximately 70 species found in both the New and Old Worlds, geographically centered in southeastern Asia. The *Flora of China* (Wu et al. 1994 to present) alone provides treatments for 31 species found within their political boundaries. Though a few species, namely *M. aquifolium*, *M. repens*, and *M. bealei*, have been embraced fully in American horticulture, numerous highly ornamental species and hybrids deserve vastly more appreciation. Many of these are suitable to the summer-sticky states of the Southeast as well as the inner-mountain regions of the Southwest. So where to begin?

In Taiwan, I suppose. There in 2007 I saw the first early-winter flowers of *Mahonia oiwakensis*. This species—with elegant, frondlike leaves to 20 in. (50 cm) along stems to 15 ft. (4.6 m) capped by erect racemes of yellow flowers that glowed in the late afternoon shade like coals from a hot fire—is the same taxon I have grown for many years under the illegitimate moniker of *M. lomariifolia*. In addition to Taiwan, it is known to naturally occur in many provinces of western China, from relatively low to rather high elevations over 12,000 ft. (3660 m). In its undiluted state as well as through the hybrids created with it, this species is perhaps the most appreciated for winter floral interest in my garden at Windcliff. *Mahonia oiwakensis* has been paired with other species, mostly notably *M. japonica*, to create some of the finest aristocrats among shrubs for the mild climates of North America.

Elegant, long, pinnate foliage and midwinter flowers of *Mahonia oiwakensis* in my garden. (Photo by Daniel J. Hinkley)

Mahonia japonica is itself a splendid shrub, but curiously, although it has long been cultivated in Japan, it does not occur in that country at all. Instead it shares the same haunts in Taiwan as *M. oiwakensis* and has possibly been collected on the mainland as well. The species, as I know it, is easily recognizable when in flower, with pendulous, rather than upright, terminal racemes of flowers that exude a spellbinding scent of jasmine when in blossom in late winter. It is still used to great extent in landscapes throughout Japan, most notably in municipal plantings in Tokyo.

Though it would be of interest to know if natural hybrids of these two species have ever been reported, the first known pairing occurred spontaneously at the legendary, no longer extant, nursery of Slieve Donard in Ireland. From a thousand potted plants resulting from seed of *Mahonia oiwakensis*, three distinct and obvious hybrids were noted and selected by the king's gardener, Sir Eric Savill. The best of these, christened *M. ×media* 'Charity', still grows as a magnificent specimen at Savill Garden in Great Windsor Park outside of London. I have paid homage to this celebrated specimen on numerous occasions where it now grows as a deep green globe of 15 ft. by 15 ft. (4.6 m by 4.6 m) with toothsome textural qualities. The clear yellow flowers carry a lovely jasmine-like fragrance, although it must be said that the scent is not carried far from the plant. The lovely floral show is often in full swing by Christmas, if not much earlier during mild autumns. 'Hope' and 'Winter Sun' are near equals, though neither have become as popular in North America.

Later, intentional crosses between the same two parents were made by Lionel Fortescue of southwestern England, and the best of the lot bears his name: *Mahonia ×media* 'Lionel Fortescue'. A rather expansive planting of this fine selection entertains us for several weeks each winter, being dependably in full blossom by Thanksgiving Day and carrying on into January. Deep green, pinnate leaves to 18 in. (45 cm) are produced along a narrow, upright framework to 8 ft. (2.4 m) in height, while the bright yellow flowers are found on dense clusters of ter-

The brilliant red new growth of *Mahonia ×media* 'Charity' is reason enough to cultivate this plant. (Photo by Daniel J. Hinkley)

Mahonia ×media 'Charity'. (Photo by Lynne Harrison)

minal racemes to 14 in. (36 cm); as many as 50 racemes in each cluster may crowd the top of each stem.

It was an unusually harsh winter in Seattle in the late 1950s that selected a hybrid from a flat of *Mahonia oiwakensis* seedlings accidentally left outdoors at Washington Park Arboretum. All but a single plant perished from the cold, and this was named *M.* 'Arthur Menzies', commemorating the assistant director of the San Francisco Botanical Garden at Strybing Arboretum, who had provided the seed. It has become a locally celebrated selection and creates a sensational, broad, bold-foliaged specimen to 15 ft. by 10 ft. (4.6 m by 3 m) over many years. The bright yellow flowers borne in dense, upright trusses are generally in peak blossom by New Year's Day. Unfortunately, the frigid temperatures we sometimes experience in mid-December can ruin the floral display.

This is an apparent, yet spontaneous, hybrid believed to be a cross between *Mahonia oiwakensis* and another Chinese species known for, above all else, its identity crisis. *Mahonia bealei* is widespread throughout China and widely cultivated in Japan, Europe, and southeastern North America, where it has become naturalized. Over the years this species has made the rounds under the names *M. japonica* 'Bealei', *M. japonica* var. *bealei*, and *M. japonica* var. *planifolia*. It is handsome and durable, seemingly more content in summer-warm areas of this continent than in the coolness of the Pacific Northwest.

I have long grown *Mahonia duclouxiana* but under the name *M. mairei*. It was under this moniker that I received it from J. C. Raulston at what was then the North Carolina State Arboretum in Raleigh. J. C. had amassed a number of *Mahonia* species and selections,

Mahonia ×media 'Lionel Fortescue' blossoming in early December in my garden. (Photo by Daniel J. Hinkley)

Mahonia 'Arthur Menzies'. (Photo by Daniel J. Hinkley)

Identities Lost, Ornaments Found: *Mahonia* and *Berberis*

Mahonia bealei. (Photo by Lynne Harrison)

and had characteristically distributed them throughout North America to keen gardeners and assorted nurseries.

Mahonia duclouxiana is perhaps the most splendid of all the flowering plants in my garden, possessing the longest and most elegant foliage of all the mahonias we cultivate, with pinnate, sharply textured fronds to 3 ft. (0.9 m) long. Erect, spidery trusses of orange flowers appearing in midwinter present a striking bicolored effect when opening from scarlet buds. This species possesses the gestalt of an evergreen shrub more suited to a warm, sultry climate but has never been seriously harmed by the sharp frosts thrown its way during the past 20 years in my gardens. I have not encountered it in the wild, though I have certainly been within its natural

Mahonia calamicaulis subsp. *kingdon-wardiana.* (Photo by Lynne Harrison)

Mahonia duclouxiana is probably the most handsome and least appreciated of the winter-flowering mahonias. (Photo by Daniel J. Hinkley)

range, 6000–11,000 ft. (1800–3350 m) in Guangxi, Sichuan, and Yunnan Provinces, as well as in India, Myanmar, and Thailand.

It is within the natural range of *Mahonia duclouxiana* that I have collected four additional species that deserve mention and cultivation.

In a dense thicket of bamboo at relatively low elevation in Sichuan Province in 1996, en route to the base of Mount Emei, I found *Mahonia calamicaulis* subsp. *kingdon-wardiana*, which I grew under the name *M. veitchiorum* var. *kingdon-wardiana* for numerous years. Very distinctive in foliage, this species (DJHC 751) offers notably glossy foliage of light green centered with an accentuated bright yellow leaf axis. The stubby terminal racemes of bright yellow flowers are produced in February and March and are not particularly showy, at least in the clone I drew from that immense botanical lottery.

Mahonia fortunei has a rather long history of use in gardens of the Pacific Northwest and has, from time to time, been readily available on a commercial basis. It is distinctive in foliage, with a dull bluish green, pinnate leaf comprised of numerous narrow leaflets that are sadly and extremely susceptible to powdery mildew. The wimpy racemes of yellow flowers produced in late autumn are among the least effective of the genus.

Interestingly, however, my collection of this species from Sichuan in 1998 (DJHC 98484) has provided a phenotype that seems completely resistant to this blight and that, if grown in full sun, takes on a pleasing note of muted orange-red in winter, lightening to bright yellow

My collection of *Mahonia fortunei*, showing bright red foliage during the winter. (Photo by Daniel J. Hinkley)

The foliage of the same collection of *Mahonia fortunei* transitions to bright yellow in spring. (Photo by Daniel J. Hinkley)

Roy Lancaster with his original collection of *Mahonia gracilipes* from Mount Emei in Sichuan, revealing the brilliant white undersurface of the leaves. (Photo by Daniel J. Hinkley)

Mahonia gracilipes. (Photo by Lynne Harrison)

before growth resumes in spring. It deserves to be distributed and trialed more extensively.

I am particularly fond of *Mahonia gracilipes*, which I first saw in Roy Lancaster's garden in Hampshire, United Kingdom, representing his collections, and later saw growing on limestone cliffs at midelevations on Mount Emei. This habit of growth in nature shows off one of its paramount ornamental traits: a brilliant white, waxy undercoating, somewhat variable from seedling to seedling. In autumn, spidery racemes carry coral red and creamy yellow flowers, while the foliage, despite being evergreen, develops good tints of orange and red if grown in full sun. As its wild habitat of choice would suggest, this species appreciates a high pH soil, which can be promoted by the use of lime. My collection of this species (DJHC 755) has done surprisingly well in the Pacific Northwest, flowering and fruiting consistently. As the growth habit of this species is somewhat gawky and thin, selections or hybrids with more density would encourage a more loyal following.

Growing side by side in nature with *Mahonia gracilipes* is *M. eurybracteata*, which I first admired, again, in Roy Lancaster's garden, where it grew under its previous name of *M. confusa*. This is a variable species with regard to foliage, with some individuals possessing an arresting platinum sheen, effective in autumn when erect racemes of yellow flowers appear. My collection of this species from Emei in 1996 (DJHC 837) is particularly good in this regard, receiving high marks from numerous plantsmen who have seen it; subsequent seedlings have inherited this trait to varying degrees. *Mahonia eurybracteata* has been afforded numerous varietal names, whether valid or superfluous only time will tell. Good friend, frequent traveling companion, and fellow *Mahonia* devotee Ozzie Johnson cultivates in his near-unparalleled plant collection outside of Atlanta, Georgia, a splendid example of *M. eurybracteata* subsp. *ganpinensis*; its flower expresses the gestalt of *M. japonica*, while in foliage it appears remarkably similar to that species growing in pots along our hotel balcony in Sichuan, *M. eurybracteata*.

In addition, Ozzie flaunts a beautifully grown specimen of *Mahonia sheridaniana*, known (a relative term) formerly as *M. fargesii*. This moderate-sized species grows in thickets of bamboo in broad-leaved evergreen woodlands of moderately low elevation in south-central Hubei and Sichuan Provinces. In foliage it is reminiscent of *M. calamicaulis*, but when in flower, with lax trusses of pale yellow flowers, it is deceptively similar to *M. japonica*.

Mahonia ×*savilliana* results from a marriage between *M. gracilipes* and *M. eurybracteata*; though first recognized at the Savill Garden near Windsor, England, it has subsequently been found to occur naturally in the mountains of Sichuan where its parent species coexist in the same habitat. Good forms of these two species could be artificially combined to enhance the overall growth habit.

In the mountains of central and eastern Nepal as well as in Sikkim and Bhutan, I have marveled at the daz-

Mahonia eurybracteata, a good form with pewter foliage from Mount Emei in Sichuan Province. (Photo by Daniel J. Hinkley)

Elegant, finely textured fronds of *Mahonia eurybracteata* subsp. *ganpinensis* in the garden of Ozzie Johnson in Atlanta, Georgia. (Photo by Daniel J. Hinkley)

zling ruby new growth of treelike specimens of *Mahonia napaulensis* in late autumn, handsome indeed as the upright trusses of bright yellow flowers open in early to midwinter. Himalayan texts offer both this and *M. acanthifolia* as species encountered in the wild, but they are assuredly one and the same. Occurring at low altitudes where temperatures and humidity are lofty, *M. napaulensis*, in its raw form, would only be suitable for

the most benign climates of the Southeast and Southern California. Though I have cultivated material under this name, to the best of my knowledge the true species is not in cultivation in North America, or if it is, it is extremely rare.

It is not just the Old World, however, that offers up *Mahonia* species deserving use in our gardens. In the New World the genus is found naturally occurring only along the west coast, from British Columbia south to Central America, and only as far east as the Great Basin, where the common name of Oregon grape still adheres. No fewer than 15 taxa exist, though numerous intergrades occur between species where their ranges overlap; these relationships require further study. In addition, though the species that occur in Mexico have garnered considerable taxonomic study, very little is known of the taxa further to the south in the higher elevations of Guatemala, Nicaragua, and Costa Rica.

As a youngster on vacation with my family at Mount Rushmore in South Dakota, I excitedly came upon my first *Mahonia*, *M. repens*, though at the time I believed I was seeing my first *Ilex* in the wild. *Mahonia repens* is certainly the most rugged of the clan and naturally inhabits the climatically brutalized western interior of North America. The suckering stems rise to no more than 1 ft. (0.3 m) in height, with the leathery, evergreen foliage taking on good hints of bronze and red if grown in full sun, especially intense in winter. I have seen this grown as a superlative groundcover at the Denver Botanic Gardens, while it is also effectively employed in the more benign climate of the Pacific Northwest as a drought-tolerant garden subject. *Mahonia repens* subsp. *rotundifolia* makes its horticultural rounds as "spoonleaf" and is distinctive in texture, possessing near-orbicular leaflets.

Growing natively on our land near Indianola is *Mahonia nervosa*, which extends from northern California to British Columbia and possesses a much longer compound leaf than *M. repens*, with 7–23 leaflets. These take on a striking deep purple coloration in winter if grown in full sun, though the species is typically found growing

Mahonia napaulensis in Sikkim, northern India. (Photo by Daniel J. Hinkley)

in moderately moist, shaded positions at low elevations. The terminal racemes of yellow flowers are produced in late winter and result in comely crops of blue fruit. *Mahonia nervosa* has a much more devoted following among gardeners in Europe than in its homeland.

The tall Oregon grape, *Mahonia aquifolium*, caused a certain degree of horticultural twitter when introduced into British horticulture in 1823, setting back the typical obsessive-compulsive gardener of that time frame by some 10 quid. It is a plastic species in nature, making certain identification difficult, as it readily unites with both *M. repens* and *M. pinnata* where their natural digs overlap. Where it is found (infrequently) growing on the Kitsap and Olympic Peninsulas in Washington State, it forms a vigorous, suckering shrub to 8 ft. (2.4 m) or taller, with glossy, pinnate, spiny-edged leaves. Erect, though short, racemes of butterscotch flowers appear in late winter, resulting in sets of blackish blue fruits.

There are handsome selections based, at least primarily, on this species. *Mahonia aquifolium* 'Atropurpureum' is sensational and should be available much more than it currently is. The glistening purple suffusion of its evergreen foliage does not ripen until the onslaught of low winter temperatures, adding a delicious, rich, gleaming presence to the off-season landscape. In February of 2001 I was privileged to take a walk through the unpretentious yet profoundly loved garden of Graham Stuart Thomas two years before he died. Together we admired *M. aquifolium* 'Moseri', which develops fertile tones of burgundy in its winter foliage. I am perplexed as to why this handsome and durable shrub has not made its way into broader use in American horticulture. In the early 1990s I received from J. C. Raulston a selection known as *M. aquifolium* 'Orange Flame' that remains quite compact in growth, to 3½ ft. by 3½ ft. (1.1 m by 1.1 m), with more deeply saturated flowers of rich yellow-orange in late winter.

Closely allied to *Mahonia aquifolium* is *M. pinnata*, which extends from Baja to British Columbia. Because it so readily hybridizes with *M. aquifolium*, it possesses a checkered past with regard to both its taxonomy and its

The sensational, deep burgundy foliage of *Mahonia aquifolium* 'Atropurpureum' in winter. (Photo by Daniel J. Hinkley)

Mahonia aquifolium 'Moseri' in the garden of Graham Stuart Thomas. (Photo by Daniel J. Hinkley)

Mahonia aquifolium 'Orange Flame'. (Photo by Lynne Harrison)

Mahonia pinnata 'Ken Hartman'. (Photo by Lynne Harrison)

horticultural application. Known hybrids between the two in cultivation, which are perhaps more plentiful than first imagined, have been provided the umbrella title of *M. ×wagneri*. True *M. pinnata* generally possesses more than the five to nine leaflets per leaf of *M. aquifolium*, with seven to eleven leaflets per leaf. The leaflets are of a finer texture and have more spines along the margin. I am particularly fond of a selection known as 'Ken Hartman', whose dense, rounded form and textural, spiny, glossy leaves are as handsome as this sun- or shade-adaptable shrub is utilitarian.

Mahonia pinnata subsp. *insularis* represents one of the rarest of plants in North America, with only two extant individuals alive on Santa Cruz Island in California. Fortunately, propagules of this taxon have been distributed, frequently encountered by way of the cultivar 'Schnilemoon'. This has proven to be a handsome and adaptable plant in the coolness of the Pacific Northwest, where I cultivate it in full sun in draining soils.

Mahonia nevinii is a striking, blue-foliaged, finely textured species to 6 ft. (1.8 m). Hailing from California, it is rare in nature and listed as federally endangered, though it is well preserved in gardens. It is closely allied to *M. fremontii* and *M. trifoliolata*, and the triad is superb in a hot, baking site with sharply drained soils. The year-round interest of ever-present, spiny, glaucous foliage is joined by a lovely display of yellow flowers in spring and colorful crops of edible red fruit in late summer. Superb specimens of *M. nevinii* at the Denver Botanic Gardens offer a glimpse of its ornamental appeal and adaptability to a rugged gardening climate.

Further south, the Mexican species of *Mahonia* await a further embrace by gardeners to the north. Introduced to the United States and Canada primarily through the efforts of Yucca Do Nursery in Hempstead, Texas, three in particular deserve illuminating.

Mahonia pallida offers a distinctive texture with short, compound leaves comprised of rounded leaflets. In late summer (an unconventional time of year for mahonias to flower), sprays of creamy white flowers gracefully arch from the apex of each stem. Those familiar with the genus *Nandina*, or heavenly bamboo, will find the similarity in floral effect to be uncanny, yet this should not be surprising, since *Nandina* is found within the same family, Berberidaceae.

Tony Avent of Plant Delights Nursery grows another Mexican species, *Mahonia gracilis*, to perfection in his exciting garden outside of Raleigh, North Carolina. Clad with glossy green leaves, its stems rise to 6 ft. (1.8 m) or more, and its yellow flowers, borne in midwinter, fill the garden with a heady redolence of jasmine. Though this species survives in the Pacific Northwest, its performance is weak compared with how it functions in summer-warm regions of North America and Europe.

Nick Macer of Pan-Global Plants in the United Kingdom, a highly regarded woody plants specialist and self-avowed *Mahonia*-phile, has observed numerous under-known species south of our border, including the poorly understood *Mahonia moranensis*, which he found deep in northern Puebla, west of Teziutlán. This species is indeed handsome in foliage and flower, and is closely allied to *M. pinnata*.

Further to the south in the páramo of Costa Rica, I have collected fruit of both *Mahonia chochoca*, with ethereally blue foliage on stems to 10 ft. (3 m) (though much less if grown in full sun) and racemes of creamy yellow flowers, and at higher elevations, *M. volcanica*. Despite its probable light neutral requirements, I am giving both species a fair trial under cultivation in my Indianola garden.

One attribute of all *Mahonia* species is that they invite wildlife into the garden. Butterflies and birds are attracted to their nectar-rich flowers, which are offered at a time of year when there is often little else in blossom. The fruits of many of the species are among the first ripening berries of the season, ready to greet newly arriving birds hungry from a long migration north. I have witnessed large flocks of Bohemian waxwings devour the colorful crops of *Mahonia* fruit, which I am only too happy to share, while throughout the winter months, Anna's hummingbirds and Townsend's warblers visit the flowers daily for nectar.

Because a few species of *Berberis* (by far *not* a majority) play alternate host to wheat rust fungus, the amal-

Nick Macer's collection of *Mahonia moranensis* from north of Mexico City. (Photo by Nick Macer)

Mahonia chochoca showing its ripening fruits at moderate elevation in Costa Rica. (Photo by Daniel J. Hinkley)

gamation of *Mahonia* and *Berberis* has tainted the legal status of *Mahonia* in some states. Hopefully, over time, adequate testing will acquit those judged guilty by association. Still, it is better to play the good citizen and contact your local extension agent for restrictions, especially if you live in wheat country.

As I attempt to more accurately assess the hardiness and adaptability of the species in this highly ornamental genus, I will appreciate hearing from anyone regarding their experiences. If you, however, have not yet tried growing these evergreen shrubs, I encourage you to do so.

HARDINESS: As a general rule, American species from the arid, inner-mountain regions are extremely hardy, zones 4–9. Coastal species from the Pacific Northwest will thrive in zones 6–10. The Mexican and Central American species, as well as most Asian species, are only appropriate for zones 7–10.

CULTIVATION: Full sun to partially shaded sites in well-draining soils, slightly acidic to slightly alkaline. Winter color of the foliage is embellished in full-sun situations, which will also promote a neater habit of growth. Hard pruning of the taller species directly after flowering will encourage growth from the base and promote a more pleasing density to the shrub; this is especially important on youthful plants even though it requires sacrificing floral effects for the first two or three seasons. Strawberry root weevil will damage the leaf margins, especially with the more thinly textured American species. Powdery mildew can be problematic on some species, particularly if air circulation is diminished.

PROPAGATION: Seeds sown fresh in autumn will readily germinate the following spring. Obviously, the hybrids and named forms will not come true; however, in my experience the mahonias are not as promiscuous in this regard as are the barberries, which are downright iniquitous. Hardwood cuttings taken from mid-August to November are successful. Though single-node cuttings (one leaf, one bud, and a short piece of stem) are appealing in terms of increasing the number of cuttings offered up from each stock plant, the axillary bud will often remain dormant for 18 months. A tip cutting, on the other hand, can result in a gallon-sized plant by the end of the first season.

A Quintet of Barberries

Horticulturally there is little challenge in distinguishing those plants that have historically represented the genus *Berberis* from species of *Mahonia*, since they have simple leaves alternately arranged along the stem. But this is an erroneous observation, as botanists explain, since the leaves of *Berberis* are actually tightly compressed and compound.

Despite the fact that barberries remain popular landscape plants, the genus comes with a good amount of baggage. First, many in the genus, though not all, lend themselves as alternate hosts of *Puccinia graminis*, the fungus causing wheat rust. Known as a heteroecious fungal species, it requires both a cereal crop and a susceptible species of *Berberis* (or *Mahonia*) to complete its life cycle.

Though this fungus has historically had a devastating impact on wheat production (the Romans prayed to Robigus, the stem rust god, while both the Soviets and the Americans stockpiled spores during the Cold War as a biological weapon), rust-resistant wheat varieties have alleviated much of the problem. However, a rise in virulent strains of this fungus may bring the issue back to the fore.

A more ominous threat to the good name of the genus may be the Japanese barberry, *Berberis thunbergii*, wreaking havoc in the woodlands and meadows of northeastern North America. Fecund in regard to fruit production under cultivation, and readily distributed by birds, the species has been banned for sale in several states.

The taxonomy of the genus is difficult, with only a few possessing the courage to take it on. One of those brave souls, Julian Harber of the Royal Botanic Gardens, Kew, has been enormously helpful in sorting out those species I have observed in China, Vietnam, Taiwan, Nepal, and Japan. In China alone, in one of two centers of diversity—the other being South America—there exists some 215 species.

Under cultivation, the plot thickens further, as *Berberis* species readily hybridize. Hybrids raised from cultivated seed have been marketed under erroneous species names for so long that they are hopelessly muddled. This ease of hybridization may ultimately serve well this frequently discredited genus through the production of sterile plants, with breeding programs already underway to realize that goal.

I am conflicted about writing about, and thus promoting, these plants, despite the fact that in the Pacific Northwest, seed production under cultivation is infrequent, so there is little risk of plants escaping the garden. As a means of acknowledging the genus without singing too loudly its praises, I have chosen only five of my favorites to discuss: two from China, two from South America, and one whose origin will probably never be known.

It was in the late 1980s during our first Grand Garden Tour in England that we visited Sissinghurst Castle and the celebrated garden of Vita Sackville-West. Showcased in one of the hedged gardens not far from the tower grew a powdery-blue-foliaged shrub that shook my socks when I saw it from a distance. Here, in this garden, combining plants for greatest impact was a high art form, so perhaps, I thought, it was not the shrub but the composition that I found so exciting. As I got closer and learned its identity, by crassly stepping over the hedge and reading the label at its base, I found that *Berberis temolaica*, a deciduous shrub to 10 ft. (3 m) in height, was every bit as dramatic as a singular noun than as an adjective from a distance. The quest was on to find this plant, and it took me to some very interesting places.

First came a realization of the promiscuity of this genus as whole. For three years I ordered seed of this species through various seed lists and exchanges. What resulted not only looked unlike *Berberis temolaica*, it did not even remotely possess the character of anything I wanted in my garden.

Native to Tibet and Yunnan Province at elevations over 14,000 ft. (4300 m), this shrub has enormous potential in terms of hardiness. It was during my 1998 trip to far northeastern Yunnan outside of Dêqên that I believed I would have the greatest likelihood of finding it, on an astonishingly beautiful trek across Beima Shan. There were barberries aplenty, many ablaze in autumn color, but virtually all were *Berberis angulosa*, the species we had come upon so often along the Jaljale Himal in northeastern Nepal. Skunked again.

Oddly enough, it was during a short visit to Western Hills Nursery in Occidental, California, that the signature foliage color of this species caught my eye. A single pot of it sat on a far table, near a fellow traveler and very keen plantsperson who happened to be ahead of me in the aisle, and whose eyes would fall upon this rarity at any moment. I believe I screamed either "Killer bees!" or "Rattlesnake!"—I do not remember which. At any rate, *Berberis temolaica* has proven to be as beautiful in my garden as I remember it that day at Sissinghurst Castle.

Berberis temolaica. (Photo by Daniel J. Hinkley)

Interestingly enough, it was during that same day hiking the precarious back alleys of that celebrated nursery that I found a small pot of a barberry brandishing narrow evergreen leaves of a most arresting translucent burgundy. On the pot itself in wax pencil, as was customary to this enterprise, was written its name and price: *Berberis replicata*, $3.00. What was written across the shrub itself, to my mind, was "too beautiful to possibly be hardy."

Ten years later this species had verified my initial assessment of beauty but steadfastly denied any tenderness, at least in our hardiness zone. Its arching canes rise quite quickly to 6 ft. by 5 ft. (1.8 m by 1.5 m), carrying elegantly narrow evergreen foliage that emerges in spring, in fact whenever in growth, in tones of ruby red. The yellow flowers, so typical of the genus as whole, offer a somewhat funky perfume that in my garden has proven to be highly attractive to diptera (that would be houseflies); however, the odor is an ephemeral distraction from the beauty provided the remaining 11½ months of the year.

The actual name of this fine shrub, though, continues to vex. *Berberis replicata* is a valid name for a species collected by George Forrest in Yunnan in the early years of the 20th century, at above 5500 ft. (1700 m) in elevation. His voucher specimens of this at the Kew Herbarium, however, bear no physical resemblance to the plant we grow under this name, nor have I ever during my time in Forrest's stomping grounds, primarily on Cang Shan in Yunnan Province, seen anything that bears resemblance to what I grow.

I have been tempted to prepare an herbarium specimen of this taxon to settle the matter once and for all. However, I recall Roy Lancaster telling of a gentleman who appeared at Kew one day with stems cut from his garden of barberries he wished to have identified. The staff taxonomists, it seems, upon hearing his request, evaporated into the crooks and crannies of the building and did not again emerge until the man had safely departed. With that in mind, for the time being I will content myself in growing this under the name *Ber-*

beris replicata, as it is fully worth growing, all the while remaining fully cognizant of the degree of entertainment that exists within the extended game of identification itself.

I had grown, in fact propagated and sold, *Berberis prattii* for several years before I happened to stumble upon the real thing during yet another trip to England, while in the garden of the late, great plantsman, gentleman, and scholar Jack Elliot. Over the years, Jack introduced me to and provided me propagules of many good plants, and during that time I came to realize that he did not expound upon a plant subject unless it was well deserved. In the far corner of his garden, during a July visit, I believed I saw a very late blossoming specimen of a golden chain, *Laburnum anagyroides*, until a flabbergasting closer inspection brought the identity of the genus into full view. The pendulous terminal panicles of soft yellow flowers were nearly 1 ft. (0.3 m) in length, while the deciduous, orbicular, spiny-edged foliage was a pleasing blue-green along a narrow framework to 15 ft. (4.6 m).

Realizing how awestruck I was by what I was seeing, Jack promised to root a cutting to share with me during my next trip abroad. Sadly, that visit with Dr. Elliot was my last, as he passed away the following spring. His wife, Jean, moved from their splendid home and garden, and now I am left, along with my appreciation for having known this couple, to wonder if that specimen of *Berberis prattii* still exists. Hailing from over 12,000 ft. (3660 m) in Sichuan Province and Tibet, it would assuredly be a candidate for the northern Midwest if testing proved its stability under cultivation. In its favor is the fact that its crops of red fruit have never been touched by birds where it is under cultivation in England; this both extends its season of ornament and lessens the possibility of unintended distribution.

It was at the Garden House, the estate and plant collection of Lionel Fortescue near Tavistock in Devon, that I first became acquainted with both *Berberis valdiviana* and Keith and Roz Wiley, curators and managers of the estate. While this initial meeting of the Wileys has matured into a friendship and my continued admi-

Berberis replicata. (Photo by Daniel J. Hinkley)

Berberis prattii. (Photo by Daniel J. Hinkley)

A Quintet of Barberries

ration of this couple's profound horticulturally artistic abilities, my relationship with *B. valdiviana* has been one of unrequited love lasting more than two decades.

In the walled garden grew a tall evergreen shrub with narrow, deep glossy green leaves that boasted so loudly of its aristocracy that one might have been tempted to cut it down out of envy. To make things yet more

unbearable, pendulous clusters of orange-yellow flowers tumbled from the ends and axils of each branch. It was not an inconsiderable amount of chemistry I was feeling between myself and this species. Since I had not yet procured a permit allowing the importation of *Berberis* and *Mahonia* into North America, I spent a moment contemplating some means of felonious smuggling. Fortunately, there were no plants available, and I came to my senses.

I later met up with more imposters of *Berberis valdiviana*—physically ridiculous caricatures of the real McCoy—offered by honest nurserymen who did not understand the loose morals of the genus as a whole. And later still, a concerted effort was made to locate the

Berberis valdiviana. (Photo by Daniel J. Hinkley)

My collection of *Berberis darwinii* from Chiloé Island, where it was collected by William Lobb in 1849, blossoming in my garden. (Photo by Daniel J. Hinkley)

species near its namesake of Valdivia along the coast of southern Chile. My traveling partners and I did find extraordinary plants there, though absent from them was *B. valdiviana*, which is now considered extremely rare due to extensive habitat loss. Of course, I am perfectly okay with not yet having this splendid species in my new garden, where it would be so well accommodated by our climate. Truly. Not.

The story of my five favorite barberries ends somewhat south of Valdivia, on the island of Chiloé, where my friends Jennifer Macuiba and Kevin Carrabine crossed tidal waters on a four-man scow to the very landing where William Lobb collected *Berberis darwinii* in 1849 (though the species was first described by Charles Darwin in 1835). I can recall something quite ethereal in walking among these shrubs, as one might feel on a stroll amidst the columns of the Roman Forum.

Berberis darwinii is already greatly favored in horticulture, though I believe much better forms can be achieved through selection. A chance seedling from my collections, under HCM 98129, has proven to be the best I have seen—an observation with an obvious bias—with dense, globular, terminal clusters of orange-red flowers amidst deep black-green, tiny, hollylike leaves. It can be vigorous under cultivation, to 15 ft. (4.6 m) tall, though generally smaller. It seems as approving of open relationships as the rest of it brethren and is especially attracted to fellow countrymen. With the low, finely textured *B. empetrifolia* that we collected on the steaming volcanic slopes of Termas de Chillán at 5500 ft. (1700 m), it has produced *B. ×stenophylla*, which appears, too infrequently to my mind, in a sublime assemblage of selected cultivars. And a marriage between *B. darwinii* and *B. trigona* (syn. *B. linearifolia*), a splendid, hardier evergreen species with narrow, deep green leaves and a confection of orange late-winter flowers, has resulted in *B. ×lologensis*.

HARDINESS: *Berberis temolaica* and *B. prattii* are hardy in zones (4)5–9; *B. replicata* in zones 7–10; *B. valdiviana* in zones 8–12; and *B. darwinii*, *B. trigona*, and *B. empetrifolia* in zones 7b–10.

CULTIVATION: The barberries enjoy a full-sun position, especially if a flowering effect is to be encouraged. However, I will admit to having deliberately grown the evergreen species in too little light to achieve a more lax habit of growth while taking pleasure in the foliage. The deciduous species will offer little ornament in less than full sun. The soil requirements are forgiving as long as they are free draining. Production of viable seed is greatly diminished if plants are isolated; however, most barberries will eagerly seek out a pollen partner if within reach. It goes without saying that until concerns about the reemergence of virulent strains of wheat rust fungus are put to bed, barberries should not be cultivated in wheat-growing regions.

PROPAGATION: I have hammered home the inappropriate choice of seed from cultivated sources to attempt to replicate the barberry species. Yet through this means, an exciting array of potential ornamental (and possibly sterile) hybrids is possible. I hope this is achievable. Propagation of most species by cuttings is easy enough (evergreen species in mid- to late autumn on bottom heat, deciduous species as softwood cuttings under mist). *Berberis temolaica* does not readily root, which might explain why it is so infrequently found in commerce. Where it is in commerce in Europe, it is often found as grafted plants, presumably using hybrid seedlings raised from the species under cultivation, as rootstock.

A Quintet of Barberries

Endearing, Elegant, and Unexpected:
Metapanax and Other Araliaceae

I pick up the second bag in my tent, glare at the fruit inside, and grimace to myself when I squeeze the first kernel and nothing gives. I think of how the hard, mealy fruits of Schefflera *are designed for slow avian digestion; they will give up their seed stubbornly in between two layers of 5-mil plastic. It is a job that I would not mind doing while mindlessly watching* The Sopranos *or listening to music while sitting in front of the fire with the dogs snoring by my side. But going seed by seed surrounded by darkness and coldness and with hip joints cementing into place, I find no joy or satisfaction in the process.*

Now Venus begins to settle beyond the ridge to the west. It just so happens that it is the brightest I have ever seen Venus; in fact this is the brightest I have ever seen any planet in my life. I am keeping the door to my tent open to watch it plummet to the horizon. As it dips beyond the mountain in the distance, above the river, I can make out the silhouettes of flat-topped firs, Abies spectabilis, *lined up like wise scouts along the ridge to spy the valleys and distant snows. Resentfully, I begin again to massage the fruit inside the bags in front of me, coaxing each seed out of its flesh.*

The color of Queen Anne cherries, the fruit of Schefflera bengalensis *took me off guard this morning, glowing like hot coals amidst black-green pools of foliage. It was a climbing* Schefflera *and one I had hoped to see after reading of it in the* Flora of Bhutan. *It was like coming across some minor ruin in Athens or Rome after reading of it in a guide and thinking, "How exciting," and then forgetting it entirely.*

I briefly examine the Schefflera *seed I have squeezed from its fruit. I hold it to the candle on the pad of my thumb, this tiny seed, and wonder if this one, this tiny fleck of carbohydrate and oil and protein, will actually become a plant. What exact molecule of water will be the first to be imbibed and begin the process of germination? Where will that molecule of water have been before? In what thunderstorm, what glacier? Will this become the plant that will ultimately grow in my garden, or that which will grow in yours? I hope it won't end up in your garden, I think to myself smugly: you will kill it.*

One hundred forty-three miles
east of Thimpu, Bhutan
November 6, 2005

THERE IS NO QUESTION THAT A FAMILY the size of the Araliaceae is going to make trouble, especially when an entire regiment of newly trained taxonomists is on the move looking for fertile fields to plough and names to make. For example, during the relatively short amount of time that has passed since I began writing this book (short in relation to the age of the universe, that is), the entire genus of *Schefflera*—but one species, *S. digitata* from New Zealand—has evaporated, only to reappear months later with a

The scrambling *Schefflera bengalensis*, with bright orange fruit, growing at moderate elevation in Bhutan. (Photo by Daniel J. Hinkley)

more bizarre slant, a genus bigger and better than ever. Now it is suggested that the genus *Aralia*, those prickly-stemmed trees and herbaceous woodlanders so many of us have cultivated, has taxonomically transmuted into *Schefflera* as well.

As I have said before, this earnest attempt to better understand and articulate the relationships of life on our planet does not trouble my stars; however, I would also like my efforts in discussing these taxa to remain relevant for at least a few weeks after this printing is complete and the ink has dried. Time will ultimately unravel the story; until then, I offer my observations with full cognizance of my utter inability to sway taxonomic opinion in any fashion. The disclaimer is thus: the plants I write about here will not exist in the future, at least not under these names.

The aralia family, Araliaceae, holds in its ranks numerous trees, shrubs, and vines, both evergreen and deciduous, that are worthy of integration into our gardens. The landscapes of North America and Europe already abound in members of the family, including the criminalized thug *Hedera helix* (English ivy) and the more polite, barely hardy *Fatsia japonica* (Japanese aralia). Fortunately, most members of the family have not proven themselves problematic in regard to invasiveness and can be relied on for fantastic textural effects from foliage, from the simple, deeply lobed leaves of *Sinopanax* to the palmately or pinnately compound leaves of *Schefflera*.

The family is bound by its distinctive compound inflorescence, generally panicles of globe-shaped umbels, with fertilization resulting in fleshy drupes or berries. These fruits are, in numerous instances, only produced after a polymorphic midlife crisis, when the entire veneer of the species changes phenomenally from juvenile to adult.

There exists a sizeable number of native North American members of the genus, and my exclusion of these may seem dismissive or snobbish. As a matter of note, I consider our native devil's club, *Oplopanax horridus*, with its bold, papery-textured leaves and brilliant heads of orange-red fruit in late summer, to be among the most sensational plants in our natural landscape. Sadly, however, it simply refuses to survive the transition to a garden setting. From eastern North America, another deciduous, angrily stemmed small tree or large shrub known as *Aralia spinosa* has in the past been highly recommended for attracting native bird species into the garden. For that I might put up with its suckering habit and biting bristles; but I have omitted it from major discussion here, and in my defense, I have also left out its numerous Asian counterparts, finding them too coarse and unruly.

It was probably in China, in Yunnan Province above Lichiang, in 1996, that I became fully infatuated with the potential of the small, hardy evergreen species found in the Araliaceae as a whole. It was there that I first met

Oplopanax horridus near Juneau, Alaska. (Photo by Daniel J. Hinkley)

Metapanax delavayi (collected as *Nothopanax delavayi* DJHC 181), a handsome, rounded shrub to 15 ft. (4.6 m) in height with finely textured, palmately compound leaves. At the apex of each branch was an erect, narrow infructescence carrying succulent blue-black fruit. Interestingly, though I returned to the general vicinity of that excursion on four different occasions, I never again encountered this species.

Metapanax delavayi has performed admirably in our garden, where in full sun it has formed an attractive, rounded specimen to 8 ft. by 7 ft. (2.4 m by 2.1 m) with a dense shag of highly textural leaves that have suffered no significant damage by temperatures as low as 10°F (−12°C). It grows, as one might expect, in a more lax manner in shaded sites; in so doing, it reveals its annual

Metapanax delavayi. (Photo by Daniel J. Hinkley)

shedding of older leaves, which to my mind somewhat diminishes its comely appearance. The racemes of small white umbels are produced in late summer.

The same autumn of that trip in 1996, Frank Bell, Darrell Probst, and I continued on our own to Sichuan Province, which resulted, in retrospect, in some of the most exciting botanical exploration I have ever taken part in. It was not so much the plants, though they were fantastic: it was the freshness and rawness of China just beginning to reveal again its potential, without the jadedness on my part that ultimately accumulates when afforded the luxury of constant travel.

During our time near Baoxing, northwest of Chengdu —the geographical center of the remaining wild population of giant pandas—I collected seed of what I believed at the time to be the same taxon I had collected in Yunnan, *Metapanax delavayi*, though it possessed a decidedly coarser expression in foliage, with leaves more consistently three- to five-lobed rather than five- to seven-lobed.

As this matured, however, it became increasingly apparent that it was another taxon entirely, one ultimately identified as *Metapanax davidii* (formerly in the genus *Pseudopanax*), honoring Père Armand David, the gentle French missionary and naturalist who so diligently inventoried his surroundings. It has made a splendid specimen in my current garden, forming a rounded specimen of primarily trifoliate leaves, each leaflet narrow and to 5 in. (12.5 cm) long. It has proved to be as hardy and as adaptable to the chill of the Pacific Northwest as my Yunnan collection.

In both China and Japan, I have been thrust by default—sometimes in aggravation, often in ambivalence—into association with the genus *Acanthopanax*, which in recent times has been dissected to recognize as well the genus *Eleutherococcus*. These taxa are rather easily identified in the field by their compound, deciduous foliage, generally bristly or barbed stems, and often startling umbels of black fruit following a quiet floral season of greenish to ivory white, globe-shaped inflorescences.

Metapanax and Other Araliaceae

Metapanax davidii. (Photo by Lynne Harrison)

These species often represent handsome trees (inexplicably scarce in cultivation), while the lion's share represent what are sincerely shrubs. My aggravation comes from the often insidious task of extricating my raingear from their stems while hiking through dense vegetation; my ambivalence is primarily due to their notoriously lackluster response in the marketplace. For numerous years my excitement in describing these species I had brought home from Asia, with the expectation that my prose would somehow translate into experimentation on the part of the gardening public, seemingly fell flat on its face. After years of experiencing this snub while having to discard yearly excess onto the burn pile, I began to bypass their beautiful orbs of glistening black fruit while confronting them in the wild, realizing that they would have a greater shot at fame and fortune if left precisely where they belonged.

If there is one star in this genus, it is *Eleutherococcus sieboldianus* in its neatly white-edged-leaf form 'Variegatus'. The species itself is quite handsome, with finely textured, palmately compound, medium green leaves and somewhat barbed stems. I first encountered it in the wild in northern Honshū in 1995, slightly above Lake Towada amidst an opulent inventory of shrubs and trees in autumn color. It is appropriate to note that on the same day, my companions Barry Yinger and Masato Yokoi, two of the most passionate variegated-plant aficionados I have ever known, found a variegated sport of *Acanthopanax sciadophylloides*, a species larger in all aspects, growing as a tree to 40 ft. (12 m) or more. They marked the location to return and gather it at a more appropriate time of year.

While on Mount Sorak, on the northeast coast of South Korea, I spotted *Acanthopanax sessiliflorus*, with glistening umbels of jet black fruit held by very short pedicels, sufficiently profuse to draw the branches—to 10 ft. (3 m) in height and still clad in mostly trifoliate leaves transitioning to brilliant yellow autumnal tones—nearly to the ground.

The fruits of *Acanthopanax sessiliflorus* were similar in effect to the splendid inky black crops of *A. setchuenen-*

Eleutherococcus sieboldianus 'Variegatus'.
(Photo by Daniel J. Hinkley)

sis that I encountered on the higher elevations of Mount Emei in Sichuan; they were also distinctively held along unarmed branches, which, in addition to the plant's trifoliate nature, allowed for a rather easy identification. I long considered this to be the finest of the genus that I had collected, though despite my florid descriptors and aggressive persistence, it too found few admirers.

Two years later, during my first trip to Chile, I met two species of the genus *Pseudopanax*, in fact the only two that occur in South America. By 2005 I already had visits to New Zealand and Tasmania under my belt and was thusly ready to encounter both shrubs and vines in this genus. Of the 50-odd genera belonging to the Araliaceae, *Pseudopanax* is found only in the Southern Hemisphere, though it possesses a wide distribution: New Zealand, New Caledonia, Tasmania, and South America.

It was exciting to meet *Pseudopanax laetevirens* in its native haunts, where it proved itself a commonly encountered, large, evergreen shrub at midelevations along the lower forested slopes of the many volcanoes of southern Chile. It has bright green, palmately compound foliage, each leaflet to less than 3 in. (7.5 cm), along stems to 15 in. (38 cm). It is also known to occur in southern Argentina.

In Chile, at 1200–1500 ft. (370–460 m) and generally beneath an overstory of *Nothofagus*, it associated with *Drimys winteri* var. *andina*, *Desfontainia spinosa*, *Berberis trigona*, *Myrceugenia chrysocarpa*, and *Pernettya*, while its distinctive spidery texture and gloss of foliage were apparent from a significant distance. In late February the terminal panicles of deep lavender fruit were perfectly ripe. From those first collections, I have come to appreciate this species a great deal and expect its terminal yellow-green flowers to appear in mid- to late May. Though this species has bravely tolerated temperatures as low as 12°F (−11°C) without damage, I have inexplicably and quickly lost two specimens with symptoms that would suggest a root pathogen.

Pseudopanax valdiviensis is the other species that occurs in Chile; unremarkably, I first encountered it in the rain forests just north of Valdivia on the west coast in the winter of 2005. Unlike the former species, this species behaves more as a scrambling shrub or vine, with four to five broad, ovate, glistening green leaflets per leaf. Also unlike its more upright cousin, which grew on sharply draining volcanic grit, this species grew in hummocks of perpetually moist moss in rather dense shade.

Traveling due east to Tasmania from Chile, some 6000 miles (9700 km), the genus *Pseudopanax* expresses itself with an extraordinarily similar accent. Demonstrating Tasmania's Gondwana heritage, the endemic *P. gunnii* possesses a great superficial resemblance to Chile's *P. laetevirens* and is encountered in the moist forests of the west and southwest. I have not had experience with this species under cultivation.

The subtle green flowers and handsome, finely textured, palmate foliage of my collection of *Pseudopanax laetevirens* growing at Windcliff. (Photo by Daniel J. Hinkley)

Metapanax and Other Araliaceae

It would not be a stretch to say that if you recognize the overall design of a *Schefflera*—that is, a shrub or small tree with evergreen, palmately compound foliage—then you can recognize any *Pseudopanax* species in the wild. Unless, that is, you happen to be in New Zealand and first encounter the so-called lancewoods.

Most island ecosystems have a rather intriguing flora and fauna, but New Zealand sets the standard on peculiarity. In theory at least, most fingers point to the moa, a dominant flightless bird, as the guilty party. The 15 or so species of this bird—all of which were extirpated after the arrival of the Polynesians—were relentless browsers, with some rising to 15 ft. (4.6 m) in height. Adapting to this pressure, the plants of New Zealand evolved strategies to outwit the ravenous beak of a bird the size of a Bradley tank. Enter heteromorphism.

As gardeners, many of us are familiar with the physical changes of plants as they morph from juvenile to adult. Euonymus, English ivy, and eucalyptus are just three of many taxa that demonstrate profound physical changes while maturing. However, I am hard pressed to think of any plant species more whimsical than *Pseudopanax ferox* or *P. crassifolius* in its transformation from youth to maturity.

Pseudopanax ferox, from a limited range on the North Island, and *P. crassifolius*, more widely distributed on both islands, spend the first chapter of their lives as an extremely constricted, unbranched structure more closely resembling a marine invertebrate than a higher form of plant life. Both are clad with narrow, linear, jagged-edged, strongly deflexed leaves to 15 in. (38 cm) long in muted tones of rusty green (with a handsome yellow stripe down the middle of the blade in *P. crassifolius*). The otherworldly effects these plants deliver are no less than if Salvador Dali were left alone with tin snips and strips of rusted metal.

After a decade or longer of beanpoling and, presumably, outmaneuvering the moa's reach, these two species of *Pseudopanax* shift to adult normalcy by beginning to branch while producing shorter, compound, less-armed foliage. As the branching occurs at such an ungainly

height, the ornamental desirability of the plant diminishes in middle age, a reality most gardeners themselves must ultimately confront.

Though reliably hardy only in the mildest coastal climates of the Pacific, *Pseudopanax ferox* and the hardier *P. crassifolius* are adaptable, in fact sensational, as container plants. As they establish, their growth rate is surprisingly fast, with 8–10 in. (20–25 cm) gained in height annually; both develop into living sculptures that will provoke double takes as well as offer the gardener a glimpse into the marvels of plant biology and evolution.

While in New Zealand, I used my outdated field guides in an attempt to sort out the other endemic species of *Pseudopanax* and the genus *Neopanax,* with

Pseudopanax crassifolius on the South Island of New Zealand. (Photo by Daniel J. Hinkley)

which it has been amalgamated. Without the prompting of an attending botanist, with a native species of *Schefflera* thrown into the mix, and with juvenile and adult growth habits as well as ample natural hybridization underway, I will admit to having been quite perplexed by the lot. (As an aside, it was relatively easy to identify *whauwhaupaku*, or *Pseudopanax arboreus*, as its life cycle begins by germinating in the crowns of tree ferns; its root system then drops to the soil surface while becoming the supporting "trunk" after the fern dies.)

With that said, I could identify *Pseudopanax lessonii*, possessing a thick, leathery, boldly textured, palmately compound leaf on an upright framework to 25 ft. (7.6 m). I had come to know this species primarily from its popular golden-variegated form, 'Gold Splash', fre-quently seen in mild coastal gardens of Cornwall, England. Even in a highly protected alcove in my garden in Indianola, my sizeable specimen succumbed to temperatures of 17°F (−8°C) in the winter of 2006–2007. There is also a purple-foliaged form, 'Purple Warrior', although it warrants mentioning that I have seen a purple-foliaged selection of *P. discolor*, another New Zealand species, offered under the same name. There are numerous other cultivars of *P. lessonii* in commerce.

Showing considerable hardiness in my garden are some novel hybrids between the lancewoods, *Pseudopanax crassifolius* and *P. ferox*, and *Pseudopanax* species with more traditional, palmately compound foliage. *Pseudopanax* 'Sabre' has proven itself tough and durable, with nearly black-green, narrow, linear foliage to 6 in.

Pseudopanax crassifolius adult. (Photo by Daniel J. Hinkley)

Pseudopanax ferox. (Photo by Lynne Harrison)

Metapanax and Other Araliaceae

(15 cm) possessing a bright red central vein held along what I consider a somewhat disappointing lax habit of growth; it would probably benefit from a brighter position than where I currently have it trialed. *Pseudopanax* 'Cyril Watson' is an extremely handsome and popular hybrid in the nursery trade of southern England, representing a hybrid between *P. crassifolius* and *P. lessonii*. The three-lobed leaves of leathery constitution are held concentrated on an upright, rounded framework to 8 ft. (2.4 m).

It was *Schefflera digitata*, the only species to occur in New Zealand, that occasionally made its appearance on forest margins at low to moderate elevations, and after a month of self-questioning, I ultimately came to distinguish its glossy leaves and less leathery texture from the numerous *Pseudopanax*, most notably *P. colensoi*, that attempted to waylay my confidence. By 2004 I had already entered into my obsession with this genus, and though I knew *S. digitata* would not prove remotely hardy in the Pacific Northwest, I nonetheless was excited to observe it in the wild.

I suspect that anyone who was first drawn into gardening by tending plants on a windowsill knows the genus *Schefflera*. The glossy green, palmately compound leaves of tropical species such as *S. arboricola* and *S. actinophylla* were requisites for the containerized interior garden, sharing digs with macramé, *Dieffenbachia*, and mealy bugs.

The genus name commemorates J. C. Scheffler, a botanist from Gdańsk, Poland, in the 19th century. *Schefflera* is just one of numerous plant genera that have been historically ignored as a hardy shrub or tree simply because no one bothered to actually put them to the test. It brings to mind the late J. C. Raulston's assertions that we as gardeners are not doing our job if we are not out there killing plants on a yearly basis. Sometimes they live, and that is how we learn.

The species that piqued my interest initially was probably *Schefflera delavayi*, which grew for a time in the Asian woodland of the UBC Botanical Garden in Vancouver. That this could actually make it through winter there unharmed seemed irrational and very exciting. Though that plant did eventually succumb during a particularly harsh winter, I received a clone of a taxon under this name from Steve Hootman, exemplary plant explorer, who had collected it in western Sichuan. I am now uncertain of its nomenclature, but undoubtedly it drew me further into the genus at large. This handsome tree sailed through every winter in my first garden and was more than 18 ft. (5.5 m) tall by 2006. The enormous, palmately compound foliage, with each of the five to seven leaflets extending to 1 ft. (0.3 m) in length, possesses a slight grayish cast. The clone of *S. delavayi* growing at Windcliff is seemingly more glabrous in effect, producing vigorous growth and enormous leaves, with each leaflet to 18 in. (45 cm) long. Late in the season, tall, branched racemes of creamy white flowers add a dash of texture.

Along with *Schefflera delavayi*, an additional 35 species are found in China, primarily in the southwestern provinces. I count one of these, *S. bodinieri*, among the most splendid species to seek out, though it is unfortunately scarce in cultivation. On a branched framework to 15 ft. (4.6 m) are carried compound leaves comprised of 7–11 elegantly long, narrow leaflets to 10 in. (25 cm). Something so exquisite should at least be grown in interior spaces if proven to be unreceptive to local climatic conditions.

In 1999 I observed *Schefflera taiwaniana* for the first time in the wild, growing at a very high elevation, over 11,000 ft. (3350 m), in north-central Taiwan alongside the Japanese red pine, *Pinus densiflora*. This beautiful and finely textured small evergreen tree carries elegant compound foliage comprised of 7–12 narrow, deep green leaflets. In spring the foliage emerges bedaubed by a startling white indumentum, later transitioning to a deep matte green along a rounded framework 15–20 ft. (4.6–6 m) high.

From my seed collections, the specimen in my garden now tops 15 ft. (4.6 m) and has been undisturbed by temperatures as low as 7°F (−14°C). I consider it one of the most exciting broad-leaved evergreens I grow.

Late-summer panicles of *Schefflera delavayi* in my garden. (Photo by Daniel J. Hinkley)

Schefflera bodinieri, an elegant species too rare in cultivation, growing in the Temperate House at the Royal Botanic Gardens, Kew. (Photo by Nic Macer)

The new growth of *Schefflera taiwaniana*. (Photo by Daniel J. Hinkley)

During that same autumn in Asia, I spent time in northern Vietnam for the first time, near Sa Pa on the border with China, atop the highest mountain in southeastern Asia, known as Fan-si-pan. It is here that numerous species of *Schefflera* grow, all of which have thus far proven themselves hardy in our zone 8 garden. *Schefflera alpina*, which occurs at the highest elevations, over 10,000 ft. (3000 m), will probably prove as hardy as *S. taiwaniana* and may give it a run for its money with regard to ornamental effects. It is more shrub than tree, to 8 ft. (2.4 m) or less, with small, very glossy green foliage that emerges with a handsome reddish pigmentation in spring.

Distinct from this species, and growing slightly lower in elevation, is *Schefflera fantsipanensis*. An extra whorl of foliage is produced in the center of each compound leaf along a rounded framework to 15 ft. (4.6 m). This too has been completely unfazed thus far by the low temperatures thrown in its face.

Schefflera gracilis is a small shrub that grows adjacent to streams and rivers in the same area of Vietnam at moderate elevations. Though some specimens observed were as tall as 15 ft. (4.6 m), most were less than 5 ft. (1.5 m) and offered ample fruit at that height. Interestingly, this species demonstrates this precociousness in my garden as well, where three-year-old specimens less than 1 ft. (0.3 m) tall have blossomed and produced viable seed.

I have been surprised by the survival of a fourth species from Vietnam, which grew at decidedly lower elevations, and which does not possess the gestalt of a hardy plant. Very large, deeply veined, compound foliage

Schefflera taiwaniana. (Photo by Daniel J. Hinkley)

Foliage of *Schefflera alpina* in my garden.
(Photo by Daniel J. Hinkley)

emerges on *Schefflera macrophylla* covered in a handsome reddish fur that ultimately wears thin. Admittedly I have this planted in a sheltered position on the north side of my home; however, it has tripled in size in two years and continues to tick. I will be delighted should my conservative estimates about the hardiness of this species prove false, though with that said, it will make a stunning addition to the inventory of garden plants in coastal Oregon to Southern California.

In Sikkim as well as Bhutan, with traveling mates Dave Demers and Scott McMahan, I became acquainted with yet another hardy species that has proven to be a top dog thus far in zone 8. *Schefflera rhododendrifolia* demonstrates the juvenility factor seen in the *Pseudopanax* species of New Zealand in that the leaflets of the palmately compound leaves in youth possess a clever and highly ornamental serrate margin. This serration is completely absent from specimens approaching procreative age, like those we saw approaching heights of 25 ft. (7.6 m). Impressively, *S. rhododendrifolia* accepted temperatures below 15°F (−9°C) as a youthful plant in my garden in Indianola without even minor leaf damage.

While in Bhutan, I excitedly came upon the hot orange fruit of *Schefflera bengalensis*, a climbing or scrambling species growing at low elevations. It would not prove to be a hardy species, yet I was intrigued by its unique habit of growth.

I returned to Taiwan in the autumn of 2007 with Bleddyn Wynn-Jones and our mutual friend from Ireland, Finlay Colley, enticed primarily by the opportunity to

My loyal and perennial guide in northern Vietnam, Uoc Le Huu, assisting in the collection of *Schefflera fantsipanensis*. Note the inner whorl of foliage. (Photo by Daniel J. Hinkley)

Schefflera rhododendrifolia at moderate elevation in Bhutan, with the far eastern and diminishing range of the Himalaya in the distance. (Photo by Daniel J. Hinkley)

Metapanax and Other Araliaceae

A robust specimen of *Schefflera rhododendrifolia* adjacent to our first night's accommodation during our trek in southeastern Sikkim in 2005. (Photo by Daniel J. Hinkley)

re-collect the aforementioned *Schefflera taiwaniana* from the highest occurring populations on the island, a proposition that ultimately took us to a trailhead leading to the summit of Yü Shan—which at nearly 13,000 ft. (4000 m) is Taiwan's (in fact one of Southeast Asia's) highest peaks. A predawn departure on a chilly early-winter day led us through an irritatingly nasty series of ladders, bridges, stairs, and chains with an abrupt exit to an abyss to our right always one misstep away. After three hours of a vertiginous climb, we were again among expansive colonies of this *Schefflera*, whose 15 ft. (4.6 m) stems were, satisfyingly, heavily weighted in pendulous racemes of ripened purple fruit.

Since it was my second trip to Taiwan and I had come primarily for *Schefflera*, I was not mentally prepared to be bombarded by so many other refined members of this family, including those with which we involve ourselves here.

The landmass of Taiwan, some 249 miles (401 km) long and 89 miles (143 km) wide, is separated from the mainland by 150 miles (241 km) of the Taiwan Strait, while situated between the southernmost islands of the Japanese Archipelago to the north and the Philippines to the south. Along its eastern front, a sharp and unstable geography thrusts abruptly from the sea, with more than 100 peaks rising above 9800 ft. (3000 m). Frequent violent aftershocks following the devastating earthquake of September 21 during our first trip here in 1999 repeatedly underscored this dynamic geology, while giving the experience a palpable edge.

During our three intense weeks in Taiwan, we circumnavigated the island one and a half times in addition to traversing the only three routes carved into the mountainous terrain: the South, Central, and Northern Cross-Island Highways. All, incidentally, while being monotonously reprimanded for

Schefflera bengalensis. (Photo by Daniel J. Hinkley)

The late flowers and enormous leaves of *Tetrapanax papyrifera* at moderate to low elevations in Taiwan. (Photo by Daniel J. Hinkley)

speeding, in Chinese, by a malfunctioning onboard navigator.

At mid- to low elevations, the enormous deciduous leaves of *Tetrapanax papyrifera*, to 3 ft. (0.9 m) across, never fail to catch the eye. It is a species with which I first acquainted myself at Wave Hill in the Bronx during the years that Marco Polo Stufano was at the helm. In Taiwan in late November it was in full blossom and admittedly handsome, with erect panicles of white flowers catching low-angled rays of late-afternoon sun. From its pith is produced so-called rice paper, which has been traditionally used to make artificial flowers, though its use as a deciduous component in the landscape is on the rise. Few semihardy shrubs or trees can offer such sensational folial texture as does this species, though I resolutely regret having planted it in my garden. It is not so much its annoying suckering habit of growth but its brown-felted leaves and stems, which dis-

pel irritating dustlike hairs, that I find not only disagreeable but downright venomous during autumn cleanup. Asthmatics should proceed with caution.

It should be noted that a selection of *Tetrapanax papyrifera* called 'Steroidal Giant', made by Sean Hogan and Parker Sanderson of Cistus Nursery in Portland, is considered to be a nonflowering, nonsuckering seedling with imposingly large leaves to 5 ft. (1.5 m) across.

Throughout the island at moderate to high elevations, *Fatsia polycarpa* came into play, with deeply lobed, evergreen leaves to 1 ft. (0.3 m) across held on a branchwork to 15 ft. (4.6 m) or more. This exceedingly handsome endemic species superficially differs from the more commonly cultivated *F. japonica* by the accentuated lobing of its leaf blade. From my experience, and contrary to literature, this species is as hardy if not more so than its Japanese counterpart, though the deepest and

Metapanax and Other Araliaceae

therefore most handsome lobing is often seen on young plants, once again demonstrating juvenility.

Adjacent to the *Fatsia* grew another most arresting, large, evergreen shrub in the same family. *Sinopanax formosanus*, like the *Fatsia* found here and nowhere else, appears to the eye to be a cross between *F. polycarpa* and *Tetrapanax*, with large, angular leaves to 10 in. (25 cm) across and textured rather than glabrous. Its appearance at such high elevations would suggest hardiness, making a collection of ripened seed, after several days of looking, a notable event.

HARDINESS: Though numerous exciting evergreen members of the Araliaceae are turning out to be much hardier than previously believed, it is doubtful that many will survive in zones below 7b unless provided a particularly protected site. This should not preclude gardeners from growing these as containerized specimens—protecting them in a cool greenhouse or sun porch in winter, integrating them into the garden in summer—nor should it suggest that these species not

be trialed to ascertain actual low-temperature tolerance. Though I had expected *Schefflera taiwaniana* to be perfectly adapted to much of southeastern North America, initial reports indicate that it is significantly damaged by winter temperatures.

Tetrapanax papyrifera is extremely root hardy, taking temperatures below 0°F (−18°C) and returning from below ground the following spring. The numerous species of *Acanthopanax* are particularly tough and can be used to provide the same visual cue as *Schefflera*, *Metapanax*, and *Pseudopanax* in zones 4–9; however, most of these come with the disadvantage of thorny stems and a loss of leaves during the winter months.

CULTIVATION: The evergreen species will benefit from some shade in hot positions, yet I continue to be more impressed with their habit of growth if provided more, rather than less, direct sun. The spectacular large leaves of *Fatsia*, *Sinopanax*, and *Tetrapanax* are superlative candidates to add a punch of texture to a vignette of smaller-foliaged minions. All will thrive in slightly acidic,

Tetrapanax papyrifera 'Steroidal Giant'. (Photo by Daniel J. Hinkley)

Fatsia polycarpa grows with *Schefflera taiwaniana* where their ranges overlap at moderate elevations in central Taiwan. (Photo by Daniel J. Hinkley)

well-drained, humus-rich soils with some supplemental water during the growing season. Scheffleras tend to grow as straight, unbranched specimens until their first blossoming, at which time lateral branches are produced. In an open situation where the plant would tend to elongate less, this is not a concern; however, in a shaded and thus more protected site, it does become problematic. I recommend encouraging branching from the base at an early age by removing the apex of the stem in late winter. *Metapanax* branches from the base naturally and is more balanced under brighter conditions. *Acanthopanax* species are excellent candidates for cutting back to encourage larger leaves; as they do blossom on second-year wood, this would preclude the autumn effects of fruit. *Tetrapanax* suckers considerably and is difficult to eliminate once established; consideration of this fact should be made before integrating it into the garden.

PROPAGATION: Hardwood cuttings taken in late summer and autumn on bottom heat root readily, though unless plants have been maintained by regular pruning, one will find a paucity of appropriate cutting material on each plant. Obviously, leaf reduction is necessary in those taxa possessing large leaves, such as *Fatsia* and *Sinopanax*. Air layering of larger branches on all taxa will be successful. Root cuttings and divisions of *Tetrapanax*, of course, are reliable methods to increase the number of plants and maintain named cultivars. Seeds of the Araliaceae generally germinate after a single cold treatment; those sown fresh in autumn will germinate the following spring. *Schefflera* seeds are small, and separating them from the pulp of the fruit—a necessity for the plant import regulations of the USDA—is an immensely tedious process. Unlike most viable seeds, which sink in water while the pulp rises to the surface, making decanting a straightforward process, these seeds float and commingle with the flesh. Cuttings from flowering-aged lancewoods, *Pseudopanax crassifolius* and *P. ferox*, will produce adult plants in much the same way as with propagation of adult forms of *Hedera helix*.

The characteristic deep lobing of the leaf blade sets *Fatsia polycarpa* apart from the more commonly encountered *F. japonica*. (Photo by Daniel J. Hinkley)

The handsome, scalloped, evergreen foliage of *Sinopanax formosanus*, found only on Taiwan. (Photo by Daniel J. Hinkley)

Metapanax and Other Araliaceae

Straight Up with an Olive:
Osmanthus and Other Oleaceae

For the last four days and nights, we [Scott McMahan, Dave Demers, and I] were at high altitude, above 12,000 ft., and though the scenery was dramatic, we were well above the zone we wished to be botanizing in. Collectively, I believe our spirits were as low as the temperatures at night, as the skies were crystalline and brought an unshakably bitter, cold wind down from the surrounding peaks. Yesterday we arrived in camp by midafternoon. To take advantage of the remaining light, Scott and I circumnavigated the deceivingly large alpine lake below our camp, through a tangle of tall rhododendrons, the standard high Himalaya inventory of Rhododendron thomsonii, R. barbatum, and R. campylocarpum surrounded by dense thickets of R. anthopogon. It was an exercise that appeared from a distance quite feasible. The rhododendrons had hidden from view our intended route, which was, in many places, blocked by sheer walls of rock falling to the water below. Not until we were well into the thick of things did we realize our folly: should we continue or return through the hard-fought snarls of closely spaced branches that caught our packs?

We continued, back to camp, for the most part without any collections of merit and with numerous shallow lines of blood across our noses from the sharp branches. Sonam built a robust fire from bits and pieces lying about the camp, and we huddled near it for a considerable time after dinner; I do not think I have ever experienced such a brutal coldness and could barely bring myself to retreat to my tent and bag.

Today we went up higher still in the morning, over a pass at 14,553 ft., then dropping quickly into a valley, soon after with Thimpu visible far in the distance. By midday we were low enough to shed some clothes as we ate our lunch beneath a cacophony of colorful prayer flags being ripped to shreds by warm winds rising up the slope.

After lunch, I attended to bodily rhythms and lost track of the rest of the party while a maze of livestock paths led me further astray. The trail I followed took me to the rear quarters of a rather large, somewhat disheveled monastery. There were a few monks about in the inner courtyard, dressed in traditional wine-colored robes, disconnected from my presence yet not unfriendly. I did not loiter but paused for a few moments in the saluted warmth of sun in the cloister while listening to an extended heated discussion between two of the brothers that ended, after apprehension on my part, in the uproarious laughter of many voices.

At the center of the courtyard, where I stood and smiled at the jocular outcome of this exchange, existed an ancient, physically corrupted, white-washed circular planter, in which grew an equally ancient specimen of Osmanthus suavis. I had not realized, until that moment, what a splendid small tree it would make, and will rethink the consideration of our collections of this species from Nepal in 1995. I suspect that I will never look at it quite the same way again.

I heard hollers in the distance downslope and made my way toward my comrades, who realized I had gone missing.

Thimpu, Bhutan
November 3, 2005

Osmanthus suavis growing in the courtyard of a temple in Bhutan. (Photo by Daniel J. Hinkley)

THERE IS A LOT TO BE SAID of this family in a very short distance, and I must be uncharacteristically concise. No other assemblage of plants has made such an impact on my "being" as a plantsman as has the Oleaceae, or olive family. For that matter, most winter-bludgeoned citizens of the far north, whether or not they are botanically inclined, would be familiar with at least one member of this family, even if just the olive in the martini they sip while trying to make peace with the blizzard outside.

It was in my zone 4 horticultural adolescence that *Forsythia* was the only possible harbinger of spring, presenting a jarring but welcome charge of yellow not a minute too soon. During Memorial Day weekend, in this zone, our winter was at last put down by the fragrance of lilacs, with stems of nonfancy, four-petaled *Syringa vulgaris* found tabletop in nearly every home, while in the deciduous woodlands of my first stomping grounds, our yearly hunt for morels led us to the base of *Fraxinus americana*, whose late-leafing tendencies encouraged the development of these fine mushrooms.

The ash would later play central figure in a mnemonic I employed to help students in my plant identification classes recall what genera or families generally possess leaves that are paired and opposite along their stems. MAD CAP HORSE (that is, maple, ash, dogwood, the Caprifoliaceae, and horse chestnuts), though a lean gathering of possibilities in a universal sense, remains a useful tool while vetting identities of plants afield.

Indeed, members of the Oleaceae nearly all have leaves that are opposite, a diagnostic that, when paired with flowers possessing four petals and (often but not always) fleshy berries or drupes, readily announces its familial associations.

The family represents a genealogy of lionized ornamentals and culinary staples, including, among numerous obscure genera in tropical and subtropical parts of the globe, *Fraxinus*, *Forsythia*, *Syringa*, *Abeliophyllum*, *Jasminum*, *Ligustrum*, *Osmanthus*, *Chionanthus*, and the type genus *Olea*. Of these I have had numerous if not somewhat desultory close encounters in the wild. Despite growing and appreciating a large number of these collections in my garden, I am not up to the task of examining each genus in the thorough fashion they might deserve.

If this seems a hurried or flippant exercise, I apologize in advance. In the case of *Forsythia* and *Syringa*, it might

Our camp at high elevation in Bhutan amidst *Daphne*, *Rhododendron*, *Viburnum*, and *Berberis*. Scott McMahan and I circumnavigated the lake in the distance, deceivingly small in appearance, and became entangled in dense vegetation in the process. (Photo by Daniel J. Hinkley)

be argued, the genera are now so broadly represented in cultivation, with hybrid selections far removed from their forebears, at least in that blowsy, overblown sense, that the species themselves garner scant interest. I take umbrage with the notion that these have been significantly improved upon.

The sprawling, ropy stems of *Forsythia suspensa* that I have found in northeastern Sichuan translate to superlative effects if grown into open trees in a garden setting. The bright yellow bells presented among the powder blue needles of *Cedrus atlantica* 'Glauca' in late winter make for an elegant composition.

Though I cannot say for certain that most *Syringa* species are more resistant to powdery mildew than the severely afflicted *S. vulgaris*, I can report that those I have grown suggest this to be the case. In addition, the hardiness inherent to the genus as a whole, with many rated hardy to zone 2, suggests that the species themselves should be more methodically trialed for the icy landscapes of central United States.

On several instances, I have collected the signature woody capsules of the wild lilacs, most notably *Syringa yunnanensis* (DJHC 406, 0182, 0545), at very high elevations in northwestern Yunnan Province as well as on Mount Emei in Sichuan Province. This 4–12 ft. (1.2–3.6 m) shrub can be quite variable in regard to flower color; the flowers range from white to wine red in moderate-sized, slightly nodding panicles. Seedlings of many wild-collected lilac species farmed out to numerous friends over the years continue to garner high marks for their swarthy and fragrant blossoms in early May. In addition, our collections of *S. reticulata* subsp. *amurensis* HC 970410 from Mount Chiri, South Korea, have proven to be extremely durable, handsome additions to the inner-mountain regions, with panicles of fragrant white flowers on a tidy framework to 8 ft. (2.4 m). *Syringa wolfii* DJH 103, collected from Mount Odae, Korea, in 1993, was planted in the perennial borders of my original garden, where it always inspired comment when in blossom, with distinctively nodding, open trusses of purple flowers. This species represented by this same collection is equally appreciated in Frank Cabot's garden, Les Quatre Vents, in Quebec, Canada, attesting to its hardiness.

There are other taxa in the genus of lilacs that I have not yet seen in the wild but would still not be without in my garden. Topping that list is *Syringa protolaciniata*. Its fine pinnate foliage delivers a good dose of texture to the garden and is extremely unlike the foliage of the prototypical lilac, making for good fun during tours of the garden with fellow plantsmen.

I could not possibly do justice in these pages to the genus *Jasminum*, despite the fact that I have collected numerous species and continue to enjoy many of these collections under the euphonious name of *Jasminum* sp. in my Indianola garden. The clusters of glistening black fruit held among arching canes or twining stems make not collecting them virtually impossible while in the field, all the while knowing that I will be adding yet another quite unidentifiable plant to my garden. Of the 43 species known to occur within China proper, the only species I have been able to identify with certainty is *J. polyanthum*, adaptable to zones 7–10, which I collected in Yunnan in 1996 under DJH 056 and again later in Sichuan Province. It presents an unyielding display of white flowers opening from pink buds that pulse fragrance in the early evening throughout summer.

From Nepal, the very pretty *Jasminum humile* HWJK 2101—a blanket name for a confused mishmash of innumerable described varieties—blossoms along our water feature with arching canes to 5 ft. (1.5 m) and pendulous clusters of delicate, slightly fragrant, yellow flowers, recalling the day I hiked alone to the remote village of Ritak in October of 2002. It is hardy in zones 6–9.

Privetly speaking. The genus *Ligustrum*, composed of about 20 species, is hackneyed in cultivation, primarily due to overutilization of *L. vulgare* as privacy hedging in Europe and eastern North America. In fact it was on account of this function that privet was applied as a common name for the entire genus.

The "privetization" of America was due primarily to the ease with which this European native thrived, its overall hardiness, its fragrant white spring flowers, and its ability to withstand a yearly brutal assault by an arsenal of pruning tools. With such a superinfection of ligustrums adjacent to the natural landscape of eastern North America, it was simply a matter of time before they escaped to the wild. The fruits of *Ligustrum vulgare* are favored by numerous bird species, and I have seen endless miles of these plants in the woodlands of North Carolina and adjacent states, where they are quite likely to remain.

Before I fully appreciated the degree of this problem, I collected *Ligustrum delavayanum* at Sheng So Po in Yunnan Province above 8000 ft. (2400 m) in elevation. It quickly established in my garden, and I was briefly taken under its spell. It had small, glistening evergreen leaves

My collection of *Jasminum polyanthum* from Sichuan is a particularly good form. (Photo by Daniel J. Hinkley)

along elegantly arching stems, and terminal clusters of fragrant white flowers in spring that, even with a single clone, resulted in astonishing crops of shiny black fruit that weighted the branches nearly to the ground. This fecund nature, though initially titillating, soon enough raised its ugly head when hundreds of seedlings began to appear at the base of the shrub. I will admit to feeling considerable disappointment in having to dispose of this species, which we promptly did.

At Sheng So Po a close ally of this *Ligustrum*—indeed, from a distance it was a dead ringer—grew side by side with it. Though by that time I was already very familiar with the genus *Osmanthus* in a horticultural context, it was thrilling to finally meet up with one on its own turf. (As a matter of historical note, it was *Ligustrum* that offered up its roots for grafting scions of numerous *Osmanthus* species before they became commonly propagated by cuttings.)

I find *Osmanthus* (Greek, meaning "fragrant flower"), with about 30 species of evergreen shrubs and small trees, to be an aristocratic and highly refined member of the olive family. Many of the species are uncannily similar in appearance to *Ilex*, from which, of course, they can be readily distinguished by an opposite leaf arrangement. *Osmanthus* is distributed in both the Eastern and Western Hemispheres but is geographically centered in Asia, with 23 species in China alone.

America claims only two: the so-called devilwood or American olive, *Osmanthus americanus*, and the highly endangered *O. megacarpus* from scrub habitat in central Florida, both hardy in zones 6–9. The demonic common name of the former is due to its extremely hard wood, which defies use in construction. It is found, sparingly so, from southeastern Virginia to Texas as well as in northeastern and southwestern Mexico. I have resoundingly failed in my attempts to grow this species, perhaps due to the provenance of the material received, but it has a growing number of devotees in the Southeast for its bird-attracting attributes.

One of the charms of the genus as a whole is that more than half of the species have evolved to delay their blossoming until months after the fray and frenzy of high spring, instead spicing the cooling autumn air with their redolence.

I will long cherish my memories of introducing plant identification students to *Osmanthus heterophyllus* in full, sweet blossom on warm autumn days in Seattle. This species from Taiwan and Japan, hardy in zones 6–9, carries hollylike, black-green leaves along stems rising to 15 ft. (4.6 m) or slightly more. In late September through much of October, densely packed clusters of small white flowers, secreted away along the stems, open to emit a beguiling and most unexpected fragrance. It has long been cultivated in both of its countries of origin as well as in the West, and numerous cultivars can be encountered in local nurseries.

The foliage of *Osmanthus heterophyllus* 'Purpureus' emerges in spring with a purplish bruise, later fading to purple-green, while *O. heterophyllus* 'Variegatus' brandishes creamy-white-edged foliage that is truly striking throughout the year. The bamboo-leaved osmanthus,

O. heterophyllus 'Sasaba', is a fantastic textural selection with foliage deeply divided into three overlapping lobes. Though most of these selections would be considered intelligent choices for a low-maintenance hedge, the pyramidal form *O. heterophyllus* 'Fastigiata' would be ideal for cramped quarters where privacy is needed.

While in Taiwan during the autumn of 2007, I came upon *Osmanthus heterophyllus* in two natural forms, which helped clarify a question I have long held regarding its taxonomy. Those with the spiny teeth associated with this species are referred to by Chinese taxonomists as *O. heterophyllus* var. *heterophyllus*, while those lacking these teeth at somewhat higher elevations are *O. heterophyllus* var. *bibracteatus*. Whether this is the original source of the handsome selection occasionally seen in cultivation as *O. heterophyllus* 'Rotundifolius', we will probably never be certain.

While in Japan in 1995, I first made my acquaintance with *Osmanthus fragrans* in blossom in early to late October, generally in gardens, over fences incapa-

Osmanthus suavis. (Photo by Daniel J. Hinkley)

Osmanthus heterophyllus 'Variegatus'. (Photo by Lynne Harrison)

ble of containing its intoxicating fragrance. It is a species that occurs naturally throughout the southern Japanese Archipelago as well as in western China. The fragrance is sweet, similar to that of Juicy Fruit gum, while the axillary clusters of flowers are white (or a pale orange in *O. fragrans* 'Aurantiacus'). The linear-ovate foliage of this species, to 6 in. (15 cm) long, is somewhat more papery in texture than most other members of the genus with which I have interacted. Unfortunately, it is not a plant I can grow well in my garden, despite the fact that I have not yet thrown in the towel. For optimum performance it needs a much more sultry climate than we can provide, in zones 7–10. I may have to content myself with enjoying it secondhand through many of the Chinese tea blends that use the flowers to impart its distinctive sweet aroma to the brew.

Osmanthus fragrans 'Aurantiacus'. (Photo by Daniel J. Hinkley)

Osmanthus ×*fortunei* and *O.* 'San Jose', both representing separate hybrid clones between *O. heterophyllus* and *O. fragrans*, are considerably muddled in commerce. The former parent conveys the lion's share of the blood, giving *O.* ×*fortunei* leathery, spiny-edged leaves along a vigorous, upright chassis to 20 ft. (6 m) and autumn flowers with a sweet scent. This hybrid is adaptable to zones 7–10. I grew it for many years in a difficult situation, against the southern side of our home in soil that often became dusty-dry by summer's end, yet it never seemed bothered.

I fear that *Osmanthus* ×*fortunei* is often sold under the name *O. armatus*, a distinctive species with long, narrow, very leathery leaves whose margins are severely armed, as the epithet implies. *Osmanthus armatus* occurs naturally in Hubei and Sichuan Provinces. I was delighted to encounter it at 8000 ft. (2400 m) on Mount Emei in the autumn of 2008. It is appropriate for zones 7–10.

I was with friends Bob Beers and Richie Steffen in northeastern Turkey in 2000 when I met up again with *Osmanthus decorus*, a charming species that I have long considered in need of greater recognition within zones 6–9. The elegantly narrow, linear leaves of 5–6 in. (12.5–15 cm) are carried densely on a rounded framework of yellowish stems to 6 ft. by 6 ft. (1.8 m by 1.8 m). In early spring, clean white axillary clusters of flowers appear partially hidden among the foliage, emitting a pleasing punch of fragrance. What this species lacks in strength of floral presentation, it more than makes up for in durability and adaptability. I have grown it in rather dense, dry shade, where it appeared as content and handsome as that specimen I now grow in a blustery exposed site in full sun. This was for many years grown under the name *Phillyrea decora*, a factoid that may seem more cogent in a moment or two.

First, enter *Osmanthus delavayi*. It was this species that I found growing alongside *Ligustrum delavayanum* at Sheng So Po, Yunnan, where I collected its seed at over 8000 ft. (2400 m) in elevation, collecting it again in 2000 on the border with Sichuan and Yunnan at over

10,000 ft. (3000 m). The latter collections, which created some measure of second-guessing on my part, were from specimens that I noted as being substantial in size, to 15 ft. (4.6 m) in height. Those clones currently in cultivation in the Pacific Northwest tend toward a more demure growth habit, to 6 ft. (1.8 m) or less, and are often diced, cubed, or globed by regrettable pruning practices.

Yet the small, rounded, ovate, dark green foliage and substantial serration on the leaf edge offer a sure-enough identifying tool, as do the masses of powerfully fragrant white flowers crowded both along the stems and at their tips in spring. It is interesting to note that I can discern remarkable (and, I think, sensational) differences between the 12 clones that I have in my garden from the 2000 collection (DJHC 0490), with flower color ranging from a slight blush of pink to a startling chartreuse. This species is considered hardy in zones 7–9.

In 1930 at the now-defunct, yet once-prestigious Surrey nursery of Burkwood and Skipwith, at Kingston-upon-Thames, a hybrid was raised between *Osmanthus delavayi* and *Phillyrea decora*, resulting in the ephemeral binomial ×*Osmarea burkwoodii*. *Phillyrea decora* was soon enough reassigned to *Osmanthus*, and this hybrid was thusly renamed *Osmanthus* ×*burkwoodii*.

It is nonetheless a handsome and worthy shrub to grow in zones 7–9, especially so as a moderate-sized informal hedge. Its somewhat larger, less serrate foliage, held densely on a rounded framework to 15 ft. (4.6 m), and its fragrant albeit short-lived eruption of clean white flowers in late winter, show considerable allegiance to *Osmanthus delavayi*. A lovely specimen of this hybrid grows adjacent to the Seattle Asian Art Museum, trained as a single-stemmed, rounded-crowned tree, fully exposing the elegance this shrub is capable of providing the garden.

Of the closely related *Phillyrea*—so closely related, in fact, that finding any explanation for retaining both genera as separate entities seems impossible—I have experience with only one of the two known species. Essentially, *P. latifolia* and *P. angustifolia* are the southern

Osmanthus decorus. (Photo by Lynne Harrison)

Several seedlings of my collection of *Osmanthus delavayi* from Sichuan Province, showing remarkable variation between siblings. (Photo by Daniel J. Hinkley)

Osmanthus ×burkwoodii. (Photo by Daniel J. Hinkley)

European and northern African counterparts to *Osmanthus*. I have retained *P. latifolia* in my collection, after admiring it for many years in my first woodland garden, primarily due to its toughness and adaptability, now employing it for screening in a difficult soil in partial shade. It might be added, rather embarrassingly, that I maintained in my first garden, and propagated for sale for several years, a plant I had received under the name *Phillyrea angustifolia*, without bothering to note that the long, narrow leaves of the plant were arranged alternately rather than in pairs. When at last it blossomed, irritatingly as a *Pittosporum*, my blunder was conveyed to those who had purchased it; however, I am certain I blamed a computer glitch for the error at the time.

There could be volumes written on the genus *Chionanthus*, and perhaps someday there might be, but they won't be penned by me. Despite the fact that only two species appear to any degree in cultivation, this genus is a large conglomeration of 80 species hailing primarily from the tropics and subtropics of both hemispheres. None the matter, as I am denied the satisfaction of successfully cultivating any *Chionanthus* due to the cool embrace of the northern Pacific.

Chionanthus virginicus, known colloquially as granny graybeard or American fringe tree, is highly celebrated, particularly east of the Mississippi, with well-seasoned and jaded plantsmen, who consider it to represent the finest of native American flowering shrubs or small trees. It grows to 20 ft. (6 m) in height and is hardy in zones 3–9. As with other members of the family, it carries its leaves in pairs, while from the axils in spring erupt loose panicles of white flowers, each with four to

Phillyrea latifolia. (Photo by Lynne Harrison)

Chionanthus virginicus. (Photo by Daniel J. Hinkley)

five long, narrow petals. These result in crops of blue, one-seed drupes that are readily consumed by birds. A federally endangered species from the sandy pine scrub of central Florida, *C. pygmaeus* is lilliputian by comparison, as its name would imply. It has evolved to resprout from the roots following periodic wildfires and would correspondingly recover from extreme cold.

The Asian counterpart to this, also deciduous, is *Chionanthus retusus*, which is widespread across much of China, Taiwan, Japan, and Korea. This species, hardy in zones 6–8, differs primarily by blossoming on the current year's wood. It develops handsome effects with regard to exfoliating bark and is known to blossom more torridly every other year.

It was a red-letter day in the spring of 2008 when I was led to an ancient natural stand of this species in full and splendid blossom, its frothy load of flowers as sharp as ice against a vivid blue sky. The experience came with both a revelation as to the beauty of the species and a certain amount of regret that the coolness of my climate prevents me from cultivating it to the degree it deserves.

An enlightening revelation regarding this genus came via e-mail from Richard Olsen just prior to my departure to Ecuador and Peru in December of 2006. As he had just returned from the same area, he teased me with photos of an evergreen shrub or small tree he had seen, with a startling froth of pink flowers. Native to the mountainous regions of northwestern South America, *Chionanthus pubescens*, a species possessing both pink- and white-flowering forms, has been ignored for too many years by the horticulturists of North America. I do not suggest it deserves attention for its actual cultivation, a remote possibility at best, but for the deliverance of its pinkness to our American species via hybridization. The first seedlings of this species are now in the apt hands of Tom Ranney, a talented individual who I am certain will do just that if it is remotely possible. The species itself, which I made a point of seeking out while in Quito, where it is commonly utilized as a street tree, would only be appropriate for consideration in zone 12 and above.

Naturally occurring stands of *Chionanthus retusus* at peak blossom in mid-May in the mountains north of Nagoya, Japan. (Photo by Daniel J. Hinkley)

A cultivated plant of the pink form of *Chionanthus pubescens* in Quito, Ecuador. (Photo by Richard Olsen)

HARDINESS: A quick-reference guide to the hardiness of selected members of the Oleaceae follows. Please note that I have indicated those that are appropriate only in summer-warm areas.

Chionanthus pubescens: zone 12
Chionanthus retusus: zones 6–8 (summer-warm)
Chionanthus virginicus: zones 3–9 (summer-warm)
Forsythia: zones 3–9
Jasminum: zones 6–10
Osmanthus: zones 6–10
Phillyrea: zones 7–10
Syringa: many rated to zones 2–8

CULTIVATION: *Syringa* does best in full sun on well-draining soils. Though literature on the subject of soil pH continues to suggest that alkaline soils are ideal,

I have never seen any indication of a resentment to slightly acidic conditions. Powdery mildew, particularly severe with *S. vulgaris* and its hybrids, takes primarily an aesthetic toll; despite midsummer defoliation on particularly bad years, it does not seemingly reduce the vigor or blossoming potential of the plant the following year. Avoid using chemicals unnecessarily.

Jasminum prefers full sun and draining soils, exhibiting remarkable drought tolerance when fully established.

I do not recommend the cultivation of any *Ligustrum*. Breeding of sterile triploid forms is on the horizon, which may result in benign, if not banal, candidates for privacy hedging.

Osmanthus is best cultivated in full sun, or very light shade with some direct sun during the day, in well-draining soils. It is extremely drought tolerant when fully established. Whereas *Osmanthus* species as a whole provide superb choices for unclipped informal hedges, I do not consider them ideal candidates for shearing; this is based primarily on personal bias but also because shearing leads to the loss of flowering wood.

Phillyrea is a highly adaptable genus for full sun or shade in any draining soils. The habit of growth will obviously be more dense under brighter conditions.

Chionanthus prefers full sun in draining soils with some supplemental water throughout the growing season. Both *C. virginicus* and *C. retusus* are polygamodioecious, meaning that sexes are primarily found on separate plants while some individuals possess both. The male-flowered forms are considered the showiest, while the females provide crops of bird-attracting fruit. To my knowledge, neither species is offered as sexed plants through the nursery trade.

PROPAGATION: *Syringa* species are readily germinated by seed after a single cold treatment, though it must not be presumed that seed will come true if collected under cultivation. Propagation by softwood cuttings under mist is successful yet often challenging, with high rates of attrition after the first winter. Removal of rooted suckers can be employed for small numbers but is impossible in the case of grafted plants.

Fresh seed of *Jasminum* sprouts like proverbial cress after a single season, while cuttings of the deciduous species taken in early summer and put under mist readily root, with survivability high. The evergreen or semi-evergreen species can be taken as hardwood cuttings in mid- to late autumn.

I do not recommend propagating or distributing any species of *Ligustrum*.

Seed is not readily produced under cultivation from any *Osmanthus* species. I have had considerable viable seed set from one clone only of *O. suavis*, but these seedlings may ultimately prove to be hybrids between this species and *O. delavayi* growing nearby. As I have several clones of *O. delavayi*, I anticipate good crops of seed. These germinate after a single cold treatment. Cuttings of any of the species, taken in mid- to late autumn and placed on gentle bottom heat, present few challenges. This genus was once grafted on *Ligustrum* rootstock.

I have no experience in collecting or sowing seed of *Phillyrea*. As with *Osmanthus*, cuttings taken in autumn will readily root.

With *Chionanthus*, seed is the most prevalent manner of propagation, though collecting the ripening fruit before it is consumed by birds is a challenge. Cuttings from both species are known to offer a very short window of opportunity; they must be taken just as the new growth begins to harden, and then placed under mist. It is probably due to this difficulty with asexual propagation that sexed plants are not offered in the trade.

Cloaked and Bejeweled:
Pittosporum and *Billardiera*

Tonight I am in a small cabin at the base of Cradle Mountain, surrounded by a sublime early-summer evening in an enchanting, unearthly lifescape. Surprisingly cool in temperature! On our drive here we stopped several times to admire open meadows comprised of expanses of bleached button grass, in the genus Gymnoschoenus, *that reflect the ambient twilight tonight with a Middle Earth ambiance. At dusk, Rachel and Stephen alerted me to a visitor on our porch and I met my first Bennett's wallaby, a doe with an inquisitive joey snug in her belly bag. I fed her a piece of apple and might well have boxed the pair up on the spot to bring home. We are off for a long hike* in the morning, *though what I have thus far seen is exciting enough to get me out of bed at daybreak. Almost as if contrived for my benefit, there is, adjacent to our lodging, a natural hummock of* Telopea truncata *(in blossom no less) and* Tasmannia lanceolata. *And as though that were insufficient welcome, someone has woven a tangle of* Billardiera longiflora *through the entire scene; the flowers have long gone and the beauty of its fruit is not what it will be, yet I could not have conjured a more perfect Tasmanian tableau had I tried. Tonight the bed is warm, my belly is full, and I am as filled with anticipation as a child on Christmas Eve.*

Cradle Mountain–Lake Saint Clair National Park
Tasmania
November 22, 1998

I T WAS THROUGH GROWING and killing houseplants as a kid in Michigan that I first became familiar with the genus *Pittosporum*. At that time, terrariums were all the rage, most notably the kind put together in oversized brandy snifters without drainage. It was into just such a death chamber that I forced *P. tobira*, whose reaction to the ordeal a few weeks later was as predictable as it was tragic.

Later in my life, after I moved to western Washington, this same species again demanded my attention; it was very much at home in the open ground of our mild zone 8 landscapes, though hardly standard fare. I came to appreciate its rhododendron-like foliage and habit of growth, along with its jasmine-scented flowers that appear in early spring. Even then, however, I did not reckon that this genus would come to play such a profound role in my life as a wide-eyed wanderer and semitalented horticulturist.

The family Pittosporaceae has been charged with the care of 10 genera and some 200 species of shrubs, trees, and vines, almost all of Australasian origin. Although I have had limited experience with the genus *Sollya* in my garden, and have encountered its scrambling stems plastered with pretty, nodding, blue flowers in the

Cradle Mountain–Lake Saint Clair National Park in northwestern Tasmania is home to a fantastical inventory of plants, marsupials, birds, and reptiles. (Photo by Daniel J. Hinkley)

Grampians of western Victoria, my attentions are biased toward the two genera with which I have interacted the most: *Pittosporum* and *Billardiera*.

The genus *Pittosporum* is as broad in its physical attributes as it is widespread, with 150 species ranging throughout tropical and temperate Africa (including Madagascar), Indochina, the Himalaya, Papua New Guinea, Australia, New Zealand, and certainly China, where *of course* 33 species are endemic. Interestingly, one now exceedingly rare species exists on Madeira (technically placing the genus in Europe), and another can be found in the Canary Islands. It is appropriate to note that some species, most notably those adaptable to tropical climates, have proven to be potentially bioinvasive.

It speaks rather loudly of the lengthy association of the British horticultural scene with its South Pacific colonies (and hotbed of *Pittosporum* speciation), combined with a paucity of the hardier Asian taxa of the genus introduced into the West, that the lion's share of species in classical literature are the notoriously tender plants from New Zealand and Australia. As a note for future reference, however, these same tender species are now seemingly surviving our winters in direct proportion to the level of carbon dioxide in the atmosphere.

The genus *Pittosporum* represents an assemblage of entirely evergreen shrubs, subshrubs, or trees with leathery, alternate foliage often presented in a false whorl at the end of each branch. The flowers are presented in a near-universal medley of inflorescences, while the individual flower nearly always swings both ways, possessing both male and female functions. What is noteworthy of the resulting fruit is its omnipotently, annoyingly greasy surface. As one who has been forced to prepare my collections in as orderly a manner as possible for inspection by the USDA during importation into our country, I can attest to the fact that the pittosporums as a whole thwart the process by soiling the envelopes with dubious smears and blots. Attempting to clean the seed of its coat is as daunting as the seed is gummy and hydrophobic.

There is no question that my admiration of the genus has come primarily from the New Zealand species, in particular *Pittosporum tenuifolium*, now offered in more flavors than designer ice cream. For several years I tenuously cultivated this species in my first, rather cold, garden where my efforts were consistently subverted by arctic outbreaks from the Gulf of Alaska. In due time, the selections I was attempting to grow aligned to our climate, or, sadly, visa versa, and I came to fully explore the breadth of this taxon.

Known as *kohuhu* in the Maori language, *Pittosporum tenuifolium* is found naturally on both the North and South Islands, though only in the scrub of the eastern, drier sides of both. I encountered it first in the wild during a memorable hike one late spring day in the hills slightly south of Christchurch, growing amidst a contingent of species seemingly adapted to human disturbance. The characteristic jet black young stems carried glossy green foliage on a framework to 25 ft. (7.6 m); though these specimens were not in blossom during my visit, they were lovely in texture and exciting to see in their raw form.

It was while visiting the late, great plantsman Jack Elliot in Kent, England, during the mid-1990s that I was introduced to what I still consider the hardiest, and finest, cultivar of this species: *Pittosporum tenuifolium* 'County Park Dwarf'. Creating a dense, rounded mound of black-purple foliage, this selection is among the very best of the lot. Its name commemorates County Park Nursery, a small but inspired devotion to New Zealand flora on the eastern flank of London. Similar in appearance, though in my estimation not as good in performance, is 'Tom Thumb'.

Since then, having changed gardening digs from a dank, cold sink to a windy, virtually frost-free locale, my appreciation of this species and its multitude of apparitions has grown accordingly. The dense, pyramidal, variegated tower of *Pittosporum tenuifolium* 'Ruffles' is a favorite, while *P. tenuifolium* 'Nanum' and 'Golf Ball', with their tight mass of tiny, pewtered leaves, beg greater use. There is no question that this immensely popular species in cultivation in both New Zealand and Australia will become increasingly popular on the western coast of North America.

For numerous years I grew *Pittosporum eugenioides* in a mild, shaded spot in my first garden. Another species from New Zealand with limited use in North America, it is technically a small tree rather than a shrub. I find the undulate edge of the leaf and the high gloss of the leaf blade particularly pleasing, a combination that captures and casts light in a beguiling fashion. *Pittosporum eugenioides* grew along the same ridge as *P. tenuifolium* above Christchurch, where its flowers betrayed its presence by filling the air with the scent of honey. This same floral fragrance, along with the characteristic fresh scent of its crushed leaves, has been noted in my garden in Indianola, though my affection for the species itself has been hijacked by a deservedly popular variegated form with the unremarkable name 'Variegata'.

Pittosporum tenuifolium 'County Park Dwarf'. (Photo by Lynne Harrison)

Pittosporum tenuifolium 'Nanum'. (Photo by Lynne Harrison)

Pittosporum eugenioides 'Variegata'. (Photo by Lynne Harrison)

Cloaked and Bejeweled: *Pittosporum* and *Billardiera*

I have also grown *Pittosporum bicolor* from Tasmania and southeastern Australia. Its short, linear leaves are held along a narrow framework to 20 ft. (6 m) under cultivation, taller in the wild. The solitary flowers of a swarthy maroon are exceedingly fragrant, especially in the evening. From my experience, this would perform at its best along a warm wall. As with *P. eugenioides*, it showed considered damage when temperatures fell below 20°F (−7°C).

An array of species can be found much further to the north, and though they are not as abundant or varied in appearance as those in the South Pacific, they are more adaptable to temperate climates in North America and Europe. These species have presented a steep learning curve with regard to putting proper names to my collec-

tions and realizing their potential in our landscapes. So steep, in fact, that one of my first collections of note—from northwest Yunnan in 1998, under the number 98119—was collected, and possibly sold, as a euonymus. It was a dull-witted error that I chalk up to the excitement of the moment and a surfeit of ripened seeds.

This euonymus ultimately transmuted upon its inaugural blossoming into a highly ornamental species known as *Pittosporum parvilimbum*. A shrub to 6 ft. (1.8 m) in height, the linear, leathery, acuminate foliage is carried in an alternate arrangement, while charming, tiny, pale yellow, exceedingly fragrant flowers result in a globose green "berry" opening to reveal bright orange-skinned seed. This has received high marks from fellow plantsman Tony Avent, in the sassy Piedmont cli-

The distinctive, narrow, glossy foliage of *Pittosporum illicioides* var. *angustifolium* readily makes itself known at moderate to high elevations throughout Taiwan. (Photo by Daniel J. Hinkley)

My collection of *Pittosporum illicioides* var. *angustifolium* putting on a remarkable showing of autumnal fruit at Windcliff. (Photo by Daniel J. Hinkley)

mate of his garden and nursery near Raleigh, North Carolina.

In Sichuan and northern Yunnan, one encounters the variable *Pittosporum heterophyllum*. From my collections of this species, as well as those of Peter Wharton of the David C. Lam Asian Garden at the UBC Botanical Garden, I have developed an admiration for its deep green, glossy, lanceolate leaves, quiet-yet-fragrant display of creamy white flowers, and squat, leathery berries opening to reveal orange seed. It may prove ultimately too large for the average landscape, though a clever variegated clone from Japan is less intimidating in this regard while proffering handsome two-toned foliage throughout the year.

In Taiwan, on two occasions, Bleddyn Wynn-Jones and I collected the seed of three species, one of which I find to be the most distinctive and ornamental of all the Asian species trialed thus far in my garden. *Pittosporum illicioides* var. *angustifolium* possesses spidery fingers of foliage to 8 in. (20 cm) long and tiny, creamy white flowers resulting in colorful crops of berries that reveal orange-red seed. It is common in the interior of the island at relatively high elevations, seen and collected on the Central Cross-Island Highway near Tayuling. Collections from 1999 have proven to be a sensational, hardy, broad-leaved evergreen shrub, though seedling selection could result in a denser, perhaps even more textural form.

Pittosporum daphniphylloides, like *P. illicioides*, occurs not only on Taiwan but also throughout much of western mainland China. It possesses broad, ovate-linear, glossy, deep green leaves along a framework to 15 ft. (4.6 m); yellow flowers appear in spring on relatively long axillary racemes, resulting in fruit spilling showy orange-red seed. My 1999 collections of this species, under the number DJHT 99111, were from the Wuling Farm area along the Northern Cross-Island Highway, though I noted it was not common in the area. In the autumn of 2007, we collected this again not far from our initial collection, at just over 2000 ft. (600 m) in elevation.

Pittosporum viburnifolium is found in thickets along the coast of Taiwan, just south of Hua-lien, and is also endemic to the adjacent but isolated botanical wonder of Lan Yu (Orchid Island). Occurring only at low elevations, and growing with *Viburnum odoratissimum*, it would be appropriate as a salt- and wind-tolerant shrub for mild climates only.

Seeing this species in the autumn of 2007 reminded me of another *Pittosporum* I had encountered four years earlier along the Cape beaches of South Africa. Amidst dense hummocks of *Myrica* grew thickets of *P. viridiflorum*, providing just a bit of familiarity to a landscape that seemed too fantastic to be of this world, while in the surf beyond, southern right whales vaulted themselves from the sea in a manner that seemed to stem from pure joy. The sweetly scented yellow flowers of *P. viridiflorum* were just opening in the early-spring days of September.

While in Bhutan at moderate elevations in 2005, with traveling companions Dave Demers and Scott McMahan, I observed *Pittosporum napaulense*, a species that occurs across the Himalaya from Pakistan east to Bhutan at elevations up to 2000 ft. (600 m). A long history of medicinal use, overzealous collection, and habitat loss have resulted in concern for its status in the wild. It is a handsome species that will form a small evergreen tree over time with ovate, lanceolate, glossy green foliage to 4½ in. (11 cm) long and terminal panicles of creamy yellow flowers.

HARDINESS: This genus is uniformly inappropriate for climates below the niceties of zone 7. Numerous species are appropriate for the hot and humid climate of the Southeast as well as the less humid, cooler conditions of the West Coast.

CULTIVATION: If using nature as a guide, the Asiatic species are appropriate as understory shrubs or in positions with partial sun. The southern Pacific species, contrarily, sail under conditions of direct sun and good air circulation. No species appreciate a waterlogged soil profile, though all are seemingly tolerant of sandy, weak soils if provided adequate summer water until fully established.

PROPAGATION: Semihardwood or hardwood cuttings taken in autumn or early winter on gentle bottom heat will readily root, with first-winter survivability high. Micropropagation protocol has been developed to increase species threatened in the wild, most notably *Pittosporum napaulense*. The seed coats of all *Pittosporum* species are tacky and greasy to the same degree often seen in parasitic plants that rely on viscidity to adhere to the limbs of host plants. It does not appear to be necessary to completely remove this seed coat to effect germination.

Billardiera

I am utterly unsure as to when and through whom I first became acquainted with the genus *Billardiera*. *Billardiera longiflora* was one of those numerous plants that, sadly, became integral to my garden without an acknowledgement of the process. What I do recall, absolutely, is choosing to site it directly outside the front door on the north side of our home in my first garden. There, its wiry, snaking stems clad with squat, linear, evergreen foliage went unnoticed throughout much of the year, with perhaps a scant bit of notice during its blossoming season in early summer, when pastel yellow, violet-tinged tubes were plastered among the foliage. It was much later, however, from late September through much of early winter, that its leathery, blueberry-sized fruit ripened to a seductive hue of glistening indigo, and visitors began to pause at our front door to ask its identity.

As time carried on, I acquired cultivars of this species with different-colored berries, most notably a white form (why bother?) and the cultivar 'Cherry Berry', whose exuberant name was not supported by its actual tones of murky puce. And perhaps like many before me, as I have with so many plant genera, for years I naively

carried on believing that this one species of *Billardiera* was the only show in town.

These myopic idiocies are cured soon enough by looking at native plants while traveling, which is what I did during my first trip to Australia in 1998. My time spent in New South Wales, Victoria, and Tasmania was brief, yet long enough to expose me, at least in conversation, to a world of plants I had never imagined. It was during that time that the genus *Billardiera* blossomed into nine species, three of which were native to the states I was visiting.

In addition to seeing the beloved *Billardiera longiflora* in both Tasmania and along the Great Alpine Road of Victoria, during this time I was introduced to *B. scandens*, both as a scrambling, drought-tolerant plant with pretty, nodding, bell-shaped flowers of soft yellow, and as a rather "interesting" fruit served during an evening meal coinciding with the hollow calls of koalas from the forest of eucalyptus surrounding our bed-and-breakfast. Unlike *B. longiflora*, whose colorful fruit is comprised chiefly of a thin, leathery skin surrounding numerous

Billardiera longiflora in fruit. (Photo by Lynne Harrison)

seeds, *B. scandens*, known as apple dumpling (or less appealingly as snot berry), has a long history of human consumption by both aboriginal tribes and subsequent European transplants. It possesses an acceptable flavor of peach and kiwi integrated into a textural flesh of acquired taste.

During further botanizing in Victoria through the spring months of 2007, I rode my bike through the Grampians, a mountainous national park in the north-central part of the state. Though wildfires had decimated much of the area a year prior, recovery was well underway and the wildflower display was probably better than it had been for decades. Below the towering flower stems of *Xanthorrhoea australis* were displays of starry, Wedgwood blue flowers along scrambling stems that I ultimately identified as *Billardiera versicolor*. Unfortunately, the altitude and general attitude of the flora here suggest this species would not translate to climates beyond the milder areas of California.

Certainly this is true of the other six-odd species that hail from the arid western side of the Australian continent. I have observed these in flower, under cultivation only, in perpetually drought-stricken southeastern Australia, and have been taken by the small shrublets of *Billardiera lehmanniana* smothered in white, periwinkle-like flowers, and the showy, orchidesque floral display of the painted billardiera, *B. bicolor*. Perhaps most aberrant of the lot was the Chapman River climber, *B. ringens*, with large, ovate, leathery leaves of gray-green held along scrambling stems brandishing clusters of showy orange-brown blossoms. It remains to be seen whether I will ever have the opportunity to cultivate these species, as my current garden cannot provide the aridity they deserve. In any case, the genus *Billardiera* has opened before my eyes, as genera are known to do, again providing the enlightenment and excitement of an ever-expanding universe of plants.

HARDINESS: *Billardiera longiflora* and *B. scandens* are hardy in zones 7–10, while the other species, though mostly not trialed in cultivation, are appropriate for dry, warm areas in zone 9 and above.

CULTIVATION: Interestingly, in my experience *Billardiera longiflora* seems to be self-fertile, with large, colorful crops of berries set with only a single plant; having said that, however, two clones will probably guarantee a better show. I was successful in cultivating this species on the north side of our home on a vine arbor for many years, but I also grew it through a small shrub in a brightly shaded position in our woodland. Nonetheless, the fruiting and floral attributes are best appreciated "up close and personal," since these effects are easy to miss without careful siting in the landscape.

PROPAGATION: Semihardwood cuttings taken in late summer or early autumn are easily rooted and maintained through the first winter. Sowing the numerous seeds, when fresh, results in good germination after only two cold periods. References cite germination difficulties with the western Australian species, an issue with which I have had no experience.

Boxed Fragrance: *Sarcococca*

The tiny village of Topke Gola, the endpoint of our 1995 trek, was our next destination, and we arrived to only a sprinkling of occupied houses, most villagers having departed with their yaks for lower winter pastures. The large monastery, festooned with prayer flags, along with a waterfall cascading into an enchanting mountain lake, made this isolated hamlet a near Shangri-la-like environment. The village was surrounded by a rich, undisturbed forest dominated by a true fir, Abies densa, whose startling blue cones had already begun to fall from the limbs high above. We were also glad to collect seeds of Betula utilis, a birch species whose sensational peeling bark is copper-colored rather than white. The species name, utilis, refers to its utilitarian value, and indeed its resplendent bark could be easily recognized throughout the region in a multitude of applications, from bridges to paddocks for livestock.

Our descent from Topke Gola five days later was both exciting and supremely disappointing. For reasons we were never able to decipher, the porters seemingly had their noses pointed toward home and proceeded hours beyond our agreed-upon camping site. We had no choice but to catch up with our belongings, and in the process dropped over 3000 ft. in elevation in one long, frustrating, rain-soaked afternoon, taking us well out of the range of reasonable hardiness. We set up camp in the rain, all in quite a foul mood, surrounded by large specimens of Edgeworthia.

We were still able to collect ample quantities of seed of numerous plant species over the remaining days of hiking; however, these will more than likely prove to be ill-adapted to the Pacific Northwest. Of particular note was Sarcococca coriacea, a gargantuan and handsome species of winter box, forming boldly textured, glossy green mounds to 15 ft. by 10 ft. while possessing the same intensely fragrant blossoms in early winter.

Tonight we have arrived at the airstrip in Taplejung, scheduled to fly in two days, greeted by a frustrated contingent of stranded mountaineers who have been unable to procure seats aboard the ever-decreasing number of planes due to the political instability. It is rumored the Maoists are planning an attack on this airstrip, and we are required to be in our tents by nightfall and remain until morning. Coke bottles are tied in bundles on the fence surrounding the airport as early warning devices.

Taplejung, eastern Nepal
November 11, 2002

THOUGH I HAVE BEEN CONNECTED with plants in one way or another for my entire life, 1983, when I moved to Seattle, was a pivotal year for my appreciation of the ever-expanding universe of the floral kingdom. It was during that first winter, while living in the Stone Cottage at Washington Park Arboretum, that I came to know so many previously unfamiliar plant genera, many of which I continue a deep and meaningful relationship with today. On a sunny, mild winter day in January of that year, I drove through the

Encountering a team of yaks carrying goods from Tibet into Nepal on a high pass between Thudam and Topke Gola in 2002. The fresh snow had fallen on our camp the night before. (Photo by Daniel J. Hinkley)

arboretum and was confronted with the most delicious of fragrances. Though I stopped my car and explored the area to attempt to find the source, I noticed nothing in flower.

It was two weeks later, while walking the arboretum with my professor of taxonomy, Art Kruckeberg, that I was formally introduced to the bearer of this perfume. The scent was emanating from a handsome, expansive planting of a 3 ft. (0.9 m) evergreen shrub clad with very dark, glossy green foliage. I was told this was *Sarcococca confusa*, commonly called winter box. I can be somewhat forgiven for not having initially found the source of the fragrance, since the racemes of rather small white flowers, often with showy anthers, are produced from the leaf axils and tend to disappear into the foliage.

During that January day with Dr. Kruckeberg, I recall another student asking him to what plant family *Sarcococca* belonged. His response—"Why do you think it is commonly called winter box?"—has remained with me. Indeed it is in the boxwood family, Buxaceae, a concise assemblage of five genera—*Buxus*, *Notobuxus*, *Sarcococca*, *Pachysandra*, and *Styloceras*—with

approximately 130 species that are cosmopolitan but for Australia.

Since that January day, my relationship with *Sarcococca* has grown significantly. Much of my appreciation for its breadth has come from my association with Bleddyn Wynn-Jones of Wales, whose interest in this genus borders on obsession.

Over a decade after I first made acquaintance with *Sarcococca* and learned to distinguish between the four or five species put to use in landscapes of the Pacific Northwest, I began a more serious relationship in encountering, deciphering, and collecting species from the wild.

Those familiar with the dense and handsome groundcovering expanses of *Sarcococca* under cultivation might be disenchanted with their demeanor in the wild. Thus it was when my traveling companions first came upon *S. hookeriana* var. *hookeriana* in eastern Nepal in 1995. Sparse, suckering stems of this species were found in densely shaded sites along the lower elevations of the Milke Danda, with characteristic leathery, lanceolate foliage, axillary flower buds already formed in autumn, and dark purple drupes just beginning to ripen in

Sarcococca confusa. (Photo by Lynne Harrison)

Sarcococca hookeriana. (Photo by Lynne Harrison)

late autumn. These fleshy (*sarcos*) seeds (*kokkos*) are the Greek namesake of the genus. Under the collection number HWJCM 92, this ultimately proved to be, under cultivation, what passes in the Pacific Northwest as *S. hookeriana* var. *humilis*, with stems less than 2 ft. (0.6 m) in height and scented white flowers with purple anthers from January to April.

Nearly another decade later, again in Nepal along the Mewa Khola drainage at much lower elevations below 6000 ft. (1800 m), we encountered a gargantuan species known as *Sarcococca coriacea*. Forming a dense thicket of slightly arching stems to more than 15 ft. (4.6 m) in height and large, leathery, acuminate leaves to 3½ in. (9 cm), it is an imposing species with application to warmer regions only. Our collections (HWJK 2425) did not survive the harsh winter of 2006–2007, when temperatures dropped to 17°F (−8°C).

It was not far from the Mewa Khola, on the eastern side of Kanchenjunga, the third-highest mountain peak and geographical boundary between Nepal and Sikkim, that I first came upon *Sarcococca wallichii*. Growing at relatively low elevations, this species is as handsome and imposing in foliage as *S. coriacea* but possesses a much hardier disposition. I had already admired it in my garden through Bleddyn and Sue's original collections from north of Darjeeling, northern India, under the collection number BSWJ 2291. Deep green, leathery foliage to 3 in. (7.5 cm) along suckering stems to 4 ft. (1.2 m) provide a splendid foil for the showy, fragrant flowers, each possessing bright red-tipped stamens.

While in Yunnan Province in 1996, in a mountain range north of Dali known as Ninety-Nine Dragons, at 9100 ft. (2800 m), I collected what I believe to be *Sarcococca hookeriana* var. *digyna*. This has long been cultivated in Europe, less so in North America, and is aptly referred to as 'Purple Stem' by the English gardening community. Under the collection number DJHC 492, it has proven to be a sensational plant, with light green foliage contrasting well with the dark purple stems, and a steady progression of intoxicatingly fragrant flowers from Christmas through February; indeed, we deliber-

Sarcococca hookeriana var. *humilis*. (Photo by Lynne Harrison)

The cut stems of *Sarcococca wallichii* in a market in Thimpu, Bhutan. (Photo by Daniel J. Hinkley)

Boxed Fragrance: *Sarcococca*

ately planted this along our driveway at Windcliff for a direct olfactory hit while driving past. The flowers are followed by crops of glistening black-purple fruit ripening in late summer.

On the same trip to China in 1996, though further north in Sichuan Province, just above Baoxing at 4000 ft. (1200 m), I collected the red fruit of what I believe to be *Sarcococca ruscifolia* var. *chinensis*, with vigorous, suckering green stems to 4 ft. (1.2 m) clad with glossy, dark green, undulating foliage. This plant, grown under the number DJHC 717, appears to be identical to what is offered in commerce as *S. ruscifolia*. With that said, this species appears to be hopelessly muddled in the trade with *S. confusa*, a rather confounding species collected by Ernest Wilson in western China in 1908 and not seen in the wild since. It may be a naturally occurring hybrid.

Additional species of *Sarcococca*, including *S. longifolia*, *S. longipetiolata*, and *S. vagans*, exist within China,

occurring further to the east and north, and to my knowledge these have not been introduced into cultivation. They may represent sturdier species that can expand their application in gardens of North American and beyond. Bleddyn Wynn-Jones has collected and offers *S. balansae* from Thailand under BSWJ 7265, considered synonymous with *S. vagans* by the *Flora of China* (Wu et al. 1994 to present). It is a handsome and robust species with extremely fragrant, creamy white flowers held amidst bold, broad-lanceolate, glistening green foliage on stems to 4 ft. (1.2 m), perhaps taller.

In 1999 on Fan-si-pan, the highest mountain in Indochina, I collected a few seeds of *Sarcococca* aff. *confertiflora* while in the heavily shaded valley of our base camp. Although my collection data refers to the day, the altitude (6500 ft. [2000 m]), and the general location, uncharacteristically enough it does not recall in even the vaguest terms exactly where I encountered this species. This fact frustrated both Bleddyn and me for the

Sarcococca ruscifolia var. *chinensis*. (Photo by Lynne Harrison)

next seven years; we have returned to this valley eight times, between the two of us, in an attempt to find this species again, but to no avail.

Fortunately the seeds did germinate and have begun to blossom, filling the air with a delicious scent for the first time during the holiday season of 2007–2008. These have formed a suckering colony of 2½ ft. (0.8 m) stems carrying densely arranged, dark green, and glossy leaves. It suffered minor damage in the winter of 2006–2007, when temperatures dropped to 17°F (−8°C) in early December after a month of mild temperatures.

While in Taiwan during the autumn and early winter of 2007, Bleddyn Wynn-Jones and I returned to a small area along the Southern Cross-Island Highway where the only known stand of *Sarcococca* aff. *saligna* occurs, a spot that Bleddyn had stumbled upon years earlier.

As an aside, every plant at this site was heavily infested with a species of mealy bug that was obviously taking a toll on the vigor of the population. Botanists, in particular Aleck Yang from the National Museum of Natural Science in T'ai-chung, have removed plants from the wild in an attempt to eradicate the pest and ultimately reestablish a healthy colony in the wild.

Although I won't cover the entire genus *Pachysandra*, a brief mention can be made here pertaining to *P. axillaris* var. *axillaris*. It was during this same trip to Taiwan in 2007 that we came upon a tiny colony of this superb evergreen groundcover. This is noteworthy only because, despite the fact that it was known to occur in Taiwan, no precise locations had previously been recorded in Taiwan's flora. Seeing this in the wild, with its distinctive jagged-edged leaves on succulent, spreading stems to 1 ft. (0.3 m), reminded me of the extent of admiration I have for this species, in particular a selection I have made from a prior collection in Sichuan Province that is not only as beguilingly fragrant as its winter box brethren, but that also has the charming habit of blossoming in late summer as well as early spring.

HARDINESS: From a base hardiness of zones 7–9 for the more commonly cultivated species, a general rule of thumb would indicate that the larger the leaf, the less hardy the species. *Sarcococca wallichii* has been severely damaged at 18°F (−8°C), though recovers completely from the base, while other *Sarcococca* species have been killed outright at the same temperature.

CULTIVATION: All *Sarcococca* species take kindly to shade and in fact are rather dependent on it. If put in too much direct sun, their leaves scald. Once fully established, they display an admirable degree of drought tolerance, though we find they are most content in humus-rich, evenly moist soils. Consider siting them near a door, window, or courtyard on the north side of your home where you are most apt to gather their fragrance on those chilly winter days when you are huddled indoors. All of the lower-growing species make superb groundcovers. Sarcococcas are alkaline tolerant and may benefit from applications of lime in strongly acidic soils. Other than the natural mealy bug infestation, I have never encountered a harmful insect on any under cultivation. Occasionally one does find individual stems of winter box collapsing within a colony, but this is perhaps cultural, due to improper pH levels, and does not appear to be caused by an infectious agent. In such cases simply remove the stem, and another will soon replace it from ground level.

PROPAGATION: As all *Sarcococca* species are suckering by nature, the easiest method of propagation would be to simply lift a colony and divide the clump. That said, the easiest method does not always translate into the best method. Divided stems will take a considerable amount of time to establish and generate new growth from the base. It is better to take semihardwood or hardwood cuttings in early autumn to early winter and place them on gentle bottom heat. Rooting hormone is beneficial. Seeds readily germinate after a single cold treatment, and seedlings often appear at the base of the parent plant, particularly if growing in an ideal shady location in cool, humus-rich, neutral to alkaline soil.

Aromatic Aristocracy:
Sassafras and Other Lauraceae

It has been another day, and I am spent but in the kindest of ways. Last night, outside our window, the river splashed and thundered, agitated from seemingly endless days of rain, transfigured in our dreams to opened heavens while revealing a break in the weather. This morning our curtains opened to Waterford skies and the prospects of at last seeing where it is we have been for the past week. It was an early departure from our lodging, leaving our transport at the trailhead before 7:00 a.m. As we hiked toward the pass, our trail twisted through titillating forests of Persea, Machilus, Lindera, Liriodendron, Tilia, Idesia, Tetracentron, *and numerous species of oaks and maples whose identities remain a mystery. Yet it was* Sassafras tzumu, *above any other species, that was the cause*

célèbre and the reason I have returned to this area. Last year only a tiny number of fruits were found still intact. The hunch to return a full month earlier has proven gratifyingly wise. Female specimens, rising to 75 ft., with enormous three-lobed leaves just beginning to transform to the red-burgundy of a ripe nectarine, were weighted down with glossy black fruit. Scott and I were in happy spirits as we made easy pickings of the fruit, often from the ground below our quarry. Tonight after dinner my mates surprised me with a cake for my birthday, brought from an adjacent village: a true confection, a memorable day.

Tao Yuan, northeastern Sichuan Province
September 6, 2004

B ECAUSE I HAVE SPENT an inordinate part of my adult life in natural landscapes of the world studying the flora for possible introduction into Western horticulture, it is no surprise that I am frequently asked what it is I see in a plant that makes it "good." I must admit that, despite having had many opportunities to do so, I have never fully articulated the criteria that set some plants apart from and above others. There are the obvious parameters of foliar texture, autumn color, and effects from flower and fruit. Yet undeniably there exists an elusive quality, some silent but perceivable pedigree that anoints nobility. It is this under-

Autumn color of *Sassafras albidum*. (Photo by Lynne Harrison)

stated yet tangible essence of quality that I have come to associate with every member of the rather large plant family known as the Lauraceae. In evolutionary terms, this family is considered relatively ancient, comprised chiefly of evergreen trees in the tropics and subtropics. Ecotourists in Central America who have caught a glimpse of the fabled resplendent quetzal can probably thank the ripening of fruit of laurel family members for bringing this avian masterpiece into view.

The Lauraceae is saturated, however, with hardy deciduous and evergreen shrubs and trees supremely suitable for temperate gardens. These are primarily dioecious—that is, having male and female flowers borne on separate plants—while possessing aromatic oils in their always alternately arranged leaves, which often exhibit a prominent parallel venation. These esters offer a handy identification tool while in the field, as the crushing of a single leaf from this family will reveal a signature fragrance best described as somewhat pungent or lemony with overtones of root beer. Camphor (*Cinnamomum*), bay leaf (*Laurus*), and California bay (*Umbellularia*) are widely recognized genera, each possessing their own distinctive fragrance.

Across the board, the small greenish or yellow flowers are generally unisexual on separate male and female plants, although research by the Missouri Botanical Garden indicates that some species may be capable of switching sexes. The flowers give rise on female specimens to fleshy fruits (technically drupes) held close to the branches by short, stubby pedicels known as cupules, which expand in width where they meet the fruit, offering yet another reliable characteristic for field identification.

Most of the numerous members of this family that I have cultivated with satisfaction over the years, including *Phoebe*, *Nothophoebe*, *Laurus*, *Umbellularia*, *Machilus*, and *Persea*, would not be considered shrublike in habit of growth, even by the most liberal standards. And many of the plants forced here under my artificial grouping are represented not by virtue of their stature but because of my overall enthusiasm, which supercedes all matters of size. In this way, I have chosen the genera *Sassafras*, *Lindera*, and *Litsea*.

Sassafras

I grew up on the boundary of the northernmost limit of *Sassafras albidum* in north-central Michigan. In my youth I considered it a very special tree, probably due to its general rarity and distinctive leaf pattern. My earliest mentor, a remarkable 80-year-old naturalist by the name of Mrs. Neuman, introduced me to the species when I was eight years old. Together we harvested the young green stems to take to her home and steep in boiling water for sassafras tea (no longer advised, I am

told). In autumn we would revisit the small population to admire the bold, lobed foliage at its autumnal peak, in radiant shades of rosy red with yellow overtones. (Incidentally, this population grew alongside the last remaining specimen of the American chestnut, *Castanea dentata*, in the region, which has since succumbed to chestnut blight.)

The leaves of *Sassafras albidum* are probably the most recognizable of all North American trees. The foliage of each tree can be unlobed (most common in young plants), two lobed (right- or left-handed mittens), or three lobed (mittens for mutant two-thumbed hands), and to 6 in. (15 cm) or more in length. Though this type of lobing can also be found in Asian representatives of the genus *Lindera*, also in the laurel family, there are no New World linderas with which *Sassafras* can be confused. *Sassafras albidum* offers a framework with a distinctive horizontal planing of the lateral branches, forming a short suckering shrub or tall tree to 60 ft. (18 m) depending on the conditions where it grows. I find the winter silhouette etched upon the winter sky a starkly beautiful effect.

In early spring, greenish yellow flowers are borne in condensed racemes along the branches, with male and female flowers found on separate plants. On female plants, blackish blue fleshy fruits (eagerly consumed by numerous bird species) ripen on thick red pedicels in autumn. In nature and in the garden, the American species of *Sassafras* have a tendency to sucker and will form multistemmed colonies over time.

Plant species with aromatic oils have found their way into human culture more quickly than those whose mysteries are cataloged without the benefit of the nose, and *Sassafras* is no exception. Though there appears to be some disagreement over the root of the genus name, it appears to have arisen from the Latin *saxum fragans*, meaning "stone breaker," referring to its early use as a treatment for kidney stones. Stems, root, and leaves were exported to Spain from Florida in the 16th century, representing one of America's earliest agricultural exports.

The essential volatile oil found in all species of *Sassafras*, with its distinctive root beer flavor, is known as safrole. It also occurs in varying quantities in nutmeg, camphor, star anise, and black pepper. Sassafras oil was once a popular folk remedy, as was the tea brewed from young twigs and roots (the same tea I first tasted as a young kid), drunk as a spring tonic. In 1960 the FDA banned the use of safrole as a flavoring or pharmaceutical ingredient after studies revealed its carcinogenic properties, though the oil continues to be used by the perfume industry. In the past 15 years, safrole has taken on a more miscreant role with its use in the manufacture of MDMA, known on the street as ecstasy or Adam. It is important to note that concentrated sassafras oil is known to be extremely toxic, with a few drops being of sufficient quantity to kill a young child.

Sassafras albidum. (Photo by Daniel J. Hinkley)

Crushed, dried sassafras leaves, first used in cooking by the Choctaw Indians of Mississippi and Alabama, are still marketed as "gumbo filé," an essential flavoring and thickener in authentic Cajun gumbo.

Sassafras albidum is distributed in roughly all states east of the Mississippi, though it is now considered extinct in southeastern Wisconsin, where it was once found. It is considered a colonizing species, thus its habitat of choice is disturbed, somewhat acidic soil in full sun. As the flora of any area matures, sassafras, which is shade intolerant, tends to be eliminated from the mix, though it will readily resprout from root suckers should disturbance once again occur many years later. Safrole, found in all plant parts, plays a role in the allelopathy of sassafras, inhibiting the germination of competing tree species in close proximity and thereby extending the plant's dominance in any one area. For this reason, planting sassafras adjacent to a vegetable garden should probably be avoided, though there is no literature supporting this assertion.

Worldwide, the three species of *Sassafras* help illustrate the fascinating similarities of the floras of eastern North America and eastern Asia. In the autumn of 2003, at approximately 8000 ft. (2400 m) on a mountain pass above the village of Tao Yuan, China, my traveling companions and I stopped for lunch before dropping to the village below. During a brief walk, I found upon the ground the burgundy, lobed, 9 in. (23 cm) leaves of what could be nothing other than the Chinese *S. tzumu*. Since it was late in the day, there was insufficient time to explore the area, but we returned a week later to spend a full, though disappointingly very wet, day on the mountain. It took little time to find impressive specimens of this species and determine the lavish diversity of plants inhabiting the general area. The sassafras grew among towering specimens of *Idesia*, *Tetracentron*, *Cyclocarya*, *Cercidiphyllum*, and *Liriodendron*, while smaller and numerous species of maples, *Lindera*, and *Rhododendron* were included among an opulent lower story.

Disappointingly, by late October the specimens of sassafras here had long jettisoned their seed for the year, so

The foliage of *Sassafras tzumu* from northeastern Sichuan, where I collected its fruit, remains burnished purple throughout the growing season in my garden at Windcliff. (Photo by Daniel J. Hinkley)

Sassafras randaiensis. (Photo by Aleck Yang)

plans were made for a repeat visit the following autumn. Arriving in mid-September of 2004, long before the monsoon had come to an end, presented its own challenges, including endless miles of rutted, muddy roads. Yet my traveling companions, Ozzie Johnson, Scott McMahan, Riz Reyes, and Dave Demers, and I reveled in collecting copious quantities of the sassafras seed that had recently dropped to the ground. The resulting plants now at Windcliff have shown remarkable vigor, growing to 12 ft. (3.6 m) in three years, while brandishing handsome burgundy-toned foliage throughout the growing season.

My attempts to see *Sassafras randaiensis* in its natural habitat in Taiwan in 1999 and 2007 proved to be less productive. Access to the only known populations of this very rare species, which grows at high elevations above 8000 ft. (2400 m), is highly regulated by the Taiwanese government. Despite applying for permission to visit its range long in advance of our trip, we were denied access, along with Aleck Yang of the National Museum of Natural Science in T'ai-chung.

Had I encountered this species on my own, however, without prior knowledge of its presence, it is unlikely I would have had the same epiphany I had experienced with *Sassafras tzumu* in northeastern Sichuan. The stature of *S. randaiensis*, to 15 ft. (4.6 m) or less, is decidedly more shrublike than its brethren, while the linear-ovate foliage to 4 in. (10 cm) is mostly (though not always) unlobed. Though these distinctions provide some justification for taxonomists erecting the new monotypic genus *Yushania* to house this rarity, genetic analysis has shown that all three taxa share common ancestors, so *S. randaiensis* will stay put in its original digs for the time being. I was genuinely pleased to have received as a parting gift in the autumn of 2007 a generous quantity of fresh *S. randaiensis* seed.

HARDINESS: With the range of *Sassafras albidum* being so wide, from Maine to Louisiana, the provenance of the material is likely to correspond to general hardiness. It is safe to say that specimens from the northerly populations will tolerate temperatures well below 0°F (−18°C). The same is true for *S. tzumu*, whose range is believed to include high elevations of Vietnam, much of Yunnan, Sichuan, and most of central China. My earlier experiences with *S. tzumu* of unknown provenance suggested some tenderness with winter dieback of unhardened wood. This has not been apparent with my northeastern Sichuan collections, which have tolerated early-winter temperatures of 15°F (−9°C) without any significant damage. *Sassafras randaiensis* has not yet been adequately tested; however, the altitude from which it hails would suggest adaptability in zones 6–9.

CULTIVATION: As the autumn color of these species is more splendid in full sun than in shade, I would suggest the former, or at least a site with several hours of direct sun. Any well-draining soil is appropriate. Obviously, male and female specimens must be present for fruit set to occur.

PROPAGATION: Seed is the most reliable method of propagation. Softwood cuttings under mist will probably root, but there is considerable attrition after the first winter. The suckering nature of *Sassafras albidum* would suggest that root cuttings taken in midwinter would work; however, this method employed with *S. tzumu* proved a sincere failure.

Lindera

Though *Lindera benzoin* is native to Michigan, where it is most apparent in the woodlands of the southern parts of the state, I am quite certain I remained unaware of the genus until my arrival in Washington State, more precisely in the backyard of Washington Park Arboretum. It was the handsome three-lobed leaves of *L. obtusiloba*, turning to resplendent tones of yellow that first autumn in my new home, that invited me into the genus. Later I would come to appreciate the plastering of soft yellow flowers among the branches of this and numerous other species in late winter and early spring.

Considering the staggering number of taxa in the genus *Lindera*—estimated at between 80 and 100 deciduous and evergreen species—I find it somewhat surprising that so few are known and appreciated in the gardens of North America or even Europe.

Of the three recognized *Lindera* species native to North America, two of them—*L. melissifolia* and *L.*

Autumn color of *Lindera obtusiloba*. (Photo by Daniel J. Hinkley)

subcoriacea—are rarely encountered either in cultivation or in the wild and have been red-flagged for conservation.

The most gregarious native species, *Lindera benzoin*, or spicebush, is certainly the best known, inhabiting moist, shaded woodlands in every state east of the Mississippi and into the northeastern provinces of Canada. It is a pleasing deciduous shrub adorned in early spring by a diaphanous haze of exceedingly fragrant, small, yellow flowers that bloom along its 8 ft. by 8 ft. (2.4 m by 2.4 m)—or more—framework.

The young twigs and foliage of spicebush give off a lemony aroma when bruised, and the leaves (along with those of its relatives *Sassafras albidum* and *Persea borbonia*) are a primary food source for the larvae of the spicebush swallowtail butterfly. It is of further entomological interest that the rarest bee species in the world, *Andrena lauracea*, has been collected only twice, 100 years apart, on *Lindera benzoin* in Carlinville, Illinois. In late summer to early fall, berries on female plants turn bright red and the leaves take on a cheerful shade of yellow. Spicebush was once used medicinally by indigenous tribes and served as an allspice substitute for American colonists.

Lindera melissifolia, or pondberry, also called southern spicebush or Jove's fruit, is a smallish, upright, deciduous shrub native to seasonally flooded depressions and swamps from southern Missouri and North Carolina south to the Gulf Coast. It is listed as endangered both nationally and in several states, and according to the Center for Plant Conservation only 40 scattered populations are known, principally in Arkansas and Mississippi.

Lindera subcoriacea, or bog spicebush, also deciduous, is found in scattered moist woods and wetland areas from Virginia south to the Gulf Coast. It is listed as endangered in North Carolina and Florida. According to Bill Cullina, author of *Native Trees, Shrubs, and Vines*, its leaves are smaller and more leathery than those of *L. benzoin*, and the mature leaves lack the characteristic spicy aroma.

Though more unsung *Lindera* taxa are certainly awaiting discovery in the mountains of Mexico and Central America, there is no argument that the genus is geographically centered in eastern Asia, where more than 80 species have been documented.

The mountains of Japan and Korea play host to a trio of exceptional deciduous *Lindera* species that I count among my favorites. It was on the east coast of Korea on Mount Chuwang that I collected fruit of *L. glauca*, a relatively small, rounded shrub to 6 ft. (1.8 m) with simple, ovate leaves to 4 in. (10 cm) long, dark green above and glaucous white beneath (hence the specific epithet). These leaves transition to delicious tints of orange and red in midautumn, at which point the show has only just begun. Adhering firmly to the branches until late winter, the leaves ripen to a crispy tawny brown, a color best compared with the fresh spring pelt of a white-tailed deer. A closely allied species with a nebulous natural history, *L. salicifolia*, which some references list as a synonym or subspecies, offers equally fine winter effects on a more formidable subject to 15 ft. by 15 ft. (4.6 m by 4.6 m).

The jet black fruits of *Lindera glauca* are somewhat lost in the autumn landscape; however, the same cannot be said for those of *L. erythrocarpa*. It was this species that we found as a common component of the deciduous oak forests of South Korea and northern Japan. Female specimens offer startling crops of red fruit, which are made even more startling in autumn when set against blazing yellow leaves—in my estimation, an effect unparalleled by any other deciduous shrub. A rather narrow framework of dark purplish brown stems rises to 15 ft. (4.6 m) or slightly taller and is cloaked by greenish yellow flowers in late winter, followed by long, lance-shaped leaves.

The last of the three linderas sharing both continental and archipelagic territory is *Lindera obtusiloba*, the species I first noticed in Washington Park Arboretum. To my mind, this plant is reason enough to embrace the entire genus without questioning. In late winter its spreading, multibranched skeleton, to 15 ft. (4.6 m), carries a vivid and beguiling display of yellow flowers. As this corresponds with the flowering of the precocious *Cornus mas*, a comparison can be made between the two, with *L. obtusiloba* emerging victorious by any account. The three-lobed leaves, very similar in appearance to its sassafras kin, emerge soon after and sear to a sizzling yellow in autumn as female specimens exhibit ripening crops of glistening ebony fruit. I can still recall snapping photo after photo of this glorious autumn concoction plastered upon pellucid Korean autumn skies, believing each image would supercede the previous in conveying the utter beauty of this shrub.

In northeastern Sichuan in 2003, during the time of my first encounter with *Sassafras tzumu*, I met up again with *Lindera obtusiloba* in the wild, many thousands of miles to the west. In China it is delineated by taxonomists as *L. obtusiloba* var. *heterophylla*, with an implication of varied leaf shapes. It is an apt name indeed. So heterogeneous were the individuals—from those appearing precisely like the Korean forms to individuals with near-orbicular leaves possessing three very short

lobes—that I believed I was confronting entirely different species.

The characteristic leaf lobing of *Lindera obtusiloba* is not without precedent in the genus as long as one does not figure into the equation the puzzling, ever-changing parameters of plant nomenclature. *Lindera triloba*, which flits about from this genus to *Parabenzoin*, is altogether a similar beast, and although I consider it vastly more refined and elegant, the real McCoy is difficult

Lindera salicifolia. (Photo by Daniel J. Hinkley)

Autumn color of *Lindera glauca*. (Photo by Daniel J. Hinkley)

Late-winter flowers of *Lindera triloba* provide a soft yellow haze contrasting nicely with burgundy stems. (Photo by Daniel J. Hinkley)

Autumn color of *Lindera triloba*. (Photo by Lynne Harrison)

to locate. Before collecting the seed of this species in the high mountains of Shikoku, Japan, I had received numerous specimens of *L. obtusiloba* under this name. Rather than possessing the dazzling yellow fall color of *L. obtusiloba*, however, my garden specimens of *L. triloba* yield a panoply of reds and oranges in autumn, and the drupes split open in a curious fashion to expose the seeds atop a jagged, waxy white star.

Parabenzoin praecox deserves a brief mention here, as it too comes and goes from beneath the umbrella of *Lindera* as science refines its take on plant genealogy. I grow this fine plant in my garden and find its small, multistemmed habit of wiry stems and nicely textured leaves to be among the most elegant of the shrubs I cultivate. Travelers to Japan and admirers of Japanese garden fences crafted from natural fibers would recognize this species as one of the most often used in traditional Japanese architecture. I have frequently encountered it growing in the rich deciduous forests of Hakone in central Honshū, where on a clear day Mount Fuji rises—too perfect, too large, and too white to possibly be real.

Deciduousness in this family is the exception rather than the rule, and the same applies to the genus *Lindera*. The evergreen *Lindera* species are many, and I approach the subject with the humility that the limit of my knowledge on the subject merits. The first evergreen species I grew came from the late J. C. Raulston, who had germinated seed of *L. aggregata* and sent me a specimen to trial. It sulked in the coolness of my Pacific Northwest garden for many years, yet it has provided me an entrée into the puzzling and overwhelming realm of the evergreen *Lindera* species. Its glossy, dark green foliage is indeed handsome, though better adapted to the sultry climate of the Southeast.

Jamie Blackburn, curator of woodland gardens at the Atlanta Botanical Garden, promotes *Lindera aggregata* as a good choice for southern gardens because it stays reliably evergreen. "The undersides of the leaves have a silvery sheen, and emerging new foliage has a silvery look that is very ornamental," says Blackburn (personal communication). At the Atlanta Botanical Garden, where there is a fine collection of other evergreen *Lindera* species, the specimens have matured at about 8 ft. (2.4 m) tall and wide, and are relatively slow growing.

The glossy green leaves of many of the species are prominently parallel-veined and not dissimilar in appearance to their sister genus *Cinnamomum*. When one ventures forth into the territory where these grow, however, all bets are off. In Sichuan Province, I have hiked amidst thickets of evergreen linderas that appeared superficially quite identical, but the fruits of some ripened to black while others ripened to red. With some 30 evergreen species to consider, it will take many more years of study before I can intelligently comment on them.

In 1996, while in China's Yunnan Province, I was attracted to a handsome evergreen shrub growing adjacent to the now-celebrated grove of the exceedingly rare *Calocedrus macrolepis* at An Feng Ying. It was to 12 ft. (3.6 m) tall and clad with quantities of bright red, fleshy fruit. I later identified it as *Lindera communis* and have found it to be a top-notch, hardy constituent of the Pacific Northwest garden. Three specimens planted in my new garden have yet to flower or fruit ten years on, though both the foliage and form of these are indeed handsome. Interestingly, current research into biofuels shows that the oils found within the seed and seed coat of this species hold promise.

While in the staggeringly rich lower elevations of Tao Yuan, Sichuan Province, we encountered a tantalizing species known as *Lindera fragrans*. It offers spidery evergreen foliage to 5 in. (12.5 cm) long along multibranched stemmery to 15 ft. (4.6 m), so sensational that I spent an entire three days, to no avail, inspecting each specimen I came upon for a few fruit that had not yet been carried away by birds. In the same area grew *L. megaphylla*, which, as its name would imply, has large and long, glossy green leaves, though on what could be safely defined as a tree, to 50 ft. (15 m) in height. *Lindera megaphylla* is planted at Windcliff, where it seems quite content in the perpetual winter fog it is provided.

My time in Dêqên in 1998, at the headwaters of the Mekong River in extreme northwestern Yunnan Province, will long be remembered. As if a titillating inventory of plants I had never before seen and an authentic, time-forgotten Tibetan frontier town were not enough, we were subjected to days of torrential rains that threatened to destroy all roads leading to and from this remote outpost. Despite the rain, I was content to use the time to systematically untangle the vegetation in the general vicinity, representing the transition zone encountered at this latitude at approximately 10,000 ft. (3000 m). Ironically, an abundance of *Clematis* aff. *orientalis*, with masses of coppery-tinged yellow flowers late in the season, served as a bioindicator of the general aridity of the vicinity.

On that day my traveling companion Ozzie Johnson and I hauled ourselves 1000 ft. (305 m) or more above the village and engorged river below. In the dim light I made out a trio of shrubs that set themselves apart from the surrounding vegetation by means of their radiant golden autumn color.

The few remaining fruits as well as the pungent lemony scent of the foliage gave little doubt that these were in the Lauraceae; however, it was not until these collections ultimately blossomed in my garden that I identified the shrubs as belonging to the genus *Litsea*.

As a genus, *Litsea* differs very little from *Lindera*, possessing four rather than two pollen sacs on each anther. It is a genus that has done particularly well for itself, prominent in floras of both the New and Old Worlds as well as both Northern and Southern Hemispheres, with nearly 400 species worldwide.

From its ranks, the best known is *Litsea cubeba*, known as *may chang* in Chinese, whose seeds are commercially harvested for the production of an aromatic oil used primarily in the production of violet-scented perfumes. This evergreen species has a widespread range throughout southern China and Indochina at low altitudes. I have attempted it without success in zone 8.

My collection from northwestern Yunnan under the number DJHC 98159, however, though without a species name, has proven to be a lovely and hardy garden plant. The bright red twigs of this plant contrast nicely with its consistently good, buttery yellow autumn color, developing on 4 in. (10 cm), narrow, ovate foliage. Interestingly, my female specimen sets large crops of glistening black fruit without a male companion (besides the masculine-minded linderas that lurk nearby).

Our departure from Dêqên to the Salween was ultimately thwarted due to landslides, though botanizing continued on our backtrack to Judian and ultimately to Weixi to the south. En route, at 9500 ft. (2900 m), our botanists identified a similar-appearing collection, under the number DJHC 98281, as *Lindera nacusua*, although this lacked the handsome reddish tints in its young bark. The resulting seedlings have yet to blossom to provide a definitive identification; my suspicions remain that this is the same *Litsea* I had collected days earlier.

Despite the paucity of taxonomic backbone I possess regarding *Lindera* and its relatives, my commitment to this splendid genus of deciduous and evergreen shrubs remains intact. For effects of flower, foliage, and fruit, brought to the garden by both North American natives and exotic taxa, few genera offer such breadth of ornament.

HARDINESS: Of course the deciduous species will prove hardier than the evergreens, yet there exists a difference of hardiness even among those that choose to undress in winter. *Lindera benzoin* is certainly hardy in zones 5–9, while *L. obtusiloba*, *L. triloba*, *L. glauca*, and *L. erythrocarpa* are more appropriate in zones 6–9.

CULTIVATION: *Lindera* and *Litsea* species fare best where they receive some shade and are ideal for naturalizing at the edge of a woodland garden, in well-draining, evenly moist, neutral to slightly acidic soil. Those grown for their autumn foliage will provide a loftier effect in full sun. Both male and female selections are required for fruit set, so plan on planting two or more if fruit is desired.

PROPAGATION: Seeds cleaned of flesh and sown fresh will germinate the following spring if provided at least six weeks of cold treatment. Softwood cuttings of the deciduous species, under mist, will root, but first-year survivability is low. Evergreen species propagated by hardwood cuttings with bottom heat present little challenge.

A Tale of Tails: *Stachyurus*

The last 48 hours have been an emotional and physical overload, and unfortunately I have had neither time nor energy to devote to the details. We arrived quite late to a very small village last night and found the porters mulling about the settlement rather than setting up camp. Sonam spoke with them sharply, and there was a palpable agitation among them for reasons we did not understand. He stayed in the village while Pemba led us and the porters across a very wet pasture where the loads were unpacked and tents erected; a troupe of very wary monkeys could be seen in the trees above us. Sonam finally returned to explain what we had already assumed to be the case: we had entered into a Maoist rebel–controlled area, and in order to move ahead in the morning we would be required to pay a "ransom."

It was an uncomfortable evening, though I did not feel threatened in any manner; a contingent of very solemn men came into our camp before dinner and negotiated with Sonam over what we should pay ($320). There was chang fermented in the village—offered after dinner were our own wooden mugs of the vile brew—and we could hear singing long into the night, which presumably included our entire allotment of porters, as they all appeared rather green this morning.

Sonam insisted, nervously we thought, that we leave camp immediately after a hurried breakfast, with our hungover porters lingering behind to break camp. After a mile, he unexpectedly led us to the right, over the Arun by way of a tenuous, ill-maintained footbridge. Once on the other bank, he pointed toward a tall, steep ridge

hours ahead, while explaining we would now take this route and, by so doing, avoid passing through three additional villages under Maoist control.

We gained in altitude all day and nearing 6000 ft. began to encounter an interesting association of plants, stopping for lunch at a traditional resting point with a splendid specimen of Acer oblongum as well as a very handsome form of Stachyurus himalaicus providing us a bit of shade. The Stachyurus was impressive in the length of the infructescence, to 7 in., and we collected its fruit (HWJK 2035) while waiting for water to be boiled for tea.

At 5:00 p.m., we entered into a small hamlet where I assumed we would spend the night. Sonam told us we would continue ahead despite the fact that we had yet to spot our porters behind. A local man who had obviously heard rumor of our approach stood along the trail waiting for us, holding out his hand to display the badly infected stump of the right index finger he had somehow managed to remove. We did our best to clean and bandage it before carrying on. Sonam was irritated that we took the time.

It was quickly approaching dusk when he found the only bit of level ground, adjacent to a very active landslide. It had been recently used for grazing, mostly overrun by Artemisia, and was literally moving with leaches. The climb to this point had been steep and unstable and the four of us were spent to our bones. With a splendid crescent moon rising, we could see the entire concave arc of the trail we had just hiked and, in the dimming light, the reassuring glint of torches of our porters pausing where we had taken our lunch— still hours behind us.

Approaching Ritak, northeastern Nepal
October 10, 2002

Overleaf: My guide, Pemba, on a woven bamboo bridge above a frightening torrent of water we crossed during our trek to Ritak, a small village in remote northeastern Nepal directly on the Tibetan border. (Photo by Daniel J. Hinkley)

I EQUATE MY FIRST WINTER living in the tempered climate of the Pacific Northwest with waking up in a terrarium after years confined to a Sub-Zero. As a native Michigander I had been propelled in this move from the yearly regimen of months of frosted sterility to four seasons of flowers and vibrant green. On that winter in 1983, I first came to know a genus of Asiatic shrubs that have since held me in their charms. On a midwinter's walk in the southern end of Washington Park Arboretum, I spied a tall arching shrub, devoid of foliage, carrying long, pendulant racemes of yellow flowers held on burgundy pedicels. My relationship with *Stachyurus* was sealed.

Twenty years later, my comprehension of the genus has certainly evolved, while my appreciation remains undaunted. There are few more beautiful flowering shrubs for the garden in late winter, though it is probably due to this blossoming time that so few people have encountered its charms.

The family Stachyuraceae is monotypic, housing only nine species of deciduous or evergreen shrubs in its type genus, whose name is taken from the Greek *stachy* ("spike") and *oura* ("tail"). The leaves are borne alternately along the stem, and wiry racemes of flower buds appear from the leaf axils in late summer, expanding into full blossom in mid- to late winter. So distinctive is this latter attribute, especially so when the buds open to reveal soft yellow to greenish yellow flowers, that there is virtually no challenge in identifying this genus.

Pinning down the proper species is somewhat more work, but recent revisions of the genus have made the job less painful by significantly downsizing the number of potential possibilities. Only two of the nine species occur outside the political boundaries of China, and one of those, *Stachyurus praecox*, is the most widely known and grown. The genus is split 50:50 with regard to a deciduous versus evergreen nature.

It was *Stachyurus praecox* that I encountered on that brisk February day in Seattle and through which I acquainted myself with the genus. The Japanese refer to this deciduous shrub as *kibushi* or *kifuji*, since the seeds

were used for black dye, while they have traditionally used the wood for toothpicks and the stem pith for lamp wicks. I have since encountered *S. praecox* in its native haunts of Japan, in the Chiba Prefecture south of Tokyo and much further north on the island of Hokkaidō. There it produces a multistemmed, arching shrub to 20 ft. (6 m) tall and as wide. The new wood retains a lovely burgundy blush during its first year, which contrasts nicely with the pendulous albeit stiff racemes of soft yellow flowers. The seed I collected while in Japan was by means of this shrub's small, leathery fruits, which do not possess ornamental value.

For exaggerated floral effects, a celebrated form of *Stachyurus praecox* var. *matsuzakii*, found naturally on the southern and Pacific sides of the Japanese Archipelago and differentiated from the norm by its somewhat larger leaves and more ovoid fruit, remains unnamed in cultivation in the United States. With drooping racemes to a staggering 14 in. (36 cm) long, it was selected at the South Carolina Botanical Garden on the campus of Clemson University. It deserves wider recognition and distribution, remaining up to this point more a plant of urban myth than reality.

On the Bonin Islands (Chichi-jima) south of Tokyo, a rare variant of *Stachyurus praecox* precariously hangs on to existence. Once given species rank, *S. praecox* var. *macrocarpa* has been downgraded to varietal status and reduced to a few remaining individuals due to predation by feral goats and introduced rats. Rats!

I brought into cultivation from Japan in 1989 a variegated selection of this species and propagated it for numerous years under the invalid name of *Stachyurus praecox* 'Aureovariegata'. Rightly renamed 'Oriental Sun' by plantsman Eric Hsu, its foliage is brightly suffused with irregular patches of gold, providing summer value from a species that is otherwise quite shallow in content during that time of year. The rather stubby, pendent racemes of soft yellow flowers are reasonably fetching in late winter but would not proffer sufficient reason to cultivate this plant without the spring and summer dress of variegated foliage.

Stachyurus praecox. (Photo by Daniel J. Hinkley)

Stachyurus praecox 'Oriental Sun'. (Photo by Lynne Harrison)

The frequently encountered *Stachyurus praecox* 'Rubriflorus' is known, indeed, to have flowers opening in shades of smoky-pink fading to soft yellow; however, what is not certain is whether this is not simply a selection of *S. himalaicus*, which often displays this color sequence naturally. It is appropriate to note that I have purchased selections under this name from nurseries in selection of *S. himalaicus*, which often displays this color sequence naturally. It is appropriate to note that I have purchased selections under this name from nurseries in Japan with the plants in full bloom and exhibiting sensationally saturated flowers of pink, only to never have them exhibit this effect in blossom again in my garden.

Stachyurus chinensis, at least from clones historically in cultivation, differs little from *S. praecox*, most notably

The pink-suffused flowers of *Stachyurus praecox* 'Rubriflorus'. (Photo by Daniel J. Hinkley)

Stachyurus chinensis. (Photo by Lynne Harrison)

Stachyurus chinensis 'Magpie'. (Photo by Lynne Harrison)

by blossoming, at least in the Pacific Northwest, approximately two weeks later. The raceme is also reportedly somewhat longer and the foliage somewhat larger. Taking into account my collections from Sichuan Province (DJHC 98397 from Mount Emei and DJHC 0603 from Baoxing), it appears thus far that these generalizations might be valid. However, this species, considered the most widespread and variable of the genus, certainly holds considerable potential in its gene pool that has not been fully revealed. On my own collections, the younger branchlets are a deep burgundy, and the anthers, noticeably deep in color, contrast with the pale yellow flowers on 4 in. (10 cm) racemes borne mid-March to early April.

'Magpie', an exceedingly handsome variegated clone of this species with a creamy-white-edged leaf—some-

A Tale of Tails: *Stachyurus*

Winter buds and retentive foliage of *Stachyurus himalaicus*. (Photo by Daniel J. Hinkley)

Stachyurus retusus. (Photo by Daniel J. Hinkley)

times throwing entire branches of pure white foliage—is often cohered to *Stachyurus praecox* in literature, but in truth it appeared in a seedling batch of *S. chinensis* at Hillier Nurseries of Hampshire, United Kingdom, in 1945. It is highly recommended for positions sheltered from intense direct sunlight.

It may certainly have been *Stachyurus chinensis* that we collected under the name *S. himalaicus* in southwestern Taiwan in the autumn of 2007 (DJHT 7074). Though Taiwanese botanists have not yet made accommodation for a second species in their flora, recent work suggests that the foliar variation within *S. chinensis* would allow the inclusion of the stachyurus on Taiwan where the foliage, though somewhat more narrow, is essentially the same as those plants from the southern Chinese mainland. Further work may ultimately have *S. chinensis* absorb *S. himalaicus* entirely (one less thing to worry about, to my mind).

On numerous levels I would prefer to have this name change, as I have developed a (perhaps unjustified) negative association with this taxon. What is referred to as *Stachyurus himalaicus* is frequently encountered at low elevations in eastern Nepal, northern India, Bhutan, and Yunnan; indeed, I have made collections from all four locations but have never retained any for my own garden. Though technically deciduous, in truth it is one of those shrubs that can never really decide to undress in autumn, and thus it stays cloaked and bedraggled in appearance. For this reason I have had little interest in cultivating it. The racemes, in the clones I have cultivated, are relatively short—to 3½ in. (9 cm) long—and possess a slight rosy-red appearance when first opening. This shrub is certainly more appropriately cultivated in mild, summer-warm localities, at least when it comes to those clones collected at lower altitudes.

Certainly more showy in flower is *Stachyurus retusus*, or at least what I grew in my first garden under this name, having received it from the late J. C. Raulston many years ago under the erroneous name of *S. szechuanensis* (it was also distributed for several years under the misspelling *S. suetchuanensis*). This has been a fabulous clone, possibly deserving of a cultivar name, with a profusion of long, pendulous racemes of yellow flowers, to 8 in. (20 cm) long, appearing in late March. Vigorous in growth, my plant quickly produced a vaulting 15 ft. (4.6 m) framework while carrying in summer its distinctively rounded, deciduous leaves to 3 in. (7.5 cm) long and nearly as wide. Hailing from Sichuan and northeastern Yunnan from relatively high elevations, it deserves trialing in climates thus far considered too frigid for *S. praecox*, and additional clones should be sought from the upper reaches of its range.

I first came to know *Stachyurus yunnanensis* from a plant growing at the David C. Lam Asian Garden at the UBC Botanical Garden and later encountered it briefly in its natural state, without fruit, while in northeastern Vietnam directly on the border with Yunnan in 2006. The cuttings Peter Wharton gave me in 1995 have ultimately thrived, forming a handsome, rounded shrub to 6 ft. by 5 ft. (1.8 m by 1.5 m), clad with glossy, evergreen leaves to 4 in. by 1 in. (10 cm by 2.5 cm). Very short axillary racemes of soft yellow flowers are produced in March and April. Though certainly not showy, it possesses a distinctive texture and color while providing year-round substance to the shaded garden.

In the spring of 2008, I encountered under cultivation in Japan a most arresting form of what I believe to be *Stachyurus yunnanensis* (Eric Hsu, personal communication), though I am not familiar with its actual provenance. It has glistening, metallic silver leaves, and if it proves to be as hardy as the species, it will make a splendid addition to gardens of the maritime West Coast and southeastern states.

If the foliage of *Stachyurus yunnanensis* is interesting, then that of *S. salicifolius* is nothing short of sensational. I observed this species on midelevations of Mount Emei in the transitional zone between temperate and subtropical floras. The bamboolike, leathery, green foliage can extend to a full 8 in. (20 cm) in length while never achieving more than ¾ in. (1.9 cm) in width. Even though the flowering effect is understated, there is no more outstanding shrub in our garden with regard to

Stachyurus yunnanensis. (Photo by Lynne Harrison)

Stachyurus salicifolius in my garden. (Photo by Daniel J. Hinkley)

folial texture. Another evergreen species from Emei, *S. obovatus*, is reported to at times confound taxonomists with foliage that can look deceivingly similar to *S. salicifolius*. I have not, to my knowledge, interfaced with this species in the wild.

The genus *Stachyurus*, like so many genera in the plant kingdom, reveals its diversity of form and merit with just a bit of study. Numerous species deserve a wider audience, for both flower and foliage, in the ebullient climate in which we garden. It would be a gratifying experience indeed to see these shrubs garner the appreciation they deserve.

HARDINESS: The evergreen and partially evergreen species are adaptable to gardens in zones 7–10 and will tolerate summer heat and humidity. The deciduous species are hardy in zones 6–10. Collections from northeastern China and higher elevations of Sichuan and Yunnan may push the envelope of hardiness of the genus as a whole.

CULTIVATION: Slightly acidic, humus-rich soils and light shade seem to be ideal for *Stachyurus*, which resents heavy clay soils. The exception seems to be *S. praecox* var. *matsuzakii*, which thrives in heavier soils while tolerating the heat and humidity of southeastern North America. Flowers are produced on second-year wood; "heading back" will diminish floral effects the following year.

At Washington Park Arboretum in Seattle, a mature specimen of *Stachyurus praecox* creates a natural arch over a trail entering the winter garden and offers a truly superlative effect when in full blossom. When this plant is sited in my region in full sun, autumn pigments of red and orange are brought forth, an effect substantially quieted if grown under shadier conditions.

PROPAGATION: Seed is of little challenge and is often produced, to some degree, under cultivation. Each rounded berry contains numerous seeds that will germinate in a single season if sown fresh in autumn. Softwood cuttings and semisoftwood cuttings of both the deciduous and evergreen species root readily, though due to the fact that next year's flower buds are formed so early, it is challenging to find appropriate wood; cuttings comprised chiefly of flowering wood often fail. The one-year survivability of the variegated forms of *Stachyurus praecox* is low; it will improve if a flush of late-summer growth can be achieved after potting the cuttings in midsummer by artificially extending the day length and lightly feeding with a nitrogen-based fertilizer.

In Search of Perfection: *Viburnum*

This morning I arose from a deep sleep on a warm futon on the island of Hokkaidō and dressed sleepily for a long hike up the mountain behind my lodging. This was an active volcano and all about the base were sizable steam vents that veiled the sunrise colors in a primordial deportment. It was a steep hike in young soil that slipped considerably with every step, but still I made good progress and could watch the unfolding of the floral strata as I gained each foot of elevation. At lower levels, the burgundy autumnal leaves of Viburnum wrightii, *a 6 ft. shrub carrying in quantity among its framework clusters of very large orange-red fruit, had me stop often to admire and photograph it. Midelevations brought its superficial look-alike,* V. dilatatum, *which I had once labored to distinguish, though now, to me, they seem miles apart. Its leaves, too, were nicely colored, while the large, flattened heads of small orange-red fruit again impressed me. It grew adjacent to an extremely steep and deep funnel-shaped steam vent that seemed to be dormant. By 2:00 p.m. I neared the summit, where I startled a pair of enormous woodland birds that I assumed to be the Japanese counterpart of the American woodcock. The size of seagulls, they possessed narrow beaks nearly a foot in length and exquisite plumage in intricate coppers and grays. I followed their short flight paths to gain a better vantage and soon came upon a magnificent fruited specimen of* Viburnum opulus var. calvescens. *Its bold, maplelike foliage had intensified to illuminating tones of golden yellow while still holding large, pendulous clusters of succulent, translucent red fruit. This I gathered while again the pair of birds took flight. I sat and ate my lunch and looked out to the poetic scene far below, beyond the rising plumes of steam.*

Hokkaidō, Japan
October 2001

T HE FIRST *VIBURNUM* WITH WHICH I became acquainted was *V. sieboldii*, by way of a wizened treelike specimen at the W. J. Beal Botanical Garden on the campus of Michigan State University. I convinced myself at the time that this ancient Spartan must have been the oldest and largest in North America, and without a bit of evidence, I continued in this fantasy until the summer of 2007. In that year on a mid-August day on the eastern end of Long Island, a walk along the lanes of East Hampton, where avenues of street "trees" revealed themselves as this species, with branches weighted in splendid crops of orange-red fruit, rather deflated the reverence of my original introduction.

Despite my false champion's fall from grace, it was a brilliant introduction to a genus of deciduous and evergreen shrubs that I have since encountered so frequently during my travels, whether in Alaska, Costa Rica, Vermont, or Nepal.

Overleaf: Autumn colors develop early on the botanically rich mountains of north-central Hokkaidō, Japan. Lending to the panoply are *Viburnum furcatum, V. sargentii*, and *V. wrightii*. (Photo by Daniel J. Hinkley)

Without exception, the genus offers leaves held in pairs and axillary corymbs of sometimes scented flowers (scented should not in this case be construed to mean fragrant), resulting in fleshy fruit of red, yellow, black, or various shades of metallic blue. The distinctive flattened seeds held within each berry will erase any doubt of its identity if the above characteristics fail to convince you.

Once placed in the honeysuckle family, Caprifoliaceae, along with a bevy of highly ornamental brethren, the genus *Viburnum* has more recently been banished to the Adoxaceae along with the elderberries, *Sambucus*, and two genera of hedgerow weeds, *Adoxa* and *Sinadoxa*. The reported number of *Viburnum* species from North and South America, Europe, and Asia varies dramatically from 150 to 250, further grouped by 8 taxonomic sections. The genus name *Viburnum* is believed to be derived from *vieo*, meaning "to tie," due to the flexible nature of the stems of many species.

As a whole it offers the merits of autumn coloration, beauty and fragrance of flowers, fruit, and graceful habit. Unfortunately, despite active and ongoing breeding programs, such as Don Egolf's especially noteworthy results from the U.S. National Arboretum, the prototypic species that unites all of these virtues does not yet exist, due to chromosomal incompatibilities between sections. Recently published monographs, most notably *Viburnums* by Michael Dirr, do a much greater service to this fine genus of shrubs than I can in this chapter. It is my intention to elaborate only on those species with which I have had considerable interaction.

Though 22 *Viburnum* species are naturally occurring in North America, these are found primarily in the eastern deciduous woodlands, far from my tromping grounds in the Pacific Northwest. *Viburnum opulus* var. *americanum*, with its lobed, maplelike leaves and colorful crops of tart, edible fruit in autumn that provide the common name of highbush cranberry, extends across the country and reaches the Pacific by means of the Columbia River Gorge.

Another edible and closely allied species, *Viburnum edule*, extends west to the North Pacific from Hudson Bay. I collected seed of this species from along a glacier-fed waterfall in 1997 near Cordova, Alaska, where it was commonly found with crops of orange-red, fusty-smelling fruit (its resulting jams fortunately lack this smell, which I compare to that of dirty socks). As this short trip to Prince William Sound was based on witnessing the accelerated breakup of Childs Glacier, I will forever associate with this species the crack and thunder of blue ice exploding into a river at its base.

Viburnum sieboldii. (Photo by Lynne Harrison)

In Search of Perfection: *Viburnum*

Viburnum ellipticum is the only member of the genus to occur solely on the western coast of North America, though to the best of my knowledge it has never been promoted as a shrub possessing sufficient ornament to cultivate in the garden. I have encountered this only in the botanically fascinating area along the Columbia River Gorge east of Portland, Oregon, where its oval, toothed leaves and purple fruit readily distinguish it from the highbush cranberry that often grows adjacent to it.

Traveling west from *Viburnum ellipticum*, one ultimately encounters the Japanese Archipelago, where this genus has done particularly well for itself, both in terms of the number of taxa represented as well as the qualities offered to the garden.

Since the late 1980s I have visited Japan, from the very far north of Hokkaidō to Yaku Shima in the far south, on 16 different occasions. I have never returned from that remarkable cluster of islands without believing I could spend two lifetimes there and never fully unravel and reveal its botanical and horticultural treasures.

One cannot speak of *Viburnum* and Japan without

Viburnum plicatum var. *tomentosum*. (Photo by Lynne Harrison)

mentioning the doublefile viburnum, *V. plicatum* var. *tomentosum*, arguably the most popularly cultivated of its brethren in North America. Although its flower lacks fragrance, it comes as close to the ultimate *Viburnum* as any.

Taxonomically speaking, this represents a fine example of the rule of priority in nomenclature. A sterile-flowered (snowball) form of this species was described by Carl Peter Thunberg as *Viburnum plicatum* and was introduced into cultivation by Robert Fortune in 1846. Its natural (lacecap) form was described, also by Thunberg, as *V. tomentosum*. For a short period after this misstep was illuminated, the sterile-flowered plant became *V. tomentosum* f. *plicatum* (it is proper to note that contemporary taxonomists would have simply provided a cultivar name). In 1946, however, Alfred Rehder pointed out that the name *V. tomentosum* had been used earlier for *V. lantana*. The end result is that the species has become nomenclaturally a botanical variety of one of its own mutant offspring. Interesting. The stuff of science fiction.

Viburnum plicatum var. *tomentosum* can be readily seen in Honshū, Shikoku, and Kyūshū, especially if one visits the mountains of these three islands during May and early June when this shrub is in blossom. Though I have not yet seen the Taiwanese counterpart, *Viburnum plicatum* var. *formosanum*, in blossom, I have collected the red-turning-to-black fruit of this close look-alike near Taipingshan at 7200 ft. (2200 m). This fruit follows double lines of pure white flowers along the entire stem as leaves are emerging in spring. The flowers on the perimeter of the corymb, as with many other species of *Viburnum* as well as hydrangeas, have sacrificed their fertility for the common good, putting their all into a larger corolla to flag down passing pollinators.

The foliage, indeed plicate or pleated, is a good identifying characteristic of the species, as is its horizontally tiered habit of growth. (Though water sprouts often occur, they should be removed in summer to accentuate this becoming feature). Under cultivation, fruit is seldom produced if only a single clone is planted, especially in the Pacific Northwest where our cool climate inhibits fruit production of any sort.

There are numerous good selections of *Viburnum plicatum* var. *tomentosum* and *V. plicatum* var. *plicatum* to choose from. Though it is not my intention to recognize each and every cultivar (see Dirr's *Viburnums* for further reading), I cannot bypass mention of *V. plicatum* var. *plicatum* 'Roseum'. Known as the pink Japanese snowball, it remains to my mind one of the most breathtaking deciduous shrubs available, with rich pink globes nestled amidst coppery-hued foliage in late May, on a tidy framework to 6 ft. by 6 ft. (1.8 m by 1.8 m).

The handsome presentation of two rows, or files, of "hydrangea-like" flowers is replicated by *Viburnum furcatum* (syn. *V. sympodiale*), though much earlier in the year, just as the leaves are emerging. On a memorable hike near Kusatsu on central Honshū, at relatively high elevation, Ozzie Johnson and I hiked through spring snow, then slush, and ultimately through mud as we dropped in altitude, watching spring unfold as our altimeters plummeted. *Viburnum furcatum* grew side by side here with, and in equal quantity to, *Clethra barbinervis*. At the bases of these shrubs grew dense colonies of *Shortia uniflora* that were, sadly, still weeks away from blossoming.

As we dropped in altitude, we watched plump buds slowly opening, ultimately unfurling at lower elevations to a pristine white on sensationally tiered shrubs to 15 ft. (4.6 m). The leaves on the lower-elevation specimens had just begun to unfold, and would ultimately expand

The so-called pink Japanese snowball, *Viburnum plicatum* var. *plicatum* 'Roseum', is among the loveliest of spring-blossoming shrubs in my garden. (Photo by Daniel J. Hinkley)

A large specimen of *Viburnum furcatum* in autumn color in northern Japan near Lake Towada. (Photo by Daniel J. Hinkley)

In Search of Perfection: *Viburnum*

to broad, orbicular, deeply veined blades to 5 in. (12.5 cm) across. In autumn the leaves transition to spectacular tints of red, orange, and yellow. I cultivate a pink-flowering form of *Viburnum furcatum* received from a fellow nurseryman and friend in Japan, and I consider it to be among the most beautiful flowering shrubs in my garden.

I have long admired *Viburnum furcatum*, although it is poorly represented in cultivation. This is at least partially due to its early flowering habit, which results in a correspondingly early ripening of its red-turning-to-black fruit. For years I came up empty-handed during trips within its range, in Japan, China, and northern India, as well as at high elevations in Vietnam, due to the fact that, by early October—when I am generally in the field—the fruits had long been devoured by birds. In 2001, shortly after the events of September 11, I left for Japan earlier than usual and collected the seed of this species in quantity on northern Honshū near the splendidly forested shores of Lake Towada; its foliage was resplendent in spirited autumn colors of red, orange, and yellow.

On Hokkaidō, during the same trip, I collected the fruit of three species of *Viburnum* that grew side by side along steam vents of a steeply graded, very active volcano near Mount Daisetsu National Park.

The first was *Viburnum opulus* var. *calvescens*, which represents the Asian variety of this circumboreal taxon. The five-lobed, maplelike leaves of this shrub, rising to 8 ft. (2.4 m), were somewhat larger than its American counterpart and had developed comely red tones, while terminal cymes of red berries were plentiful and handsome.

A splendid pink-flowered form of *Viburnum furcatum* blossoming in late March at Windcliff. (Photo by Daniel J. Hinkley)

The fruit of *Viburnum furcatum* ripening in early summer. (Photo by Daniel J. Hinkley)

Indeed I have collected close allies of this species in Alaska, Michigan, and the Pontic Alps of northeastern Turkey. It was in the latter that I first met up with the closely related *Viburnum orientale*, an attractive deciduous species to 5 ft. by 5 ft. (1.5 m by 1.5 m) with boldly textured, maplelike leaves to 6 in. (15 cm) wide and striking clusters of glossy coal-orange fruit in autumn. One of my seedlings from this collection holds good promise by possessing a burgundy blush to the foliage throughout the growing season. But I digress. Back to Japan.

Growing nearby *Viburnum opulus* var. *calvescens* was *V. dilatatum*, which can be distinguished from its look-alike, *V. wrightii*, by its tomentose young branches and large, attractive clusters of small orange-red fruit. This represents one of several *Viburnum* species that emit a rather foul, fetid odor when in blossom (Art Kruckeberg described it as one not to mention in mixed company), and for this reason it has never been particularly high on my list. With that said, the yellow-fruited *V. dilatatum* 'Xanthocarpum' is very good with regard to fruit effect if sited adjacent to *Callicarpa* 'Profusion'.

Viburnum dilatatum 'Xanthocarpum'. (Photo by Lynne Harrison)

A particularly good form of *Viburnum orientale* from my collections in northeastern Turkey. (Photo by Daniel J. Hinkley)

In Search of Perfection: *Viburnum*

A close relative of this species, *Viburnum wrightii*, was the third seen that day on Hokkaidō, where it bore small clusters of large, glistening orange-red berries and ovate leaves picking up good autumn tints of orange and yellow. This encounter was hardly a first for me, as my path intersected often with this species in South Korea in 1993 and 1997. A single representative of my 2001 collection resides in my garden, where it fruits very well despite its isolation from other clones. Since this is out of the norm for viburnums, which generally require two clones for successful pollination, I assume it has found an unknown partner to its liking from the assemblage of viburnums I cultivate in the garden.

My notes from both trips to South Korea refer to numerous collections of *Viburnum wrightii*, and although Korean botanists have delineated two varieties, I was blissfully ignorant of both during my time there. Of greater excitement during this time was finding a single specimen, in fruit, of *V. carlesii*, the so-called Korean spice viburnum. This occurred on the island of Ulleung, which sits in the middle of the East Sea, a six-hour ferry ride from the peninsula's eastern coast. It grew there in open shrubland with nearby specimens of *Camellia japonica*, its felted, grayish green, ovate leaves beginning to develop yellow tints in early October. I later observed *V. carlesii*, whose mainland populations have plummeted due to habitat loss, on the island of Taehuksan off the country's southwestern tip. From my collections during that trip, a seedling with a dense habit of growth and larger heads of ethereally fragrant, tubular, pink flowers appeared, and we propagated this form by cuttings for several years without providing it a cultivar name.

It is timely to mention the closely allied *Viburnum bitchiuense*, the Japanese counterpart to *V. carlesii* that is in all ways larger in format. Despite the fact that I have never encountered it in its rightful place, it remains one of my favorite deciduous, "fragrant" viburnums.

We were on Taehuksan Island primarily as a point of transfer to the significantly more isolated Sohuksan Island. As ferry service was inconsistent, my compan-ions and I spent several days botanizing on Taehuksan as we waited. Unfortunately, our 5:00 a.m. departure was cancelled at the last moment due to an approaching typhoon, and we hightailed it for the mainland on the next ferry. (Sadly, this very storm capsized a ferry on this run the following day, resulting in a large loss of human life.)

J. C. Raulston and others had botanized on Sohuksan in the late 1970s, resulting in numerous important plant introductions made to American horticulture. During this trip, J. C. collected seed of *Viburnum awabuki* that he named 'Chindo', commemorating the small island he was on at the time. It is a splendid evergreen shrub, with large, glistening green leaves along stems to 15 ft. (4.6 m) or taller over time. The rather large, pyramidal cymes of creamy white, fragrant flowers rest handsomely among the foliage in early spring, resulting in crops of red fruit.

Although *Viburnum awabuki* 'Chindo' is a superb choice as a shrub for mild climates, it continues to cause a minor disturbance in taxonomy. There is no question it is very closely allied to *V. odoratissimum*, whose handsome gloss can be appreciated in low-elevation scrub in Japan, Taiwan, the Philippines, and northeastern India. The latter was, at least at one time, not considered ade-

Viburnum carlesii. (Photo by Lynne Harrison)

quately hardy for gardens in zone 7 and below; however, this might be due to the provenance of the material tested. J. C.'s collection has not just survived but sailed through winter assaults in the Pacific Northwest, enduring temperatures as low as 5°F (−15°C) without suffering even minor leaf burn.

Considering the number of viburnums that exist in China proper, it is rather curious that despite the number of times I have visited the country, only a few of my encounters with the genus stand out as memorable. Much of this is probably due to the general lack of appreciation I had for the genus during my travels on the mainland.

Certainly one of the most widespread species (and thus often hard to decipher), and most handsome in regard to fruiting effects, is *Viburnum betulifolium*. I have frequently encountered this species during various forays into Sichuan, and have found it (if indeed I was looking at a single taxon) to be very variable with regard to size of leaf and infructescence. On one memorable occasion, I encountered a particularly fine specimen of *V. betulifolium* on a road above Baoxing, Sichuan, in 2000, not far from the monastery of 19th-century French missionary Père Armand David. It glowed red from a great distance, with enormous clusters of fruit along stems carrying heavily veined, ovate leaves. Seedlings resulting from this form have not thus far, at least in the coolness of the Pacific Northwest, proven to have inherited this generous habit of fruiting. Other collections of what I believe to be this species have comparatively tiny leaves, with some smaller than a nickel.

During my second trip to the Tao Yuan area, while trekking at Peng Jia Ba (which, with its granite chimney stacks smothered with pines, is almost a cliché of romantic Chinese landscapes), my cohorts Ozzie Johnson, Scott McMahan, Dave Demers, Riz Reyes, and I collected large corymbs of red fruit from a handsome and robust evergreen species to 15 ft. (4.6 m), with narrow, leathery foliage to 6 in. (15 cm) long. Currently in my garden under the number DJHS 4251, it has yet to flower, though it brings comment from everyone who

Viburnum bitchiuense. (Photo by Lynne Harrison)

Viburnum awabuki 'Chindo'. (Photo by Lynne Harrison)

In Search of Perfection: *Viburnum*

sees it in foliage. My colleagues and I are certain this is closely allied to *Viburnum henryi*, which I have long admired for its similarly crafted, dark green foliage and clusters of white, honey-scented flowers in early summer.

While at the base of Stone Bell Mountain, not far from Lichiang in northeastern Yunnan Province, I collected the glistening turquoise fruit of what I believed to be *Viburnum atrocyaneum*. This neat evergreen species, with short, ovate, dark, glossy evergreen foliage on mounding shrubs to 8 ft. (2.4 m), has long grown in the collections of Washington Park Arboretum, though due either to a lack of different clones to enhance pollination, or to the inhibiting coolness of our maritime climate, it has been lackluster with regard to fruiting effect.

This same sapphire blue is the signature color of the fruit of numerous evergreen species found within the genus. *Viburnum davidii* and its more robust (and in my opinion, more comely) counterpart *V. cinnamomifolium*, along with the vulgarized and mildew-ridden *V. tinus*, are among those who embrace this tincture. The best of the lot, however, is *V. propinquum*, a tastefully elegant evergreen that I would not be without in my garden. I first encountered this relative rarity (in cultivation) during my days studying plant identification on the campus of the University of Washington. Its ovate-linear, dark glossy green leaves are held by handsome red petioles, while the lacey white corymbs in late spring result in sparkling lapis-colored heads of fruit.

Though I have long admired *Viburnum propin-*

Viburnum betulifolium in fruit. (Photo by Daniel J. Hinkley)

Viburnum henryi. (Photo by Daniel J. Hinkley)

quum, it was not until our time on the Southern Cross-Island Highway in Taiwan in the autumn of 2007 that I observed it (excitedly) in the wild. The foliage of this handsome shrub, at nearly 8000 ft. (2400 m) in elevation, was substantially different in size and texture than the clone that has been in cultivation, though it certainly fell within the parameters offered in literature.

Growing nearby this species, and throughout Taiwan at moderate to high elevations, was the distinctive and, I think, highly ornamental *Viburnum urceolatum*. The deciduous, lanceolate foliage of this small shrub, to 5 in. (12.5 cm) long, provides superb texture, while the 3½ in. (9 cm) lacy heads of white flowers result in a lasting and ornamental crop of red fruit held on wiry red pedicels. The Taiwanese forms of this taxon are distinctive enough, especially those I observed on southern Honshū and Yaku Shima, Japan, to have prompted some to retain their original moniker, *V. taiwanianum*.

Though Taiwan does share a number of its viburnums with Japan, mainland China, the Philippines, and Indochina, several species occur nowhere else. In 1999 I collected seed of *Viburnum parvifolium* on a hike toward Snow Mountain in the Wuling Farm area near the Northern Cross-Island Highway. It is now firmly established in my garden and, in late December, is heavily weighted with crops of dark red fruit. As the name implies, it carries very small deciduous leaves, less than 1 in. (2.5 cm) long, sometimes three-lobed and frequently carried in whorls of three on vigorous new growth.

Viburnum arboricolum is another handsome endemic

Foliage of *Viburnum propinquum*. (Photo by Daniel J. Hinkley)

The semievergreen foliage of *Viburnum urceolatum* picking up autumn color at moderate elevation in north-central Taiwan. (Photo by Daniel J. Hinkley)

In Search of Perfection: *Viburnum*

Possessing the smallest leaves of the genus, *Viburnum parvifolium* is striking in both flower and fruit. (Photo by Daniel J. Hinkley)

Lovely evergreen foliage emerges with a burnished tint on the treelike *Viburnum arboricolum* growing in my garden from seed collected in Taiwan. (Photo by Daniel J. Hinkley)

common throughout the moderate to lower elevations. It is a small tree to 30 ft. (9 m) clad with leathery, light green, bold, ovate foliage to 4 in. (10 cm), upon which rest wide, white cymes of honey-scented flowers in June, followed by crops of orange-red fruit that ripens to black. Despite its widespread distribution on this island, *V. arboricolum* is surprisingly little known in cultivation. It has suffered brutal climatic assaults in my garden, including temperatures as low as 5°F (−15°C), without suffering damage of any kind.

Perhaps the most intriguing of the endemic viburnums on Taiwan is *Viburnum taitoense*, a species that I did not come to appreciate until early December of 2007. During this visit, especially evident at moderate to high elevations, this 8 ft. (2.4 m) shrub, carrying glossy, dark green, ovate foliage to 3 in. (7.5 cm), was just commencing flower, with terminal, narrow, somewhat pendulous clusters of fragrant white flowers. Far from bold and brash, it would probably not set the horticultural world on fire, yet I found its understated charms to my liking, similar in effect to *V. chingii*, an evergreen species shared with me by Roy Lancaster, who collected it in Sichuan Province numerous years ago.

Throughout China, Indonesia, and the Himalaya I have frequently encountered *Viburnum cylindricum*, generally at moderate to low elevations. It is a durable, robust evergreen often found in xeric conditions. The ovate-lanceolate, gray-green foliage, to 6 in. (15 cm) or more, is coated with a thin, waxlike cuticle allowing one to etch on its surface with any reasonably pointed object. This superb field identification tool was pointed out by Roy Lancaster years before I first encountered the species in the wild, and I have used it numerous times since to verify my suspicions of what I might be looking at. The broad, flattened cymes of white flowers are followed by beady blue-black fruits that possess little flesh (and that are, incidentally, irritatingly difficult to clean before importation).

Though I have collected this species in northern Vietnam and western China, and have observed some defoliation of these types during especially cold winters, the hardiest type that I grow is from my first collection, found in eastern Nepal in 1995, at just over 6000 ft. (1800 m), while with friends Bleddyn and Sue Wynn-Jones, Kevin Carrabine, and Jennifer Macuiba.

Memorable, too, on that first trek through the high Himalaya was encountering for the first time *Viburnum grandiflorum* in the wild. This grew at moderately high elevations, above 10,000 ft. (3000 m), on a ridge called the Milke Danda. However, like much of the vegetation at this elevation, nearly all specimens observed had been nipped back to neat, rounded hummocks by yaks.

The deeply impressed, dark green, ovate foliage of *Viburnum grandiflorum* is unmistakable, especially by those who have cultivated its most famous offspring, *V. ×bodnantense*, a mid-20th-century cross between it and a closely related species, *V. farreri*. As with both parent species, the flowers of *V. ×bodnantense* begin to appear in mid-December in temperate climates and continue throughout much of the depths of winter. Even if hard freezes occur and damage flowers that have already opened, unopened buds remain unmolested and continue to unfurl as temperatures rise.

The three best-known selections of *Viburnum ×bodnantense* are 'Dawn', 'Deben', and 'Charles Lamont'. 'Dawn', with pink flowers, is the most commonly cultivated, although I find it the least acceptable. 'Deben' is white with a hint of rose blush to the freshly opened flowers, but is not particularly floriferous. The best, in my opinion, is 'Charles Lamont', with substantially larger clusters of pink flowers produced over many weeks.

The other parent, *Viburnum farreri*, occurs much further northeast in Gansu, Qinghai, and Xinjiang Provinces of China at relatively high elevations. It was the Russian Grigorij Potanin who first observed this species in the wild in the mid-19th century, although Reginald Farrer popularized it through his writings from his lengthy forays into Gansu in the early 20th century. In *On the Eaves of the World* (1917), Farrer paints purple this shrub with his characteristic prose: "this most glorious of flowering shrubs . . . all over North China, probably the best-beloved and most universal of garden plants."

I have not shared the same pleasure in seeing this plant in the wild, though I must admit that Farrer's excitement over the shrub was not unfounded. A superb dwarf form, *Viburnum farreri* 'Nanum', develops a dense, twiggy globe of reddish young branches plastered with clusters of fragrant white flowers from November until April. It begs to be employed by breeders in a revisit

Viburnum grandiflorum. (Photo by Lynne Harrison)

Viburnum ×bodnantense 'Dawn'. (Photo by Lynne Harrison)

In Search of Perfection: *Viburnum*

My collection of *Viburnum erubescens* from eastern Nepal. (Photo by Daniel J. Hinkley)

of the original crosses that resulted in *V. ×bodnantense*. *Viburnum farreri* 'Candidissimum' is also top-notch and tough as nails, producing a steady progression of pure white, fragrant flowers on an arching framework to 12 ft. (3.6 m). I have admired this selection in the climatically challenging state of Michigan in full blossom in mid-March, long before the frosts of winter had relinquished control.

It was during another memorable trek in eastern Nepal that I first encountered *Viburnum erubescens* and collected its fruit. In the autumn of 2003, the Wynn-Joneses and I were accompanied by my friend and novelist Jamaica Kincaid on a journey up the Arun River. Two weeks into the trek, just days before we were to leave the valley for the higher lands to the northeast, we were confronted by Maoist rebels in a small village where we were meant to spend the night. Though we paid our ransom and were given passage without incident, our guide chose to leave the river valley and proceed cross-country to avoid any possible confrontation.

It was during this difficult detour, at midelevations of 7000–9000 ft. (2100–2700 m), that we walked among thickets of a tall *Viburnum* having the overall gestalt of

V. grandiflorum, with ovate, deeply veined leaves and bright red petioles. Unlike the yak-nipped hummocks of *V. grandiflorum*, these were physically intact and quite heavy with ripened red fruit, despite the fact that at this altitude we were in an area heavily denuded by goats and dzo (yak-cow hybrids that can survive below 10,000 ft. [3000 m] in elevation).

It was not until these collections blossomed for the first time in my garden in 2007 that I was able to confirm my suspicion that this deciduous shrub was *Viburnum erubescens*. The very pretty, slender, and pendulous 6 in. (15 cm) panicles of tubular pink flowers appear in late winter and early spring, resulting in clusters of red fruit.

As an aside, the flowers of this species are close in appearance to those of *Viburnum taitoense*, the winter-flowering species I first observed in flower in Taiwan in the autumn of 2007.

During our 1995 trek to Topke Gola via the Jaljale Himal, returning via the river drainage directly west of Kanchenjunga, we collected the bright red fruit of *Viburnum mullaha* at lower elevations, especially around heavily grazed thickets near the villages we passed through. These too have matured to blossoming age in my garden, though other than the crops of edible red fruit, I do not expect an enormous demand for this species in its raw form anytime soon.

HARDINESS: As a very general rule of thumb, the evergreen species of *Viburnum* are appropriate only in temperate areas (zones 7–10), while many of the deciduous species can tolerate frigid temperatures (zones 4–7). I urge you to be adventurous and share the successes (and failures) in your garden with other gardeners in your climate. The benevolence of the Pacific Northwest climate is particularly welcoming to the evergreens; however, the inherent coolness reduces the splendid effects fruit set can bring to the autumn garden.

CULTIVATION: Fruiting can indeed be enhanced in nearly all instances by planting more than one clone in the garden (or in the same planting hole!). This rather obvious statement suggests that it is in fact possible to acquire individual clones; however, because so many viburnums are vegetatively propagated in the nursery trade, this is not the case.

It is often suggested that the deciduous viburnums are less tolerant of shaded conditions than their evergreen brethren. Though this may be true to some extent, the best form and function of this genus can be achieved by planting in bright or full-sun positions. A few exceptions apply, most notably *Viburnum rhytidophyllum*, which looks downright miserable in too sunny a position.

Whereas there is a degree of plasticity with regard to the pH requirements of viburnums, which will tolerate slightly acidic to slightly alkaline conditions, there is a greater case to be made for a uniformly well-draining soil with moderate fertility. Avoid saturated soils.

With respect to pruning, avoid heading cuts when at all possible, instead thinning canes from the base and removing water sprouts as necessary. A few viburnums, such as *Viburnum farreri*, *V. grandiflorum*, and *V. ×bodnantense*, possess a naturally awkward habit of growth that can be tamed somewhat by cleaning the inner framework of unnecessary branches. This approach will embellish the naturally tiered habit of growth of many species, especially *V. plicatum* and its numerous selections.

The evergreen species are susceptible to damage by the adult strawberry root weevil, which feeds on the leaf margins at night, leaving unsightly notches. Success in controlling this pest during the relatively short period in which the adult is active and feeding depends on vigilance; hand removal of the weevil at night with a flashlight is successful, as is inoculation of the soil with parasitic nematodes that kill this insect in its larval stage.

The viburnum leaf beetle, introduced from Europe, is also of concern. The larvae and adult of this insect feed on the foliage tissue between the veins and greatly reduce the vigor of the shrub within three years of infestation. Though all *Viburnum* species are fair game, this pest tends to prefer deciduous viburnums in the *V. opulus* complex. Where infestation is noted, use of resistant species is recommended, including *V. plicatum*, *V. carlesii*, *V. ×burkwoodii*, and *V. rhytidophyllum*.

Powdery mildew can be problematic on a few species, most notably—in the Pacific Northwest—on *Viburnum tinus*, from Europe. Planting in an open area with good air circulation may alleviate the problem.

PROPAGATION: Most viburnums in the trade are propagated vegetatively, through softwood or hardwood cuttings. The evergreen species provide little challenge in this regard; simply take the cuttings in late summer to late autumn and provide gentle bottom heat. Cuttings of deciduous species should be taken as soon as they begin to firm in late spring to early summer, using rooting hormone, on gentle bottom heat and under mist. *Viburnum grandiflorum*, *V. farreri*, and their hybrids will readily root in early April (leaving a bit of heel on the short cuttings), whereas cuttings from the same shrub will prove more belligerent by midsummer. While most of the deciduous viburnums readily root from cuttings, not all are as eager to commence growth the following spring. Encouraging a flush of growth from the cuttings by providing artificially long days in late summer (either with untransplanted cuttings still in the rooting tray or after transplanting) will increase survival after the first winter.

The flattened seeds of viburnums should be removed from the flesh of the berry and sown fresh in autumn. Though a few seedlings may appear in the tray the following spring, viburnums as a rule require two cold periods—that is, two winters—before germinating. These can be transplanted after the first true leaves appear, and should be established in a container for a season before planting out.

Notable Orphans: Some Personal Favorites

Well, so much for the comforts of Hong Kong, from where I last wrote you. What a trip it has been, a string of pearls and dregs that I cannot possibly assimilate into one cohesive experience while I am here. I have thought of you during the past four nights in my room in Tao Yuan. My en suite room had a combo shower/latrine with a sizeable slot in the concrete floor. This fell away beneath my room to a rather rowdy pen of pigs beneath. I have never been extremely talented at squatting—I blame my ruined knees—so I moved the desk chair from my room to the toilet and positioned it precisely for unambiguous dispatch. I must have looked like a very severe secretary taking dictation. This was working particularly well until one of the legs of my chair slipped into the slot and I fell over into the wall with my pants around my ankles, kicking in squalor, desperately fearful that a pig was going to bite

my behind. The bath towel on the rack was (I am not kidding) growing fungal fruiting bodies of sufficient size that I could have chopped up the entire towel and stir-fried it for dinner. There was no heat and it was freezing. Electricity came on between 6:00 p.m. and 9:00 p.m., and hot water from 9:00 p.m. to 10:00 p.m. I attempted a shower on the second night, waited for a gush of hot water to rinse over my soaped-up exterior, and it just dripped. I never even got my hair wet. This morning, after having gone to bed exhausted and too cold to take my socks off, I woke up with the foot of the bed soaked in blood, as I had a leach under my sock and didn't know. It was like a scene from The Godfather; I started looking for a big horse head under the blankets. Am I getting too old for this?

E-mail to Nedra Dayton
from Nan Guan, Sichuan Province
October 3, 2003

S OME THINGS JUST DON'T FIT together neatly yet cannot possibly be set aside and ignored. Despite their incongruity to the whole, their presence is needed to enhance the collective experience. Thus it is with a few orphans I find myself with at the end of this exercise of writing. It is these to which are associated many good, at least notable, experiences during the times of our chance encounters, subsequent collection, and successful cultivation. Some of these are sincerely obscure, inhabiting inappreciable families, while others may represent a tiny fraction of hardiness from a much larger aggregate of tropical or subtropical plants inappropriate for most gardeners in North America and Europe. Yet there are here, too, some representatives from behemoths in the floral kingdom that I have come to value highly for the effects they bring to the garden, although I lack the mental faculties to tackle them as a whole. Despite the desultory tenor of this final chapter, to my mind these plants are a short string of individual pearls that should be granted more attention than they currently receive, in climates where they can be accommodated.

Colletia spinosissima in southern Chile.
(Photo by Daniel J. Hinkley)

Colletia

The Rhamnaceae is a remarkable congregate of 55 genera saturated with highly ornamental species, many of which are put to good use in gardens of western North America. Among these is the genus *Ceanothus*, which transforms my garden and the dry hills in California and Mexico into a surreal wash of blue each spring. *Rhamnus purshiana*, the so-called cascara, represents the type genus and is common throughout the Pacific Northwest, where it is still gathered by a cottage industry for use in the manufacture of a purgative.

My first introductions to the genus *Colletia*, with five species, came by wandering the plant collections of Van-Dusen Botanical Garden in Vancouver, British Columbia, and later through an exemplary 15 ft. (4.6 m) specimen of the red-flowering *C. hystrix* 'Rosea' at Western Hills Nursery in Occidental, California. By the time I was able to see *Colletia* in its rightful habitat, I knew the genus quite well.

This is not meant to be self-congratulatory. How could one be? The near-leafless, spiny (in some cases severely so), upright, oppositely arranged branches are quite

A pink-flowered variant of *Colletia spinosissima* growing on the rock walls of Machu Picchu. (Photo by Daniel J. Hinkley)

Colletia hystrix 'Rosea'. (Photo by Daniel J. Hinkley)

Scutia is closely allied to *Colletia*. (Photo by Daniel J. Hinkley)

unlike any other shrub we can successfully cultivate in zone 7 and above. So when provided the opportunity to collect seed of *Colletia spinosissima* along the Bío-Bío River in south-central Chile in 1998, I dipped in. I will say truthfully that I collected its seed with a considerable degree of hesitation. The plants I had seen under cultivation were certainly intriguing texturally, though they did not exactly exude ornament through their stomata.

The inherent beauty of a plant under cultivation is often 90% horticultural practice and 10% genetic potential. My collection of this species was, by chance, planted in dry, troublesome soil, where it has thrived, creating a dense, sea green column of sharp-tipped, leafless stems to 8 ft. (2.4 m), while smothered in fragrant, white, tubular flowers comprised chiefly of cup-shaped calyces in mid- to late summer. Given this plant's stout character and brilliant year-round interest from stem and flower, I would not be without it in my garden.

I have since come upon additional species while in the mountains of Peru. Indeed anyone visiting the ruins of Machu Picchu will assuredly find low barbed specimens of *Colletia* growing amidst the rock walls of the ruins itself, in blossom midwinter. As a note of interest, its close ally and superficial look-alike, *Scutia*, will be seen frequently by visitors to the Galápagos Islands off the coast of Ecuador; in fact, it is often the only source of green pigment in the frequently parched and bleached landscapes of this remarkable archipelago.

HARDINESS: Zones 7–10.

CULTIVATION: Full sun and poor, draining soils.

PROPAGATION: From nutlets produced (rarely in cultivation), the seeds readily germinate in a single season. Hardwood cuttings taken in mid- to late autumn will readily root if placed on gentle bottom heat.

Indigofera

The Fabaceae, or so-called pea family, contains a surfeit of plant species that are part of our collective consciousness. Clover, peanuts, and sweet peas are among an incalculable assortment of plant species that share the telltale traits of this family: often pinnately compound foliage, a characteristic keeled, zygomorphic (irregularly shaped) flower, and an elongated seed pod known technically as a legume. Spines and tendrils are not uncommon.

Armed with a tiny bit of training, gardeners will find it hardly a difficult task to identify any plant considered parcel to this family, whereas venturing a guess as to which of the 600 genera and 12,000 species within the family the plant belongs presents a bit more of a challenge.

The genus *Indigofera* represents in itself a virtual minefield of plant taxonomy, with more than 800 species worldwide, primarily native to warm regions of the world. The classical rich violet dye indigo lent its name to the genus by the fact that the "type" species, *I. tinctoria*, was a traditional source of this pigment (a similar color is derived by numerous other plant genera). Despite the fact that most species hail from the tropics, a handful of highly ornamental indigoferas are adaptable to temperate climates of North America and have caught the eye of keen horticulturists.

As a general rule of thumb, the hardy indigoferas are subshrubs, those indecisive creatures that are uncertain whether to remain above ground during the winter or retreat to safety. They are notoriously late to come into growth in spring and often confuse greenhorn gardeners with their sincerely dead appearance. Growth ultimately resumes from close to ground level (higher on mild years), and thusly most species should be pruned to ground level as a matter of routine late-winter maintenance.

The first of the lot with which I became acquainted was *Indigofera incarnata* 'Alba' (syn. *I. decora* 'Alba'), hardy to zones 5–9, which grew in the rock garden at the UBC Botanical Garden in Vancouver, British Columbia. This polite, low, somewhat suckering species rises to only 2 ft. (0.6 m) in height and is clad with bright green, pinnate foliage throughout the growing season. In midsummer, when presenting its lax, elongated clusters of

Indigofera incarnata 'Alba'. (Photo by Lynne Harrison)

white flowers, it is a near dead ringer for a diminutive, ground-hugging wisteria. The typical form with pink flowers, though equally stunning and certainly garden worthy, is for some reason less frequently encountered in North American horticulture.

Indigofera heterantha (zones 5–9) was next on my dance card. We first met on a walk through the garden of Highgrove, the country home of Prince Charles, with Rosemary Verey. There was a large swath of it growing near the terrace, and Ms. Verey—being privileged to do such things in the garden of His Royal Highness—offered me some seed. The resulting plants have entertained me for two decades, rising to 3½ ft. (1.1 m) by summer's end, carrying finely fretted pinnate foliage and an endless progression of pink flowers presented in short racemes. We have it planted in a gravelly, summer-parched meadow near our home in Indianola, where it

Indigofera heterantha. (Photo by Lynne Harrison)

Indigofera pendula. (Photo by Lynne Harrison)

looks as becoming as it might planted next to a future monarch's castle. *Indigofera kirilowii*, which I have collected from mountains of South Korea, is similar in effect but probably hardier, to zone 4.

I had read of *Indigofera pendula* (zones 7–10) in Roy Lancaster's classic *Travels in China* long before I encountered it growing amidst open pineland near Lichiang, Yunnan Province, in 1996. It is, in short, a spectacular species, although sadly it is culturally restricted to gardens with more benign climates in North America and Europe. Specimens of my seed collections from Yunnan (DJH 077) continue to garner admirers, blossoming for a full 12 weeks throughout summer and early fall. Long, elegant chains, ultimately expanding to 15 in. (38 cm) by summer's end, carry light pink flowers along an open, upright framework to 12 ft. (3.6 m) or more. This species often befuddles visitors to our garden, who believe

Indigofera amblyantha. (Photo by Daniel J. Hinkley)

they are seeing an aberrant form of wisteria trained into a small tree. Though this might be cut back hard in late winter like other indigoferas, I believe it is best considered a freestanding, multistemmed small tree.

While touring Chanticleer Garden near Philadelphia with the garden's director, Bill Thomas, I paused to admire another *Indigofera* I had not yet had the pleasure of encountering. I was immediately smitten. *Indigofera amblyantha* (zones 5–9) forms a small, upright subshrub to 4 ft. (1.2 m), cloaked in summer with the usual pinnate foliage but with densely packed racemes carried perfectly upright on the stems, like an elegant candelabra. The trait of this species that most pleases the talented gardeners at Chanticleer is one that is common to the genus: a steady progression of flowers for an extraordinarily long period from midsummer to late autumn.

HARDINESS: *Indigofera amblyantha*, *I. heterantha*, and *I. incarnata* 'Alba' are hardy to zones 5–9; *I. kirilowii* to zone 4; and *I. pendula* to zones 7–10.

CULTIVATION: The *Indigofera* species as a whole thrive in a sharply draining soil in full sun. Richness in soil or conditions that are too wet in winter will adversely affect their long-term survivability. Though viable seed is set in our garden, we have had little to no self-sown seedlings. Cutting the stems back hard in late winter is the only task you will find yourself obliged to undertake in order to admire this marvelous, often overlooked genus in your garden. Not only do these plants offer a near-endless blossoming sequence during the growing season, but the spent flowers also self-cleanse. Simply put, these shrubs need virtually no maintenance to look terrific.

PROPAGATION: Easy by seed, which is often produced under cultivation. If seeds are allowed to dry completely before harvesting, soaking them in water for 24 hours will result in more consistent germination the following spring. Softwood or semisoftwood cuttings under mist will root; however, their attempts at blossoming should be forfeited to preserve vigor.

One Potato, Two Potato:
Solanum and *Fabiana*

The Solanaceae, or so-called potato family, is a botanical aggregate few if any humans alive today could assert they have never encountered. Tobacco, tomato, mandrake, petunia. Plants whose names are inextricably linked with vice-presidential spellings or misspellings, and plants whose ability to set the tongue aflame is measured in Scoville units.

Despite this family's enormous ethnobotanical intrigue, of its 85-odd genera and 3000 species, there are two shrubs I would not garden without.

Solanum crispum, occupying the same genus as that of the potato and tomato, is frequently encountered in southern Chile, primarily on forest margins in the coastal province of Valdivia. An evergreen shrub or rambler, this has for many years been promoted as a vine or wall shrub in Europe, with considerable whisperings of its tender nature propagated from one reference book to another. Unfortunately, even keen gardeners shy away from this plant, as its name is muddied by a first cousin, the noxious and poisonous nightshade, *S. dulcamara*. Miles apart from *S. dulcamara* in ornamental aspect, and certainly not toxic nor noxious, *S. crispum* is one of the best value plants in our garden due to its enormously long period of blossom.

Though I did easily raise my own collections of this shrub (HCM 98043), *Solanum crispum* 'Glasnevin', selected at the National Botanic Gardens, Glasnevin, in Dublin, is that which should be sought out and grown. Beginning in mid-April, clusters of porcelain-blue, butterscotch-centered flowers are presented in large clusters amidst arching canes carrying glossy, evergreen foliage.

I first met up with this plant in the garden of the late, highly regarded horticultural artist Kevin Nicolay of Seattle, Washington. He grew it on the columns of his front porch in tandem with *Rosa* 'Alchemist', a combination that divulged his artistic talents. In early June, the rose repeats the color of the center of the *Sola-num* flower, making for a resplendent combination. Yet months after this rose retreats to foliage, the *Solanum* forges onward, producing an astonishing progression of flowers until the first frosts of autumn.

Though I plagiarized this scene for many years in my garden, upon moving to Windcliff I experimented by considering *Solanum crispum* a freestanding element. To say that I have not regretted the decision would be an understatement; in fact, I now wonder why I so methodically subdued the strength of this species by plastering it against our carport wall.

As a bonus, as in "if you order now," the flowers self-cleanse and infrequently set fruit under cultivation, insuring against invasiveness inside or outside the garden.

HARDINESS: Though *Solanum crispum* is probably root hardy in zones 6b–10, one can push the hardiness by siting it in a warm position against a wall. It will

Solanum crispum 'Glasnevin'. (Photo by Daniel J. Hinkley)

remain evergreen and unblemished by all but the most severe of frosts in zones 7–10, often continuing to blossom through the winter on mild years.

CULTIVATION: In full sun in draining soils with some supplemental water. Though apparently very tolerant of alkaline conditions, *Solanum crispum* certainly does not appear to suffer from slightly acidic soils. When content, it is vigorous in growth and will easily reach its ultimate height of 15 ft. (4.6 m) in two years or less. To keep it in bounds, I prune heavily each spring, removing nearly all of the top growth to 2 ft. (0.6 m) above ground. Dormant buds readily appear along older wood, and flowers commence shortly after growth resumes.

PROPAGATION: This can be readily propagated by a simple stern stare; however, for those less inclined to such abusive tactics, semisoftwood under mist or hardwood cuttings on bottom heat will root readily.

Not particularly far from where *Solanum crispum* occurs naturally, a most remarkable small evergreen shrub can be found that, in the Northern Hemisphere, assuredly and perpetually must confront identity crises. It is the tiny, imbricate, waxy foliage of this species, *Fabiana imbricata*, closely adhered to upright stems to 4 ft. (1.2 m), that virtually guarantees the uninitiated to ask the same question: "What species of heather is this?"

It is this foliage, whose waxy overlay possesses the scent of lacquer, that makes *Fabiana imbricata* supremely adaptable to the brutally hot and arid valleys along the northeastern slopes of the southern Andes. There you will find it frequently in communion with low mats of cactus (*Maihuenia poeppigii*) in rocky, poor soils. In midsummer the tubular, lavender or white flowers betray its true identity, although even then few beyond those with a keen taxonomic background would readily place this in the Solanaceae at first glance.

Fabiana imbricata growing in my garden with full sun and well-draining soil. (Photo by Daniel J. Hinkley)

One Potato, Two Potato: *Solanum* and *Fabiana*

Despite the fact that this species has been in cultivation for numerous decades, with prostrate as well as named color forms offered for sale, it is remarkable how little known it is. For its textural folial qualities, drought tolerance, and stalwart ability to make visitors to your garden feel unworthy in your presence, there are few better shrubs to be had.

HARDINESS: Zones 7–10.

CULTIVATION: Full sun in poor soils. Once fully established, *Fabiana* will compete admirably with the greedy root systems of our native coniferous trees.

PROPAGATION: My wild collections of this (HCM 98007) readily germinated the following spring, but I have yet to have viable seed set under cultivation. None the matter, as it roots readily from hardwood cuttings taken in mid- to late autumn and placed on gentle bottom heat.

Desfontainia spinosa

It is often those plants with which I have faced repeated failure that most intrigue me, as if perhaps polishing them with purple prose will make them more amenable during my next attempt.

With this monotypic genus in the obscure family of the Potaliaceae, a small splintering from the gentians, there will assuredly be further attempts. *Desfontainia spinosa* is extremely common throughout the southern Andes, forming dense thickets in the shade of *Nothofagus* at moderate elevations. In a nutshell, and with considerable academic aplomb, I would propose this to be visually a cross between a holly, an *Osmanthus*, and a bag of candy corn.

The spiny-edged, shiny leaves to 3 in. (7.5 cm) long are held in pairs along stems to 5 ft. (1.5 m), though frequently less. I have collected its mature fruit in Chile while the shrub was still in full flower; for seemingly months on end, pendulous, waxy, bicolored flowers are produced in tones of red-orange fading to yellow.

Though there is certain to be future taxonomic revision, the specimens that I have observed in the páramo of Costa Rica, considered by botanists to be the same taxon, appear to the naked eye quite identical.

Despite my shortcomings with this species, other keen gardeners along the West Coast have reported success, a fact that I am loathe to report. I will keep trying.

HARDINESS: Disturbingly, in zones 8–12.

CULTIVATION: The key to success with *Desfontainia spinosa* is seemingly providing bright shade in draining yet evenly moist, slightly acidic soils, which sounds eerily similar to the conditions under which I have killed this species numerous times.

PROPAGATION: The seed I have collected from this shrub, with Kevin Carrabine and Jennifer Macuiba under the numbers HCM 98118 and 98162, and with Richie Steffen under HS 049 and 089, all readily germinated the spring after sowing. These grew modestly well in containers after transplanting. Though I have not been granted the privilege, I can only presume that hardwood cuttings taken in autumn would be successful, a theory supported by the existence of at least one

Desfontainia spinosa. (Photo by Daniel J. Hinkley)

clonal selection of this species in cultivation, 'Harold Comber'.

Asteranthera ovata

The Gesneriaceae, though certainly not in its entirety, has been hijacked by the blue rinse brigade, those sturdy and passionate comrades devoted to the African violets, genus *Saintpaulia*, as well as *Streptocarpus*, known colloquially as the Cape primrose. Though I resolutely reserve my right to grow these two fine genera under fluorescent lights when my joints are perfectly solidified, I am more interested for the time being in the numerous underknown family members with applications in temperate gardens.

North America is naturally devoid of the family, although *Ramonda* and *Jankaea*, both herbaceous contingents from the European branch, have secured a position of importance among the cognoscenti of keen plantsmen on the East Coast. I have tried these genera in the coolness of the Pacific Northwest with mixed, mostly unfortunate results.

Imagine, then, my encounter with *Asteranthera ovata* in a shaded, cool woodland in southern Chile in 1998, in fact on Chiloé Island south of Puerto Montt. Along the trunks of trees in low-pitched shade grew a self-adhering vine of tiny, ovate leaves held in pairs along chocolate-colored stems. Presented with no flowers, and being the taxonomic sleuth I am known to be, I was transfixed by this tiny-foliaged yet unknown species of *Hydrangea* I had come upon. Indeed, this might have been the discovery that would guarantee my legacy.

Less than 24 hours later I was confronted with its very non-hydrangeaceous nature: a plastering of ludicrously large, flaring, in-my-face vermillion flowers. I attempted a weak regrouping of my taxonomic strength among attending colleagues.

In truth I was smitten at first sight with this too-infrequently-known plant, which remains rare even among connoisseurs of the ranks of the Gesneriaceae. I did not collect seed during that trip, as none was granted; however, I took cuttings of numerous clones chanced upon in the Alerce Andina, east of my departure city of Puerto Montt, the day before I returned home. These readily rooted, and I remain entranced by the species to this day.

HARDINESS: Zones 8–10.

CULTIVATION: In cool, moist soil in shade, and provided a substrate on which to adhere. This species will tolerate little frost and will fail in hot or dry climates.

PROPAGATION: Easily rooted by semisoftwood or hardwood cuttings in late summer. As with the climbing hydrangeas, the adventitious roots present along

Asteranthera ovata growing with *Luzuriaga polyphylla*. (Photo by Daniel J. Hinkley)

the stem will not translate into a ready-made root system.

Grevillea victoriae

Despite the fact that I have had considerable one-on-one time with members of the Proteaceae, attempting to deal with the mammoth expanse of this family is an exercise in futility. Though I have hiked in the lustrous, silvery forests of *Leucadendron* on Table Mountain near Cape Town and amidst the charmingly dwarf *Protea nana* in the Drakensberg, collected seed of *Embothrium*, *Lomatia*, and *Orites* in South America, and admired numerous species of *Banksia*, *Grevillea*, and *Hakea* in Australia and impressive specimens of *Knightia* in New Zealand, I must let this family jell. I will return for a rematch when tackling trees in my next book.

If there is one, however, that I cannot possibly omit from this extended essay on my appreciation for shrubs, it is *Grevillea victoriae*. The genus itself is mountainous in scope, with 360 known species occurring in Australia, Papua New Guinea, and New Caledonia. Had I the gardening climate to more fully embrace this genus, I believe I would ditch all current efforts and fall headfirst into the abyss. Nevertheless, I can grow a few grevilleas in my zone 8 garden, and probably more than even I realize. In fact the North Willamette Research and Extension Center near Portland, Oregon, is evaluating nearly 100 species and hybrids that have survived in their climate.

It might have been more predictable, during my last foray into Australia in the autumn of 2007, to have wished to see the Wollemi pine, *Wollemia nobilis*, a monumental discovery made in the Blue Mountains near Sydney in 1994. However, my excitement in encountering a plant in the wild is derived mostly from my respect for its ornamental attributes and its reliable performance in my garden. And few shrubs offer the length of blossom and ornament of evergreen foliage offered by *Grevillea victoriae*.

This dense, rounded shrub grows to 5 ft. (1.5 m) tall, with tawny orange flowers, rich in nectar, formed along pendulous racemes that bloom for months, from late October until April. In the Pacific Northwest our winter resident Anna's hummingbird finds the flowers a reliable food source, especially during frosts. Interestingly, this species has received high marks for its garden performance in the southeastern states, bucking the general trend of most Australian plants, which resent heat and humidity.

It was therefore with great excitement that during my last days in Australia, along the Great Alpine Road in the state of Victoria (Her Royal Highness was indeed indulged), I at last found that which I had so hoped to see. A sizeable colony of *Grevillea victoriae* grew within hummocks of *Podocarpus lawrencei* and *Drimys xerophila* at over 7000 ft. (2100 m). As I might have expected, even with remnant banks of snow still present, this species was in full flower.

Protea nana, a subshrub from high elevations in alpine meadows of the Drakensberg Mountains of South Africa. (Photo by Daniel J. Hinkley)

Grevillea victoriae. (Photo by Lynne Harrison)

Grevillea victoriae. (Photo by Lynne Harrison)

Some taxonomists treat *Grevillea victoriae* var. *miqueliana* as a separate species. (Photo by Daniel J. Hinkley)

Grevillea victoriae

HARDINESS: Zones 7–12.

CULTIVATION: Full sun and draining, poor soils. Deprive of water during the growing season and particularly during periods of high temperatures. The Proteaceae as a whole exhibits a sensitivity to phosphorus; fertilizing of this shrub in any event should be avoided entirely. There are several naturally occurring varieties as well as named forms of this species; 'Murray Valley Queen' is top-notch, with larger racemes of flowers of a deeply saturated orange-red, while *Grevillea victoriae* var. *miqueliana* offers a very long winter display of spidery pink-red flowers.

PROPAGATION: If more than one clone exists in the garden, seed will be readily set and easily germinated. With that said, the genus is highly promiscuous, and spontaneous hybrids will occur in a garden setting if other species are present. Hardwood cuttings taken in midautumn and placed on gentle bottom heat root consistently well; however, there is some attrition from root disturbance upon potting, during which time fertilizer with phosphorus should be avoided.

Philesia magellanica

Anyone who travels in search of something, whether it be plants or antiques, knows full well the dangers of false expectation. This has happened to me numerous times afield, when conversations or books read prior to departure assured me I would see drifts of this and expansive colonies of that, whereas in the end I never saw a single specimen. Such it nearly was with *Philesia magellanica*, an evergreen, scrambling, shrubby monocot from the Valdivian cloud forests of southern Chile.

In a small family known as the Philesiaceae, although retained by some in the Liliaceae, it shares its ranks with two other genera, one of which is considered to be the most beautiful flowering plant in all of South America. I was afforded numerous opportunities to marvel at the near-iridescent red bells of *Lapageria rosea* presented along vigorous vining stems, carrying ever-

Philesia magellanica. (Photo by Daniel J. Hinkley)

Lapageria rosea. (Photo by Daniel J. Hinkley)

green foliage, which grew high into the overstory, and readily collected its chunky fruit during the few times it was offered. In addition, I found both species in the genus *Luzuriaga*, evergreen ground- or trunk-covering shrublets with leathery, pinnately compound leaves to 3 in. (7.5 cm) long. The habitat of *Luzuriaga radicans* overlaid that of the superficially similar *Luzuriaga polyphylla*, yet the former's orange-red fleshy fruit readily distinguished it from the latter's yellow-green berry.

On the day before my departure from Puerto Montt, and already accepting the fact that I had been skunked in my attempts to see *Philesia* in its native habitat, I took one last hike into the Alerce Andina National Park. It was during that hike that I came upon a family enjoying a walk together on a pleasant, sunny Sunday afternoon. As I passed by, I noticed the youngest daughter carrying a petite bouquet of lipstick-red tubular flowers. After I stole these from her and pushed her from the trail . . . No, I did not.

Within a few hundred yards, in a damp mossy position in shade, I was surrounded by shrublets growing through a mossy substrate on the stems of trees and rotting logs. These were smothered in the most outlandishly beautiful flowers that I believed, at that moment, I had ever encountered in the wild. I whooped and hollered, and feeling quite full of myself, sang a refrain of "Philesia Navidad," composed directly on the spot.

HARDINESS: Zones 7b–9, in summer-cool, humid areas only.

CULTIVATION: I have successfully established this plant in a mossy, acidic, perpetually moist soil in shade, although it is doubtful that we possess enough humidity in the greater Puget Sound area to suit its desires. This is a shrub for coastal English and Irish gardens or for western slope landscapes from southern Washington to northern California.

PROPAGATION: I was able to gather sufficient seed in Chile during that trip and on subsequent forays into South America, and did not find the germination requirements as sticky as the ensuing cultivation of the species itself. Hardwood cuttings taken in late summer root quite easily.

HARDINESS ZONES

USDA Plant Hardiness Zones Average Annual Minimum Temperature

ZONE	TEMPERATURE (DEG. F)			TEMPERATURE (DEG. C)		
1		below −50		−45.6	and below	
2a	−45	to	−50	−42.8	to	−45.5
2b	−40	to	−45	−40.0	to	−42.7
3a	−35	to	−40	−37.3	to	−40.0
3b	−30	to	−35	−34.5	to	−37.2
4a	−25	to	−30	−31.7	to	−34.4
4b	−20	to	−25	−28.9	to	−31.6
5a	−15	to	−20	−26.2	to	−28.8
5b	−10	to	−15	−23.4	to	−26.1
6a	−5	to	−10	−20.6	to	−23.3
6b	0	to	−5	−17.8	to	−20.5
7a	5	to	0	−15.0	to	−17.7
7b	10	to	5	−12.3	to	−15.0
8a	15	to	10	−9.5	to	−12.2
8b	20	to	15	−6.7	to	−9.4
9a	25	to	20	−3.9	to	−6.6
9b	30	to	25	−1.2	to	−3.8
10a	35	to	30	1.6	to	−1.1
10b	40	to	35	4.4	to	1.7
11	40	and above		4.5	and above	

To see the USDA Hardiness Zone Map, go to the U.S. National Arboretum site at http://www.usna.usda.gov/Hardzone/ushzmap.html.

Temperatures

$°C = 5/9 \times (°F − 32)$

$°F = (9/5 \times °C) + 32$

Viburnum furcatum near Aomori, Japan, on northern Honshū. (Photo by Daniel J. Hinkley)

KEY TO COLLECTORS' REFERENCES

The significance of the known provenance of plants cannot be overstated when attempting to fully comprehend plant taxonomy and natural distribution. Historical reference aside, once this record is lost, though the ornamental characteristics remain intact, the plant becomes valueless in terms of helping us interpret or more broadly appreciate the botanical resources of our planet as they existed at any one moment in time. The following list represents a subset of my collection initials, which includes all of those mentioned in this book.

These have been applied to my collections from surveys, and those of close associates, over the past twenty years. The initials are generally followed by the year as well as the sequential number of collection. The year is sometimes given as two digits, other times as a single digit, as in DJHTu 0048 (collection 48 made in 2000) and DJHC 0612 (collection 612 made in 2000); some numbers, however, include the collection number only, minus the year the collection was made.

BSWJ	Bleddyn and Sue Wynn-Jones
DJH	Dan Hinkley, Korea, Japan, Mexico; 1993, 1994, 1995
DJHC	Dan Hinkley, China; 1996, 1998, 2000, 2003
DJHS	Dan Hinkley, Sichuan; 2004
DJHSi	Dan Hinkley, Sikkim; 2005
DJHT	Dan Hinkley, Taiwan; 1999, 2007
DJHTu	Dan Hinkley, Northeastern Turkey; 2000
EDHCH	Eric Hammond, China; 1997
HC	Hinkley, Probst, Korea, Japan; 1997
HCM	Hinkley, Carrabine, Macuiba, Chile; 1998
HS	Hinkley, Steffen; Chile; 2003
HWJ	Hinkley, Wynn-Jones, Vietnam; 1999, 2003
HWJCM	Hinkley, Wynn-Jones, Carrabine, Macuiba, East Nepal; 1995
HWJK	Hinkley, Wynn-Jones, Kincaid, East Nepal; 2002

PLANT SOURCES

I have frequently found interesting, well-grown shrubs and vines, true to name and reasonably priced, through the following ethical sources. This list is not meant to be comprehensive, however. There are numerous small, local specialist nurseries and independent garden centers that deserve your patronage. Support them!

Please note that not all nurseries listed here provide mail-order services. Note, too, that from 2009 onward numerous plants mentioned in this book will be available throughout North America and Canada at independent garden centers under the Monrovia label.

United States

ArborVillage
P.O. Box 227
Holt, Missouri 64048
www.arborvillagellc.com

Arrowhead Alpines
P.O. Box 857
Fowlerville, Michigan 48836
www.arrowhead-alpines.com

Broken Arrow Nursery
13 Broken Arrow Road
Hamden, Connecticut 06518
www.brokenarrownursery.com

Camellia Forest Nursery
626 Highway 54 West
Chapel Hill, North Carolina 27516
www.camforest.com

Cistus Nursery
22711 NW Gillihan Road
Sauvie Island, Oregon 97231
www.cistus.com

Digging Dog Nursery
P.O. Box 471
Albion, California 95410
www.diggingdog.com

Far Reaches Farm
1818 Hastings Avenue
Port Townsend, Washington 98368
www.farreachesfarm.com

Forestfarm Nursery
990 Tetherow Road
Williams, Oregon 97544
www.forestfarm.com

Garden Vision
10 Templeton Road
Phillipston, Massachusetts 01331
home.earthlink.net/~darrellpro
Mostly rare woodland perennials, with some interesting woody plants. The Web pages are primarily an image gallery of epimediums offered by the nursery, but you can request a catalog by contacting Darrell Probst.

Gossler Farms Nursery
1200 Weaver Road
Springfield, Oregon 97478
www.gosslerfarms.com

McMahan's Nursery
5727 Cleveland Highway
Clermont, Georgia 30527
www.mcmahansnursery.com

PendulousPlants.Com
P.O. Box 814
Horse Shoe, North Carolina 28742
www.pendulousplants.com
Online mail-order company specializing in weeping plants.

Plant Delights Nursery
9241 Sauls Road
Raleigh, North Carolina 27603
www.plantdelights.com
Mostly rare perennials, with some interesting woody plants.

SmallPlants.Com
P.O. Box 814
Horse Shoe, North Carolina 28742
www.smallplants.com
Online mail-order company specializing in small trees and shrubs, including dwarf conifers.

Song Sparrow Perennial Farm
13101 E Rye Road
Avalon, Wisconsin 53505
www.songsparrow.com

Western Hills Nursery
16250 Coleman Valley Road
Occidental, California 95465
www.westernhillsnursery.com

Yucca Do Nursery
P.O. Box 907
Hempstead, Texas 77445
www.yuccado.com

United Kingdom

Blackthorn Nursery
Kilmeston, Alresford
Hampshire, SO24 0NL
Limited openings. Exceptional Daphne
hybrids and others.

BlueBell Arboretum and Nursery
Annwell Lane
Smisby
Ashby de la Zouch
Leicestershire LE65 2TA
www.bluebellnursery.co.uk

Crûg Farm Plants
Griffith's Crossing
Caernarfon
Gwynedd LL55 1TU
www.crug-farm.co.uk

Great Dixter
Northiam
Rye
East Sussex TN31 6PH
www.greatdixter.co.uk/nursery.htm

Hardy Exotics
Gilly Lane
Whitecross
Penzance
Cornwall TR20 8BZ
www.hardyexotics.co.uk
*Many rare shrubs and vines, and many
tender species.*

Hopleys Plants
High Street
Much Hadham
Hertfordshire SG10 6BU
www.hopleys.co.uk

Pan-Global Plants
The Walled Garden
Frampton Court
Frampton-on-Severn
Gloucestershire GL2 7EX
www.panglobalplants.com

Wildside Nursery
Green Lane
Buckland Monachorum
Yelverton
Devon PL20 7NP

Wisley Plant Centre
RHS Garden Wisley
Woking GU23 6QB
www.rhs.org.uk/wisleyplantcentre

Netherlands

De Hessenhof
Hessenweg 41
Ede 6718 TC

Piet Oudolf
Kwerkerij Oudolf
Broekstraat 17
Hummelo 6999

Pieter Zwijnenburg Jr.
Botanische kwekerij
Halve Raak 18
Boskoop 2771 AD

Rein en Mark Bulk
Rijneveld 115
Boskoop 2771 XV
www.bulk-boskoop.nl

France

The Plantsman Nursery
1 Brantirat, Route de Coutras
Sablons 33910
*An extraordinary collection
of vines from Guy Sisson.*

New Zealand

Matai Nurseries
52 Harris Street
Waimate
www.nznatives.co.nz
*An extensive selection of New Zealand
natives.*

Texture Plants
P.O. Box 111-86
Sockburn
Christchurch
www.textureplants.co.nz
*A nurseryman's nursery run
by Tim and Hamish Prebble.*

Woodleigh Gardens and Nursery
1403 South Road
Oakura, RD 4
New Plymouth
www.woodleigh.co.nz
Specializing in hydrangeas.

Australia

Heronswood
105 Latrobe Parade
Dromana
Victoria 3936
www.diggers.com.au

Kuranga Native Nursery
118 York Road
Mount Evelyn
Victoria 3796
www.kuranga.com.au
*The best native plant nursery
in Australia.*

BIBLIOGRAPHY

Adams, N. M., and A. L. Poole. 1980. *Trees and Shrubs of New Zealand*. Wellington: P. D. Hasselberg, Government Printer.

Aniśko, T., and U. Im. 2001. Beware of butterfly bush. *American Nurseryman* 194 (2): 46–49.

Bean, W. J. 1914. *Trees and Shrubs Hardy in the British Isles*. 8th ed. London: J. Murray, 1980.

Biswas, K. 1967. *Plants of Darjeeling and the Sikkim Himalayas*. Vol. 1. West Bengal Government Press.

Bondurant, C. S. 1887. Botanical medicine monographs and sundry. *American Journal of Pharmacy* 59 (3).

Coats, A. M. 1992. *Garden Shrubs and Their Histories*. New York: Simon and Schuster.

Costermans, L. 1981. *Native Trees and Shrubs of South-eastern Australia*. Adelaide: Rigby.

Cullina, W. 2002. *Native Trees, Shrubs, and Vines: A Guide to Using, Growing, and Propagating North American Woody Plants*. Boston: Houghton Mifflin.

Curtis, C. M., and D. I. Morris. 1994. *The Students' Flora of Tasmania*. Parts 1–4b. Hobart, Tasmania: Saint David's Park Publishing.

Dirr, M. A. 1983. *Manual of Woody Landscape Plants: Their Identification, Ornamental Characteristics, Culture, Propagation and Uses*. Champaign, Illinois: Stipes.

Dirr, M. A. 2007. *Viburnums: Flowering Shrubs for Every Season*. Portland, Oregon: Timber Press.

Dirr, M. A., and C. W. Heuser Jr. 1987. *The Reference Manual of Woody Plant Propagation: From Seed to Tissue Culture: A Practical Working Guide to the Propagation of Over 1100 Species, Varieties, and Cultivars*. Athens, Georgia: Varsity Press.

Farrer, R. J. 1917. *On the Eaves of the World*. London: E. Arnold.

Floridata. www.floridata.com.

Gentry, A. H. 1993. *A Field Guide to the Families and Genera of Woody Plants of Northwest South America*. Washington, D.C.: Conservation International.

Grant, J. A., and C. L. Grant. 1990. *Trees and Shrubs for Pacific Northwest Gardens*. 2nd ed. Portland, Oregon: Timber Press.

Hammel, B. E., M. H. Grayum, C. Herrera, and N. Zamora, eds. 2003. *Manual de Plantas de Costa Rica*. Vols. 1–3. Saint Louis: Missouri Botanical Garden Press.

Hara, H., A. O. Chater, and L. H. J. Williams, eds. 1982. *An Enumeration of the Flowering Plants of Nepal*. Vol. 3. London: Trustees of British Museum (Natural History).

Haworth-Booth, M. 1984. *The Hydrangeas*. 5th ed. London: Constable and Company.

Hilliard, O. M., and B. L. Burtt. 1987. *The Botany of the Southern Natal Drakensberg*. Cape Town, South Africa: National Botanic Gardens.

Hillier Nurseries. 1992. *The Hillier Manual of Trees and Shrubs*. Melksham, Wiltshire, United Kingdom: Redwood Press.

Hitchcock, C. L., and A. Cronquist. 1973. *Flora of the Pacific Northwest*. Seattle: University of Washington Press.

Hoffmann, A. J. 1978. *Flora Silvestre de Chile: Zona Central*. Santiago: Imprenta Salesianos.

Hoffmann, A. J. 1982. *Flora Silvestre de Chile: Zona Araucana*. Santiago: Imprenta Salesianos.

Hoffmann, A. J. 1998. *Plantas Altoandinas en la Flora Silvestre de Chile.* Santiago: Imprenta Salesianos.

Integrated Taxonomic Information System. 2008. Hydrangeaceae. Taxonomic Serial No. 24093. http://www.itis.gov/servlet/SingleRpt/SingleRpt?search_topic=TSN&search_value=24093.

Lancaster, R. 1989. *Travels in China.* Woodbridge, Suffolk, United Kingdom: Antique Collectors' Club.

Lancaster, R. 1991. *Shrubs Through the Seasons.* London: HarperCollins.

Lancaster, R. 1995. *A Plantsman in Nepal.* Woodbridge, Suffolk, United Kingdom: Antique Collectors' Club.

Lane, C. 2005. *Witch Hazels.* Portland, Oregon: Timber Press.

Lawson-Hall, T., and B. Rothera. 1995. *Hydrangeas: A Gardener's Guide.* Portland, Oregon: Timber Press.

Lee, Y. N. 1996. *Flora of Korea.* Seoul: Kyo-Hak.

Li, H. L. 1963. *The Woody Flora of Taiwan.* Narbeth, Pennsylvania: Livingston.

Lord, T., ed. 2007. *RHS Plant Finder, 2007–2008.* London: Dorling Kindersley.

Malla, S. B., A. B. Shrestha, S. B. Rajbhandari, T. B. Shrestha, and P. M. Adhikari. 1997. *The Flora of Phulchoki and Godawari.* Kathmandu: Ministry of Forests and Soil Conservation, Department of Plant Resources.

Mallet, C. 1994. *Hydrangeas: Species and Cultivars.* Vol. 2, Centre d'Art Floral. Varengeville sur Mer, France.

Mallet, C., R. Mallet, and H. van Trier. 1992. *Hydrangeas: Species and Cultivars.* Centre d'Art Floral. Varengeville sur Mer, France.

McCann, I. R. 1994. *The Grampians in Flower.* Melbourne: Victorian National Parks Association.

McClintock, E. 1957. A monograph of the genus *Hydrangea. Proceedings of the California Academy of Sciences* 29 (5): 147–256.

National Taiwan University Herbarium. Flora of Taiwan. http://tai2.ntu.edu.tw/fotdv/fotmain.htm.

Ohwi, J. 1984. *The Flora of Japan.* Ed. Frederick G. Meyer and Egbert H. Walker. Washington, D.C.: Smithsonian Institution.

Phillips, C. E., and P. Barber. 1981. *Ornamental Shrubs.* New York: Van Nostrand Reinhold.

Phillips, R., and M. Rix. 1989. *Shrubs.* New York: Random House.

Polunin, O., and A. Stainton. 1984. *The Flowers of the Himalaya.* Delhi: Oxford University Press.

Radford, A. E., H. E. Ahles, and C. R. Bell. 1968. *Manual of the Vascular Flora of the Carolinas.* Chapel Hill: University of North Carolina Press.

Ranney, T., and N. P. Lynch. 2007. Clarifying taxonomy and nomenclature of *Fothergilla* (Hamamelidaceae) cultivars and hybrids. *HortScience* 42 (3): 470–473.

Riedemann, P., and G. Aldunate. 2003. *Flora Nativa.* Chile, Zona Sur: Corporación Jardín Botánico Chagual.

Ruedda, R. M. 1993. The genus *Clerodendrum* (Verbenaceae) in Mesoamerica. *Annals of the Missouri Botanical Garden* 80 (4): 870–890.

Sargent, C. S. 1894. *Forest Flora of Japan: Notes on the Forest Flora of Japan.* Boston: Houghton Mifflin.

Staff of the Liberty Hyde Bailey Hortorium. 1976. *Hortus Third: A Concise Dictionary of Plants Cultivated in the United States and Canada.* New York: Macmillan.

Thomas, G. S. 1994. *Ornamental Shrubs, Climbers, and Bamboos.* London: John Murray.

Van Gelderen, C. J., and D. M. Van Gelderen. 2004. *Encyclopedia of Hydrangeas.* Portland, Oregon: Timber Press.

Watson, L., and M. J. Dallwitz. 1992 onward. Hydrangeaceae. The families of flowering plants: descriptions, illustrations, identification, and information retrieval. http://delta-intkey.com/angio/.

Wu, Z. Y., P. H. Raven, and D. Y. Hong, eds. 1994 to present. *Flora of China.* Beijing: Science Press. Saint Louis: Missouri Botanical Garden Press. http://flora.huh.harvard.edu/china/.

Yang, C., ed. 1997. *The Distribution of the Woody Plants in Sichuan.* Guiyang: Guizhou Science and Technology Publishing House.

INDEX